Praise for David Dary's *The Oregon Trail*

"[Dary] sets the flesh-and-blood human figures who actually trod the trail against a detailed backdrop of war, diplomacy, and politics. What makes this book so readable and rewarding, however, is Dary's eye for color and detail: ox commands; the terrifying spectacle of a buffalo stampede; and the ideal caliber of the weaponry one should carry on the trail."

—*Los Angeles Times*

"It is Dary's depiction of the great and awful everyday that will grab the reader. A thoroughgoing chronicle, told with generous enthusiasm, skill, and an eye for plain truths as well as detail."

—*Kirkus Reviews*

"An epic American story of limitless hopes, searing losses, pioneers, missionaries and not a few bad characters. It's hard to imagine a more informative introduction to the westering itch along the Oregon Trail and to those who responded to it."

—*Publishers Weekly*

"Dary eschews embellishment and hews to fact, permitting readers an unadorned but palpably realistic rendition of what traveling the trail was like."

—*Booklist* (Starred Review)

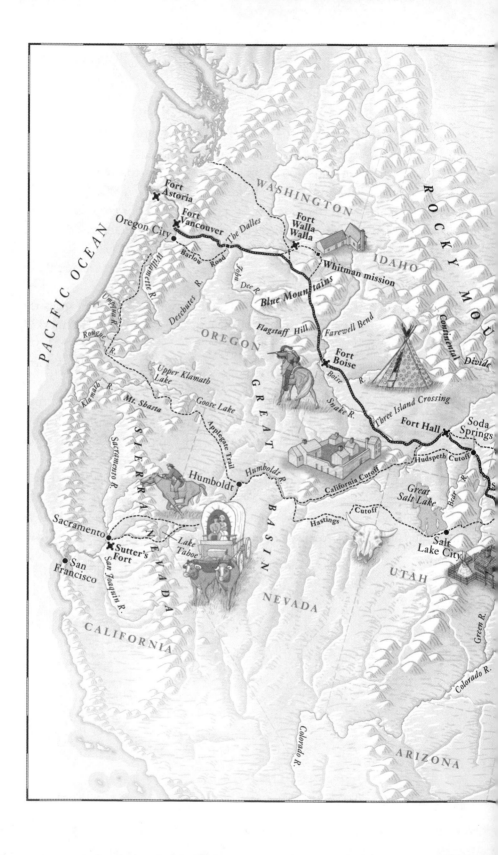

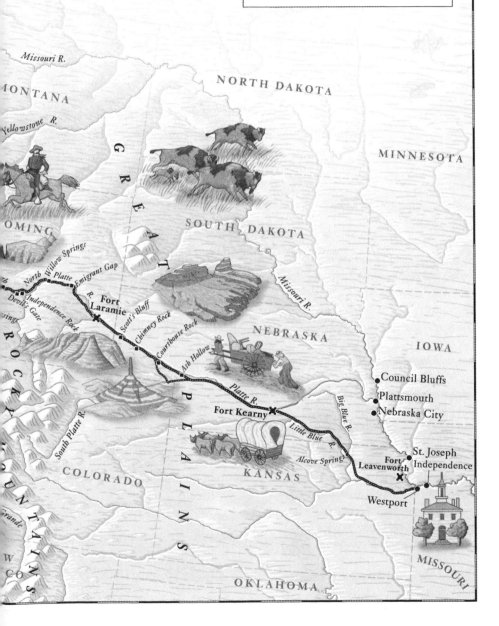

THE
OREGON TRAIL

AN AMERICAN SAGA

DAVID DARY

OXFORD
UNIVERSITY PRESS

OXFORD

UNIVERSITY PRESS

Oxford University Press, Inc., publishes works that further
Oxford University's objective of excellence
in research, scholarship, and education.

Oxford New York
Auckland Cape Town Dar es Salaam Hong Kong Karachi
Kuala Lumpur Madrid Melbourne Mexico City Nairobi
New Delhi Shanghai Taipei Toronto

With offices in
Argentina Austria Brazil Chile Czech Republic France Greece
Guatemala Hungary Italy Japan Poland Portugal Singapore
South Korea Switzerland Thailand Turkey Ukraine Vietnam

First published in the United States by Alfred A. Knopf,
a division of Random House, Inc., New York, and simultaneously
in Canada by Random House of Canada Limited, Toronto.

First issued as an Oxford University Press paperback, 2005
198 Madison Avenue, New York, New York, 10016

Oxford is a registered trademark of Oxford University Press

Library of Congress Cataloging-in-Publication Data
Dary, David.
The Oregon Trail : an American saga / David Dary.
p. cm.
Originally published: New York : Knopf, c2004.
Includes bibliographical references and index.
ISBN-13: 978-0-19-522400-9
ISBN-10: 0-19-522400-0
1. Oregon National Historic Trail—History.
2. Frontier and pioneer life—Oregon National Historic Trail.
3. West (U.S.)—History—1848–1860.
I. Title.
F597.D37 2005   978'.02—dc22   2005015176

Title page illustration: A wagon train on the Oregon Trail, from Albert Richardson's book *Beyond the Mississippi*, by an unknown artist. *Courtesy of the Kansas State Historical Society*

1 3 5 7 9 8 6 4 2
Printed in the United States of America on acid-free paper

To the memory of those pioneers
who traveled the Oregon Trail

Faithfulness to the truth of history involves far more than a research, however patient and scrupulous, into special facts. Such facts may be detailed with the most minute exactness, and yet the narrative, taken as a whole, may be unmeaning or untrue. The narrator must seek to imbue himself with the life and spirit of the time. He must study events in their bearings near and remote; in the character, habits, and manners of those who took part in them. He must himself be, as it were, a sharer or a spectator of the action he describes.

Francis Parkman

Contents

Maps

Introduction

The Oregon Trail probably should be called "the Oregon-California-Utah-Colorado-Nevada-Montana-and-Other-Points-West Trail," because from the 1840s until 1869 travelers used all or part of it to reach these places at one time or another. It began, however, as the road to Oregon, and even though many travelers soon followed much of it west to California or someplace other than Oregon, it is best remembered today as the Oregon Trail, and that is what I call it between these covers.

To write that the Oregon Trail was not a trail may surprise some readers. While it did begin as a trail, by the middle 1840s it was becoming a well-worn road as large numbers of people with their wagons followed it west from the Missouri River. For travelers bound for Oregon or California, it was a journey of more than 2,000 miles, and they averaged about three miles per hour in their wagons drawn by oxen, some by mules or horses. It took about four and a half months for emigrants to reach Oregon or California. For others the journey was longer. The travel time was less for Mormons bound for Salt Lake City, or gold-seekers bound later for Colorado, Idaho, and Montana. Of course, some people never reached their destinations. Many died from cholera, other illness, or accident. Their graves, some marked but many unmarked, still lie along what remains of the roads in the corridor they followed. For those who completed their overland journeys, the trip was shorter than for those who traveled by ship around Cape Horn from the East Coast. It took them about six months to reach California or Oregon.

During the years of peak travel, from 1843 until the early 1850s, the Oregon Trail was followed by at least a quarter of a million people who wanted to reach Oregon or California. Others, heading for Utah, Colorado, Nevada,

Montana, and other points in the West, used much of the road until 1869, when the transcontinental railroad was completed. Until then the Oregon Trail was the major overland route from the Missouri River to the Pacific coast. Independence, Missouri, was the first starting point for emigrants, but in time other towns along the Missouri River also became jumping-off points. From each place, trails were blazed to the principal corridor of travel along the Platte River in modern Nebraska, and like roads anywhere, intersections or junctions with other trails developed, either running to the Oregon Trail or starting from it. Some of these trails were called cutoffs. Today we call them shortcuts.

The purpose of this book is to chronicle the saga of the road's history from long before it came into being to the present day, and to relate its history and the stories of the people involved, including explorers, Indians, fur traders, trappers, traders, emigrants, gold-seekers, soldiers, pleasure-seekers, freighters, those who carried the mail, and finally the "turnarounds," those people who gave up and returned east for one reason or another.

Unlike the self-sufficient mountain men, fur traders, and other individualists in the frontier West, most of the thousands of emigrants were more ordinary men, women, and children who banded together and traveled in moving communities on wheels to cross the plains, prairies, mountains, and deserts to reach their promised lands. For many it was a monumental event in their lives. More than 2,000 travelers kept diaries or journals or later wrote down their recollections, probably sensing that their experiences were of historic importance. They were important, but it is doubtful that any of them realized they were participating in the longest voluntary migration in history. Their experiences have provided historians, fiction writers, and makers of Hollywood films and television shows with countless stories that capture the romance, hardships, and emotions of the people going west.

Today one can fly to the same destinations reached by the emigrants in a few hours or leisurely make the drive by auto from the Missouri River westward in a matter of days. Modern highways follow or parallel many of the roads the emigrants traveled in their wagons, with their handcarts, by horse or mule, or by walking. Traveling the route today by auto and visiting the historical sites gives one a true appreciation of the land they crossed, the hardships they overcame, and what they accomplished in helping to settle the American West. The story is truly an American saga.

David Dary
Along Imhoff Creek
Norman, Oklahoma

The Oregon Trail

CHAPTER ONE

THE EXPLORATION
OF OREGON

One man's exploration is another man's home ground.

Anonymous

BEFORE THE FIRST Europeans arrived, people had lived in Oregon for more than 10,000 years. Anthropologists believe as many as 180,000 natives in about 125 tribes once made modern Oregon their home. Of these the best known today are the Chinooks, who lived along the lower Columbia River and on the narrow coastal plains between the rugged Cascade Mountains and the Pacific Ocean from Shoalwater Bay, north of the Columbia, to Tillamook Head, about fifty miles south of the river's mouth. They also ranged inland from the mouth of the Columbia to a large rapids first called The Dalles by French-Canadian trappers, who gave it a French name meaning "rapids of a river going through a narrow gorge."

The Chinooks, named for the warm, moist southwest wind blowing in from the Pacific Ocean, included the Cooniac, Cascade, Clatsop, Clackamas, Multnomah, and Wasco tribes, which all spoke the same language. Many lived in multifamily cedar-plank houses forty to sixty feet long and twenty feet wide that were roofed with bark or boards. Trading with other tribes was their pleasure. Their livelihood came from fishing, hunting, and gathering nuts, berries, and plant food. They hunted game with bows and arrows, and they were skilled boatbuilders, shaping their canoes from single cedar logs. Their smallest canoe carried only one person and the largest as many as sixty. Using a homemade twine seine made from nettles, the crew of a large canoe could catch two tons of salmon on a single outgoing tide on the Columbia River.

The Chinook society was highly stratified and based on voluntary cooperation and association. Socially, men were considered superior to women, which was reflected in what women wore—often nothing at all, although both sexes wore furs for warmth in the winter. They flattened the foreheads of their children's heads with headboards on their cradleboards. They were among the wealthiest natives north of Mexico, so wealthy that they could afford to devote two months each winter to artistic and spiritual pursuits. Their culture was rich.[1]

But then the Europeans came. The events leading to their discovery of Oregon began centuries earlier when Marco Polo, at the age of seventeen, joined his father and uncle, both Venetian merchants, on a long overland journey to China. They left Venice in 1271 and were gone about twenty-four years, seventeen of which were spent in China. They returned to Venice in 1295, and when they recounted stories of their travels, the Venetians found them difficult to believe, many thinking they were fables. Marco Polo soon entered the military and about three years later was taken prisoner while commanding a Venetian galley during a battle in a war between Venice and Genoa. While in a prison at Genoa, Polo dictated the story of his travels to another prisoner, a writer of romances named Rustichello da Pisa. After Venice and Genoa made peace in 1299, Polo and Rustichello were released from prison. Polo's manuscript was widely copied, translated, and circulated in many versions. When mass printing developed late in the fifteenth century, Polo's manuscript appeared in book form and reached an even wider audience. His descriptions of jewels, silks, porcelain, and spices such as cinnamon, pepper, and cloves, plus paper money, eyeglasses, ice cream, spaghetti, and other Oriental discoveries fascinated readers. These Europeans found it difficult to believe that there was a civilization larger and more advanced than theirs. In fact, it took nearly a century before Polo's account was accepted as more fact than fiction. His book became the basis for some of the first accurate maps of Asia produced in Europe.[2]

The fifteenth century marked the beginning of the great age of Western discovery and exploration that took place along with the Renaissance, the revival of the classical forms developed by the ancient Greeks and Romans, and the intensified concern with secular life, humanism, and the importance of the individual. Apparently inspired by Polo's belief that the Orient and its riches might be reached by sailing west from Europe, Christopher Columbus set sail in three small caravels, the *Santa María,* the *Niña,* and the *Pinta,* in 1492. Columbus carried with him a copy of Marco Polo's book in which he had made notations on the margins of some pages. Columbus, of course, found the Americas and not the Orient, but believing he had reached India or the East Indies, he labeled the natives as "Indians." It was a few years later that Amerigo Vespucci, an Italian navigator, sailed along the northern coast of South America and concluded in 1499 that the lands discovered by

Columbus belonged to a new continent and not the Orient. Martin Wald-seemüller, a German geographer and mapmaker, read Vespucci's journal and suggested the new lands be called America, an adaptation of Vespucci's first name. By then King Henry VII had sent John Cabot, the English navigator and explorer, to find a direct western route to the Orient. Aboard his ship the *Matthew* with a crew of eighteen, Cabot left Bristol in May 1497 and in late June landed on what must have been Cape Breton Island, now part of Nova Scotia, and then sailed along what are today the coasts of Labrador, New-foundland, and New England. Cabot claimed his discovery for England.

As the sixteenth century began, the Portuguese navigator Ferdinand Magellan sailed around the tip of Africa to India and later followed the same route on a voyage to the East Indies. By then Magellan had concluded that one should be able to sail southwest from Europe around or through South America to the Orient. After the Portuguese king turned down Magellan's request for a fleet of ships with which to prove his theory, Magellan renounced his Portuguese citizenship and persuaded the king of Spain to finance the journey. Magellan got his ships, left Spain, and sailed southwest to South America and then along its coast. He found no passage through the continent, but at the tip of South America he discovered a passage around the continent that became known as the Strait of Magellan. Once on the west coast of South America, he named the calm ocean he had entered the Pacific.

Although Magellan did not find a water route through South America, for the next two centuries Europeans continued to believe that such a passage existed. Spaniards came to call the imagined route the Strait of Anian, while English and French explorers, searching in North America, called it the Northwest Passage.[3] King Francis I of France sent Jacques Cartier in search of the route in 1534. After twenty days at sea, Cartier sighted New-foundland and soon discovered the Saint Lawrence River, giving France a claim to what is now Canada. Beginning in 1576, a succession of English explorers searched for the Northwest Passage starting with Sir Martin Fro-bisher, who was followed in 1585 by John Davis. Next was Henry Hudson, who in 1610 found Hudson Bay but no Northwest Passage. Robert Bylot followed in about 1615, with Luke Fox and Thomas James sailing into Hud-son Bay in 1631. All of them had been encouraged to seek such a passage by English merchants and statesmen who wanted to establish trade with the Orient, but none found it.

As the French and English were exploring the east coast of North Amer-ica, the Spanish were searching the east coast of Central America for the Strait of Anian. In September 1513, Vasco Núñez de Balboa found the Pacific Ocean after crossing the swampy Isthmus of Panama. Spain then sent Her-

nando Cortés around the tip of South America and up the west coast of
North America seeking the Strait of Anian. In 1532, Cortez discovered the
southern tip of what is now Baja California, but he probably did not name it
California. The earliest known reference to the name "California" appears
in a 1539 diary written by a Spaniard on one of three ships sailing up the
Pacific coast under the command of Francisco de Ulloa, who apparently
believed Baja California was an island. Whether the writer of the diary,
Ulloa, or someone else named it California is not known, but most authorities believe the name was taken from an early-sixteenth-century novel written by a Spaniard, García Rodríguez Ordoñez de Montalvo. The novel's
English title is *The Exploits of Esplandian,* and one of the characters is beautiful Calafia, the queen of California, a mythical island inhabited solely by
black women who lived in the manner of Amazons.

In 1542 another explorer, Juan Rodríguez Cabrillo, began sailing up the
coast of what is now California, mapping the shoreline, naming prominent
landmarks, and going ashore in some areas. But on what is now Catalina
Island, Cabrillo suffered a broken limb and soon died from complications.
Cabrillo's chief pilot, Bartolomé Ferrer, took control and continued north,
perhaps reaching the coast of present-day Oregon. But Ferrer, like the others, failed to find the fabled Northwest Passage. Most of the names Cabrillo
gave to landmarks have since been forgotten because about sixty years later,
the Spanish explorer Sebastián Vizcaíno, sailing north from Acapulco,
renamed the places named by Cabrillo in order to give himself credit for
new discoveries. Vizcaíno and his men went ashore at a fine bay and held
mass. Since it was the day of St. Didacus, who in Spanish is called San Diego,
Vizcaíno so named the bay. *San Diego* was also the name of his ship. Sailing
up the coast, Vizcaíno named what is now San Pedro Bay after the saint who
had been martyred in Constantinople; gave an island off the coast the name
Santa Catalina, after St. Catherine, patron of Christian philosophers; and
named Santa Barbara after the patron of artillerymen and all men in danger
of sudden death. Later he named Monterey Bay after the viceroy who had
sent him on the voyage. Nearby, his Carmelite friars named the Carmel
River after their own order. Aside from Monterey Bay, Vizcaíno used little
imagination in naming places and things. He either looked at the religious
calendar or asked his friars which saint's day it was and gave the places that
name. Because Vizcaíno's names were hallowed, the padres who came later
preserved them in reverence, while those given by Cabrillo disappeared.[4]

At the time Vizcaíno was sailing up the coast, ship traffic in the waters off
California was pretty much limited to the somewhat regular Spanish vessels
loaded with riches returning from Manila in the Philippines. The Spanish

navigators found Pacific currents favorable for reaching North America just north of Baja California. There they turned their ships south and sailed to their destinations. It was the treasure these Spanish ships carried that attracted Sir Francis Drake to these waters aboard his ship the *Golden Hind* in 1579. Drake was secretly commissioned by Queen Elizabeth I to undertake an expedition against Spanish colonies on the Pacific coast and also to seek the Northwest Passage. After sailing through the Strait of Magellan into the Pacific, Drake plundered Valparaiso and other Spanish ports. He then captured Spanish treasure ships returning from the Philippines before sailing as far north as the present U.S.-Canadian border looking for an inland passage across North America. Not finding one, he sailed south and anchored his ship for repairs at an inlet north of present-day San Francisco, which is now called Drake's Bay. He claimed the region for England and named it New Albion.

By then European explorers were sailing in ships much larger than those used earlier by Columbus and others. The ships had four or five masts, high forecastles, poop decks, and two or more tiers of guns. They were the great ships that traveled the oceans during the sixteenth and seventeenth centuries. Drake's *Golden Hind* was such a ship. The maps Drake and other early explorers brought with them from Europe were of little help. In fact, they were not reliable and contained mostly imagined details of the Americas. Some of these maps showed North America as no more than a land extension of Asia, with the Gulf of Mexico opposite the Bay of Bengal. Cuba was even portrayed as an island off Asia. Only after explorers returned to Europe with their charts did mapmakers begin to produce more accurate maps. When Sir Francis Drake captured Spanish treasure ships in the Pacific during the late sixteenth century, he took their charts, since they were more accurate than his own. The belief that America was an extension of Asia disappeared early in the eighteenth century when Vitus Jonassen Bering proved that the Asian and North American continents were not joined. Bering, who entered the Russian navy under Czar Peter the Great in 1724, explored the water routes between Siberia and North America, sailing through what became known as the Bering Strait into the Arctic Ocean in 1728. Bering and another Russian explorer, Alexi Chirikov, discovered rich furs in the region, which quickly overshadowed their quest for the mythical Northwest Passage. Their discoveries led Catherine the Great, ruler of Russia, to organize a trading company in 1766 to establish a trading post on Kodiak Island in the Gulf of Alaska.

The arrival of Russians along the far northwest Pacific coast prompted Spain to send Juan Pérez to the area in 1774, and the following year Bruno de

Hezeta and Bodega y Quadra sailed into the region from the south. As Hezeta sailed near the mouth of what is now known as the Columbia River, he felt a strong current and saw discolored water, but with the fog and because his men were sick with scurvy, he did not discover the river. Next came Captain James Cook. After two successful voyages in the Pacific the English Parliament offered to give him 20,000 pounds if he discovered the Northwest Passage. With two ships, the *Resolution* and the *Discovery*, Cook sailed south from England in July 1776, around the continent of Africa, across the Indian Ocean, and into the Pacific and then northward. He discovered and named the Sandwich Islands in honor of his friend and sponsor, the Earl of Sandwich. These islands later became known as the Hawaiian Islands. Cook then sailed toward the east and sighted the coast of modern Oregon in March 1778, but he never found the fabeled Northwest Passage. He did land on the west coast of present-day Vancouver Island and established a fort and spent time repairing his ships, obtaining supplies, and trading with the natives. He bought furs at sixpence each and later sold them in China for about 160 percent profit. John Ledyard, an American sailing with Cook, would later inform Thomas Jefferson, the United States minister to France, of the fur-trading potential of the Pacific Northwest.

Another Englishman, John Meares, a retired naval officer who sailed for various nations, explored the Pacific coastline in 1786 and for two years engaged in the fur trade between the Pacific Northwest and China. When he sailed into Nootka Sound, Meares traded two English pistols for a plot of land from an Indian chief. With laborers brought from China (the first Chinese in North America), Meares constructed a small fort and then built the *Northwest America*, the first ship built in what is now British Columbia. The vessel was launched in September 1788. Returning to China, Meares sold the furs and his ship and joined several others in forming a new trading company that secured a British license to carry on the fur trade. The trading company outfitted two new ships, the *Argonaut* and the *Princess Royall*, which flew the British flag. Meares's trading fort at Nootka Sound soon came to the attention of Spain and Russia. Spain sent an expedition led by Don Esteven José Martínez to Nootka in 1789 to build its own fort and to defend Spanish claims to the region. Martínez captured some English ships near Nootka, which angered the British. Tensions mounted between Spain and England, but the Spanish realized they could not control the whole coastline along what is now the western United States. They simply did not have the resources needed. In 1794, Spain signed a treaty with Britain abandoning all claims to Nootka, but the two nations failed to set the dividing line for Spanish and English claims.

By the early seventeenth century, explorers began to search for what was called the River of the West. It first appeared on European maps after Spanish explorer Martín de Aguilar, like Hezeta before him, had reported he thought they had located a major river running into the Pacific near the 42nd parallel. Mapmakers then began labeling the River of the West as an estuary to the mythical Straits of Anian or Northwest Passage but located it anywhere from the 42nd to the 50th parallel. In 1765, British Major Robert Rogers called the as yet unseen river "Ouragon," apparently its Indian name. Later it was spelled "Oregon" by Jonathan Carver in 1778 as a derivative name referring to the Ouisconsink River in present-day Wisconsin.

As Spanish and English ships were plying the Pacific coast, dissatisfaction with English rule in the thirteen colonies along the Atlantic coast exploded, and in 1775 the American Revolution began. After declaring independence from England, the rebellious colonists created in 1781 a loose union under the Articles of Confederation. England finally recognized the new independent nation in 1783 with the Treaty of Paris. Even before the Constitution was ratified in 1788, American merchants moved to challenge the British in trade in the Pacific Northwest. Robert Gray, an American sea captain who may have served in the Continental Navy during the Revolutionary War, was hired by a Massachusetts trading company. He and Captain John Kendrick were sent by Boston merchants in 1787 to the northwest Pacific coast to trade with the natives and then to sail to China and trade. Kendrick commanded the *Columbia Rediviva,* while Gray commanded the sloop *Lady Washington.* Their ships carried buttons, beads, blue cloth, and other trade items. Arriving on the coast of what is now Oregon ten months later, they traded the goods for the pelts of sea otters, and Kendrick and Gray exchanged ships. While Kendrick remained with the *Lady Washington* to trade, Gray sailed to China on the *Columbia Rediviva,* sold or traded the pelts for tea and perhaps spices and silk, and continued west through the Indian Ocean into the Atlantic and back to Boston. He arrived in Boston in August 1790, becoming the first American to circumnavigate the globe. The *Columbia* was overhauled and made ready for another voyage.

On September 28, 1790, Gray again sailed out of Boston Harbor in command of the *Columbia Rediviva,* bound for the northwest Pacific coast. About nine months later, in early June 1791, he arrived on what is today Vancouver Island. This time Gray remained to trade. He erected a fort while Kendrick sailed the *Lady Washington* to China to trade furs obtained from the natives. Gray then sailed down the Pacific coast, only to sight and greet Captain George Vancouver, the English explorer who had served under Captain James Cook. Vancouver was given his own command in 1791 to explore the

Pacific. Gray visited Vancouver aboard the *Discovery* and then returned to the *Columbia* and departed. A few days later Gray sailed into a bay and soon saw what appeared to be an entrance to a large river between sandbars. As Gray started to sail up the river, he saw natives on the bank who then ran along the shore following the ship. John Boit, one of Gray's crew members, wrote in his journal, "Without doubt we are the first Civilized people that ever visited this port, and these poor fellows view'd us and the Ship with the greatest astonishment, their language was different from any we have yet heard. The Men where entirely naked, and the Women, except a small apron before, made of Rushes, was also in a state of Nature."[5]*

Indians later recalled that at first they were much surprised and alarmed. Some imagined that the ship must be some overgrown monster, come to devour them, while others supposed her to be a floating island, inhabited by cannibals, sent by the great spirit to destroy them and ravage the country. But when the mild-mannered crew went ashore and distributed a few trinkets, the Indians realized they would not be harmed.[6] Soon natives in canoes filled with furs and dried salmon went to the ship. Gray and his men were soon trading nails, copper, cloth, and other things for the furs and salmon. A few days later John Boit wrote in his journal:

> The River, in my opinion, wou'd be a fine place for to sett up a Factory. The Indians are very numerous, and appear'd very civill (not even offering to steal). during our short stay we collected 150 Otter, 300 Beaver, and twice the Number of other land furs. the river abounds with excellent Salmon, and most other River fish, and the Woods with plenty of Moose and Deer, the skins of which was brought us in great plenty, and the Banks produces a ground Nut, which is an excellent substitute for either bread or Potatoes. We found plenty of Oak, Ash, and Walnut trees, and clear ground in plenty, which with little labour might be made fit to raise such seeds as is necessary for the sustenance of inhabitants....[7]

Robert Gray apparently did not realize that he had discovered a great river, but before leaving he named it the *Columbia* after his ship. Whether Gray wondered if the river was the fabled Northwest Passage or the rumored River of the West, no one knows. For reasons known only to him,

---

*John Boit's grammar and spelling are awkward in spots. Other quotations from writers of the eighteenth and nineteenth centuries contain such errors, but here, and throughout, quotes have been reproduced as they appear in the original sources and without the use of "[*sic*]." Bracketed interpolations appear only where explanation is needed.

Gray did not sail up the river to explore it, but soon after his discovery, George Vancouver heard the news and sent Lieutenant William Broughton up the Columbia more than a hundred miles, and he produced the first detailed map of the lower river. Broughton, however, thought the river was not suitable for major commerce. Like Gray, he had no way of knowing that the Columbia River flows for more than 1,200 miles from the base of the Canadian Rockies in southeastern British Columbia along a convoluted course to the Pacific. When Gray returned to Boston in July 1793, he told of finding the river, but no one made much of it. Gray may not have realized the importance of his find, which would be the basis for the first U.S. claim to the Pacific Northwest by right of discovery. He never sailed again to the Pacific Northwest but spent the remainder of his career commanding merchant vessels along the Atlantic coast. In 1806, at about fifty-one, he died, apparently from yellow fever, and was buried either at Charleston, South Carolina, or at sea.[8]

LONG BEFORE the United States acquired the Louisiana Territory in 1803 and Thomas Jefferson sent Lewis and Clark to explore it, there was curiosity among many Americans about the vast region west of the Mississippi River. Americans knew the Spanish had explored and occupied southern portions of the territory where Indians lived, and that fur-bearing animals populated the mountainous areas. Therefore many Americans assumed that both Indians and fur-bearing animals could also be found in the northern areas of the Louisiana Territory. These things seem to be confirmed when a small booklet titled *New Travels to the Westward, or, Unknown Parts of America: Being a Tour of Almost Fou[r]teen Months, Containing, an Account of the Country, Upwards of Two Thousand Miles West of the Christian Parts of North America*... was published at Boston in 1788. The forty-five-page work told of the first overland journey to the Pacific coast undertaken by a white man, who was named Alonso Decalves and claimed to have traveled up the Mississippi River in the spring of 1786 with his brother, John Decalves, Peter Vanshutes, and an Indian named Tomhegan. Decalves relates how after thirty-one days on the Mississippi his party traveled overland to the west. Decalves wrote: "The woods in general was filled with all sorts of game fowl, as the rivers were with Otters, Fish, &c.... We seldom traveled one hour before we had frequent opportunities of killing every kind of game."

Decalves describes how, after crossing the prairie and plains, the party crossed "a great chain of mountains which extended from north to south, whose height was truly astonishing." Descending the mountains, they struck

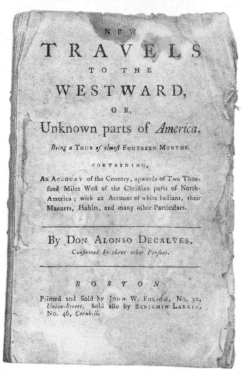

*The cover page of the fictional tale of Don Alonso
Decalves's travels from the Mississippi River westward to the Pacific during the 1780s. The work was
first published in Boston in 1788.* (Author's collection)

a stream and followed it to the Pacific Ocean, where they wintered among
Indians. There Decalves found a white captive named John Vandelure. In
the spring of 1787, Decalves's party returned east laden with gold and furs,
arriving at New Orleans on July 27, 1787. If Decalves's story had been true, he
would have been the first white man to cross the continent, but his account
was entirely fictional, all except the part relating to John Vandelure, who
apparently was a crew member from a Dutch ship captured on the Pacific
Northwest coast in 1784. Vandelure married an Indian woman and then lived
with her family. The booklet became quite popular and by the early nineteenth century had gone through at least twenty-one printings. Exactly who
read Decalves's narrative and what influence it had on them is not known,
but the journey was presented as a factual account. Many readers undoubtedly believed what they read and that a treasure in furs was waiting to be
harvested in the vast region west of the Mississippi.[9]

Certainly animal skins and pelts have been traded by man since ancient times. Henry Hudson discovered what is today Hudson Bay in 1610 on the very edge of what turned out to be one of the greatest hunting grounds for furs and pelts. But Hudson died before he became aware of what he had found. It remained for Sieur des Médard Chouart des Groseilliers, a Frenchman, and his brother-in-law, Pierre-Esprit Radisson, to realize the land's potential for the fur trade. Groseilliers arrived in French Canada about 1639 and worked as an assistant to Jesuit missionaries until 1646, when he settled in Quebec and married. After his wife died, he remarried. His second wife was the half-sister of Pierre-Esprit Radisson. In 1859 both men traveled into the country north of Lake Superior after hearing stories from the Huron, Cree, and Sioux Indians of the wealth of beaver pelts. A year later they returned to Montreal with a cargo of prime furs, only to be charged by French authorities with illicit trading without a license and forced to pay a series of fines. Irritated by how their countrymen had treated them, Groseilliers left Canada and sought redress in France. Finding none, he traveled to Boston and then England, where he sought support for their fur-trading venture. A group of London merchants agreed to put up the money, and in 1668, Groseilliers, who was called "Mr. Gooseberry" by the British, sailed to James Bay, at the southern end of Hudson Bay, and established Fort Charles, the first permanent white settlement on the bay. Groseilliers and his party were so successful in acquiring furs that two years later King Charles II of England granted a royal charter to his cousin, Prince Rupert, and seventeen other Englishmen to establish the Hudson's Bay Company. The chartering of companies by the Crown had by now become an established method of trade and territorial expansion for nearly a century. But the charter granted to the Hudson's Bay Company included privileges no other company had ever enjoyed. It had absolute proprietorship and supreme jurisdiction in civil and military affairs over all the lands whose rivers emptied into Hudson Bay, or nearly half of modern Canada. The Hudson Bay Company had the power to make laws and to declare war against the natives.

The company's development of the fur trade, however, was very slow. In 1749, seventy-nine years after it received its charter, the Hudson's Bay Company had only four or five coastal forts and no more than 120 employees, who annually bartered from the natives three or four shiploads of English goods for about the same weight of furs and skins. Still, the annual trade was highly profitable. It was not until England gained control of what had been French Canada following the French and Indian Wars, and after the Treaty of Paris in 1763, that the Hudson's Bay Company's trade increased tremendously and attracted competition from private trappers. By the time the American Revolution started, private trappers in Canada were penetrating the region from the Great Lakes westward up the Saskatchewan River toward the Rocky Mountains. In 1783 a group of private fur traders organized the North West Company in Montreal to compete directly against the highly profitable Hudson's Bay Company. Alexander Mackenzie, a member of the North West Company, explored what is now northwest Canada from Great Slave Lake to the Arctic Ocean, traveling on the great river that now bears his name. Four years later, in 1793, Mackenzie took a small expedition up the Peace River, crossed the Rocky Mountains, then followed the Fraser River and its tributaries before moving overland to near the Pacific Ocean. Mackenzie, a native of Scotland who immigrated with his family to New York City in 1774 and then moved to Montreal in 1779, became the first white man north of Mexico to explore overland the North American continent. His journals were published in book form as *Voyages from Montreal* in London in 1801 and a year later in Philadelphia. Mackenzie's book contains the first published account of Robert Gray's discovery of the Columbia River.

President Thomas Jefferson read the journals during the summer of 1802 and apparently learned for the first time of Gray's discovery. Jefferson apparently was convinced that if the United States did not stake and survey Gray's discovery, it might lose its claim and the reported rich resources of the Pacific Northwest. Jefferson was also influenced by reading the published accounts of the explorations of Cook and Vancouver. Jefferson began to envision an official expedition that would combine scientific, diplomatic, and commercial goals. About six months before the United States acquired the Louisiana Territory, Jefferson proposed to Congress that the lands west of the Mississippi River should be explored. Congress agreed. But to conceal the nation's expansionist aims from England, France, and Spain, Jefferson suggested the expedition's journey be presented as a "literary pursuit." By the time Meriwether Lewis and William Clark left St. Louis heading up the Missouri River, the United States had purchased New Orleans and the Louisiana Territory from France for $15 million. Lewis and Clark reached the Columbia River in December 1805, established Fort Clatsop near the mouth of the river, and remained until March 1806, when they started their return journey to Missouri. In St. Louis they confirmed that America's new territory was rich in furs.

Until the colonies were granted independence, the fur trade in North America had been controlled by the English and French, who had traded goods for furs trapped by natives for more than a century. When independence came, enterprising individual Americans began to pick up where the

British and French had left off. They might have developed a large fur trade had George Washington not argued that British fur-trading companies along the Canadian border might be able to turn the Indians against the independent Americans. Washington also argued that private American traders were too small to compete against the large and more experienced Hudson's Bay and North West companies. Washington convinced Congress in 1795 to build, stock, and operate a series of fur-trading posts called factories in the American South and West. This became known as the factory system, and the fur trade became the first industry in United States history to be subsidized by the government. Congress created the Office of Indian Affairs to handle it. The first factory was established in 1795 at Colerain on the Saint Marys River in Georgia. Another came soon after in what is now central Tennessee, but between 1795 and 1802, no other factories were established. The government planned to have all furs obtained in trade with Indians sent to Washington, D.C., where they would be sold at public auction. The money obtained from sales would then be used to buy more trading goods and to fund the factory system. But from the beginning the system did not work well. The factories were poorly managed. Employees were not of the same quality as those in the private fur companies, and the quality of goods offered to Indians was poor. Many Indians refused to use the government factories.[10]

The factory system was started about a decade before Lewis and Clark returned from their exploring journey across the continent. When they related that there were great commercial possibilities for the fur trade in the regions they had visited, they confirmed what a Spaniard named Manuel Lisa already suspected. Late in 1808, Lisa and nine other men in St. Louis, including William Clark of Lewis and Clark fame, organized what became known as the Missouri Fur Company, headquartered in St. Louis. They sent their first expedition up the Missouri River in the spring of 1809. Lisa, who had gone up the Missouri the previous year, had learned that it was easier and faster for his men to trap and skin beaver than to trade for beaver pelts from the Indians, since many western tribes, unlike their eastern counterparts, moved frequently and were not full-time trappers. Then, too, Lisa and other fur traders would learn that in the West they would have to adapt to the vast unsettled country and also to the demands of the growing markets in the East and in Europe for pelts. While he probably never realized it, Lisa created the concept of the western "mountain man" years before that label came into use.

Lewis and Clark's accounts of the commercial fur-trading potential west of the Mississippi River to the Pacific apparently confirmed what John Jacob

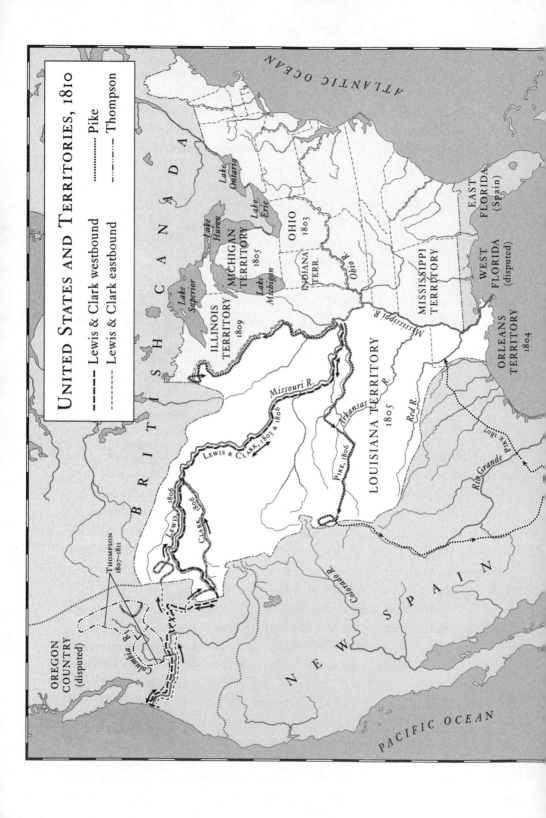

UNITED STATES AND TERRITORIES, 1810

----- Lewis & Clark westbound   ·········· Pike
----- Lewis & Clark eastbound   —·—·— Thompson

Astor also suspected and resulted in his organization of the American Fur Company in New York City. Some background: Astor was the third son of a German butcher. His oldest brother, George, immigrated to London, where he began manufacturing and selling musical instruments. The next son, Henry, soon left for America and became a butcher in New York. John Jacob remained at home in Germany until relations with his stepmother became strained. He left home, walked to the Rhine Valley, got a job on a timber barge, and worked his way down the Rhine River to Holland, adding to the small savings he had already accumulated. When he had enough money, he sailed to London, where he went to work for his brother George, learning to make musical instruments, learning the English language, and again saving his money. He also gathered as much information as he could about the American Revolution, which was then under way in the American colonies. After the Revolution ended, Astor sailed to America, in November 1783, carrying seven flutes and $25 in his pocket. After a voyage of about eight weeks, his ship entered Chesapeake Bay only to be frozen in the ice for about two months. Astor made good use of the time by talking with another German immigrant who had been to America earlier. The man, who had previously dealt successfully in American furs, told Astor about wonderful opportunities in the field. By the time the ice melted and the ship docked, Astor was convinced the fur trade was for him. From Baltimore, Astor headed north to New York to join his brother Henry.

John Jacob Astor was twenty-one years old when he reached New York in March 1784. He worked as a baker's assistant before opening a small shop, where he sold musical instruments and bought and sold furs. One day a woman, Sarah Todd, entered the shop to purchase furs for a coat. Her ability to judge furs and to make them into coats won the heart of Astor, and soon they were married. The marriage brought young Astor into higher Dutch New York society—and a dowry of $300. From a store on Water Street, Astor and his wife gradually expanded their trade in furs. Not infrequently, Astor would leave the store in his wife's care and head for the frontier to buy pelts and make contacts with others engaged in the fur trade in America's northwest territories and in Montreal, then the center of the trade in North America. John Jacob became friends with Alexander Henry, an American who had worked in the English fur trade in Canada and then retired to Montreal. Henry knew the trade well, and he educated Astor about the value of western trading posts.

While the headquarters of Astor's American Fur Company was in New York City, the center of its operation soon became Mackinac Island in Lake Huron, in what is now northern Michigan. The British had started building

Fort Mackinac in 1780, but in 1783 when the Treaty of Paris was signed, giving independence to the American colonies, the island passed to U.S. control. British troops, however, did not evacuate the fort until 1796, when the United States and Great Britain signed a treaty drafted by the American John Jay to resolve their outstanding differences. Among other things Jay's treaty called for the British to evacuate their posts on the northwestern frontier of the United States. Astor was thus able to purchase British fur-trading interests on Mackinac Island and merge them with his American Fur Company.

By 1800, Astor had become the leading American merchant in the fur trade and was worth perhaps a quarter of a million dollars. He soon became interested in trade with China and made a trip to London, where he obtained a license to trade in any East India Company port. Back in New York a friend joined Astor in sending a shipload of furs to Canton, China. The venture was successful and Astor's share of the profit was $50,000, part of which he invested in New York City real estate, which became the foundation of his fortune.

When Astor organized the American Fur Company in 1808, it was in part his response to competition from fur traders in St. Louis and his desire to develop a western entrance to the fur trade on the Pacific coast. Astor knew the English were already pushing westward across Canada to expand their fur trade. He approached the North West Company to see if it wanted to join him in a Pacific Northwest venture. Officially the North West Company said no, apparently believing that it could beat out any competition offered by Astor. But three members of the North West Company privately expressed an interest in joining Astor, understanding that he had the resources to compete against the English. Astor realized that before he could formalize his Pacific Northwest operation, he should have government support. Starting with local officials in New York, he eventually was able to meet with President Thomas Jefferson in the summer of 1808. Astor explained his plan. Jefferson was pleased that Americans were organizing to capture the Indian trade, but he did not give Astor a blanket endorsement. In his reply, sent by letter, Jefferson said that while he liked what Astor had proposed, he only promised "every reasonable patronage and facility in the power of the executive," suggesting that Astor's company would be protected from hostile actions of the North West Company, headquartered at Fort William, located on the north side of Lake Superior.[11]

With the implied government support, Astor began to formalize his plans to enter the fur trade in the Pacific Northwest. The three members of the North West Company—Alexander McKay, Duncan McDougal, and Donald McKenzie—and a little later a fourth man, a wealthy New Jersey native named Wilson Price Hunt, joined the group. On June 23, 1810, Astor and his four partners signed the necessary papers establishing the Pacific Fur Company as a subsidiary company of his American Fur Company. The agreement established Astor as head of the company. He would manage its affairs from New York City, furnishing vessels, goods, provisions, arms, ammunition, and everything else needed, provided the cost did not exceed $400,000. The stock of the company was divided into one hundred shares. Fifty shares were Astor's, while thirty-five were divided among the partners and their associates and fifteen shares were held in reserve for others who might join the enterprise. Astor then set about to put his plan into action, a plan that would lay the foundation for American settlement in what would be called Oregon Country, a name applied to the entire region west of the Rocky Mountains between California and Alaska.

CHAPTER TWO

ASTORIA

It is fortune not wisdom that rules man's life.

Cicero

JOHN JACOB ASTOR'S grandiose plan was to establish a chain of small trading posts along the route followed by Lewis and Clark and then to build a large trading post or depot near the mouth of the Columbia River to give him a fur-trading monopoly in the Pacific Northwest. Astor wanted the planned trading post at the mouth of the Columbia River to be an "emporium to an immense commerce; as a colony that would form the germ of a wide civilization; that would, in fact, carry the American population across the Rocky Mountains and spread it along the shores of the Pacific." From this post Astor envisioned his ships carrying furs to the great markets in China and returning with goods to Boston and New York. Still other ships carrying trade goods would obtain pelts from Russians living along the coast of Alaska. To implement this plan, Astor would send two expeditions to the Pacific Northwest, one by sea, the other overland. He believed later expeditions over these routes could keep his trading posts supplied.[1]

Sending an expedition by sea was the easiest part of his plan. Astor already had two ships in the Pacific, the *Beaver* and the *Enterprise*. Obtaining another ship and a captain was not difficult. Astor arranged for Jonathan Thorn, a lieutenant in the United States Navy, to take a leave of absence from the military to command a fine sailing ship named *Tonquin*, a 290-ton vessel with ten guns and a crew of twenty men. Four of Astor's partners—Alexander McKay, Duncan McDougal, David Stuart, and his nephew Robert Stuart—were to travel with the *Tonquin* along with eleven clerks, plus provisions, Indian trade goods, seeds to plant and raise crops, and even frames and timbers to build a small sailing ship for coastal trade that would be assembled once the party reached the Columbia River. The *Tonquin* set sail from New York on September 8, 1810, and followed a route around South America into the Pacific to reach the Columbia River.[2]

For Astor, sending an expedition overland was more difficult. Aside from Alexander Mackenzie's party of Canadians and Lewis and Clark's expedition, no other white men were known to have traveled overland to the Pacific. To head his overland expedition, Astor selected one of his partners, Wilson Price Hunt, a twenty-seven-year-old originally from New Jersey. While Hunt had never traveled west of the Mississippi River, he had acquired much knowledge of the western country from Indian traders in St. Louis, including Indian trading practices and the character of the different tribes. In St. Louis, Hunt operated a mercantile store in partnership with John Hawkinson from 1804 until 1810, when he became a chief agent for Astor's Pacific Fur Company.

Hunt traveled to Montreal and joined two other partners in Astor's enterprise, Donald McKenzie and Alexander McKay, to organize the overland expedition. Unlike Hunt, McKenzie had spent a decade in the West in the service of the North West Company. He understood Indians and the strategy of the Indian trade. So did McKay, who had accompanied Alexander Mackenzie overland across what is now western Canada to near the Pacific in 1793. McKay, who was older than Hunt and McKenzie, had retired from the North West Company two years earlier and joined Astor in his Pacific Fur Company venture. When Hunt arrived in Montreal in July 1810, the three men began purchasing supplies, including Indian trade goods, and recruiting Canadian voyageurs for the first leg of the expedition. When these things were done, everything was loaded aboard a great canoe typical of those used by the fur traders to navigate the intricate and sometimes obstructed rivers. One source describes Hunt's canoe as being "between thirty and forty feet long, and several feet in width; constructed of birch bark, sewed with fibers of the roots of the spruce tree, and daubed with resin of the pine, instead of tar. The cargo was made up in packages, weighing from ninety to one hundred pounds each, for the facility of loading and unloading, and of transportation at portages. The canoe itself, though capable of sustaining freight of upwards of four tons, could readily be carried on men's shoulders. Canoes of this size are generally managed by eight or ten men, two of whom are picked veterans, who receive double wages, and are stationed, one at the bow and the other at the stern, to keep a lookout and to steer. They are termed the foreman and the steersman. The rest, who ply the paddles, are called middle men. When there is a favorable breeze, the canoe is occasionally navigated with a sail."[3]

Before leaving the island of Montreal, the Canadian voyageurs, as was their custom, attended services in the ancient Chapel of St. Anne, the patroness of all voyageurs. After leaving the chapel, as was also the custom, the men had a "a grand carouse, in honor of the saint and for the prosperity of the voyage." When the party finally left Montreal in the large canoe, they made their way up the Ottawa River and along a succession of small lakes and rivers toward Mackinac Island in Lake Huron. Their progress was slow. Hunt soon realized the men recruited for the journey were a mixed lot. Some were able-bodied but inexperienced. Others were experienced but lazy. Still others were experienced and willing but were old veterans incapable of hard work. Then, too, the voyageurs frequently wanted to go ashore, build a fire, put on a pot of stew, smoke, gossip, and sing. The party arrived on July 22, 1810, at the site of old Fort Michilimackinac, built by the French in 1715 for the fur trade, located on the south shore of the Straits of Mackinac, which connect Lake Huron and Lake Michigan. The French relinquished the post to the British in 1761, and the British abandoned it in 1781. Around the old fort a settlement had grown during the years. In 1810, it was still a place where traders and trappers gathered before setting out to do their work to the north or southwest. A year or more later they would return with their pelts, dispose of them, and then let off steam by spending their profits, fiddling, dancing, and drinking, and dressing themselves in the best clothes they could buy and parading like arrant braggarts on the beach.

When the party arrived at Fort Michilimackinac, many voyageurs were in residence, and Hunt began looking for good men to join the expedition. He wanted to recruit experienced, hardworking, and trustworthy men for a period of five years. But some would not enlist for more than three years. Others wanted part of their pay in advance. Hunt had no success in hiring good men until one experienced voyageur agreed to join the expedition. That man then enticed a few others to do the same. Knowing that voyageurs with the North West Company viewed themselves with great self-importance and often wore feathers in their hats to mark them as men of the north, Hunt distributed feathers and ostrich plumes to the men who had signed up. The feathers and plumes caught the fancy of other voyageurs, and soon Hunt was able to hire a full complement of the good men he needed.

While Hunt was doing his hiring, a Scotsman named Ramsey Crooks arrived at the post. Hunt, who had sent Crooks a letter inviting him to join the expedition, was pleased to see him. Crooks had worked with the North West Company and had experience, judgment, enterprise, and integrity. Soon Hunt's expedition was ready to depart. The voyageurs, however, again wanted to celebrate before leaving. They feasted, fiddled, drank, sang, danced, frolicked, and fought until they were satisfied. Hunt apparently paid many bills to keep the voyageurs happy until, on August 12, 1810, after hugs and kisses with their wives, sweethearts, brothers, cousins, and anyone else who was on hand, the expedition left Mackinac Island and headed southwest to Green Bay and the Fox and Wisconsin rivers and to Prairie du Chien, where the Wisconsin and the Mississippi rivers meet. From there the expedition traveled down the Mississippi and arrived at St. Louis on September 3, 1810.

The arrival of Hunt's expedition in the small settlement of St. Louis was big news. It marked the entrance of a new company into the fur trade. With ample funds, Hunt was able to hire several additional men and added another partner to the enterprise, Joseph Miller, a well-educated Pennsylvanian, who had entered military service in 1799. When he was refused a furlough in 1805, he resigned in disgust and turned to trapping beaver and trading with Indians. Hunt thought Miller would be an asset to the expedition. By the time Hunt had hired the men he needed, the expedition numbered about sixty. It was Hunt's plan to follow Lewis and Clark's route up the Missouri River, but the size of the expedition required more than the large canoe that Hunt's party had used to reach St. Louis. Two other boats were acquired. One was a Schenectady barge that had seen service on the Mohawk River in New York State. The other was a large keelboat typical of the craft plying the Mississippi River.[4]

Loaded with the men and supplies, the three boats left St. Louis on October 21, 1810, and started up the Missouri River. It was late in the year for such travel, but Hunt had decided it would be cheaper to have the expedition spend the winter in camp than to hold the members in St. Louis with its temptations. The expedition traveled up the Missouri about 450 miles before the weather told Hunt it was time to make winter camp. The site selected was at the mouth of the Nodaway River, a few miles below where the borders of present-day Kansas, Nebraska, and Missouri meet. There the expedition went into winter camp, but soon several of the men hired in St. Louis deserted. Hunt returned to St. Louis to hire replacements. One of the men hired was Pierre Dorion, a half-breed Sioux interpreter who joined the expedition in the spring with his wife, Marie, an Iowan Indian, and two sons, a two-year-old and a four-year-old. Although the famous Sacagawea had crossed the northern plains with Lewis and Clark to the Pacific, Marie Dorion was the first woman known to have traveled from Missouri to the Pacific. The expedition then consisted of forty Canadian voyageurs, several American hunters, interpreter Pierre Dorion and his family, a clerk named John Reed, and five partners including Hunt. They were joined by the touring English naturalist John Bradbury and the young botanist Thomas Nuttall, who wanted to travel with the group into what is now South Dakota.[5]

As the expedition pushed up the Missouri River, a few more men deserted during the weeks that followed. They were replaced by wandering trappers met by the expedition, including Alexander Carson and Benjamin Jones, who had been trapping at the headwaters of the Missouri River for two years, and three Missouri Fur Company veterans—Jacob Reznor, Edward Robinson, and John Hoback. When these men learned that Hunt intended to follow Lewis and Clark's path up the Missouri River, they encouraged him to take a more southerly route, which was easier and did not go through hostile Blackfeet Indian country. After much discussion Hunt decided to leave the Missouri River upstream at the Arikara Indian villages near the border of present-day North Dakota, and to travel overland. Just before the expedition reached the villages, it was overtaken by a party of trappers commanded by Manuel Lisa. Hunt suspected there would be trouble with Lisa, the king of the Missouri River fur traders, but at the Arikara villages, where Lisa had much influence, he helped Hunt trade for horses from the Indians and furnished another fifty horses from his Missouri Fur Company trading post a few miles away in exchange for the boats Hunt's expedition were abandoning.

On July 18, 1811, Hunt's expedition, with eighty-two horses, left the Arikara villages and headed overland toward the southwest. The five Pacific Fur Company partners each rode a horse, as did Dorion's wife. The rest of the horses were used as pack animals for supplies and provisions while the remaining members of the expedition walked. After two or three days they reached the Grand River and found a camp of Cheyenne Indians. There Hunt bought thirty-six more horses. The expedition reached the Little Missouri River on August 14 and crossed the Powder River on August 23. A week later they came upon a camp of Crow Indians as they traveled through the Bighorn Mountains. They then followed the Bighorn and Wind rivers into the Wind River Mountains, crossing the Continental Divide, to the Spanish River, known today as the Green River, where they met a band of Snake Indians and traded for a large supply of buffalo jerky. The expedition turned west and began to look for trees large enough to make canoes, thinking they could travel down the Snake River, a tributary of the Columbia. But they learned that the Snake River was very difficult to navigate, so the expedition continued overland to Henry's Fort, then a deserted trading post on Henry's Fork of the Snake near modern St. Anthony, Idaho. There they found cottonwood trees large enough to make pirogues, and the men began to fell the trees and carve the pirogues. From what is known, one group of trappers were to remain at Henry's Fort to trap during the upcoming winter months with instructions to bring their pelts the following spring to the new trading post on the Columbia River. Other groups of trappers apparently remained at other points along the route and were instructed to do the same.[6]

Shifting to river travel meant the expedition had to abandon their horses. Many of the animals were left in the care of two young Snake Indians as the expedition, in perhaps fifteen newly carved pirogues, entered the water on Henry's Fork of the Snake on October 19. At first the river looked tame enough to carry them down to the Columbia River, but within days the river became a torrent. One voyageur was killed and several pirogues loaded with supplies and goods were lost in the roaring river. The expedition realized they could not continue their journey by water. A few miles east of what is today Twin Falls, Idaho, the expedition spent ten days discussing their fate. They decided to cache everything they were carrying except essentials that could be carried on their backs. They then split up into groups, each led by one of the partners or by clerk John Reed. In this way they hoped at least one group would locate Indians who might furnish provisions, horses, and information. Hunt's little party was the luckiest and came upon a Shoshone Indian camp and obtained food and some horses. Most of the others had to live off the land. Hunt was able to get Crooks's group to the Indian camp, but one of the Canadian voyageurs, out of his mind for lack of food, drowned in the river before they reached the camp.

Four days before Christmas, 1811, Hunt's and Crooks's parties again started west. With the help of three Shoshone guides, they made their way across the Snake River and moved northwest toward the Columbia River, following a route that traversed Baker Valley, Grande Ronde Valley, and the Blue Mountains. On January 8, 1812, they stumbled upon a large Indian camp, where they rested for six days. When they resumed their journey, it took them about seven days to reach the Columbia River. They then followed the stream to Astor's trading post, which had been constructed by the men who had arrived on the *Tonquin*, Astor's ship. There, Hunt and Crooks found McKenzie's, McClellan's, and Reed's parties waiting. They had arrived at Astoria, as the trading post became known, a few days earlier. Other stragglers from the expedition began showing up at the post during the days and weeks that followed.[7]

When Hunt arrived at Astoria, he learned that reports he had heard from Indians were true. The *Tonquin* had been destroyed at Nootka on Vancouver Island by Indians, who killed Captain Jonathan Thorn and all of his crew. While the *Tonquin* was a fine sailing ship, its captain left much to be desired. Astor had hired Thorn because he had a reputation for courage and firmness, and was accustomed to naval discipline. Thorn had distinguished himself in American naval action against Tripoli and the Barbary States in the early 1800s. But as Alexander Ross, one of Astor's partners who sailed on the *Tonquin,* recalled, Thorn "was an able and expert seaman, but unfortunately, his treatment of the people under his command was strongly tinctured with cruelty and despotism. He delighted in ruling with a rod of iron; his officers were treated with harshness, his sailors with cruelty, and every one else was regarded by him with contempt. With a jealous and peevish temper, he was easily excited; and the moment he heard the Scotch Highlanders speak to each other in the Scottish dialect, or the Canadians in the French language, he was on his high horse, making every one on board as unhappy as himself."[8]

When the *Tonquin* arrived at the mouth of the Columbia River on March 22, 1811, a violent storm was raging. The entrance to the river and the adjacent coast was wild and dangerous. "A fresh wind from the northwest sent a rough tumbling sea upon the coast, which broke upon the bar in furious surges, and extended a sheet of foam almost across the mouth of the river. Under these circumstances the captain did not think it prudent to approach within three leagues, until the bar should be sounded and the channel ascertained. Mr. Fox, the chief mate, was ordered to this service in the whaleboat, accompanied by John Martin, an old seaman, who had formerly visited the river, and by three Canadians. Fox requested to have regular sailors to man the boat, but the captain would not spare them from the service of the ship, and supposed the Canadians, being expert boatmen on lakes and rivers, were competent to the service, especially when directed and aided by Fox and Martin."[9]

Astor's partners aboard the *Tonquin* tried to persuade Captain Thorn to send seamen instead of the Canadians in the small boat, but he refused. At one o'clock in the afternoon Fox, Martin, and the three Canadians set off in the small whaleboat. All eyes aboard the *Tonquin* followed the whaleboat until it disappeared beyond the high rolling waves and among the foaming breakers. There was still no sign of the whaleboat and its crew when darkness came. During the night the wind subsided and by morning the weather was serene. Still there was no sign of the whaleboat and its crew. They did not survive.

Wilson Price Hunt learned that after Captain Thorn had crossed the bar, he had anchored the *Tonquin* in a bay about ten miles up the Columbia River. Hogs, sheep, and goats were landed on the river's north shore. Later several hogs escaped into the woods and in time bred and became a pack of bothersome wild pigs. The *Tonquin* meantime sailed farther up the Columbia, meeting many curious Indians on the riverbanks. Most of the men on the ship went ashore and set up a camp. They cut firewood and filled their

An unidentified artist's portrayal of the loss of several Canadian voyageurs in a whale-boat on March 25, 1811. Captain Jonathan Thorn of the Tonquin *had ordered them to cross the bar at the mouth of the Columbia River during a violent storm.* (Courtesy Bill Gulick Collection)

wooden water casks. Packs of ax heads were then taken off the ship and opened. Some of the men began cutting and shaping handles. Soon Captain Thorn, Alexander McKay, David Stuart, and other leaders of the ship's expedition hired a Clatsop Indian chief named Daitshowan to guide them up the river to find a good location for Astor's factory, or trading post. The men picked a site about ten miles from its mouth on the south bank at what was then called Point George (now Smith Point). The site was covered by dense trees, including Douglas fir, red alder, and hemlock. To the south there were steep hillsides and deep ravines, but the spot offered a good view up and down the river. Soon the men began clearing the ground by cutting down trees and using black powder to blast out stumps. The process was slow. Meantime, the *Tonquin* was moved and anchored in the river just off the spot where the men began to construct a large trading store and storage building under the supervision of Johann Koaster, the ship's carpenter. Later they would build a house and blacksmith shop and construct a wall, or palisade, that covered about ninety square feet around the trading post. At the front corners of the wall they constructed two bastions and mounted a cannon in each. At some point they raised the American flag over what was named Astoria, for their employer.

The Astorians were apparently unaware that to the east of their new trading post a party from the North West Company was heading down the Columbia River toward its mouth. Headed by David Thompson, a partner in the company, this party was stopping at all Indian villages and presenting British flags to the natives, proclaiming that they were formally taking possession of the country in the name of the king of England for the North West Company. On July 15, 1811, about four months after the first Americans arrived at the mouth of the Columbia aboard the *Tonquin*, Thompson and his men arrived at Astoria and learned the Americans had beaten the British in establishing a trading post.

A few weeks earlier, as Hunt learned, the *Tonquin*, with twenty-three persons, including a Quinault Indian named Joseachal as interpreter, set sail from the mouth of the Columbia River. Captain Thorn steered north and a few days later arrived at Vancouver Island, where he anchored the ship in a harbor near Nootka. The Indian interpreter warned Thorn about anchoring there because the nearby Indians were treacherous. Thorn ignored the warning. Soon many Indians in canoes carrying sea-otter skins came to the *Tonquin* to trade. Late in the day, Alexander McKay and a few other men from the ship went ashore to visit the Indians in their village, especially the chief. Six Indians were kept aboard the *Tonquin* to make sure no harm would come to McKay and the other men from the ship who spent the night in the Indian village. Before McKay and the men returned to the ship the following morning, a large number of Indians brought many sea-otter skins in their canoes to the *Tonquin*. When the Indians went aboard, Captain Thorn made a liberal offer to one man for a single skin. The Indian treated the offer with scorn and began following Thorn around on the deck. Thorn soon snatched the otter skin from the man, rubbed it in his face, and then threw the Indian over the ship's side. The trading quickly ended, and the Indians left the ship in their canoes.

McKay and his party then returned to the *Tonquin* and learned what had happened. The Indian interpreter warned McKay that the ship should sail immediately because the Indians would seek revenge. McKay, who understood Indian culture, agreed and urged Thorn to weigh anchor and sail away. Thorn laughed off the warning and assured McKay that the ship's cannon and firearms would certainly keep the ship and everyone aboard safe. During the rest of the day there were no signs of trouble from the Indians, and tensions on the *Tonquin* eased. When Captain Thorn retired to his cabin for the night, he left no more than his usual order for precautions with the crew.

At the first light of dawn the following morning, a canoe with twenty Indians came alongside the *Tonquin*. The Indians did not show any weapons, appeared friendly, and held up sea-otter skins. Captain Thorn and McKay were still asleep. The officer of the watch, having not been told to keep Indians off the ship, let them come aboard. He did the same with the Indians in a second canoe that soon came alongside the ship. As the Indians spread over the ship, the officer called Captain Thorn and McKay. They appeared and the Indians offered to trade with the captain on his terms. As more canoes with Indians were sighted coming toward the ship, Thorn became concerned and ordered the anchor lifted and seven men were sent aloft to set the sail. Thorn then made a hurried trade with the Indians, giving them mostly knives for the skins. When he next ordered the Indians to leave the ship, one man gave a yell. It was a signal. Armed with the knives they had just traded for, and war clubs they had hidden under their dress, the Indians attacked. McKay was struck with a war club and tossed into the water where Indian women in canoes killed him. Thorn made for a young Indian chief and killed him with a knife. He then tried to get to his cabin and the firearms stored there, but he never made it. He was killed, as were other crew members on deck. Of the seven men who had been sent aloft, three were killed as they tried to come to the aid of those on deck, but four of them made their way to the ship's cabin, where they barricaded the door, got muskets and ammunition, broke holes through the companionway, and opened fire. The Indians left the ship, and soon the four survivors were on deck firing guns at the fleeing natives, including Thorn's Indian interpreter Joseachal, who had not taken part in the fight. He fled the ship with the others.

At dawn, with no sign of life on the ship, several Indians, including the interpreter Joseachal, set out in canoes toward the *Tonquin*, still in the harbor. They approached the ship cautiously. After a while they saw one man on deck. He appeared friendly and invited them to come aboard. The Indians paused for some time before boarding the ship. When they did, they found the deck deserted. Soon other canoes came to the ship loaded with Indians apparently intent on taking anything they could find. Suddenly there was a tremendous noise. The *Tonquin* had exploded. The Indian interpreter was thrown unhurt into the water, but most of the Indians aboard the ship were killed. Although the evidence is hazy, it appears that one member of the crew, seriously wounded the day before, enticed as many Indians as possible to return to the ship. He then set fire to the ship's powder magazine, taking his own life as well as theirs. The four crew members who had barricaded themselves in the cabin tried to escape in one of the ship's boats but were later taken prisoner by the Indians and killed. Only the Indian interpreter Joseachal escaped death and carried the story of the demise of the *Tonquin* and its crew back to Astoria.[10]

The loss of the *Tonquin* spread feelings of doom and gloom among the men at Astoria, but when Hunt arrived there on May 11, 1812, they were recovering. The *Beaver,* another of Astor's ships, had arrived a few days earlier after an eight-month voyage from New York. Supplies and reinforcements carried by the *Beaver* made possible the establishment of new trading posts up the Columbia River, where the Pacific Fur Company had competition from the North West Company. The fresh supplies also meant they could restock Fort Okanogan, established a year earlier by David Stuart on the east bank of the Okanogan River just above its entrance into the Columbia River in what is now Washington. When Stuart left the North West Company and became a partner in Astor's new Pacific Fur Company in 1809, he apparently gave his nephew Robert Stuart two of his five Astor shares, making Robert a partner, too. Both David and Robert Stuart were among those who arrived on the *Tonquin* and constructed Astoria.

In the summer of 1812, after an attempt to send dispatches overland to Astor failed when the party lost them during an Indian attack, Robert Stuart was chosen to carry new ones east. They described the state of the company's operations, including a report on the loss of the *Tonquin,* to provide Astor some idea of what reinforcements and supplies were needed.

When Robert Stuart's party left Astoria on June 29, 1812, with another group of Astorians going up the Columbia River to trade, they were unaware that eleven days earlier, on June 18, the United States had declared

This is Astoria as it appeared in 1813. (Courtesy Bill Gulick Collection)

war on Great Britain. The War of 1812, as it became known, was the culmination of a series of problems that had developed between France and Great Britain during the course of the French Revolution and the Napoleonic Wars. Beginning in 1793, both countries had violated the maritime rights of neutral powers, as had the United States. British naval officers claimed that seamen on U.S. vessels, including naturalized Americans of British origin, were either deserters or British subjects. They were pressed into British military service. The British refused to accept that the United States had the right to naturalize foreigners. The United States challenged the British practice, and relations between both countries soon reached a breaking point when, in 1807, a British frigate fired on a U.S. ship in American territorial waters, then left the area. Later the British executed four American crewmen. At the urging of President Thomas Jefferson, Congress passed the Embargo Act of 1807, which prohibited nearly all U.S. ships from putting to sea and then banned overland trade with British and Spanish possessions in Canada and Florida. The legislation hurt the U.S. economy and was replaced in 1809, when Congress forbade any trade with France and Britain. The United States reopened trade with all nations the following year. Napoleon then lifted France's anti-neutral decrees. The United States demanded Britain do the same so that American trade could resume, but Britain refused. James Madison, who had become president, called Congress into session in November 1811. After about eight months of debate, Congress declared war on Great Britain on June 18, 1812. Word of the war took about seven months to reach Astoria.

Donald McKenzie had left the Astor trading post on the Clearwater River near the border of modern Washington and Idaho and traveled to Fort Spokane on the Spokane River in what is now eastern Washington, to celebrate Christmas and the New Year of 1813 with another Astorian, John Clarke. The Pacific Fur Company post had been built near another post operated by the North West Company. Both companies were very competitive when going after pelts, but many men on both sides were Canadians and friends. They often drank, ate, and celebrated together. McKenzie and Clarke were celebrating when John George McTavish and some other men with the Canadian North West Company arrived at Fort Spokane. McTavish informed Astor's men that Great Britain and America were at war and, to prove it, showed a copy of President Madison's Declaration of War. The document was quickly passed around. The happy faces on the Astorians became stern. McTavish's and Astor's men realized the meaning of the war even though they were on the other side of the continent. Neither group had been aware of the threat of war, but now McKenzie and Clarke heard

McTavish boast that the North West Company would soon dominate the fur trade since the British ship *Isaac Todd* was planning an attack on Astoria.

McKenzie quickly departed Fort Spokane to carry the news to Astoria. He arrived in the middle of January with a copy of the Declaration of War. Everyone at the fort was shocked by the news. Astor's chief agent, Wilson Hunt, was away on business aboard the *Beaver* in the Bering Sea. Realizing it was unlikely that Astor could send another supply ship, McKenzie and Duncan McDougal, the ranking partners on hand, made the decision to abandon Astoria. They were convinced that their agreement with the Pacific Fur Company gave them that authority. They ordered an inventory of goods and provisions. It showed that the fort's foodstuffs and Indian trading goods were in short supply. Without new supplies, trade with the Indians would not be profitable during the coming season, and any hope that one of Astor's ships would be able to deliver new supplies was abandoned. McKenzie ordered that all trade cease except to provide provisions for Indians living nearby. McKenzie wanted to notify other Astorians at Fort Spokane and Fort Okanogan of what had happened, but he delayed until March. He and others at Astoria were unaware that Astor was trying to negotiate with the British to save the Pacific Fur Company.

On April 11, 1813, two canoes carrying eighteen men from the North West Company, including John George McTavish, arrived at Astoria. The Astorians gave them a cool but decent welcome. After all, they were friends. The next day everyone drank, ate, and celebrated the birthday of Astoria. McTavish reported that within a few weeks the British ship *Isaac Todd* would arrive on the Columbia. Although no British ship had appeared by August, an American vessel, the *Albatross,* arrived from the Sandwich Islands (Hawaii) carrying Wilson Hunt. Having landed in the islands, he learned of the war between Great Britain and the United States, and instead of continuing to China as planned, he sailed back to Fort Astoria. Hunt was angry when he learned that McDougal and McKenzie had decided to abandon the settlement, and in a meeting with the Astorians, he asked that the decision be rescinded. Hunt said Astoria could be defended, but he was outvoted. A few days later he departed aboard the *Albatross,* which was going back to Hawaii. Since the ship was already under charter, it did not have sufficient space to carry all of the Astorians plus their belongings, furs, and trade goods, but the captain did find room to carry Hunt to Hawaii. There he could charter another ship to return to Astoria for the others.

With Hunt gone, McDougal and McKenzie were again in charge, and they sold Astoria, including the buildings, equipment, and its wealth in gathered furs, for the trifling sum of $58,000, a fraction of the real value, to the North West Company. McKenzie's motivations are not clear. He may have sold the fort because he feared it would simply be taken when the British warship arrived, or he may have done so with the promise that he would become a partner in the North West Company. Regardless, when the bill of sale was signed in October 1813, it provided the Astorians either employment with the North West Company or safe passage back to the states. On the last day of November 1813, a ship was sighted off the coast near the mouth of the Columbia River. It turned out to be the *Raccoon*, a British vessel that had reached Astoria ahead of the *Isaac Todd*. Even though Astoria was already owned by the North West Company, William Black, the ship's captain, took formal possession of the post for king and country and raised the British Union Jack on Astoria's flagpole. Smashing a bottle of Madeira against the pole, Black renamed Astoria Fort George. He then claimed Astoria and the country all around it for Britain by right of wartime conquest. These words would later come back to haunt British diplomats.[11]

CHAPTER THREE

DISCOVERING THE OREGON TRAIL

The more you explore, the more you find that needs exploring.

Anonymous

WHEN ROBERT STUART left Fort Astoria in the summer of 1812 to carry dispatches overland to John Jacob Astor in New York, he had no idea that the route he and his men followed would be far more important than the dispatches he carried. In fact, the route would have lasting historical significance. As has already been related, Robert Stuart and his uncle David Stuart had arrived on the Columbia River aboard the *Tonquin*. Now, about a year later, the twenty-seven-year-old native of Scotland was leading a small party of men overland to St. Louis, from where he would continue on to New York. Lewis and Clark had made the journey, and the previous year Wilson Hunt had reached Fort Astoria by blazing a new trail farther south than the one followed by Lewis and Clark. Now Stuart intended to retrace Hunt's trail to the Missouri River and follow the stream down to St. Louis.

On June 29, Stuart and his party left Fort Astoria with another group of Astorians traveling by barge and canoe up the Columbia River on trading expeditions. As has already been noted, none of them knew that eleven days earlier, on the other side of the continent, the United States Congress had declared war on Great Britain, or that the British would soon control Fort Astoria. Stuart's party consisted of six men, including Robert McClellan and Ramsey Crooks. Both had resigned from the Pacific Fur Company and asked Stuart for permission to go with him overland to St. Louis. The other men in Stuart's party were Benjamin Jones, a native of Virginia who then called Missouri his home; a Canadian half-breed named François LeClaire; the Canadian André Vallé, who had gone overland to Astoria the previous year with Wilson Hunt; and John Day, who had suffered great hardships while also going overland with Hunt. Before Stuart's party parted from the other Astorians, Day's mental condition worsened, and he tried to commit suicide. So Stuart sent Day back to Fort Astoria with the others, which meant there were only five other men with Stuart when on July 30, 1812, his party camped beside the Walla Walla River where it flows into the Columbia, close to what is today the southern border of Washington State. The following morning Stuart and his men broke camp, said good-bye to the few remaining Astorians camped nearby, mounted horses they had obtained from Indians, and ascended the hills to the south-southeast toward the Blue Mountains, in what is now northeast Oregon. In addition to the six horses they rode, they led nine other horses carrying the party's supplies and camping outfits. We know such details because Stuart kept a journal that has survived. Its pages reveal a great deal about the route followed by Stuart and his men, the country traversed, the Indians they met, the wildlife they encountered, and the hardships they endured.[1]

As the party set out on its own that Friday, July 31, the weather became hot. Stuart and his men soon began traveling over arid hills composed of sand and clay. Not a spring, pool of water, or stream did they find, and the party traveled without stopping until late afternoon. What happened next is related in Stuart's journal:

> Towards dusk the ravines became less deep and the country gently undulating, but the shallow drains still bent their course to the Columbia. [We] already had a fine young dog (our only companion of the kind) given up for want of water; and Leclaire, to preserve respiration, drank his own urine, when despairing of finding a brook, we began to talk of stopping for the night. Searching a little farther on for an eligible situation, we discovered by the faint remains of day light, at a great distance a head, something like a wood, in the vicinity of which we were confident of getting a supply of that element we so much wanted—a pace of the speedy kind took place of our common one, and at a late hour we reached the Umatalla [Umatilla River], a ripple which the horses (I suppose) hearing, rushed forward to immediately and drank immoderately, then crossed to the other side, where a gravely beach being the first dry spot near, we took up our quarters on it for the night; having come this day at least 45 miles.[2]

Pendleton, Oregon, is today located on the spot where Stuart and his party camped the night of July 31, 1812.

During the following days the party followed a trail that took them along the rugged Blue Mountains and away from the Umatilla River. Dense forests cut by deep ravines made travel slow. From time to time, the party would come upon small streams with rocky beds and had to force their horses to cross. Because of the rugged terrain they were not able to cover the same distance traveled the first day. Stuart's journal for Wednesday, August 5, contains the following entry.

> The sun had made its appearance above the cliffs when we left our nights station, the road was rugged in the extreme, and the proximity of the mountains obliged us frequently to cross the river, a business our horses are by no means fond of. We went on but slowly, and at the end of 12 miles extricated ourselves from among rocks and precipices to enter the big flat, where on account of having broke several saddles, we encamped, on the right bank one mile below the narrows, and in the evening shot two salmon and a beaver.[3]

Stuart's campsite on August 5 is where modern La Grande, Oregon, stands today.

During the following days they left the Blue Mountains and descended upon a vast plain with fine streams with willows and cottonwood trees marking the banks of the waterways. On August 10 they reached Woodpile Creek, where they saw antelope grazing. Stuart and his men tried to kill some of the animals for meat, but they were too shy and fleet and soon disappeared. On August 12, the party reached the Snake River near modern Huntington, Oregon, and made camp. There the Snake, one of the largest river systems in America, entered the mountains. The Snake begins in what is now Yellowstone National Park and threads its way southward along the eastern base of the Grand Tetons. It crosses into modern Idaho, reverses direction and flows northwest and then crosses southern Idaho before moving north again along the western border of Idaho and Oregon, where Stuart and his men camped.

While in camp, a Snake Indian visited the party and told of two white men living with his people about a day's travel away. Stuart and his men spent two days trying to locate the whites without finding them. On the evening of the second day they found a camp of Shoshone Indians who told Stuart that white men were living with their people on the other side of the river. Camping nearby, Stuart sent one of the Indians across the river to locate them. Stuart and his men got no sleep that night because of swarms of mosquitoes, and by dawn, the party was irritable, especially after the Indian returned and informed them he could not find the white men.

Stuart and his party soon set out again on their journey. They had been on the trail only a short time when a Snake Indian on horseback raced after them. Stuart stopped to see what he wanted. When the Indian reined his horse and jumped to the ground, he put his arms around the neck of Stuart's horse and gave the animal a loving hug. The Indian said the horse belonged to him, that the animal had been stolen from him by Walla Walla Indians. At that point the rest of Stuart's men rode up and some of them recognized the Snake Indian as one of two Indians hired by Wilson Hunt the previous year to care for his party's horses when they took to water travel in canoes. As Stuart and his men questioned the Indian, he informed them that the route followed by Hunt the previous year was very bad and circuitous, that he knew a much shorter and easier route for Stuart's party to travel.

Stuart promised to give the Snake Indian a pistol with powder and ball, a knife, an awl, some blue beads, a blanket, and a looking glass if he would guide them to the shorter and easier route. The Indian agreed and was in Stuart's camp on the Snake River the next morning. After traveling a few miles the Indian told Stuart that if he cut across the hills on the other side of the Snake River, they would save many miles of travel. The Indian urged Stuart and his men to camp on the spot that night, since it would be a good day's journey through the nearby hills. Stuart took his advice and camped. But the next morning the Indian was gone. So was Stuart's horse, the one the Indian claimed was his. Stuart and his men made new vows never to trust another Snake Indian, and instead of taking the Snake's advice and traveling through the nearby hills, Stuart and his men decided to follow the river. The weather was very hot, and prairie flies frequently made the party's horses frantic. When they camped at night, the heat and mosquitoes made sleep impossible.

On August 20, as Stuart's party traversed the prairie close to the Snake River, they found four trappers—John Joback, Edward Robinson, Jacob Reznor, and Joseph Miller. The first three had helped Andrew Henry construct Henry's Fort for the Missouri Fur Company in 1810. They had met Wilson Hunt coming overland from St. Louis in 1811 and guided his party to Henry's Fork of the Snake River before leaving to trap beaver. A bit later, the fourth man, Joseph Miller of Astor's Pacific Fur Company, joined them in their trapping. Not too long before the four men met Stuart's party, a wandering band of Arapaho Indians had robbed them of their furs and other possessions. Stuart's party shared what luxuries they could with the men, who then traveled with Stuart's party to Caldron Linn, a waterfall on the Snake River just east of modern Murtaugh, Idaho. There the trappers found three undisturbed caches of goods left by Wilson Hunt's party the year before. Six other caches had been robbed, and the canoes left by Hunt had been damaged. At that point Joseph Miller asked to join Stuart's party going

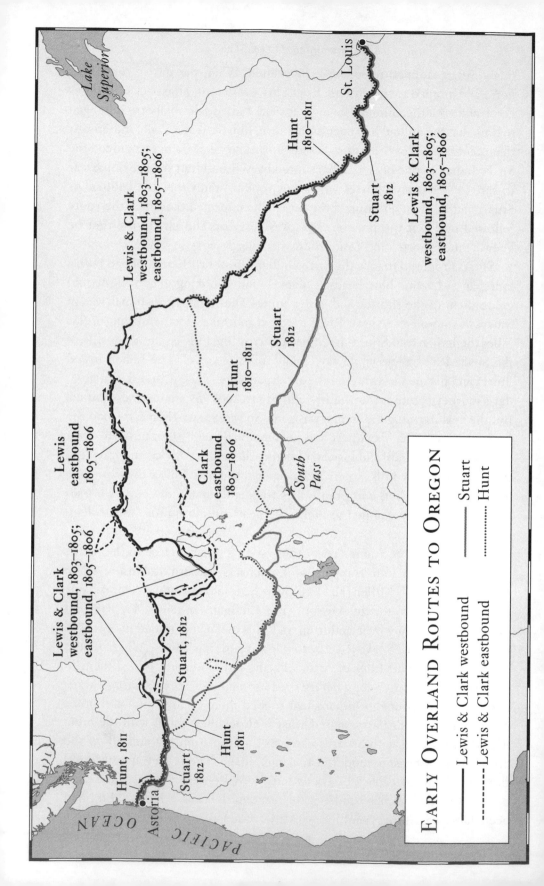

EARLY OVERLAND ROUTES TO OREGON

—— Lewis & Clark westbound —— Stuart
- - - Lewis & Clark eastbound ········· Hunt

St. Louis

Hunt
1810–1811

Stuart
1812

Lewis & Clark
westbound, 1803–1805;
eastbound, 1805–1806

Lake Superior

Lewis & Clark
westbound, 1803–1805; eastbound, 1805–1806

Lewis
eastbound
1805–1806

Hunt
1810–1811

Clark
eastbound
1805–1806

Stuart
1812

South
Pass

Lewis & Clark
westbound, 1803–1805;
eastbound, 1805–1806

Stuart, 1812

Hunt, 1811

Stuart
1812

Hunt
1811

Astoria

PACIFIC OCEAN

to St. Louis, but the other three decided to return to trapping because they did not want to return to St. Louis empty-handed. On August 25, 1812, near where Bliss, Idaho, is located today, Stuart's party found one hundred lodges of Snake Indians who were killing and drying fish on the Snake River. Stuart wrote: "The fish begin to jump soon after sunrise, when the Indians in great numbers, with their spears, swim in to near the center of the falls, where some placing themselves on rocks…assail the salmon, who, struggling to ascend and perhaps exhausted with repeated efforts, become an easy prey." Stuart added that the Indians' spears "are a small straight piece of Elk horn, out of which the pith is dug, deep enough to receive the end of a very long willow pole, and on the point an artificial beard is made fast by a preparation of twine and gum." Joseph Miller told Stuart that he had stopped at this point the previous year as he came overland with Wilson Hunt's party. He told how he was astonished at seeing the Indians in a few hours killing "some thousands of fish." Stuart and his men camped nearby that evening and from all indications enjoyed an ample supply of fish for their meal.[4]

On Tuesday, September 1, Stuart and his men resumed their journey and continued to follow the Snake eastward. Soon the country opened up, but the summer had been extremely dry. Game had disappeared. There was little grass for the horses. Two days later, on September 3, the party had reached Marsh Creek near present-day Declo, Idaho, where they found some Shoshone Indians. There Stuart's party obtained a dog, some dried salmon, and a cake made of pulverized roots and berries. In his entry for Friday, September 4, Stuart wrote: "Last night we made a hearty meal on the Dog's carcass, and between the evening's and this morning's pastime, caught a sufficiency of Trout for breakfast, which we found delicious, they being fried with the dog's fat and a little flour we had still preserved." Learning from the Indians that his party had left the trail they wanted to use, Stuart and his men found the correct Indian trail and continued their journey. But on September 7, Stuart decided not to follow Wilson Hunt's route via Henry's Fort over Teton Pass but instead to leave the Snake and turn east and follow the Portneuf River.[5]

On Friday, September 11, Stuart's party saw antelope and many geese near what is now Georgetown, Idaho. They also saw a large black bear. Although wildlife was becoming more plentiful and they had seen signs of buffalo, the party continued to rely on filling their frying pans with fresh fish. The next day, Saturday, some Crow Indians brought buffalo meat to Stuart's camp. The following day, Sunday, September 13, Stuart wrote in his journal that he and his men doubled their watches, "a precaution by no means unnecessary, for having by midnight augmented their numbers to 21, they conducted themselves in such a manner as made it requisite for all of us to keep guard the remainder of the night. At day break I traded what little meat they had with a few pieces of buffalo skin, which done, they insisted on selling us horses and demanded gun powder in return." Stuart then noted: "This I refused, but they would absolutely exchange some, and at length I acceded in one instance— Their behavior was insolent in the extreme, and indicated an evident intention to steal, if not to rob—we kept close possession of our arms, but notwithstanding our vigilance, they stole a bag containing the greater part of our kitchen furniture. To prevent an open rupture, we gave them about twenty loads of powder and departed, happy to be getting off on no worse terms."[6]

Stuart's party continued without any sign of Indians, but a few days later, on Saturday, September 19, Crow Indians stole every horse Stuart and his men had. This was devastating. After discussing their situation, the men set about to replenish their food supply. Soon the men noticed Indians watching them from some distance, probably waiting to see where Stuart's men would cache things they could not carry on foot. Stuart decided the party would not leave anything behind. They gathered together everything they planned to carry and burned or threw everything else into the river. They then set out on foot continuing east.

On September 21, after having covered only eighteen miles in two days, they decided to cross to the north side of the rapidly moving Bear River at a point about ten miles southeast of present-day Irwin, Idaho. Stuart and his men built two rafts. They quickly found their rafts sturdy enough to withstand the fast-moving water. Instead of crossing the stream, they decided to drift with the current. For a few days Stuart and his men floated with the current until nightfall, when they moved ashore and camped. Late Thursday afternoon, September 24, Benjamin Jones killed an elk as it began raining. The rain had turned to snow by the time the men set up camp. When the elk was skinned the next morning, the men found a ball and an arrow that had been in the animal's body for about a week. Stuart and his men realized the Crows had no guns, but they knew the dreaded Blackfeet did. Stuart and his men assumed Blackfeet had shot at the animal.[7]

Stuart's party rested in camp that day but took to the rafts the following morning, wanting to avoid the Blackfeet at all cost. Although the weather was cold, they continued floating down the Bear to what is now called Thomas Fork. There they followed the stream north and traveled overland to Grey's River, which they reached on September 26. They followed Grey's River north and northwest until September 28, when they turned north and then east. On October 1, the party was in the vicinity of the present-day towns of Felt and Tetonia, Idaho, located west of the Teton Mountains. Fearing they were in Blackfeet country, Stuart and his men did not attempt to shoot game for food. They crossed the Teton River and headed south toward Teton Pass. In camp, the men discussed whether or not to cross the mountain in front of them or to go around. McClellan said they should go around, but the majority voted to go over the peak in hopes of avoiding the Blackfeet. The next day the party moved out. McClellan, who had been carrying the party's beaver trap in addition to his own possessions, soon announced that he was going to leave the party. Exactly why he made the decision is still debated, but he probably was irritated with the party's progress and the decision to cross the mountain. It is known that his feet were chafed and sore. In addition, he may have thought he could survive better alone.

The day that McClellan left the party, Ramsey Crooks, who had been suffering from a high fever, could hardly travel. Stuart noted in his journal: "Mr. Crooks' indisposition increased so much this afternoon that I insisted on his taking a dose of Castor oil, which fortunately had the desired effect, but he has such a violent fever and is withal so weak as to preclude all idea of continuing our journey until his recovery." The party made a few miles but could not travel the next two days. On Monday, October 5, the party traveled eight miles with others in the group carrying Crooks's belongings. Crooks was slowly recovering. Two days later the party crossed Teton Pass, located in present-day northwest Wyoming. Even though there were nine inches of snow on the ground, the party made twenty-two miles that day. Then they hit the Snake River, which they followed to the Hoback River.[8]

By October 11, they were moving overland. Game was scarce. The remainder of the meat carried by the party was gone. Although there was nothing to eat, the party forged on and went to bed hungry on October 12. The next morning they checked the beaver trap they had set in the Green River. There was nothing except the forepaw of a large beaver that had gotten away. Later in the day they came upon the camp of Robert McClellan. Stuart later wrote: "We found him lying on a parcel of straw, emaciated and worn to a perfect skeleton and hardly able to raise his head, or speak from extreme debility, but our presence seemed to revive him considerably." When the party camped for the night, they still had not located any food. Stuart's journal for October 13 contains the following entry:

As we were preparing for bed, one of the Canadians advanced towards me with his rifle in his hand, saying that as there was no appearance of our being able to procure any provisions at least until we got to the extreme of this plain, which would take us three or four days, he was determined to go no farther, but that lots should be cast and one die to preserve the rest, adding as a further inducement for me to agree to his proposal that I should be exempted [as their leader]. I shuddered at the idea & used every endeavor to create an abhorrence in his mind against such an act, urging also the probability of our falling in with some animal on the morrow but finding every argument failed [and that he was about to convert some others in the party to his purpose] I snatched up my rifle cocked and leveled it at him with the firm resolution to fire if he persisted. This affair so terrified him that he fell upon his knees and asked the whole party's pardon, swearing he should never again suggest such a thought.[9]

The next day, Wednesday, October 14, the party, including McClellan, traveled about two miles down toward the plains when they discovered an old buffalo bull. After considerable trouble, they killed the animal at about two o'clock in the afternoon. What happened next is told in Stuart's own words: "So ravenous were our appetites that we ate part of the animal raw—then cut up the most of what was eatable and carried it to a brook at some little distance, where we encamped being hungry enough to relish a hearty meal.... We sat up the greater part of the night eating and barbecuing meat, I was very much alarmed at the ravenous manner in which all ate, but happily none felt any serious efforts there from, probably in consequence of my not allowing them to eat freely before they had supped a quantity of broth."[10]

During the days that followed, Stuart and his men found and killed more buffalo for food, and then on Thursday, October 22, Stuart wrote in his journal: "We set out at day light, and ascended about three miles, when we found a spring of excellent water, and breakfasted; five more [miles] brought us to the top of the mountain, which we call the *big horn*, it is in the midst of the principal chain."[11] Stuart and the others did not realize it, but they were crossing the Continental Divide. They were at the western end of a twenty-mile-wide gap at more than 7,400 feet in the Rocky Mountains. It later became known as South Pass, and they apparently were the first white men to cross it. Years later it would become symbolically the most important landmark on the Oregon Trail. South Pass is located nearly sixty miles northeast of what is now Rock Springs, Wyoming. In his journal, however, Stuart makes no reference to the importance of the pass he and his men crossed that day.

After crossing the pass, Stuart's party traveled east to the Sweetwater River and followed that stream to near present-day Alcova, Wyoming, where they found the North Platte River and camped there Saturday night, October 31. The next day the party saw many buffalo and deer. They killed one buffalo cow. After two more days of travel, Stuart and his men decided to make winter camp. It was cold. There was sufficient wood for their campfires, and game was plentiful for food. Then, too, the men thought if they continued on they might meet unfriendly Indians. They also liked the isolated location of their camp and thought it was concealed from Indians. The men decided they would construct two buffalo-hide canoes and then navigate down the river after spring thaws had raised the water level.

Stuart and his men went into winter camp on November 2, 1812. Their hope of not being discovered by Indians was shattered on December 11, when a party of Arapaho Indians surprised them. The Indians, who appeared peaceful, said they were a war party on foot going against the Crow Indians. Stuart noted in his journal:

The behavior of the Indians was far more regular and decent than we had any reason to expect from a war party; they threw up two breastworks of

William Henry Jackson's painting Red Buttes *shows Indians leaving Robert Stuart's campsite in what is now Wyoming, in the fall of 1812.* (Courtesy Scotts Bluff National Monument)

logs where the whole excepting the chief and his deputy betook themselves to rest tolerably early; these two we permitted to sleep in our hut,
and one of us remained awake alternately all night. They all ate vora-
ciously and departed peaceably about 10 a.m. carrying with them a great
proportion of our best meat in which we willingly acquiesced. They
begged a good deal for ammunition but a peremptory refusal soon convinced them that all demands of that nature were unavailing and they
laughingly relinquished their entreaties.[12]

It appears that the Indians offered to return in about two weeks with
horses to trade for ammunition and that Stuart agreed. But after the Indians
left, Stuart and his men decided the Indians might come back in force to
take the ammunition. The next day, Saturday, December 12, Stuart and his
men finished dressing the buffalo and deer hides they had and spent much of
the day making moccasins. On Sunday morning, December 13, the men left
their camp and walked twenty-two miles through three inches of snow. During the next several days they followed the North Platte to where Casper,
Wyoming, stands today, and then turned southeastward past the site of
present-day Douglas, Wyoming, and on to where Fort John (Fort Laramie)
would be built more than two decades later in what is now southeast
Wyoming. Near what is today Torrington, Wyoming, Stuart's party established a second winter camp in late December 1812. On New Year's Day, 1813,
Stuart wrote in his journal:

> Was solely devoted to the gratification of our appetites: all work was sus-
> pended for the day, and we destroyed an immoderate quantity of buffalo
> tongues, puddings, and the choicest of the meat. Our stock of Virginia
> weed [tobacco] being totally exhausted, Mr. McClellan's tobacco pouch
> was cut up and smoked as a substitute, in commemoration of the new
> year.[13]

Game was plentiful, and there was sufficient wood for fires in the vicinity
of their second winter camp. Early in January they cut down trees and began
to build two canoes. The river was still frozen, but they wanted to be ready to
travel once it thawed. When the first thaw came in early March, Stuart and
his men made plans. On March 7, 1813, they dragged their canoes to the riverbank in preparation for their departure the next morning. When a wild
goose appeared that afternoon, they killed the bird for dinner. The next
morning they set out in their canoes. But a few hundred yards downstream
the water was not deep enough for passage. Everyone returned to camp to

wait for deeper water. They tried again several days later and finally gave up hope of using the canoes and went on foot.

They followed the Platte eastward and on April 2 camped near where Lexington, Nebraska, stands today. Eleven days later Stuart and his party reached an Otoe Indian village located about two miles southeast of the site of what is now Yutan, Nebraska. There, Stuart and his men found two traders from St. Louis, who told Stuart and his men of the war between America and Great Britain. Stuart was able to trade for provisions and a skin canoe that the Otoes would construct for the journey down the North Platte and the Missouri rivers. In his entry of Friday, April 16, Stuart wrote:

> Our canoe was finished last evening and consists of five elk and buffalo hides, sewed together with strong sinews, drawn over and made fast to a frame composed of poles and willows 20 feet long, 4 wide, and 18 inches deep, making a vessel somewhat shaped like a boat, very steady, and by the aid of a little mud on the seams, remarkably tight. In this we embarked at an early hour and drifted 10 miles, when the wind began making oars an absolute necessary part of our equipment, [and] not to be procured at the Indian village.[14]

When they finally reached shore, Stuart and his men made camp and constructed two oars on Sunday morning, April 18. Later that day they put their boat back in the water, but the wind was too high to try to use the oars. They drifted with the current, and about thirty miles later floated into the Missouri River. Six days later they arrived at Fort Osage, east of present-day Kansas City, Missouri. Because of bad weather, Stuart's party rested at Fort Osage for a day and were given provisions by the acting commanding officer for their journey to St. Louis. On April 30, 1813, Robert Stuart and his party of six weary, worn travelers reached the town of St. Louis after their ten-month-long overland journey. Stuart estimated that they had traveled 3,768 miles since leaving Fort Astoria. Their arrival caused quite a sensation and people crowded around them to hear the news. When Stuart and others told that Wilson Price Hunt's party had reached the Columbia River the year before, it was the first news of their fate to reach St. Louis. Stuart and his men then rested, but Stuart and perhaps others in his party were interviewed by Joseph Charless, a St. Louis newspaper editor who in 1808 established the first newspaper west of the Mississippi River, the weekly *Missouri Gazette*. Stuart and his men probably enjoyed the town's offerings. To them St. Louis must have seemed luxurious, even though the young frontier town was on the far western edge of what then passed for civilization in America.

On May 8, 1813, eight days before Robert Stuart left St. Louis on horse-back for New York, 1,300 miles away, the weekly *Missouri Gazette* published the following:

Arrived here a few days ago from the mouth of the Columbia river, Mr. Robert Stuart, one of the partners of the Pacific Fur Company, accompanied by mssrs R. Crooks, Jos. Miller and Rob M'Clellen, with three hunters. We learn that Mr. Stuart is bound to N-York with dispatches. Next week we shall present our readers with an account of their journey from the Pacific Ocean to this place, a short narrative which will evince to the world that a journey to the Western Sea will not be considered (within a few years) of much greater importance than a trip to New York.

As promised, the *Missouri Gazette* on May 15, 1813, published under the small headline "American Enterprise" an interview with Stuart, who briefly described the journey. Editor Charless then predicted that from the information provided by Stuart, "a journey across the continent of North America might be performed with a wagon, there being no obstruction in the whole route that any person would dare to call a mountain in addition to its being much of the most direct and short one to go from this place [St. Louis] to the mouth of the Columbia river." Stuart apparently left the wrong impression with Charless about the terrain along his route, but Charless was correct in predicting that wagons would eventually cross the continent.

CHAPTER FOUR

JOHN McLOUGHLIN AND THE MISSIONARIES

Westward the course of empire takes its way.

Bishop Berkeley

ON CHRISTMAS EVE, 1814, about eighteen months after Robert Stuart delivered dispatches to John Jacob Astor in New York, the War of 1812 ended when a treaty was signed in the Flemish city of Ghent. It took weeks for Americans to learn the war was over because communication between Europe and America was slow. The news did not reach General Andrew Jackson until after his forces had defeated the British in the Battle of New Orleans early in 1815. The Treaty of Ghent, however, ignored the issues that had caused the war and simply proclaimed that it was over. It gave four British-American commissions the tasks of resolving the boundary questions.

Article One of the treaty called for the lands captured during the war to be given to their former owners. John Jacob Astor argued that the British should return Fort Astoria, which they had formally seized and renamed Fort George in 1813. But the North West Company insisted that the Astorians had legally sold Fort George to them. Instead of challenging the British and sending his men back to the Columbia River to trade, Astor pressed the issue of Fort George with James Monroe, secretary of state, and later with other government officials, but without success. It was not until 1818 that the British and Americans agreed to joint occupancy of the lands between Spanish California and Russian Alaska. On October 6 of that year the American flag was again raised over Fort George. By then, however, Astor had given up any plans of resuming operations in the Pacific Northwest, leaving the fur trade there in the hands of the British. Astor, now in his middle fifties, told a friend, "If I was a young man, I would again resume that trade—as it is I am too old and I am withdrawing from all business as fast as I can."[1] Astor did leave the fur-trading business, but it took him until about 1834 to dispose of his interests. In the meantime, he dealt in New York City real estate and soon gained the title "landlord of New York." Among his holdings were large sections of what is now the midtown business district. At the time of his death in 1848, Astor was the richest man in America.

The failure of the Treaty of Ghent to resolve the boundary issue gave the British a fur-trade monopoly in the Pacific Northwest. After the Hudson's Bay Company merged with the North West Company in 1821, it dominated the trade. It was then that Sir George Simpson, the Hudson's Bay Company governor in British North America, turned the entire Oregon Country into a company preserve. Dr. John McLoughlin was appointed chief factor in the Columbia District, one of the company's four administrative districts across Canada, which covered present-day British Columbia and the states of Oregon, Washington, and Idaho. McLoughlin, who stood six feet four inches in height and had a tremendous chest, was of Scottish ancestry. He was born in 1784 in what is now the province of Quebec; later, his parents moved to Quebec City to educate their children. At the age of fourteen McLoughlin began to study medicine with Sir James Fisher, a medical doctor who lived near Montreal. Four and a half years later, at the age of eighteen, he received permission to practice medicine and in 1803 became a resident physician with the North West Company at Fort William, now Thunder Bay, Ontario. In late July 1823, McLoughlin traveled from Fort William to Fort George on the Columbia River to assume his new responsibilities.

Although the Hudson's Bay Company's traders still occupied what had been Fort Astoria, McLoughlin and other officials in the company realized the southern boundary of British territory might soon be the Columbia River. They decided to construct a new post on the north bank of the river. The site selected was about a hundred miles inland from the mouth of the Columbia on a bluff about a mile above the river and six miles above where the Willamette River flows south into the Columbia. As the new post was being constructed, McLoughlin traveled by canoe back and forth between Fort George and the new post, supervising the movement of goods plus thirty-one head of cattle and seventeen hogs. By the spring of 1825, the new post was completed, and on March 19, Sir George Simpson, the pudgy little governor of the Hudson's Bay Company, broke a bottle of rum against the new post's flagpole. The Union Jack was raised, and the post was officially named Fort Vancouver after English Captain George Vancouver, the earliest explorer to penetrate the Columbia River region. It was a pointed reminder to the United States that a subject of Great Britain was the first

This photograph, made about 1851, shows Dr. John McLoughlin.
(Courtesy Bill Gulick and the Fort Vancouver National Historic Site)

white man there. The governor then sailed away, leaving Fort Vancouver in McLoughlin's hands.

It was soon evident to McLoughlin that the location of Fort Vancouver was too far above the Columbia River. Its location on a bluff about a mile from the river made it difficult to haul food and supplies from boats to the post. Also, water had to be brought too great a distance from the river. Four years later, in 1829, a new post was constructed above flood level on Jolie Prairie, or Belle Vue Point, a broad area of prairie and trees sloping upward to dense forests, much closer to the Columbia. McLoughlin supervised the construction of the new Fort Vancouver, a parallelogram about 750 feet by 450 feet surrounded by a stockade fence 20 feet high. In time, there would be a bastion in the northwest corner mounting two 12-pound cannon. In the center against the front wall were several 18-pound cannon. Two wide double gates were the only entrance and exit to the post. On the back side of Fort Vancouver, McLoughlin supervised the planting of fields of grain, fruit orchards, and a large vegetable garden. More imposing were the many buildings, including a pharmacy, a stone powder house, a chapel used as both a church and a school, warehouses for furs, English goods, and other commodities, plus workshops for carpenters, mechanics, blacksmiths, wheelwrights, tanners, coopers, and other workers. Nearer the Columbia River but outside the stockade, a village of about sixty houses was constructed in rows with streets. Here lived mechanics, laborers, and voyageurs. Their housing, however, was nothing like that enjoyed by married officers and McLoughlin inside the stockade.

Married officers had small houses, each with two rooms, but McLoughlin's house was a large one-story structure with many rooms, constructed about eight feet above the ground to provide storage space. It was palatial. A double flight of stairs led up from the ground to a verandah and into a central hallway. Off this hallway was a large dining hall with a huge mahogany dining table, damask napery, flat silver, Spode china, and Waterford glassware, all of which was used for multicourse dinners prepared in the kitchen, one of several outbuildings behind his house. The meals might include red meat or lamb, tripe, or pork, rice, vegetable soup, fowl, salmon or sturgeon, rich butter and cream sauces plus fresh bread and hot biscuits. Desserts might be rice pudding, apple pie, melons, and grapes or cheese with bread and hot biscuits. The only alcoholic beverage served was wine with dinner, and only occasionally. McLoughlin and his guests nearly always dressed for dinner, with the host wearing a black broadcloth suit with wide satin lapels. His guests might wear semi-Indian attire, jackets of tanned deerskin trimmed with beads and fringe made by their wives. After dinner, there was fellowship and good conversation on world affairs, philosophy, art, science, politics, or subjects other than fur trading in the smoking room of McLoughlin's house. McLoughlin himself did not smoke but did not mind if others did. He had a fine library, perhaps the only one west of the Rocky Mountains. There was nothing like Fort Vancouver anywhere else in the West. It was an oasis of Western civilization in the wilderness.

As chief factor, McLoughlin followed specific orders from the Hudson's Bay Company. He was to stop all traffic in whiskey. He was to develop coastal trade, which the North West Company had neglected. He was to open business with the Russian-American Fur Company, and finish constructing Fort Langley, a trading post on the Fraser River. He also was to sweep the country clean of fur-bearing animals, send brigades south to California, plant gardens, and, most important, keep expenses down. As for the Indians, the Hudson's Bay Company's policy was firm. Indians were to be treated fairly. No effort should be made to change their beliefs or way of life, but if they harmed property or personnel, the Company was to respond with vigor.

McLoughlin followed his orders. He also had no use for an idle or lazy man. If he saw a man doing nothing, McLoughlin sent him to work in the orchards or garden. Later, after mills were built, an idle worker would be sent to one of them. Sundays were days of rest and for attending religious services, but Mondays through Fridays the workdays began early and continued until six o'clock in the evening. On Saturdays the workday ended at five o'clock, at which time workers were given their rations, which consisted of eight pounds of salted salmon and eight quarts of potatoes per person per month plus a supply of tallow and peas each week. The workers received an annual wage of 17 pounds. From that they had to buy clothing and incidentals and perhaps supplement their food rations. While the workers, or *engagés*, were for the most part illiterate and lived outside the stockade, the clerks and officers who came from the British Isles lived inside the stockade and formed the gentleman class. Typical of this period, class prejudice was all-pervasive, but all enjoyed free time. Leisure activities included hunting, riding, and picnicking for gentlemen, while the workers found pleasure in footraces and competitive feats of strength. Everyone celebrated when a supply ship or a Royal Navy vessel docked below the post.

This is the chief factor's house at Fort Vancouver as it appeared in May 1860.
(Courtesy Bill Gulick and the Fort Vancouver National Historic Site)

Fort Vancouver as it appeared about 1860. The chief factor's house is on the left. The long building (right) is the Bachelors' Quarters. (Courtesy Bill Gulick and the Fort Vancouver National Historic Site)

Fort Vancouver soon became a center of intense activity as McLoughlin directed the establishment of more posts in what are now Washington, Oregon, Idaho, and British Columbia. Eventually, McLoughlin was responsible for nearly thirty trading posts that were supplied by Fort Vancouver. He had six ships, and during peak seasons as many as six hundred male employees worked for him. A majority of his officers, clerks, and trappers were from what is now the province of Quebec in Canada. The backbone of the fur trade was the trapper, or voyageur. Most of them were of French and sometimes Scottish heritage. They had their own customs and code of honor above and beyond the expectations of the Hudson's Bay Company. These voyageurs, plus freelance European and Indian trappers, would trap all winter and then in the summer bring incredible numbers of furs to Fort Vancouver.

As the trade increased and Fort Vancouver achieved a permanent presence, McLoughlin sought to make the post as self-sustaining as possible, in keeping with the Company's order to keep expenses low. He expanded Fort Vancouver's agricultural activities to cover almost thirty miles along the Columbia River and about ten miles north from the riverbank. Sawmills, gristmills, and dairies were established. Just south of the employees' village just outside the stockade, a shipbuilding business was established along with tanneries and a hospital. Surplus goods were used in trade with Russians and in the Sandwich (Hawaiian) Islands. McLoughlin soon became known as the "King of the Columbia."

When McLoughlin was about twenty-four years old, he married a Chippewa Indian, but she died giving birth to McLoughlin's first son, Joseph. Later, at Fort William, McLoughlin married Margaret McKay, the widow of Alexander McKay, who had died aboard the *Tonquin*. Margaret was part Indian. In time they would have three children—two girls and a boy. Margaret and the children joined McLoughlin at Fort Vancouver after it was constructed. Because there were few white women at the fort, many men married Indian women, who made good wives and housekeepers. Margaret McLoughlin helped to train some of the Indian wives in western household arts and in adjusting to the white man's lifestyle.[2]

LATE IN THE FALL of 1820, Dr. John Floyd, a Virginia congressman and a cousin of Charles Floyd who died on Lewis and Clark's expedition, heard stories from several Astorians telling how the British through McLoughlin and the Hudson's Bay Company were establishing dominance in the Pacific Northwest. This was only two years after the United States and Great Britain had agreed on joint occupancy of Oregon Country. Hearing glowing reports about the region from his cousin, Dr. Floyd became enthusiastic, and in December 1820 urged Congress to appoint a select committee to "inquire into the situation of the settlements upon the Pacific Ocean and the expediency of occupying the Columbia River." The motion was adopted and Dr. Floyd found himself appointed chairman. His committee's report and subsequent bill called for annexation of the vast region, stressing its value to the fur trade, and he related how communication could be more easily established between the American Atlantic coast and the Pacific than across British Canada. The measure failed to gain support, but Dr. Floyd introduced a substitute bill in 1822 stating that when the region reached a population of 2,000 it should become a territory of the United States. Dr. Floyd labeled the area "Origon." This was the first American use of the word. His bill lost by a vote of 100 to 61, probably because it was too visionary for the time.

Not discouraged, Dr. Floyd realized that if settlement of the region was to occur, his dream must be kept alive in the public consciousness. In 1828, he presented to Congress a "Memorial of Citizens of the United States," asking the government to support settlement in Oregon Country. The document was written by Hall Jackson Kelley, a Massachusetts schoolteacher who became interested in the area about 1818. Six years later he began promoting settlement there, relying on accounts of government explorers and reports from fur traders. Kelley devised a plan to colonize Oregon Country whereby a New England–style town would be established in Oregon Country much like the Puritan colony had been established in Massachusetts. The new town would serve as the nucleus for a new state. The year Dr. Floyd presented the "Memorial" to Congress, Kelley organized the American Society for Encouraging the Settlement of the Oregon Territory, which grew rapidly in membership and was incorporated in 1831.[3]

While these developments were taking place in the East, American trappers, or "mountain men," as they became known, were crisscrossing the West trapping beaver for fur companies headquartered in St. Louis. Beginning in 1825 these trappers began holding an annual rendezvous where they would gather to dispose of their beaver pelts and other furs to traders who had traveled overland with goods and supplies. William Ashley, a flamboy-

This illustration shows William Sublette and other fur traders heading to the rendezvous of 1830 on the Wind River near present-day Riverton, Wyoming. Following Sublette's two Dearborn carriages are his ten mule-drawn wagons, the first wheeled vehicles to be used on a portion of the Oregon Trail. (Courtesy Scotts Bluff National Monument)

ant Virginian who entered the fur trade in 1822, took a wagon across part of what is now Nebraska in 1824, and his men had gotten a small cannon mounted on two wheels through South Pass in 1827, but it was not until 1830 that William Sublette took ten wagons loaded with supplies to the rendezvous of 1830 held on the Wind River near present-day Riverton, Wyoming. Each of Sublette's wagons were drawn by five mules. In addition, there were two Dearborn carriages each drawn by one mule, plus twelve head of cattle and one milch cow. The wagons brought by Sublette were the first to make the long journey over the prairie and plains to what is now west-central Wyoming.

But the distinction of taking the first loaded wagons over South Pass is held by Benjamin Louis Eulalie de Bonneville, made famous by Washington Irving in *The Adventures of Captain Bonneville*, published in 1837. Born near Paris, Bonneville came to America with his family in 1803. After his initial schooling, he went to West Point, graduating in 1815. He served with New England garrisons until 1820, when he was transferred to Mississippi and later served in Arkansas, Texas, Missouri, and Indian Territory. By 1830, Bonneville was eyeing the rich fur trade in the Rocky Mountains. After gaining financial backing, he requested and received a two-year leave of absence from the army. Bonneville organized his own expedition, and on May 1, 1832, left Fort Osage, Missouri, with a party of 110 men bound for the Green River region below the Wind River Mountains in what is now western Wyoming.

In the vicinity of the town of Daniel in west-central Wyoming, Bonneville built a temporary fort, primarily of cottonwood logs, for protection. It was located a few hundred yards from the Green River. He called the post Fort Bonneville, but trappers in the region named it "Bonneville's Folly" and "Fort Nonsense" because they believed it was poorly located and offered little protection from roving bands of Blackfeet Indians. The fort was built at an elevation of more than 7,000 feet, in the high country of the upper Green River. The Wind River Range was just to the east. The fort was completed as winter arrived. Fearing that he and his men would be snowbound, Bonneville abandoned it. Bonneville spent about three years altogether in the Rockies, but he was not successful in the fur trade. He couldn't compete with the more experienced trappers. He did, however, demonstrate that loaded wagons could be taken across South Pass. Bonneville gave up his western adventures in 1835 and returned east only to learn he had been dropped from the army for overstaying his leave. Before being reinstated as an army officer in the spring of 1836, he sold the story of his adventures to Washington Irving for $1,000.[4]

UNTIL THE EARLY 1830S, Protestant missionaries paid little attention to the American West, but in 1829 the American Board of Commissioners for Foreign Missions (ABCFM) in Boston got a report from its mission in what is now Hawaii that sailors who had sailed along the coast of Oregon Country from Alaska to California and up the Columbia River had seen many unconverted Indians. The board then sent Jonathon Green, a sailing captain, from Hawaii to explore the Oregon coast. When his dispatches reached Boston in 1832, he reported there were at least thirty-four tribes of Indians that he believed needed instruction.

Not quite a year earlier three Nez Percés and one Flathead Indian had traveled east to St. Louis from their homes west of the Continental Divide beyond the Bitterroot Mountains. They came, they said, to get someone to come and preach the white man's religion to their people. They had learned of the religion from Canadian voyageurs who were Roman Catholic and perhaps from the expedition of Lewis and Clark about twenty-five years earlier. In St. Louis the Indians became celebrities, although two of them died, apparently after sampling too much of the white man's way of life. The two surviving men, disillusioned with the white world, decided to return west. At a banquet held before they left St. Louis, according to tradition, one of the Nez Percés said:

> My people sent me to get the "White Man's Book of Heaven." You took me to where you allow your women to dance as we do not ours, and the book was not there. You took me to where they worship the Great Spirit with candles and the book was not there. You showed me images of the good spirits and the picture of the good land beyond, but the book was not among them to tell us the way. I am going back the long and sad trail to my people in the dark land. You make my feet heavy with gifts and my moccasins will grow old carrying them, yet the book is not among them. When I tell my poor blind people, after one more snow, in the big council, that I did not bring the book, no word will be spoken by our old men or by our young braves. One by one they will rise up and go out in silence. My people will die in the darkness, and they will go a long path to other hunting grounds. No white man will go with them, and no White Man's Book to make the way plain. I have no more words.[5]

While there is doubt that the Nez Percé actually spoke these words, the remarks were reported in the East and published in the *Christian Advocate and Journal,* a New York religious newspaper, on March 1, 1833. The Methodist newspaper also published an editorial asking: "Who will respond to go beyond the Rocky Mountains and carry the Book of Heaven?" The Indian's purported remarks made a profound impression on many readers, as did Captain Green's report, which was widely circulated. In Middletown, Connecticut, Wesleyan University President Wilbur Fisk asked the Methodist Mission Board and the ABCFM to establish a mission among the Flatheads. Fisk asked a former pupil, the Reverend Jason Lee, to lead a caravan to Oregon and establish the mission. Lee agreed, and Fisk raised $3,000 for the purpose. Lee then toured the eastern states to gain support and to publicize his plans. To help them reach Oregon, a young fur trader named Nathaniel Wyeth agreed to let thirty-two-year-old Lee, his nephew Daniel Lee, and four assistants travel with his expedition to the annual rendezvous of 1834 being held on the Green River in present-day Wyoming. Wyeth, a native of Massachusetts, had earlier invented a horse-drawn ice cutter that put grooves outlining uniform squares on the surfaces of frozen ponds. The squares could then be easily broken apart by cutting bars. Because his invention cut the costs of harvesting ice from 30 to 10 cents a ton, Wyeth was hired by a large Boston ice company that soon gave Boston a new staple export, revitalizing Boston's trade with the West Indies. Wyeth soon enrolled in Hall Jackson Kelley's American Society for Encouraging the Settlement of the Oregon Territory, but found himself more interested in trade than in Kelley's plan, and he organized his own company to trade for furs on the Columbia River. By the time Wyeth agreed to let Lee and his party accompany him, Wyeth was about thirty-two and had already completed one fur-trading trip west and had gathered supplies to trade for pelts at the rendezvous.[6]

Wyeth agreed to send Lee's mission's supplies to Oregon aboard his ship, the *May Dacre.* Wyeth and Lee's party then gathered at Independence, Missouri, a town founded in 1827 just east of modern Kansas City, Missouri. Independence, its name perhaps inspired by the independent nature of President Andrew Jackson, was located about three miles south of the Missouri River and twelve miles from the western border of Missouri. The town was the county seat of Jackson County, named in honor of Andrew Jackson, and it was built around a brick courthouse in the town square constructed in 1829. By then Independence was the eastern terminus of the Santa Fe Trail. Merchants supplied by steamboats plying the Missouri River catered to Santa Fe traders. The town was well suited as a jumping-off point for travelers bound for Oregon Country. William Sublette and the naturalists Thomas Nuttall and J. K. Townsend joined Wyeth and Lee's party at Independence, which, Townsend wrote, had recently "been the scene of a brawl." As Townsend explained, the little town of Independence

had been for a considerable time the stronghold of a sect of fanatics, called Mormons, or Mormonites, who, as their numbers increased, and they obtained power, showed an inclination to lord it over the less assuming inhabitants of the town. This was a source of irritation which they determined to rid themselves of in a summary manner, and accordingly the whole town rose, *en masse,* and the poor followers of the prophet were forcibly ejected from the community. They took refuge in the little town of Liberty, on the opposite side of the river, and the villagers here are now in a constant state of feverish alarm. Reports have been circulated that the Mormons are preparing to attack the town, and put the inhabitants to the sword, and they have therefore stationed sentries along the river for several miles, to prevent the landing of the enemy. The troops parade and study military tactics every day, and seem determined to repel, with spirit, the threatened invasion. The probability is, that the report respecting the attack, is, as John Bull says, "all humbug," and this training and marching has already been a source of no little annoyance to us, as the miserable little skeleton of a saddler who is engaged to work for our party, has neglected his business, and must go a soldiering in stead.[7]

No attack or bloodshed occurred, and at ten o'clock on the morning of April 28, 1834, the caravan, consisting of 70 men and 250 horses, started toward Oregon under the leadership of Wyeth and Captain William Sublette, who in St. Louis had organized his own supply train for the rendezvous, before coming to Independence. Townsend recalled that Captain Wyeth and Sublette took the lead, with Townsend and Nuttall riding their horses, followed by other men on horseback leading heavily laden pack horses. The missionaries—Reverend Lee, his nephew Daniel, Cyrus Shepard, and two assistants—rode along the flanks, driving the horned cattle they were taking to Oregon.

Soon after crossing the western border of Missouri, Wyeth's party turned northwest, crossing what is now northeast Kansas. Daniel Lee later wrote:

The whole party numbered between fifty and sixty men, all mounted on horses or mules, and armed with rifles. Most of them had each a powderhorn or a flask, a large leathern pouch for bullets hung at his side, and buckled close to his body with a leathern belt, in which hung a scabbard of the same material bearing a "scalping-knife," that savage weapon whose very name is a terror. The mules and horses altogether were over one hundred and fifty. Nearly one-third were for the men, and about two-thirds carried packs, each man leading two of them. . . .

Our encampments were generally near some stream of water, where there was good grass for our animals; and our tents, eight in number, were pitched in a circular form, enclosing a space large enough to contain all our horses and mules, fastened to pickets. These are sticks more than a foot long and two inches wide, one for every horse or mule. They were driven into the ground, and are designed to prevent the escape of the animals in case of any sudden attempt of the Indians to frighten them away. A regular guard was kept up, and relieved every four hours during the night; and when the horses were without the camp feeding, morning and evening, a watch was set near them. . . .

We generally traveled about twenty miles a day, halting near noon to bait and take dinner, and encamping early to give our animals time to fill themselves without the camp before dusk, when they were all brought within, where they remained till morning; then the cry, "Turn out!" was heard from Captain Wyeth. Soon the horses were seen without, and the breakfast fires before the tents. Each of the eight messes into which the company was divided, embraced from five to eight persons. Fried bacon and dough fried in the fat, with tea or coffee, made our meal; around which we sat on the ground in good Indian style, and braced up our craving stomachs for the toils of day. Each mess now prepared to move: tents were struck, packs and saddles put in order. "Catch up!" cried Captain Wyeth, and the whole camp was instantly in motion to gather the animals, pack up, mount, and away.

When the company reached the Platte River in modern Nebraska, they followed the south bank of the river. Daniel Lee noted: "The Platte, as its name implies, is very shallow, and in some places more than a mile wide. The bottom is a quicksand, and in fording, it is necessary to keep in motion to prevent sinking. The water has a whitish appearance, and a thick sediment will deposite itself in a vessel in which it stands. The banks are low, and a level bottom, covered generally with grass, extends a mile, more or less, on either side, terminated by hills. The country is destitute of timber."[8]

Once the company entered what is now southeast Wyoming, they passed through the area where Fort Laramie was then being constructed. They continued on to Independence Rock, located about fifty miles southwest of modern Casper, Wyoming. The oval-shaped outcropping of granite rose more than 100 feet above the valley floor. Almost 2,000 feet long and 700 feet wide, it was the most prominent landmark west of Fort Laramie and was named by a party of trappers who stopped there about 1824 to celebrate American Independence Day. It already had become a stopping point for travelers, who would carve their names and messages in the rock. Wyeth, Lee, and others inspected the carvings.

From Independence Rock the caravan traveled across the Continental Divide at South Pass, and then down the Big Sandy to the Green River, where the rendezvous was held in June. Wyeth was disappointed that only a few trappers wanted to trade furs for goods from the large selection he had brought from St. Louis. Wyeth's and Lee's parties left Sublette at the rendezvous and traveled with a party of Hudson's Bay Company traders to the Snake River near present-day Pocatello in southeast Idaho. There, Lee delivered the first Protestant sermon in Oregon Country to trappers, Indians, and members of his party. Following the sermon, there was a feast and a horse race. One Canadian trapper was killed when he fell from his horse. The next day Lee conducted the first Protestant funeral service west of the Rocky Mountains.

Wyeth had planned to take his profits at the rendezvous and continue to the Columbia River, where he hoped to set up a fishery and export salmon to the Sandwich (Hawaiian) Islands and New England. Frustrated, he decided

William Henry Jackson's painting of ox-drawn emigrant wagons approaching Independence Rock, located about fifty miles southwest of present-day Casper, Wyoming. (Courtesy Scotts Bluff National Monument)

to remain in the area and build a trading post where he could dispose of his merchandise to Indians and trappers alike. On the Snake River above the mouth of the Portneuf, at what is today Pocatello, Wyeth and his men constructed Fort Hall. On August 4, 1834, the Stars and Stripes were raised over Fort Hall, the first permanent U.S. post west of the Continental Divide. Meanwhile, Lee's party continued on with the Hudson's Bay Company traders, passing through Boise Valley and then the Blue Mountains. On September 15, 1834, Lee and his party reached Fort Vancouver, where John McLoughlin welcomed them and invited Lee to hold a religious service at the post.

McLoughlin and Lee became good friends. When McLoughlin learned that Lee wanted to establish a mission among the Flathead Indians, he convinced Lee that he could be of more use by establishing a mission in the Willamette Valley near where twenty or so families of French Canadians lived with their Indian wives. The French Canadians had left the employment of the Hudson's Bay Company and turned to farming the rich Willamette Valley. With the assistance of McLoughlin, Lee and his party of missionaries became carpenters, woodcutters, stockmen, and blacksmiths. In the fall of 1834, they constructed a log house near the east bank of the Willamette River in the vicinity of present-day Salem, Oregon. By the spring of 1835, the missionaries had fenced thirty acres and planted crops. Lee also established a school and conducted religious services. He sought to improve social conditions in the settlement, the first agricultural community in Oregon Country.

Lee's mission had been constructed and was in operation when Presbyterian missionaries Dr. Marcus Whitman and Rev. Samuel Parker toured Oregon Country in 1835 to find a suitable location for a religious mission. Whitman, then about thirty-two, was a medical doctor who had practiced for four years in Canada before returning to New York, where he became an elder of the Presbyterian Church. Parker, then about fifty-four, had been a pastor of Presbyterian and Congregational churches in New York State and a teacher at Ithaca Academy. After touring the region and visiting Fort Vancouver, it was decided that Dr. Whitman should return east for helpers. While there, he married Narcissa Prentiss. In the meantime, Parker accepted an invitation from John McLoughlin to remain the winter at Fort Vancouver. Parker expected a complete lack of comfort at the wilderness post, but he later wrote:

> I am very agreeably situated in this place. Half of a new house is assigned to me, well furnished, and all the attendance which I could wish, with access to as many valuable books as I have time to read; and opportuni-

ties to ride out for exercise, and to see the adjoining country, as I can desire; and in addition to all these, and still more valuable, the society of gentlemen enlightened, polished, and sociable. These comforts and privileges were not anticipated, and therefore the more grateful.[9]

In the spring of 1836, Dr. Whitman and his new wife, Narcissa, headed west. With them were Rev. Henry H. Spalding and his wife, Eliza, an invalid. The two couples joined a fur-company caravan bound for a rendezvous on the Green River, where the missionaries and especially their wives were welcomed by mountain men, many of whom had not seen a white woman in years. By most accounts, blond, buxom Narcissa captivated the trappers, while Eliza seemed more attracted to the Indians, who seemed to sense she had a sincere interest in them. For all practical purposes, the journey west was Narcissa Whitman's honeymoon, and all indications suggest she enjoyed the journey. In a letter sent east to her husband's parents written on June 27, 1836, while camped along the Platte River, Narcissa wrote:

> It is astonishing how well we get along with our wagons where there are no roads. I think I may say it is easier traveling here than on any turnpike in the States. On the way to the buffalo country, we had to bake bread for ten persons. It was difficult at first, as we did not understand working out-doors; but we became accustomed to it, so that it became quite easy. June found us ready to receive our first taste of buffalo. Since that time I have had but little to do with cooking. Not one in our number relishes buffalo meat as well as my husband and I. He has a different way for cooking every piece of meat.... We have had no bread since. We have meat and tea in the morn, and tea and meat at noon. All our variety consists of the different ways of cooking. I relish it well and it agrees with me. My health is excellent. So long as I have buffalo meat I do not wish anything else.[10]

While Narcissa and Eliza probably did not realize it, they were the first white women to cross the continent. Their party also established another first. The wagon they brought with them was the first to travel west of Nathaniel Wyeth's Fort Hall, established two years earlier. After leaving Fort Hall, the Whitman-Spalding party traveled to Fort Walla Walla, a Hudson's Bay Company post under McLoughlin's supervision. Traveling through the region, Dr. Whitman and Spalding selected two sites for their separate missions. Then from Fort Walla Walla they followed the Columbia

River to Fort Vancouver, where John McLoughlin welcomed them and provided warm hospitality.

After two months of an almost steady diet of dried buffalo meat, the food was wonderful. The gracious dining was ambrosia, especially for the wives of Whitman and Spalding, but the Americans would not eat black pudding even when served on Spode china. Black pudding was made of "blood and the fat of hogs, well spiced and filled into a gut."[11]

McLoughlin urged the missionaries not to establish missions among the Cayuse Indians, warning that they were known to be treacherous, but Whitman felt his work was desperately needed among them and decided to establish his mission at Waiilatpu, or Rye Grass Meadow, about twenty-five miles east of Fort Walla Walla. Spalding decided to serve the Nez Percé, so named for their pierced noses, and established his mission one hundred twenty-five miles northeast of Whitman's at Lapwai, about twelve miles east of present-day Lewiston, Idaho. McLoughlin provided the missionaries with bedding and clothing, and allowed them to draw grain and flour for two years from the stores at Fort Vancouver. McLoughlin also permitted Mrs. Whitman to live at Fort Walla Walla while her husband supervised the construction of his mission.

As a child, John McLoughlin had been christened by a Catholic priest. McLoughlin's father was Catholic and his mother a Protestant who converted to Catholicism at her marriage. But John McLoughlin apparently became a Protestant, reading the Anglican service on Sundays and feast days as demanded by the Hudson's Bay Company's policy. The Indians, however, did not like the Anglican service, so McLoughlin held a separate service for them and read from a French-language Bible. By 1838, McLoughlin realized the need for a Catholic priest to exert a morally restraining force on the natives. He also knew that a Catholic priest was less likely to encourage Americans settling in the region. So in February 1838, McLoughlin requested that one or more Catholic priests be sent to Fort Vancouver. It was nearly nine months before two priests, Father François Blanchet and Father Modeste Demers, arrived in late November 1838, while McLoughlin was on a furlough. The priests established missions at Fort Vancouver, in the Willamette Valley, and at Cowlitz. Early in January 1839, Father Blanchet held the first Roman Catholic service in what is now Oregon.[12]

In 1840, Pierre-Jean De Smet, a Jesuit missionary, came west with a fur-company caravan commanded by Andrew Drips, bound for the annual rendezvous in the Rockies on the Green River near present-day Daniel, Wyoming. The caravan, however, was unlike the earlier supply trains heading for the annual rendezvous. Perhaps a fourth of the travelers were not connected to the fur trade. In addition to De Smet, there were five Congregationalist missionaries and the Walker family, the first declared emigrants to Oregon who undertook the long journey westward. In all, there were perhaps sixty people in the caravan along with thirty heavily laden two-wheeled carts, each drawn by two mules in tandem; sixty pack mules carrying trading goods; and four carts loaded with household goods and belongings. Two of the carts carried the belongings of the missionaries, while the other two carried those of Joel P. Walker, his wife, Mary, and their four children, and Mrs. Walker's sister, Martha Young. Joel Walker—on his way to Oregon—was a brother of mountain man Joseph R. Walker, who probably urged Joel to settle there. Joel Walker and his party have the distinction of being the first American emigrants to cross the continent, but they did not take wagons beyond Fort Hall.

The credit for taking the first wagons to Oregon goes to Robert Newell and Joseph Meek, who had led some missionaries to Fort Hall in 1840. When they decided to leave their wagons, Newell agreed to take them in exchange for his services. Soon Newell got the idea of taking the wagons to Oregon. Newell later recalled that on September 27, 1840,

we put out with three wagons. Joseph L. Meek drove my wagon. In a few days we began to realize the difficulty of the task before us, and found that the continual crashing of the sage under our wagons, which was in many places higher than the mules' backs, was no joke. Seeing our animals begin to fall, we began to light up, finally threw away our wagon beds, and were quite sorry we had undertaken the job. All the consolation we had was that we broke the first sage on the road, and were too proud to eat anything but dried salmon skies after our provisions had become exhausted. In a rather rough and reduced state, we arrived at Dr. Whitman's mission station in the Walla Walla valley, where we met that hospitable man, and kindly made welcome and feasted accordingly. On hearing me regret that I had undertaken to bring wagons, the Doctor said, "O, you will never regret it. You have broken the ice, and when others see that wagons have passed they too will pass, and in a few years the valley will be full of our people." The Doctor shook me heartily by the hand; Mrs. Whitman too welcomed us, and the Indian walked around the wagons, or what they called "horse canoes," and seemed to give it up.[13]

Newell and Meek went on to settle in the Willamette Valley. Newell, who had been born in 1807 in Butler County, Ohio, went west and learned the saddler's trade at St. Louis and soon had the urge to become a trapper in the Rocky Mountains. Meek, who was three years younger than Newell, had been born in Washington County, Virginia, and came west at the age of eighteen. In 1829, Newell and Meek joined William Sublette's first party of trappers heading west from St. Louis. Both men spent years in the mountains as mountain men before settling in Oregon. Once there, Joe Meek took to wearing a bright red sash like the French trappers of the Hudson's Bay Company. Since the Company's trappers enjoyed good relations with most of the Indian tribes in the region, Meek may have felt safer in his travels throughout Oregon Country imitating their appearance.

McLoughlin and the Hudson's Bay Company could not legally stop Newell, Meek, and others from settling in the area since land claims by the United States and Britain had never been settled. McLoughlin, however, had been ordered to discourage American settlement. When Americans arrived in dire need of supplies and assistance, McLoughlin found himself facing an economic and moral dilemma. As a Christian with humanitarian concerns, he arrived at a compromise. Since he did not see the emigrants as threatening the Company's fur-trading monopoly, he traded food, medical supplies, and other essentials for their produce, harvested crops, and livestock. This made the settlers dependent upon Fort Vancouver, and for a time this plan worked.

CHAPTER FIVE

THE AMERICAN OCCUPATION OF OREGON

We go westward as into the future,
with a spirit of enterprise and adventure.

Henry David Thoreau

A S THE WHITMAN-SPALDING party arrived on the Columbia River in 1836, the government in Washington was again paying attention to Oregon Country. President Andrew Jackson dispatched Navy Lieutenant William A. Slacum by ship to the Pacific Northwest on a fact-finding tour. Slacum located Indian villages and visited the American missionaries and the handful of settlers in the Willamette Valley. He was impressed with what the settlers had accomplished and the promise of the country. Slacum had some contact with the Hudson's Bay Company and learned that it generously loaned oxen to settlers for work in the fields. The Company, however, would not sell the settlers breeding stock for fear of depleting its own herds. In talking with one of the settlers, Ewing Young, a native of Tennessee, Slacum learned that cattle were plentiful several hundred miles to the south in Mexican California. After some discussion, Slacum helped Young and other settlers organize the Willamette Cattle Company to import cattle from California. The settlers then raised money to buy Spanish cattle. Young, a finely built man standing six feet two inches in height, agreed to take ten men, go to California, purchase the cattle, and drive them overland to Oregon. To help, Slacum agreed to transport Young and his men in his ship, the *Loriot*, to California.

Ewing Young was no stranger to California. In fact, he had traveled over much of the West before settling in Oregon Country. Young had joined William Becknell in his second trip to Santa Fe from Missouri in 1822, a trip on which wagons were used for the first time to carry trading goods across the prairie and plains. Young made another trading trip to Santa Fe in 1825, and then turned to trapping beaver in the West. A young Kit Carson served his apprenticeship as a mountain man under Young, who was the first man to effectively open overland trade with California. Young had made at least two overland trips to the Pacific coast before settling in Oregon Country in 1834. Yet, for reasons that are still not clear, he did not get along with John McLoughlin. With very little help from McLoughlin and the Hudson's Bay Company, Young pretty much survived on his own. Perhaps to irritate McLoughlin, Young announced in 1836 that he was going to build a whiskey distillery. He acquired a large copper kettle and began to make plans to produce whiskey, until the missionaries asked him to abandon those plans. He agreed and had just sold his copper kettle at about the time Slacum arrived by ship on the Columbia River to survey Oregon Country for President Jackson.[1]

On January 21, 1837, Young and his men, including Philip Leget Edwards, who was carrying the settlers' money, got aboard Slacum's ship and departed. After some difficulty the ship finally crossed the bar at the mouth of the Columbia River on February 10 and entered the Pacific Ocean and sailed down the coast to San Francisco. After greasing the palms of several Spanish officials, Young received permission to buy 700 head of cattle, provided he purchased them from a mission the Spanish government had seized. Young paid $3 a head for the cattle. After acquiring horses for the journey, Young and his men received 200 cattle at the mission of San Francisco rancho and about 500 head at the mission of San José. By July they were driving their cattle north.

Philip Leget Edwards, the party's treasurer, kept a diary. His entry for July 20 reads:

> This afternoon finished swimming the cattle across the San Joaquin, at which we have been engaged since the 12th. A corral had previously been made on the bank to prevent the cattle from scattering abroad. On the 12th we drove them in, and immediately made an effort to drive the cattle across, but the water being deep at the going in, they took fright and refused to swim. We now caught a few calves, and, towing them across with skin lassos, succeeded in driving their mothers across also.[2]

By August 14, the drive reached Jesús María (Buenaventura) with 729 cattle. By August 20, Young and his men were driving their cattle among the mountains of the Cascade chain that separate the valley of the Tulares from that of the Shastas. Following an old Hudson's Bay Company trail over the Siskiyou Mountains, the drive covered only a few miles a day. Young and his men lost a few cattle along the trail, but by early September they still had 680 head, more than they had expected to survive. They also encountered a few friendly Indians. In his diary entry for September 8 and 9, Edwards wrote:

> The Indians of the mountains do not appear to be numerous, having never seen more than 15 at one time. They are unoffending and friendly. I was particularly pleased with their language. The enunciation is peculiarly clear and distinct, and entirely free from the harsh gutturals to which I have been accustomed in Indian languages. Like all American savages before they have had much intercourse with white men, they exhibit a great propensity for long and high toned harangues. That we did not understand them was no consideration. One old man, after seating himself in silence and smoking his pipe with much formality, raised his voice to its highest key and began as follows: "In yonder mountains I was born. There I sucked my mother's breast. There he had grown up," and, doubtless, many other items of equal importance, could we have understood him. I never failed in getting a grave harangue when I addressed one of these mountain orators.[3]

A few days later, Indians sent a volley of arrows from their bows toward Young and his men. One horse was struck but none of the drovers were injured. The Indians then disappeared. The cattle drive continued north and finally reached the Willamette Valley in October 1837 with 630 cattle. Of that number, 135 head were owned by Young, who soon became a respected man of means in the settlements. Young built a larger cabin and a gristmill and farmed more than 150 acres of wheat. He was the first American to plant wheat in what is now Oregon. But his prosperity was short-lived. He died in 1841 from complications caused by a stomach ulcer; he was about forty-eight years old.

After leaving Young and his men in California, William Slacum continued his voyage back to the east coast of the United States, where, in December 1837, he presented to Congress a glowing report on the settlers' successes in the Willamette Valley. Slacum's report not only helped to plant Oregon fever in the minds of Americans, but it renewed lawmakers' interest in the unsettled boundary dispute with Great Britain. A few months later, in 1838, Missouri Senator Lewis F. Linn introduced a bill calling for military occupation of the Columbia River region and the creation of a territorial government for Oregon. Linn included a report that was widely distributed, describing the history of American claims to Oregon Country, how the

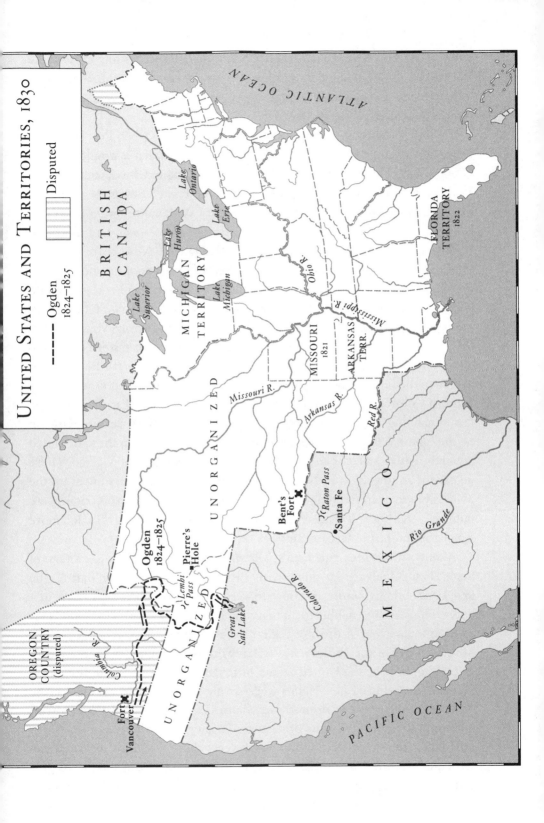

United States and Territories, 1830

— · — Ogden 1824–1825
Disputed

ATLANTIC OCEAN

BRITISH CANADA

Lake Superior
Lake Michigan
Lake Huron
Lake Erie
Lake Ontario

MICHIGAN TERRITORY

FLORIDA TERRITORY 1822

Ohio R.
Mississippi R.

MISSOURI 1821
ARKANSAS TERR.

UNORGANIZED

Missouri R.
Arkansas R.
Red R.

OREGON COUNTRY (disputed)

Columbia R.

Fort Vancouver

Ogden 1824–1825
Lembi Pass
Pierre's Hole

Great Salt Lake

UNORGANIZED

Bent's Fort
Raton Pass
Santa Fe

Colorado R.

MEXICO

Rio Grande

PACIFIC OCEAN

wives of Marcus Whitman and Henry Spalding had successfully crossed the Rocky Mountains, and glowing stories about the settlers in the Willamette Valley. Linn's bill failed in Congress, but the publicity associated with it attracted more attention to Oregon.

Easterners learned even more about Oregon in 1838 when Rev. Jason Lee returned east and toured many areas telling people what a wonderful land Oregon was. He carried with him a petition signed by settlers in the Willamette Valley praying for protection by the United States. At about this time another petition, signed by about seventy Willamette settlers, was also brought east by Thomas J. Farnham, a Vermont lawyer who had moved to Illinois and was then hired to travel to Oregon by New York publisher Horace Greeley and other easterners interested in seeing the region settled. Farnham was instructed to write down what he saw so that his report could be published and attract settlers. In the spring of 1839, Farnham took a party of nineteen men west to see Oregon Country firsthand. From Missouri they followed the Santa Fe Trail to Bent's Fort in what is now eastern Colorado and followed the Arkansas River over the divide to the North Platte River and on to the Green River. By the time the party reached what is now northwestern Colorado, many of its members had turned back. Farnham and the few remaining men completed the journey and toured western Oregon before taking a ship to Hawaii and then to California. From there he sailed down the Mexican coast and crossed overland to the Gulf of Mexico. There he caught another ship to New Orleans, where he took a steamboat up the Mississippi to near his home in Illinois. Farnham's written observations were published in a book, *Travels in the Great Western Prairies,* in 1841. It fueled more American interest in Oregon and was reprinted several times.[4]

About a year after Farnham's *Travels* was first published, Secretary of State Daniel Webster sat down with British envoy Alexander Baring, the first Lord Ashburton, in an effort to resolve their nations' boundary disputes. The Webster-Ashburton Treaty of 1842 set the eastern U.S. and Canadian boundary, but it did not address the boundary in Oregon Country. Many settlers in the Willamette Valley were disappointed with the treaty and felt ignored by the United States, but many lawmakers and diplomats in Washington believed U.S. claims were strong in Oregon. In retrospect, the American policy was to do nothing. South Carolina Senator John C. Calhoun said the policy was one of wise and masterly inactivity, and President John Tyler predicted that within a few years there would be an American settlement on the Columbia sufficiently strong to defend itself and to protect the rights of the United States in the region. American settlers in Oregon did not grasp their government's position.

THERE IS NO QUESTION that missionaries first made Americans aware of the economic advantages of Oregon Country. Their books, speaking tours, correspondence with the eastern religious press, and conversations with politicians painted a picture of an agricultural paradise. Then came a few government reports, especially one written by Lieutenant Charles Wilkes, who commanded a government exploring expedition beginning in 1838 into the West that included a journey up the Columbia to the Snake River and another down the Willamette River to what is now California. His prediction that a great state would develop in the Pacific Northwest came as easterners were still feeling the effects of the economic depression of 1837, which was followed by the collapse of the international fur trade in 1839. Businessmen and farmers were frustrated and became even more so when another depression occurred in 1841. Business failures cast dark shadows over the future of many Americans, and depressed prices for agricultural products made times hard for farmers. Poor transportation in many areas of the Middle West also made it difficult for farmers to transport their crops and produce to markets. Economic conditions were such that Oregon Country appeared to offer greener pastures for many Americans, and at least ten Oregon societies were organized in Mississippi Valley towns with members pledging to move to Oregon Country.

To a lesser degree California was also gaining the attention of some Americans. After Mexico declared its independence from Spain in 1821, the new government threw out the Spanish practice of controlling all commerce to maintain internal security. The new Mexican government welcomed English-speaking merchants who found a waiting market for their goods in California. Still other Americans saw California as their promised land. Swiss-born John Augustus Sutter had heard glowing reports from a Canadian, and wanting to escape creditors—and his first wife—in America, Sutter hired six mountain men and a Mexican servant and left St. Louis on April 11, 1838, traveling with an American Fur Company trading caravan to the annual rendezvous. From there Sutter traveled to Fort Vancouver and then sailed to the Sandwich (Hawaiian) Islands and returned east to California.

Another American who headed for California was John Marsh, a native of Salem, Massachusetts. After graduating from Harvard in 1823, he went west to Minnesota and taught in the first school there. He then became an assistant to the Indian agent at Fort St. Anthony and studied medicine with the post physician. Marsh was never certified as a doctor because the post physician died. In the meantime, Marsh became a staunch supporter of the

Sioux Indians during tribal difficulties that finally erupted into the Black Hawk War. While in Minnesota, he compiled the first dictionary of the Sioux language with the help of his common-law wife, the beautiful daughter of a French trapper. When he was accused of being sympathetic toward the Sioux, he moved to Independence, Missouri, and set up a general store, but when creditors and rumors that he had given guns to the Sioux were beginning to catch up with him, Marsh moved to Santa Fe and then to California, where he established a medical practice at Los Angeles. His fees were paid in cattle, and Marsh soon had a large herd. In 1838 he acquired a ranch in the San Joaquin Valley, where he established one of the largest herds of cattle in California. He then began sending glowing letters about California east to attract American settlers.

By 1840, other Americans, including some fur traders who had returned east following the collapse of the fur trade, also promoted California. One man who heard wonderful things about California was John Bidwell, a schoolteacher. Born in Chautauqua County, New York, his family moved to Pennsylvania in 1829 and to Ohio in 1831, where he became a teacher. By 1840, Bidwell had set out on his own and traveled to Platte County, Missouri, where he got a job as a schoolteacher. There, in the northwest Missouri town of Weston, Bidwell attended a meeting of people wanting to settle in California. How many people attended the meeting is not known, but a company was organized, and each person wanting to go signed a pledge to obtain "a suitable outfit, and to rendezvous at Sapling Grove on the ninth of May following." Sapling Grove, later called Elm Grove and Round Grove, was located in what is now Johnson County, Kansas, just west of the Missouri border. The following spring, when Bidwell reached Sapling Grove on May 9, 1841, he found sixty-nine men, four of them with families, waiting. The emigrants organized their company, electing fifty-four-year-old John Bartleson of Jackson County, Missouri, captain, and Bidwell, secretary.

It is clear that Bidwell, Bartleson, and other emigrants wanted to go to California, but it appears they were not sure what route to follow. Aside from trappers who had gone overland to California via Santa Fe or Taos, most emigrants had traveled there by ship. One can only assume that when Thomas Fitzpatrick, a well-known mountain man, arrived at Sapling Grove to guide a party of missionaries headed by Father Pierre-Jean De Smet to Oregon, the California-bound emigrants took advantage of the opportunity. Perhaps Fitzpatrick could show them the way to California. So the emigrants and the missionaries led by Fitzpatrick set out following the route that had been used for years by fur traders going west.

When their combined caravan left Sapling Grove on May 19, 1841, it consisted of five missionary carts, thirteen emigrant wagons, and about seventy people. Father De Smet recalled that fifty of the people knew how to use a rifle. Three more men and another wagon caught up with the caravan on May 23, and Rev. Joseph Williams, a sixty-three-year-old minister riding horseback and determined to Christianize the heathen Indians, joined on May 26 between the Black Vermillion and Big Blue rivers in what is now northeast Kansas. Father De Smet and others in the caravan welcomed Williams, but in his recollections of the journey published at Cincinnati in 1843, Williams wrote on Monday, May 31:

> We had two Methodists in company with us. Col. Bartleson had been a Methodist, but is now a backslider. Our leader, Fitzpatrick, a worldly man, is much opposed to missionaries going among the Indians. He has some intelligence, but is deistical in his principles. At 2 o'clock, commenced a most tremendous hail storm, with wind, which blew down most of the tents, accompanied with rain and lightning and thunder almost all night. I slept but little, the ground being covered with water. That night, dreadful oaths were heard all over the camp ground, O the wickedness of the wicked.[5]

The profanity greatly bothered Williams, as did the fact that many of the men in the caravan wanted no part of his preaching and moralizing.

When the caravan reached the Platte River in present-day Nebraska, it followed the stream westward. Spring thunderstorms in early June slowed their progress almost daily. As they pushed west, they came upon thousands of buffalo grazing on the plains. Hunters killed only as many as were needed for food. Martha Williams, then twelve, traveling with her parents, Richard and Lizzie Huckaby Williams, and their six other children, recalled years later that when the party reached Independence Rock, "one of the men in taking his gun out of the wagon accidentally shot and killed himself."[6] Martha Williams's father was no relation to Reverend Williams, who identified the man as James Shotwell. "I was called upon, by his comrades, to preach his funeral, which I did. The death of this young man caused some seriousness in his comrades for a few days." During the journey, Reverend Williams also performed two weddings. Otherwise the daily routine changed little, until one Friday evening when, as Reverend Williams recalled:

> One of our hunters [Nicholas Dawson], who was in the rear, was robbed of all he had by the Indians. They struck him with their ram-rods, and he ran from them. Soon a war party of the Sioux Indians appeared in view.

We soon collected together in order of battle, to be ready in case of an attack. The Indians stood awhile and looked at us, and probably thinking that the better part of valor is discretion, they soon showed signs of peace. Captain Fitzpatrick then went to them, and talked with them, for he was acquainted with them. They then gave back all that they had taken from the young man, and our men gave them some tobacco, and they smoked the pipe of peace.[7]

Young Martha Williams's recollections of the event are not so dramatic. She recalled that the incident occurred after the Oregon-bound emigrants left the site of present-day Soda Springs, Idaho. She recalled: "We had no trouble with the Indians. I remember one time some Indians caught one of our company away from the train, took his coat and hat and then followed him into camp. The captain of our company got them all off to themselves, the emigrants gave them their supper and they gave us no trouble."[8]

On August 10, in the vicinity of Soda Springs, at least six emigrants decided not to continue the journey and, on horseback, started back to Missouri. The rest of the caravan camped at Soda Springs, so named because of the naturally carbonated springs created by underground geothermal activity that heats water and mixes in carbon dioxide gas. It was here that the California-bound emigrants decided to turn south and follow the Bear River toward California. When Thomas Fitzpatrick advised them against trying to blaze a new route to California, some of the emigrants were persuaded to continue with Fitzpatrick and Father De Smet and his missionaries toward Oregon. Richard Williams and his family were among those who went to Oregon. But about thirty men, including John Bartleson, John Bidwell, and Benjamin Kelsey, with his wife, Nancy, and their infant daughter, were determined to go on to California. Thus the party divided at Soda Springs. Led by Fitzpatrick, Father De Smet's missionary party, along with Reverend Williams and all but one of the families, set out north for Fort Hall and Oregon.

Martha Williams remembered that a man named Cochran who joined the company at Fort Laramie persuaded her father to go to Oregon instead of California. She also recalled that the Oregon-bound emigrants went to Fort Hall, where they traded their oxen and wagons for horses. "Rode part of them and had packs on the others. Armentenger, of the Hudson's Bay Co., piloted us on to Dr. Whitman's. . . . We were short of provisions most all the time and went hungry lots of time until we got to Dr. Whitman's. There we got some wheat and ground it on a hand mill, and I think some pickled pork. . . . When we left Dr. Whitman's he sent an Indian to pilot us down to

The Dalles.... When we left The Dalles, another Indian piloted us on to Willamette Falls, what is Oregon City now."[9]

The California-bound emigrants headed south from Soda Springs with perhaps eight wagons pulled by oxen along with a few horses and mules. They followed the Bear River without a guide or a compass and with only the sun to set their course across the modern Utah and Nevada deserts toward California. They followed a route that led them to the Great Salt Lake Valley near the present-day Utah towns of Fielding, Garland, and Tremonton. When their water was about gone, they changed course and headed east to Bear River near modern Corinne, Utah, to replenish their supply. The party then pushed northwest around the north side of the Great Salt Lake. On September 11, 1841, near what is today Lucin, in northwest Utah, Kentuckian Benjamin Kelsey abandoned his wagons, slaughtered his oxen for food, and put his young wife, Nancy, and their baby on horseback. Crossing into what is now northeast Nevada, the emigrants soon came to a river that had been found by the explorer Peter Skene Ogden during the 1820s. He first called it by various names, including Mary's River. Later, another explorer, John Charles Frémont, would rename it the Humboldt River after the German naturalist and geographer Alexander von Humboldt. The emigrants followed the river southwest to its end at what is now known as the Humboldt Sink.

At some point they abandoned the rest of their wagons and tied their belongings to the backs of their oxen and followed the Carson River and then the Walker River, where they rested. A few men reconnoitered the mountains to the west and reported they were barely passable. Some emigrants thought they ought to go back to Fort Hall before winter snows arrived, but when the matter was put to a vote, a majority decided to continue their journey over the mountains. The next day they discovered the Stanislaus River flowing west and crossed over the Sierra Nevada between the Stanislaus and Walker rivers. The mountains were beautiful but vast and rugged. The emigrants had no way of knowing when they entered California, but on November 4, 1841, nearly destitute, their clothing in shreds, and near starvation, they reached John Marsh's Rancho Los Medanos near Mount Diablo, some forty miles east of San Francisco. Nancy Kelsey became the first white woman to cross the Sierra Nevada mountains to California, where she died in 1895. The Bidwell-Bartleson party, as it has become known, was the first group of emigrants to go overland to California. In so doing they established the overland route that used the Oregon Trail from Missouri to present-day Idaho before turning southwest toward California.

An unidentified artist depicted the struggle emigrants experienced in getting their wagons over the rugged Sierra Nevada. (Author's collection)

Earlier, when the Oregon-bound emigrants had reached Fort Hall, Father De Smet and his missionaries left the party and headed for Flathead Indian country to establish the Jesuit mission of St. Mary's in the Bitterroot Valley. In time, De Smet had six successful missions, which embarrassed the Protestant missionaries. From what is known, the Indians were largely indifferent to the efforts of the Protestant missionaries, who seemed to argue among themselves. The Indians noticed that the Jesuits did not argue. Thomas Fitzpatrick, the guide, went no farther than Fort Hall. As for Reverend Williams, he traveled with emigrants along the Columbia River to where the Willamette River joins it. There, Williams went to Fort Vancouver, where he met P. B. Littlejohn, another missionary, about to leave for a nearby mission. Williams later recalled:

So I brought up my baggage to the house where Littlejohn was staying, and with his consent put them in there, without asking McLoughlin. Immediately after, McLoughlin came into the house, looking very angry, he asked me if I had any recommendation to him. I told him I had not. He then told me he would not receive me. I showed him my credentials as a preacher in the Methodist Church, but he cared not for these. I then asked him to let my articles lay a few hours in his room, but it was not granted. He is an ill-natured, old Roman Catholic. I went down to the river and stayed with some people who were going to travel with me. Next day we went down to the Willamette River, then went up it in a canoe, and laid on the bank. Next day I went on foot across the mountain, in company with Samuel Kelsey. Climbing over the mountains and traversing the plains, fatigued me; and by over-heating myself, it gave me the chills and fevers for near a week.[10]

Williams recovered his health and spent the winter in Oregon. In his recollections he recalled that the greater part of the American mountain men who had settled in Oregon after the collapse of the fur trade joined the Methodist Episcopal Church. He described them as "good citizens" and noted:

In this country there are about four classes of people: First, the Hudson's Bay Company, mostly Canadians. Second, the New England missionaries. Third, the French farmers, mostly Catholics. Fourth, the mountain men who have settled along the Willamette River. At Vancouver they keep a large quantity of goods which they sell very cheap. English ships come in about twice a year. They belong to the Hudson's Bay Company and exchange their goods for beaver and other skins, flour, beef, and pork.... The Roman Catholics here appear to be buying the good will of the people by presents, and, I believe, are trying to get the control of the Indians. I fear our missionaries are too scornful toward the poor, naked Indians; indeed too much so with all the poor people.[11]

The following spring Williams and a few other missionaries started east, but to avoid Blackfeet Indians the party changed course and followed the Green River southwest until it came to a fort or trading post established by James Bridger on the river at Blacks Fork in what is now southwestern Wyoming. But Bridger had left about a month before to go to St. Louis to purchase supplies, including blacksmithing equipment. In his journal Williams noted: "We saw nothing there but three little, starved dogs. We saw the grave of an Indian woman, who had been killed by the Shiennes

[Shoshone Indians]. From here we could see the mountain-tops spotted with snow."[12]

To avoid hostile Indians, Williams and his party traveled south to Taos, New Mexico, and then followed the Santa Fe Trail back to Missouri. By then another group of emigrants had left Independence, Missouri, for Oregon. Their caravan was promoted by Dr. Elijah White, a man described as a pompous busybody, who had gone to Oregon by ship and served as a physician at Rev. Jason Lee's Willamette Valley mission from 1837 until he returned to the States by ship in 1841 after being accused of immoral conduct. White went to Washington, D.C., where Missouri Senator Lewis Linn, among others, was campaigning to make Oregon Country part of the United States. Since White was about the only person in the capital who had been to Oregon, he was offered the position of subagent for the Oregon Indians at half salary and the promise that he would be given a full salary and his own agency if Congress passed a measure calling for the occupation of Oregon. Secretly he was authorized to promote "Oregon fever" and was given funds to do so. Now he was in Missouri preparing to go overland for the first time to Oregon.

The emigrant party White had organized had gathered at Independence, Missouri, in late April 1841 and then crossed into what is now eastern Kansas and camped at Sapling Grove to await Dr. White's arrival. By then the sapling elm trees that first gave the spot its name were leafing out and growing into large trees and the gathering place was becoming known as Elm Grove. Dr. White found the emigrants waiting when he arrived on May 14, and the following day he was elected captain to serve for one month. Nathaniel Crocker was elected secretary. On that day there were about 112 people in the party, with eighteen wagons. Latecomers raised the total number of emigrants to 125, including women and children and sixty or seventy men. On May 16, the caravan set out for Oregon. Two days later Captain White issued an unpopular order that the emigrants' dogs must be put to death to prevent a feared outbreak of rabies. Twenty-two dogs were killed.

Bad weather and a sick sixteen-month-old baby slowed the caravan's progress for the first several days. On May 21, the baby died. Funeral services were held and the baby was buried near what is today Lawrence, Kansas. The next day the caravan made good time and traveled twenty-five miles. After crossing the Kansas River in the vicinity of present-day Topeka, Kansas, the caravan pushed northward to the Little Blue River and on to the Platte River where, on June 15, Lansford W. Hastings was elected captain, replacing White, whose term had ended. Whether Dr. White was irritated by not being reelected captain or for some other reason, he and a small group of the emigrants went on ahead of the main party the following day.

Until they reached Fort Laramie in late June, the parties traveled separately but were reunited at the fort. West of the fort the emigrants met James Bridger and Thomas Fitzpatrick, who had guided Father De Smet, his missionaries, and emigrants to Fort Hall the previous year. Bridger and Fitzpatrick were taking furs to the States. Dr. White hired Fitzpatrick to guide the emigrants to Fort Hall for $500, which the government paid.

The journey was mostly uneventful until the emigrants reached the area of Independence Rock, where one of them died in an accidental shooting and his funeral services were held. Then, on July 13, Hastings and another emigrant were taken prisoner by some Sioux Indians. Fitzpatrick was able to free the two men, and the caravan continued its journey, by mid-August reaching Fort Hall, where Fitzpatrick left the caravan. Dr. White and the emigrants continued by packtrain to the Willamette Valley, arriving in early October 1842.[13]

Soon after Dr. White arrived, he took a census of the men, women, and children who had settled in the Willamette Valley and at Wailatpu, near what is now Walla Walla, Washington, and he also gathered information on their crops and livestock. He accounted for 248 families consisting of 825 men, women, and children. They had 6,620 acres of land under improvement and owned 3,143 horses, 6,558 head of cattle, 139 sheep, and 1,939 hogs. During 1842, they produced more than 33,000 bushels of wheat and 16,238 bushels of other grains. This was the evidence Dr. White needed to send east to show that Americans could successfully farm in Oregon Country. Dr. White was convinced that if more American settlers did not arrive, the British and Canadians would be in the majority and Oregon Country would belong to them.[14]

BY 1842, it was obvious to the emigrants heading to Oregon that oxen were the best animals to pull their wagons. Oxen are castrated bulls of the genus *Bos* that are more than four years old, and they had advantages over horses and mules. They were sure-footed, calm, docile, less apt to be scared or to flounder in mud or snow, and not given to much sickness. Their hooves are cloven, or split, and they had to be shod. Oxen shoes were two curved pieces of metal, one on each side of the hoof. Shoeing oxen, especially on the trail, was difficult, because unlike horses and even mules, which allow themselves to be shod rather easily, oxen would lie down and tuck their feet up under themselves. It took several men to lift an ox and hold it while the animal was being shod. If the shoeing was done at one of the posts along the trail, the animal was placed in a large sling. When on a dusty trail, the noses of oxen had to be kept clean of the dust that gathered in their nostrils. Keeping the oxen's noses clean was usually a task assigned to young boys, who used a damp rag to remove the dust. Still, an ox did not cost as much as a horse to buy and keep. Oxen could be maintained on a coarser diet than horses. They could live on prairie grasses and sage, but horses could not survive on prairie grasses alone and had to be fed. Oxen also could stand idle for long periods of time with little damage to their feet and legs, and they could be trained like horses.

Mules could make better speed than oxen and horses, and could live on prairie grasses, but they did not have the staying power of oxen. Mules had a cantankerous disposition. Samuel June Barrows summed up the mule when he wrote: "If there is any one animal that can be defined only by a simple proposition of identity, that animal is a mule. A mule is a mule. When you have said that, you have defined him, stigmatized him, and given the only full and accurate description of him."[15]

Oxen were trained by leading and giving them age-old commands that included "Get up," "Whoa," "Back up," "Gee" (Go right), and "Haw" (Go left), and by using a whip or goad. No reins, bits, or halters were needed to work oxen. They were simply yoked with either a neck yoke or a head yoke, two oxen to a yoke, but a trainer had to be very forceful, if not domineering. The ox on the left was the neigh ox, the one on the right was the off ox. Emigrant Peter Burnett, who traveled to Oregon in 1843 with his wife, six children, and three wagons, proved their value. Although they traveled at only about two miles an hour, they were reliable. Burnett wrote: "The ox is a most noble animal, patient, thrifty, durable, gentle and does not run off. Those who come to this country [Oregon] will be in love with their oxen. The ox will plunge through mud, swim over streams, dive into thickets and he will eat almost anything."[16]

As OREGON COUNTRY gained more congressional attention in 1842, the route emigrants were using to reach the Columbia River also attracted the legislators' attention. John Charles Frémont, then a twenty-nine-year-old second lieutenant in the U.S. Corps of Topographical Engineers, was ordered to take an expedition and survey the Platte River route up to the head of the Sweetwater River. A native of Georgia, he got a job, early in his career, as a civilian teaching mathematics to midshipmen aboard the USS *Natchez*. He then assisted on some surveys. In 1838 he was appointed an officer with the topographical corps and went on two expeditions in the region of the upper Mississippi and Missouri rivers and received training in cartography both in the field and in Washington, D.C. There he eloped with Jessie Benton, the seventeen-year-old daughter of Missouri Senator Thomas Hart Benton. Benton was interested in Oregon. As early as 1822, he had urged that U.S. troops be sent to the upper Missouri River and even to the Columbia River to protect American fur traders, but he found no support for his proposal in Congress. By 1841, Benton was encouraging American settlement in Oregon Country and the use of Missouri as the starting place for emigrants heading toward the Columbia River. It was no surprise that Benton designed his son-in-law's expedition to publicize the overland route to Oregon.

When Frémont's expedition started west on June 10, 1842, it was about three weeks behind Dr. Elijah White's caravan. Frémont's party included the German topographer Charles Preuss, Lucien B. Maxwell as hunter, Kit Carson as guide, twenty-one experienced voyageurs hired at St. Louis, and two young men: nineteen-year-old Henry Brant, son of Colonel J. B. Brant of St. Louis, and Senator Benton's twelve-year-old son, Randolph. At their fathers' request, Frémont took the young men along for "development of mind and body." Frémont later wrote:

> We were well armed and mounted, with the exception of eight men, who conducted as many carts, in which were packed our stores, with the baggage and instruments, and which were drawn by two mules. A few loose horses, and four oxen, which had been added to our stock of provisions, completed the train.[17]

Niles' National Register, on July 2, 1842, reprinted a story from the *St. Louis Republican* reporting Frémont's departure and describing his expedition's purpose as "important." The newspaper added: "Since the attention of the country has been directed to the settlement of the Oregon territory by our able senator (Dr. Linn) and by the reports of those who have visited that region in person, the importance of providing ample security for the settlers there, and of opening a safe and easy communication from the western boundary of Missouri to the Columbia River, has been universally admitted."

Frémont's expedition followed the already established route across what is now northeast Kansas into what is now Nebraska, where it struck the Platte River. Frémont, however, called the Platte the Nebraska River, and the word "Nebraska" first appeared in print in Frémont's report. The word comes from the Otoe Indian name "Nebrathka," used to identify the Platte River. Nebrathka means "flat water." Once Frémont and his party reached the Platte, they turned west and followed the south bank. They made good time, reached Fort Laramie on July 13, and made camp a little above the fort on the bank of the Laramie River, with its pure, clear water rushing down from the mountains. Frémont wrote that the stream "looked freshingly cool, and made a pleasant contrast to the muddy, yellow waters of the Platte."

I walked up to visit our friends at the fort, which is a quadrangular structure, built of clay, after the fashion of the Mexicans, who are generally employed in building them. The walls are about fifteen feet high, surmounted with a wooden palisade, and form a portion of ranges of houses, which entirely surround a yard of about one hundred and thirty feet square. Every apartment has its door and window,—all, of course, opening on the inside. There are two entrances, opposite each other, and midway the wall, one of which is a large and public entrance; the other smaller and more private—a sort of postern gate. Over the great entrance is a square tower with loopholes, and, like the rest of the work, built of earth. At two of the angles, and diagonally opposite each other, are large square bastions, so arranged as to sweep the four faces of the walls.[18]

Fort Laramie, first called Fort William, had been built in 1834 by fur traders William Sublette and Robert Campbell. They sold the post in 1835 to

Fort John [Fort Laramie] as it appeared before the U.S. government purchased it in 1849. This scene was painted from memory by William Henry Jackson. (Courtesy Scotts Bluff National Monument)

the fur company operated by Lucien B. Fontenelle and Thomas Fitzpatrick, and the following year it became the property of the American Fur Company. After the last rendezvous in 1840 and the collapse of the fur trade, Fort Laramie became an oasis for people traveling the trail to Oregon Country and a trading center for Indians. When Frémont arrived there in July 1842, he learned that Indians in the region visited the fort two or three times a year to trade buffalo robes for blankets, calicoes, guns, powder, and lead, plus glass beads, looking glasses, rings, vermilion for painting, tobacco, and alcohol diluted with water. Frémont noted:

> I have always found [the American Fur Company] strenuously opposed to the introduction of spirituous liquors. But in the present state of things, when the country is supplied with alcohol—when a keg of it will purchase from an Indian every thing he possesses—his furs, his lodge, his horses, and even his wife and children—and when any vagabond who has money enough to purchase a mule can go into a village and trade against them successfully...it is impossible for them to discontinue its use.[19]

After reaching South Pass, Frémont traveled northwest and reconnoitered the Wind River Mountains. Throughout his report, Frémont addresses road conditions from one area to the next. At one point he writes, "From the mouth of the Kansas to the Green River valley, west of the mountains, there is no such thing as a mountain road on the line of communication."[20] There is no question that he was writing a guide for future emigrants to follow. At another point he wrote: "If it is in contemplation to keep open the communication with Oregon territory, a show of military force in this country is absolutely necessary; and a combination of advantages renders the neighborhood of Fort Laramie the most suitable place, on the line of the Platte, for the establishment of a military post."[21]

Frémont's expedition was undoubtedly designed to prepare the way for the United States' occupation of Oregon Country and to encourage settlement in the vast region of Indian country west of the Missouri River, where, it was hoped, settlers could raise crops to feed soldiers and emigrants traveling the trail. Frémont returned to Missouri in early October and then traveled east to Washington, D.C., where he finished writing his report. When it was completed, Congress ordered that his report be printed in 1843, accompanied by a map. By then an even larger number of emigrants were making plans to travel overland to Oregon Country.

CHAPTER SIX

THE EMIGRANTS OF 1843

The soul of a journey is liberty, perfect liberty,
to think, feel, do just as one pleases.

William Hazlitt

THE GRASS WAS GREENING and spring flowers were beginning to bloom along the western border of Missouri in April 1843 when emigrants intent on going to Oregon Country began arriving at Independence and nearby Westport. They came from other areas in Missouri and from nearby states. They had sold their homes, farms, and household belongings to raise money to buy or build wagons, purchase oxen or mules to pull their wagons, and to buy supplies for the journey. Most of the emigrants had only a vague idea of the route they would follow in crossing the prairies, plains, and mountains between Missouri and Oregon. Most of them probably felt uncertain about what lay ahead. But when they met other emigrants, they found some answers to their questions and some strength in numbers. They also met Dr. Marcus Whitman, who was returning to his Oregon Country mission at Waiilatpu. Whitman had hurried to Boston earlier in the winter after the American Board of Commissioners for Foreign Missions ordered some of its missions in Oregon Country closed. He had pleaded to keep the missions open, and now he was returning to Oregon Country. Delighted by Whitman's presence, the emigrants asked him to accompany them west. He agreed and told them to go ahead, saying he would catch up with them after he completed some business at Shawnee Mission, located several miles north of Elm Grove. The mission had been constructed in 1839 by Methodist missionaries after removing it from its first location near Turner, Kansas.

Encouraged that Whitman would soon join them, the emigrants decided their number was sufficient to begin their journey and gathered at Elm

Grove, a few miles from Westport and about twelve miles southwest of Independence, just across the western border of Missouri in what is now Kansas. By May 21, there were 875 men, women, and children in camp along with 120 wagons, most drawn by oxen, some by mules. In addition, there were perhaps 3,000 loose cattle, horses, and oxen. The emigrants held a meeting to establish a set of traveling rules and to elect a council of nine men to mediate any disputes that might erupt. They also decided that they would wait until after they crossed the Kansas River before electing officers.

To guide them to Oregon County, the emigrants hired fifty-three-year-old John Gantt, an experienced fur trader, trapper, and former captain in the U.S. Army. He said he would guide them for $1 per person. Some years earlier Gantt had been kicked out of the army for supposedly falsifying pay accounts. He then became a partner with mountain man Jefferson Blackwell and traded with the Indians. Later the two men built a trading post on the Arkansas River near where William Bent had established a post. The competition became stiff, and Bent won. Gantt then spent some time guiding an expedition headed by Colonel Henry Dodge charged with improving relations with Indians on the plains and the eastern slope of the Rockies. Afterward, Gantt returned to Missouri, where in 1843 the emigrants hired him as their guide.[1]

With Gantt leading the way, the wagons left Elm Grove on the morning of May 22. Because of spring rains, the mule-drawn wagons left first, to avoid getting stuck behind the slower ox-drawn wagons. Herded along with the wagons were more than a thousand head of cattle owned by Jesse and Lindsay Applegate and Daniel Waldo. For everyone it was something of an experiment. Such a journey with so many men, women, children, wagons, and livestock had never been attempted on the western prairie and plains. Travel was slow. To make matters worse, there were frequent spring rains that created much mud. About five days later the vanguard of the emigrants' wagons reached the Kansas River at the modern-day site of Topeka. The rest of the wagons caught up the following day.

Camped on the south side of the Kansas River, Rev. David Lenox and others apparently tried to make a deal with Joseph Papan, who operated a ferry to carry travelers and their wagons across the stream. Papan's ferry was nothing more than a wooden platform attached to two canoes. Papan, however, would not agree to the terms the emigrants proposed, so the emigrants began building their own ferry. Lenox's sixteen-year-old son, Edward, recalled that his father acquired three dugout canoes from a Frenchman living nearby, constructed a platform, and fastened the dugouts about four feet apart under the platform, thereby creating a primitive raft. The task of ferrying wagons one at a time across the Kansas River began.[2]

On May 31, 1843, the last of the emigrants crossed the river and joined the others who had made camp a few miles to the north along the bank of what is today Soldier Creek. The early arrivals nicknamed the place Camp Delay. There, on June 1, the emigrants began the process of electing a commander-in-chief for the caravan. Matthew C. Field, an assistant editor of the *New Orleans Picayune*, witnessed the election. He was traveling with a party of pleasure-seekers to the Rocky Mountains organized by Sir William Drummond Stewart. There were twenty "gentlemen" in the party, including William Clark Kennerly, nephew of General William Clark; Jefferson Clark, the son of General Clark; Kennerly's cousin John Radford; members of the prominent Chouteau and Menard families of St. Louis; a few army officers on leave; and a few professors of science. William Sublette was guiding the party, which also included about thirty hunters, mule drivers, and camp servants to make life comfortable for the gentlemen. Traveling faster than the large wagon train, they came upon the emigrants camped on Soldier Creek. In a letter sent back to his newspaper, Field wrote:

> It was a curious and unaccountable spectacle to us, as we approached. We saw a large body of men wheeling and marching about the prairie, describing evolutions neither recognizable as savage, civic, or military.... We found they were only going on with their elections, in a manner perhaps old enough, but very new and quizzical to us. The candidates stood up in a row before the constituents, and at a given signal they wheeled about and marched off, while the general mass *broke* after them "lickity-split," each man forming in behind his favorite, so that every candidate flourished a sort of tail of his own, and the man with the longest tail was elected! These proceedings were continued until a Captain and a Council of Ten were elected, and, indeed, if the scene can be conceived, it must appear as a curious mingling of the whimsical with the wild. Here was a congregation of rough, bold, and adventurous men, gathered from distant and opposite sections of the Union, just forming an acquaintance with each other, to last, in all probability through good or evil fortune, through the rest of their days. Few of them expected or thought of ever returning to the States again. They had with them their wives and children, and aged, dependent relatives. They were going, with stout and determined hearts to traverse a wild and desolate region, and take possession of a far corner of their country, destined to prove a new and strong arm of a mighty nation.[3]

Field and the others in Stewart's party moved on and never saw the emigrants again. After roaming through the Rocky Mountains for about three weeks, they started back to Missouri and arrived there by late October.

Although Field does not identify the winner, Peter Burnett, a native of Tennessee, was elected commander-in-chief. Burnett had been practicing law at Platte City, Missouri, where he also operated a general store. James W. Nesmith was elected orderly sergeant. Under their leadership the wagon train resumed its journey the following morning. Dr. Marcus Whitman caught up with the emigrants after having completed his business at Shawnee Mission. His presence gave the emigrants new confidence. During the weeks that followed, he would often ride along the caravan of moving wagons answering questions and giving encouragement to the emigrants.

Aside from spring rains that made the trail muddy and slowed travel, the wagon train had other difficulties caused by the large number of loose cattle and other livestock herded along with the wagons. Edward Lenox recalled: "Father and some of the other men went ahead and engaged in cutting down cottonwood trees, and felling them across the stream to make a rude bridge. We were all compelled to fall into single file. There was a vast amount of confusion and the teamsters generally got mad and raved at the Captain. 'Well,' said Burnett, 'I throw up my job right here and now.' "[4] Burnett, who later became the first governor of California, recalled years later that he quit as leader of the wagon train because of "10,000 little vexations" inherent in trying to lead so many free spirits westward. Burnett already had the responsibility of taking care of his wife and six children traveling in three wagons.

William Martin assumed command of the wagon train as the emigrants traveled west and northwest through the Kansas River valley past the site of modern St. Marys, Kansas, before climbing through the rolling hills and grasslands a few miles northeast of what is today Wamego, Kansas. Captain Gantt guided the emigrants over the route taken by Kit Carson the previous year when he guided John C. Frémont on his first western expedition. The route had been pioneered early in 1827 by William Sublette, who took wagons to the fur-trading rendezvous in 1830. By 1843, what had first been called "Sublette's Trace" was becoming known as the trail to Oregon Country. The trail turned north in the vicinity of modern Westmoreland, Kansas, and a few miles farther on turned northwest, crossing the Black Vermillion River southeast of modern Blue Rapids, Kansas. A few miles northwest of the crossing the emigrants came to a picturesque spring located seven miles south of present Marysville, Kansas. The spring, located on the east side of the Big Blue River, was already a favorite camping spot for frontiersmen. It

This 1930 photo shows Independence Crossing on the Big Blue River, located south of present-day Marysville, Kansas. (Courtesy Kansas State Historical Society)

This is Alcove Spring, located near Independence Crossing on the Big Blue River, south of Marysville, Kansas. The spring was a favorite camping site for emigrants. (Courtesy Kansas State Historical Society)

was a pleasant stop for the emigrants, who had traveled a little more than a week to reach the spot after crossing the Kansas River. A few years later it would be named Alcove Spring by another party of emigrants.

Leaving the spring, the wagons forded the Big Blue River. In 1843, the crossing did not have a name, but after another crossing of the river was established nearby at the site of present-day Marysville, Kansas, for emigrants using St. Joseph, Missouri, as their jumping-off point, the first crossing became known as Independence Crossing, since it was used by emigrants starting from Independence, Missouri. The newer crossing was referred to as the St. Joseph Crossing. Edward Lenox later wrote:

> The large bands of cattle owned by Jesse and Lindsay Applegate, and Daniel Waldo could hardly be rounded up in the morning before ten o'clock, and so delayed us in our morning start, that after a few days it was amicably agreed to divide the company. Father [Rev. David. T. Lenox] took our two teams and with thirty-one other teams, whose occupants chose to accompany us, we went ahead. Those who were left behind, chose Jesse Applegate as Captain. Soon after this separation was made, father appointed four captains of the guard to have charge on each fourth night in succession. The nights were divided into four watches each, and the men and boys generally were expected to take their turn at guard duty.[5]

Years later Jesse Applegate recalled, "There was just cause for discontent in respect to loose cattle. Some of the emigrants had only their teams, while others had large herds in addition which must share the pastures and be guarded and driven by the whole body." The emigrants with only a few cattle traveled with the light column while those with more than four or five cows joined the cow column. Applegate recalled that the cow column, being so much larger than the light column, "had to use greater exertion and observe a more rigid discipline to keep pace with the more agile consort."[6]

Having divided into two sections, the emigrants crossed into what is now Jefferson County, Nebraska, and stopped at Fremont Springs, located a little more than four miles south of modern Diller, Nebraska. The springs were named for explorer John Frémont, who had camped there the year before. His name was carved in soft sandstone nearby. The route continued northwest, passing east of present-day Fairbury, Nebraska, until it reached the Platte River, formed by the North Platte and South Platte rivers. The headwaters of the North Platte originate in what is now north-central Colorado, and the river flows northward to near modern Casper, Wyoming, then southeast through eastern Wyoming and western Nebraska. The South

The names Kit Carson and Col. John C. Fremont are carved in the limestone at what is called Fremont Springs, located just off the Oregon Trail in what is today Jefferson County, Nebraska. Frémont, Carson, and their party camped at the springs on their way west in 1842. The springs are about four miles south of Diller, Nebraska, and six and a half miles southeast of Fairbury, Nebraska. (Courtesy Kansas State Historical Society)

Platte originates on the eastern slopes of the Continental Divide northwest of present-day Fairplay, Colorado, and flows north out of the mountains through what is now Denver and continues north to Greeley. There the South Platte bends east and meets the North Platte River to form the Platte at what is now North Platte, Nebraska. From that point the Platte is wide and flat as it meanders east more than four hundred miles until it enters a gorge near modern Ashland, Nebraska, and then flows into the Missouri River. East from the point where the Platte River is formed, the wide stream often lacks a permanent channel since it flows around numerous islands creating more than one channel. The river's name comes from the French word for "broad, shallow, and flat." In time, emigrants came to describe the Platte River as "a thousand miles long and six inches deep." At times it could be forded with ease and often with dry feet, but at other times, especially when it carried the water from melting mountain snows, it was difficult to cross.

Once the emigrant train struck the Platte River, it moved west along the stream's south bank with the light column first, followed by the cow column. Years later Jesse Applegate wrote what has become something of a classic on trail life with the cow column in 1843.

It is four o'clock a.m.; the sentinels on duty have discharged their rifles—the signal that hours of sleep are over; and every wagon and tent is pouring forth its night tenants, and slow-kindling smokes begin largely to rise and float away on the morning air. Sixty men start from the corral, spreading as they make through the vast herd of cattle and horses that form a semi-circle around the encampment, the most distant perhaps two miles away.

The herders pass to the extreme verge and carefully examine for trails beyond, to see that none of the animals have strayed or been stolen during the night.

This morning no trails lead beyond the outside animals in sight, and by five o'clock the herders begin to contract the great moving circle and the well-trained animals move slowly toward camp, clipping here and there a thistle or tempting bunch of grass on the way. In about an hour five thousand animals are close up to the encampment, and the teamsters are busy selecting their teams and driving them inside the "corral" to be yoked. The corral is a circle one hundred yards deep, formed with wagons connected strongly with each other, the wagon in the rear being connected with the wagon in front by its tongue and ox chains. It is a strong barrier that the most vicious ox cannot break, and in case of an attack of the Sioux would be no contemptible entrenchment.

From six to seven o'clock is a busy time; breakfast is to be eaten, the tents struck, the wagons loaded, and the teams yoked and brought up in readiness to be attached to their respective wagons. All know when, at seven o'clock, the signal to march sounds, that those not ready to take their proper places in the line of march must fall into the dusty rear for the day.

There are sixty wagons. They have been divided into fifteen divisions or platoons of four wagons each, and each platoon is entitled to lead in its turn. The leading platoon of today will be the rear one tomorrow, and will bring up the rear unless some teamster, through indolence or negligence, has lost his place in the line, and is condemned to that uncomfortable post. It is within ten minutes of seven; the corral but now a strong barricade is everywhere broken, the teams being attached to the wagons. The women and children have taken their places in them. The pilot (a borderer who has passed his life on the verge of civilization, and has been chosen to the post of leader from his knowledge of the savage and his experience in travel through roadless wastes) stands ready in the midst of his pioneers, and aids, to mount and lead the way. Ten or fifteen young men, not today on duty, form another cluster. They are ready to start on a buffalo hunt, are well mounted, and well armed as they need be, for the unfriendly Sioux have driven the buffalo out of the Platte, and the hunters must ride fifteen or twenty miles to reach them. The cow drivers are hastening, as they get ready, to the rear of their charge, to collect and prepare them for the day's march.

It is on the stroke of seven; the rushing to and fro, the cracking of the whips, the loud command to oxen, and what seems to be the inextricable confusion of the last ten minutes has ceased. Fortunately every one has been found and every teamster is at his post. The clear notes of the trumpet sound in the front; the pilot and his guards mount their horses, the leading division takes up the line of march, the rest fall into their places with the precision of clock work, until the spot so lately full of life sinks back into that solitude that seems to reign over the broad plain.

An unidentified artist shows a man on horseback blowing his trumpet in an emigrant camp. It was the signal to break camp to resume their journey on the Oregon Trail. (Courtesy Kansas State Historical Society)

Applegate observed that the emigrants viewed the scenery as they traveled west, but it soon became so overwhelming that it was often ignored. He then continued his narrative:

The pilot, by measuring the ground and timing the speed of the wagons and the walk of his horses, has determined the rate of each, so as to enable him to select the noon place, as nearly as the requisite grass and water can be had at the end of five hours' travel of the wagons. Today, the ground being favorable, little time has been lost in preparing the road, so that he and his pioneers are at the nooning place an hour in advance of the wagons, which time is spent in preparing convenient watering places for the animals. As the teams are not unyoked, but simply turned loose from the wagons, a corral is not formed at noon, but the wagons are drawn up in columns, four abreast, the leading wagon of each platoon on the left—the platoons being formed with that view. This brings friends together at noon as well as at night.

Today an extra session of the Council is being held, to settle a dispute that does not admit of delay, between a proprietor and a young man who has undertaken to do a man's service on the journey for bed and board. Many such engagements exist and much interest is taken in the manner this high court, from which there is no appeal, will define the rights of each party in such engagements. The Council was a high court in the most exalted sense. It was a Senate composed of the ablest and most respected fathers of the emigration....

It is now one o'clock; the bugle has sounded, and the caravan has resumed its westward journey. It is in the same order, but the evening is far less animated than the morning march; a drowsiness has fallen apparently on man and beast; teamsters drop asleep on their perches and even when walking by their teams, and the words of command are now addressed to the slowly creeping oxen in the softened tenor of women or the piping treble of children, while the snores of teamsters make a droning accompaniment. But a little incident breaks the monotony of the march. An emigrant's wife whose state of health has caused Dr. Whitman to travel near the wagon for the day, is now taken with violent illness. The doctor has had the wagon driven out of the line, a tent pitched and a fire kindled. Many conjectures are hazarded in regard to this mysterious proceeding, and as to why this lone wagon is to be left behind.

And we too must leave it, hasten to the front and note the proceedings, for the sun is now getting low in the west, and at length the painstaking pilot is standing ready to conduct the train in the circle which he has previously measured and marked out, which was to form the invariable fortification for the night. The leading wagons follow him so nearly round the circle, that but a wagon length separates them. Each wagon follows in its track, the rear closing on the front, until its tongue and ox chains will perfectly reach from one to the other, and so accurate the measurement and perfect the practice, that the hindmost wagon of the train always precisely closes the gateway. As each wagon is brought into position it is dropped from its team (the teams being inside the circle), the team unyoked, and the yokes and chains are used to connect the wagon strongly with that in its front. Within ten minutes from the time the leading wagon halted, the barricade is formed, the teams unyoked and driven out to pasture. Everyone is busy preparing fires of buffalo chips to cook the evening meal, pitching tents and otherwise preparing for the night. There are anxious watchers for the absent wagon, for there are many matrons who may be afflicted like its inmate before the journey is over; and they fear the strange and startling practice of this Oregon doctor will be dangerous. But as the sun goes down, the absent wagon rolls into camp, the bright, speaking face and cheery look of the doctor, who rides in advance, declares without words that all is well, and both mother and child are comfortable....

It is not yet eight o'clock when the first watch is to be set; the evening meal is just over, and the corral now free from the intrusion of the cattle or horses, groups of children are scattered over it. The larger are taking a game of romps, "the wee toddling things" are being taught the great achievement that distinguishes man from the lower animals. Before a tent...a violin makes lively music, and some youths and maidens have improvised a dance upon the green; in another quarter a flute gives its mellow and melancholy notes to the still air, which as they float away... seem a lament for the past rather than a hope for the future. It has been a prosperous day; more than twenty miles have been accomplished of the great journey....

But time passes; the watch is set for the night, the council of old men has broken up and each has returned to his own quarter. The flute has whispered its last lament to the deepening night, the violin is silent and the dancers have dispersed. Enamored youth have whispered a tender "good night" in the ears of blushing maidens, or stolen a kiss from the lips of some future bride—for Cupid here as elsewhere has been busy bringing together congenial hearts, and among those simple people he alone is consulted in forming the marriage tie. Even the Doctor [Whitman] and the pilot have finished their confidential interview and have separated for the night. All is hushed and repose from the fatigue of the day, save the vigilant guard, and the wakeful leader who still has cares upon his mind that forbid sleep.[7]

Aside from herding so many cattle, life in the light column, which moved ahead of the cow column, was probably similar and perhaps less complicated with fewer loose cattle and horses. For persons in both columns, the daily journey was often monotonous. The sight of Indians occasionally broke the daily routine, and at one point a party of about three hundred

Sioux Indians blocked the wagons and demanded a cow. When the animal was given to them, they killed it on the spot and ate the meat raw. The emigrants were always on the lookout for Indians, who would approach the wagons when they wanted something. Nancy M. Hembree was a young girl traveling with her parents. She later recalled that once some Indians rode up to the wagons and tried to buy a white squaw. This attracted the emigrants' attention while other Indians came in from another direction to run off loose cattle.[8]

The emigrants soon saw prairie dogs and many buffalo as they traveled westward, and their hunters provided them with fresh buffalo meat. One emigrant, Sarah Damron Adair, remembered how the women would cut buffalo meat into thin slices and string it on ropes outside the wagon beds. Within three days the meat would be well dried and ready to pack away in sacks until needed.[9] John A. Stoughton, who was thirteen years old at the time, later recalled that buffalo were so thick that emigrants had to keep firing guns to prevent getting trampled. The animals' hoofs "sounded like thunder and we could hear the rattle of their interlocked horns for miles," wrote Stoughton, who remembered one buffalo stampede that missed his wagon by only half a mile.[10]

The emigrants were nooning when the stampede that occurred. Sixteen-year-old Edward H. Lenox later recalled:

We were all at lunch at the noon hour, mother as I remember her, setting in her home-made chair with a rawhide bottom, when all of a sudden, there is a rushing "as of a mighty wind." We are all on our feet in a moment, wondering if it is some cyclone, or what the roaring may mean. Our pilot shouts, "The buffalo are coming! The buffalo are coming! You women and children get behind those rocks on the right, and all of you men get out your guns and run to the rocks on the left, and shoot all you can as they come by, and I will go out and meet, and wheel in front of them, and turn them toward the men." With these words, he sprang on the back of his fine black mule, put spurs to him, and went flying round the hill that hid the buffalo from our sight. The pilot played his part grandly, for sure enough, here he came, leading a herd of over three thousand bellowing, fighting buffalo past the men. Seven of them fell dead as they passed the ledge of rock where the men were posted, and the great herd went plunging over the precipice twenty feet high, into the great South Platte River, two hundreds yards from our wagons, where scores of them were drowned. Mother exclaimed, "Just see them floating down the river" and

Occasionally, Indians would stampede a herd of buffalo through an emigrant wagon train. This painting by William Henry Jackson shows emigrants trying to control their oxen as the buffalo race between the wagons. (Courtesy Scotts Bluff National Monument)

This is Windless Hill. In the foreground is Ash Hollow, in what is now western Nebraska. Emigrants descended a 25-degree slope for about three hundred feet, letting their wagons down by ropes into Ash Hollow. Windless Hill and Ash Hollow are located just off U.S. Highway 26 northwest of Ogallala in Garden County, Nebraska. (Courtesy Kansas State Historical Society)

Dr. Whitman remarked, "Those are the drowned buffaloes, drowned from falling over each other."[11]

By this time in early July the caravan had passed the junction of the North and South Platte rivers and was preparing to cross the South Platte. One of the emigrants, William Athey, swam across the river with a small cord attached to a larger rope. Once he reached the other side, he used the cord to pull the rope across the river. The rope was then used like a cable for guiding the wagons, which were chained together to cross the stream. It took two days to get the wagons across, while the cattle and other livestock were forced to swim. The emigrants crossed the land between the South and North Platte rivers and then crossed the North Platte. Exactly where they crossed is unclear, but it was apparently west of Ash Hollow, a prominent landmark located just southeast of modern Lewellen, Nebraska. Ash Hollow was the principal entrance into the North Platte Valley for travelers coming from the south and east. There is no evidence that the emigrants in the caravan of 1843 saw Ash Hollow. Robert Stuart was probably the first white man to see the hollow, and named the creek that ran through it Cedar Creek in

William Henry Jackson's painting titled Approaching Chimney Rock *shows emigrants near the large clay and sandstone protrusion, which can still be seen today south of Bayard, Nebraska.* (Courtesy Scotts Bluff National Monument)

Courthouse Rock (right) and Jail Rock were two prominent landmarks named by emigrants, just south of the Oregon Trail. These natural sandstone formations thrust upward from the surrounding countryside and can be seen from many miles away. They are located five miles south of Bridgeport, Nebraska. (Author's collection)

1813, but later travelers found the trees to be ash and renamed the place for the trees they found.

The emigrants traveled up the south bank of the North Platte past a massive sandstone landmark that resembles a courthouse and a small protrusion to the east resembling a jail. Courthouse Rock and Jail Rock were to the south of the emigrants' route but were very visible. Both landmarks are located south of modern Bridgeport, Nebraska. Not too many miles west, Chimney Rock rose on the horizon. It was named by early fur traders because the clay and sandstone protrusion resembled a factory chimney. From the bottom of its funnel-shaped base to the top of the column is more than three hundred feet. Chimney Rock is located southwest of present-day Bayard, Nebraska. Farther up the trail the emigrants saw Scotts Bluff, a massive bluff on the south bank of the North Platte River. It was named for Hiram Scott, one of William H. Ashley's "enterprising young men" recruited in St. Louis about 1822. Scott, a promising young mountain man, is believed to have died in the vicinity of the bluff in 1828 after returning east from the annual rendezvous.[12]

This is Chimney Rock as it appeared in 1928.
(Courtesy Kansas State Historical Society)

Less than sixty miles up the trail from Scotts Bluff, the Laramie River joins the North Platte River. There the emigrants caught sight of Fort Platte, sometimes called Richard's Fort, a trading post consisting of perhaps a dozen buildings, including a blacksmith shop, surrounded by a large adobe wall. Lancaster P. Lupton started to construct the post in 1839 for the fur trade, but he never finished it. Lupton sold it to Sybille, Adams & Company, who in turn sold it to Bernard Pratte and John Cabanne about the time the emigrants were traveling through the area in 1843. If the post's reputation preceded it, the emigrants probably avoided it, since it never carried much in the way of groceries or other supplies. Its principal trade was in whiskey, which sold for $4.00 a pint. Because the emigrants needed supplies, most stopped at nearby Fort Laramie, located above the mouth of the Laramie River. Built in 1841 and first called Fort John, Fort Laramie was about a mile from Fort Platte and was more impressive. Its adobe walls were six feet thick and fifteen feet high, with bastions at the south and north corners and a blockhouse over the main gate. Here the emigrants purchased a great many

This massive bluff on the south bank of the North Platte River is called Scotts Bluff,
named for Hiram Scott, who died in its vicinity in 1828 while returning east from the
annual mountain men's rendezvous. This photo was taken in 1928. Scotts Bluff is today a
national monument. (Courtesy Kansas State Historical Society)

supplies. Flour sold for $0.25 to $0.50 a pint, sugar and coffee sold for $0.50 to $1.50 a pint, and liquor was $4.00 a pint. Even the presence of Spanish traders from Taos selling flour, sugar, coffee, and whiskey at high prices did not ease the emigrants' run on supplies at Fort Laramie.[13]

After leaving Fort Laramie, the emigrants entered the area called the Black Hills. They crossed the North Platte River near the mouth of Deer Creek, where the route followed the north side through sage plains to the Sweetwater River, located near two more prominent landmarks—Independence Rock and Devil's Gate Canyon. Looking something like a huge turtle, Independence Rock is an oval-shaped outcropping of granite oriented northwest to southeast located about 200 yards from the bank of the Sweetwater River. From the earliest days of mountain men and traders, it served as a bulletin board where travelers left messages on the stone. It got its name about 1824 when a group of Americans celebrated the Fourth of July below the massive rock. The 1843 emigrants arrived there on July 30 and rested for three days. The second important landmark west of Fort Laramie was Devil's Gate Canyon, about half a mile north of the trail in modern Natrona County, Wyoming, and only a few miles west of Independence Rock. The Sweetwater River, but not the trail, went through the canyon,

This is Devil's Gate, located a few miles west of Independence Rock and about a half mile north of the Oregon Trail. The Sweetwater River flows through the canyon. This view looks west. (Courtesy Kansas State Historical Society)

which is 370 feet deep and about 1,500 feet long. Next was South Pass, although to the surprise of many emigrants it was not a narrow gorge through the Rocky Mountains with canyon walls hundreds of feet high. South Pass was simply a valley some twenty miles wide. Coming from the east, the emigrants hardly noticed the gradual climb to the Continental Divide, but as they started down, the descent was fairly steep. The Continental Divide symbolically marked the boundary between the United States and Oregon Country, but the emigrants did little celebrating. They still had about a thousand more miles to travel.

West of South Pass the trail turned southwest toward Fort Bridger on Black's Fork of the Green River. After the collapse of the beaver trade and

This 1928 photograph shows the remnants of the Oregon Trail west of South Pass in modern Wyoming. (Courtesy Kansas State Historical Society)

the last rendezvous in 1840, James Bridger and other mountain men looked for other ways to make a living. In 1841, Bridger started building a small trading post between the mouths of the Big Sandy and Black's Fork on the Green River. When his partner, Henry Fraeb, was killed by Indians, Bridger abandoned the post. In 1842, however, he moved into the Black's Fork area and built another trading post overlooking the stream. For some reason, however, he soon abandoned it and headed east to St. Louis. During the winter of 1842 he teamed up with Louis Vasquez, an old friend, who had earlier operated a trading post with Andrew Sublette, a younger brother of William, on the South Platte River. Bridger and Vasquez returned west in the spring of 1843 with blacksmithing equipment and other supplies for a new trading post, although they did not have as many supplies as Bridger wanted. He was heavily in debt and failed to get the credit he needed in St. Louis. But by late summer in 1843, Bridger and Vasquez had constructed another trading post in a beautiful valley on Black's Fork below the snow-capped Uinta Mountains.

The last Fort Bridger was built at a spot where Black's Fork, fed by cool mountain water from melting snows, divides into several small streams. Each of the several branches was lined with cottonwoods, some willows, and other trees kept alive by the moisture from the stream. Fort Bridger was the first trading post built west of the Mississippi expressly for the convenience of emigrants traveling west. It was 1,026 miles from Independence, Missouri.

This log building is part of a replica of James Bridger's fort, located at Fort Bridger State Historic Site, just off U.S. Highway 30 in southwest Wyoming. (Author's collection)

When the vanguard of emigrants arrived in their wagons in late August 1843, they found only grass, water, and wood for fuel. Few emigrants in the wagon train made any reference to Fort Bridger in their recollections, but it may have been at Fort Bridger that Jesse A. Applegate saw Sioux Indians. Trying to recall boyhood events sixty years later, Applegate wrote:

> I saw several very pretty squaws with cheeks painted red, wearing beaded moccasins and beautiful red leggings, fringed along the outer seams. Some of them had papooses almost white and very pretty. Some were wives of white men at the fort, and some belonged to the great war party I saw there mustering to fight the Blackfeet. As I remember this army of Sioux warriors, they were all mounted on nice horses, bucks and squaws all painted about the face, and armed with bows and arrows encased in quivers slung at the back. Some had spears, some war clubs, but no guns, or if any, very few.... Several of the Amazons of this war party visited our encampment. They were dressed and painted and armed like the men. Some of them were very fine of figure, had pretty faces, and eyes as soft and bright as the antelopes on those wild plains. They were all young women, and, as I thought, made love to our young men with their eyes like city damsels, but in the excitement of battle I

suppose they became very furies and those lovely eyes flashed fire. Their small, shapely hands and small feet clad in beaded moccasins were admired even by our women, and I fear our men, bold as they were, were almost captured already by those lovely warriors.[14]

From the Green River the emigrants traveled northwest into modern Idaho, striking the Bear River valley and then coming to a series of springs. John C. Frémont and his exploring party were ahead of the emigrants. In his report on August 25, 1843, Frémont wrote:

This was a cloudless but smoky autumn morning, with a cold wind from the southeast, and a temperature of 45 degrees at sunrise. In a few miles I noticed...the first volcanic rock we had seen, and which now became a characteristic rock along our future road. In about six miles' travel from our encampment, we reached one of the points in our journey to which we had always looked forward with great interest—the famous *Beer springs*....A pretty little stream of clear water enters the upper part of the basin, from an open valley in the mountains, and, passing through the bottom discharges into Bear River. Crossing the stream, we descended a mile below, and made our encampment in a grove of cedar immediately at the Beer springs, which, on account of the effervescing gas and acid taste, have received their name from the voyageurs and trappers of the country, who in the midst of their rude and hard lives, are fond of finding some fancied resemblance to the luxuries they rarely have the fortune to enjoy.[15]

Frémont sampled the water at Beer Springs, which became better known as Soda Springs, and found it hot and with a pungent and disagreeable metallic taste, leaving a burning effect on the tongue. There were other springs in the area, including one called Steamboat Springs. The next day the emigrants arrived in their wagons, and Frémont described their arrival with these words: "A huge emigrant wagon, with a large and diversified family, had overtaken us and halted to noon at our encampment; and, while we were sitting at the spring, a band of boys and girls, with two or three young men, came up, one of whom I asked to stoop down and smell the gas, desirous to satisfy myself further of its effects. But his natural caution had been awakened by the singular and suspicious features of the place, and he declined my proposal decidedly, and with a few indistinct remarks about the devil...."[16]

Whether one of the boys was Jesse A. Applegate is not known, but years later Applegate remembered:

We camped very near one of these springs and nearly a quarter of a mile from Bear River. Here we met Fremont, with his party, and I thought their large tent, a very nice affair. There was a soda spring or pool between the camps, and Fremont's men were having a high time drinking soda water. They were so Noisy that I suspected they had liquor stronger than soda water mixed with the water.... After Fremont's men had been drinking soda water from that spring, and enjoying it greatly nearly a whole day, one of our company fished out an enormous frog from the pool, almost as large as a young papoose, and falling to pieces with rottenness. Soon after this discovery we noticed that the hilarity at the Fremont tent suddenly ceased.[17]

Dr. Marcus Whitman left the emigrants near the springs to go ahead to Fort Hall on business. Many women wanted to take time to wash things in the hot water of the springs and to rest. After a couple of days the emigrants moved on northwest to Fort Hall, owned by the Hudson's Bay Company and located in a large plain on the Snake River. It was constructed of wood and encased with sun-dried adobe bricks. Jesse A. Applegate recalled: "The walls were solid on the outside except for portholes and a gate or two. There was a square court inside, and the houses opened facing this square on the four sides. I visited the people in the fort with mother and other folks, and found women and children living there. They were very kind and sociable. I think

This view of Fort Hall was probably drawn by William Tappan about 1849. It appears in Osborne Cross's "Report of the Quartermaster General, 1850." (Courtesy Idaho Historical Society)

This drawing shows the inside of Fort Hall. (Courtesy Idaho Historical Society)

the women living there were Indians or mixed bloods." Applegate also recalled playing a game with other boys using the stomach of an ox that had been slaughtered. "The weather being warm, it was swollen to the size of a large barrel. The game...was both original and uncanny, and I am sure we never played it afterwards. The sport consisted of running and butting the head against the paunch and being bounced back, the recoil being in proportion to the force of contact." Everything was fine until one boy, Andy Baker, lowered his head and charged the swollen stomach. His head went inside, where he was stuck until the other boys pulled him out.[18]

The chief factor at Fort Hall was a jolly and rather fat Scotchman named Richard Grant, who had assumed his position the year before. He quietly tried to enforce his company's policy of discouraging Americans from settling in Oregon Country. He was friendly and sold supplies to the emigrants. The prices were high, but they were not as exorbitant as at Fort Laramie. Grant tried to persuade the emigrants to go to California instead of Oregon. If they insisted on going to Oregon, he urged them to leave their wagons at the post and trade their cattle for horses and pack in their belongings, pointing out that the emigrants of 1842 had done so. Proof of this was the nineteen wagons parked beside Fort Hall left there the previous year.

A few emigrants were already determined to go to California. One of them, Joseph B. Chiles, who had been to California two years before, met mountain man Joseph Walker near Fort Laramie and hired him to lead a party to California. Chiles's small pack company had caught up with the large train north of the Kansas River. At Fort Bridger Walker joined them.

When the emigrant train reached the Portneuf River, a tributary of the Snake, the small party split into two groups. Walker and a group including Pierson B. Reading turned southwest to blaze a new trail to California. Chiles and his group of perhaps nine or ten men continued up the Snake River and then south along the Malheur River to blaze another new trail to northern California. They were to go to Sutter's Fort and send aid to the other party. They crossed the northern end of the Sierra Nevada but suffered from great hardships. Reading was given a land grant and later established several towns in what is now Shasta County, California, and the town of Redding may have been named for him, with the spelling changed after the arrival of the railroad. The party led by Walker reached California by traveling to the Humboldt River and over what became known as Walker Pass, which he had discovered earlier in the year. It is a relatively low-lying pass at about 5,250 feet, located south of Owens Peak in modern Kern County.[19]

At Fort Hall the rest of the emigrants decided to take their wagons as far as they could toward Oregon. Dr. Marcus Whitman encouraged them to do so and reportedly gave them written directions that included a list of places where they should camp along the way. He also promised to send a Christian Indian to guide them. One emigrant, John Burch McClane, recalled that he and Whitman and others went ahead of the main body and "made some explorations" and wrote notes on slips of paper and fastened them to trees or stuck them on stakes along the route to guide the rest.[20]

The Oregon-bound emigrants left Fort Hall on August 28, following the Snake River to the southwest as the stream flows toward American Falls, where the river drops fifty feet in six to ten steps. Ten miles beyond the falls the wagons traveled through a gap of two rock masses that gained the name Massacre Rocks. Two miles beyond they passed a huge half-buried boulder on which some of the emigrants may have carved their names. Soon the emigrants began turning northwest to follow the Snake, perhaps using Three Island Crossing before reaching Fort Boise, a trading post built in 1834 on the east bank of the river below the mouth of the Boise River. It was operated by the Hudson's Bay Company. Like Fort Hall, it was built of wood and encased with adobe blocks. Near Fort Boise the emigrants again crossed the Snake River. In trying to do so Miles Ayres, a man about sixty years old, had trouble with his mules. Another emigrant named Stringer, about thirty, went to Ayres's aide. Both drowned in sight of their families.

Some days later the emigrants reached the Malheur River where it flows into the Snake River southeast of modern Vale, Oregon, and soon reached the Grand Ronde Valley and the Umatilla River. From there they continued to Whitman's mission and then to Fort Walla Walla on the Columbia River,

William Henry Jackson's painting of a wagon train using three islands, in modern Elmore County, Idaho, to cross the Snake River. Today the site is called Three Island Crossing. (Courtesy Scotts Bluff National Monument)

where they remained for three days before continuing to The Dalles. There, on November 1, 1843, many of the emigrants left their wagons and turned to water transportation. Some hired Indians to take them down the Columbia River in canoes and rafts to Oregon City. At the Great Falls on the Columbia River, Jesse A. Applegate's brother Warren and his cousin Edward Bates Applegate, Lindsay Applegate's son, lost their lives when their boat capsized. The others traveling on the Columbia continued downstream, while those herding livestock crossed it and drove their animals westward along the river.

One of the emigrants, John B. Nelson, a Virginian and a blacksmith by trade, made the journey safely with his wife and three children, carrying his blacksmithing tools in his wagon plus the root of a hop vine for yeast to make bread, and a few family keepsakes. Other keepsakes had been left along the trail because they took up too much valuable space in their wagon. When Nelson reached The Dalles on Christmas Day, 1843, his wife gave birth to their fourth child. Some days later the Nelsons and the other emigrants who had left Missouri about six months earlier arrived in the Willamette Valley after traveling 2,000 miles, a journey that would not be forgotten.

CHAPTER SEVEN

SELF-RULE AND MORE EMIGRANTS

Government is a contrivance of human
wisdom to provide for human wants.

Edmund Burke

U NTIL FORTY-EIGHT-YEAR-OLD Ewing Young died in 1841, the settlers in the Willamette Valley had little need for government in their
daily lives. There were only a few hundred Americans plus some retired
Hudson's Bay Company employees living there. But after Young's funeral,
the settlers realized they had no government to take charge of the disposition of his property. Young had accumulated some wealth from raising cattle. The settlers elected Dr. Ira Babcock from Jason Lee's Methodist mission
to be the supreme judge in dispersing Young's estate. Dr. Babcock ordered
that Young's property be sold at public auction. Mountain man Joe Meek
was the auctioneer. Sidney Smith bought Young's land and some of his livestock. Other men bought Young's tools and the remainder of his livestock.
George Gay bought seven books for $1.00, and Courtney Walker bought
Young's two-volume set of Shakespeare for $3.50. Some of the money raised
was used to build a jail, and the balance was held until final disposition of
Young's estate could be made.[1]

After the auction many settlers began talking more about the need for
government. The following year, 1842, Babcock chaired two "Wolf Meetings" ostensibly held to discuss how to protect their settlements from
wolves, but the settlers also discussed the need for a government. Other
meetings followed, and on May 2, 1843, 102 settlers met at Champoeg, on the
edge of French Prairie in the heart of the Willamette Valley, to organize a
government.

Fifty-two of the settlers were Canadians with instructions from John
McLoughlin and the Hudson's Bay Company to head off the attempt. The

remaining fifty settlers were Americans. They favored setting up a government. When the vote was taken two Canadians, François Matticaux and Étienne Lucien, who had earlier worked for John Jacob Astor at Astoria, joined the Americans in supporting the organization of a government. The vote was 52 to 50. On that day Oregon's Provisional Government was born. A legislative committee of nine men was created to write a constitution. A handful of settlers wanted Oregon to be an independent nation, but they moved to California before the constitution was adopted in a meeting on July 5, 1843. On that day the preamble was revised to read: "We, the people of Oregon Territory, For purposes of mutual protection, and to secure peace and prosperity among ourselves, Agree to adopt the following laws and regulations until such time as the USA extend their jurisdiction over us." This Organic Act, as it is called, created a legislature, an executive committee of three men, and a judicial system. The settlers were not taxed, but were encouraged to make donations through subscriptions to cover the expenses of their new government. In drawing up the laws and regulations, someone happened to have a copy of the laws of Iowa, and they were adopted.

Down the Willamette River at Fort Vancouver on the Columbia, John McLoughlin received and rejected an invitation that the Hudson's Bay Company join the new government. McLoughlin then added a bastion to the fort and increased its defenses, claiming he did so because of unrest among Indians, but many American settlers believed McLoughlin was more fearful of the organized American settlers and reports he had received telling of belligerent speeches against Britain in the American Congress. For instance, early in January 1844, Representative John Wentworth of Illinois told his colleagues in Congress that it was their duty to speak freely and candidly, and let England know that she could never have an inch of Oregon, nor another inch of what was then claimed as United States territory. The emotions were just as strong in the British Parliament, where Sir Robert Peel proclaimed that England knew her rights and dared maintain them. To emphasize their position the British sent the *Modesta,* a sloop-of-war carrying twenty guns, up the Columbia River in July 1844 and anchored her opposite Fort Vancouver. In spite of the belligerent talk in their respective capitals, both sides realized the 1818 Treaty of London remained in effect, and the vast region of Oregon Country was still jointly occupied by the British and the Americans. The two countries wrangled over the boundary question. The United States had offered to accept the 49th parallel as the demarcation line, and Great Britain had proposed that it be the Columbia River. Then a second Oregon bill introduced by Missouri Senator Lewis F. Linn was defeated by the Senate. Linn had again called for the United States to occupy Oregon Country militarily and create a territorial government. The bill's defeat irritated many Americans living in the Mississippi Valley and more emigrants headed for Oregon Country.

Only after the emigrants of 1843 arrived in the fall did they learn that a provisional government had been established in Oregon Country, but since they were tired and worn out after their long journey, most were apparently more concerned about getting land and building their homes than politics. To the east in the Mississippi and Missouri river valleys, attitudes were different. Historian Hubert Howe Bancroft wrote in 1886 that the belligerent attitude of the Americans and British

> was also as well known to uneducated western men, who were capital Indian-fighters, and who had served under Jackson and Taylor, as it was to the scholarly officers of the British fur company. The inducement to go to Oregon was not lessened by the prospect of having to drive out the nation which had been fought at New Orleans and along the border, and a large number of people collected at different points along the Missouri River, amounting in all to fourteen hundred persons. The company which rendezvoused near Weston [Missouri], at a place called Capler's [Caples] landing, was led by Cornelius Gilliam, who had conceived the idea of an independent colony, as best suited his fancy and the temper of his men. The leaders of 1844 were hardly equal to those of the previous years.... They were brave, loyal, earnest, but better fitted to execute than to command; to be loyal to a government than to construct one. Their tendencies were more toward military glory than pride of statesmanship. This spirit led them to organize under military rules for their journey to the Columbia, and to elect a set of officers sufficient for an army, with Gilliam as general.[2]

Cornelius Gilliam was never a real general, but he had served as a captain in the Black Hawk and Seminole wars. Gilliam, then about forty years old, standing five feet ten in height and weighing about two hundred pounds, was in robust health. He was an ordained minister, had been a sheriff, and had served in the Missouri legislature before deciding to go to Oregon Country. Gilliam had little education, but he had the reputation of being brave, obstinate, impetuous, and generous. Late the previous summer he had published a notice advising that he intended to emigrate to Oregon, and he told readers that if they wished to join him, he planned to leave on the first Monday of May 1844 from an area across the Missouri from what is now St. Joseph. On March 2, 1844, Gilliam and his family, including married sons and daughters along with a few other families, crossed the Missouri River at Caples Landing at the site of present-day Amazonia, Missouri, located about twelve miles north of St. Joseph. St. Joe, as people came to call the town, had been founded a year earlier by Joseph Ribidoux, who first established a trading post near there in 1827. St. Joseph was closer to the Platte River than Independence, and emigrants leaving from there did not have to cross the often hazardous Kansas River.

Once Gilliam and his party crossed the Missouri, they camped in the river bottoms on the Sac and Fox Indian reserve, probably with the permission of the Indians. There Gilliam and his party waited for other emigrants to arrive. The weather was pleasant. Spring had arrived early, but in April, rains began, and they continued on and off into early June. For about two months Gilliam's party waited in camp for other emigrants. On May 9 there were more than 300 men, women, and children in camp with perhaps 70 wagons and more than 700 head of cattle. On that day they started west. Still others would join the company during the days that followed, raising the human total to about 500.

This crossing on the Missouri River may have been in the area of St. Joseph, Missouri. The photo may have been made by Albert Bierstadt, the well-known landscape painter, who was also a pioneer photographer. If the photo was taken by Bierstadt, it probably was made in 1858 when he traveled over the Oregon Trail. (Courtesy Kansas State Historical Society)

Albert Bierstadt made this photo at the Wolf Creek crossing in what is now Doniphan County, Kansas, in 1859. Bierstadt labeled the photo "Wolf River Ford, Kansas," but the stream has long been considered a creek. (Courtesy Kansas State Historical Society)

At some point perhaps thirty miles west of the Missouri River, an emigrant named Bishop, an invalid, died. His body was carried some miles to Wolf Creek and the Presbyterian mission there, where Rev. William Hamilton conducted a funeral service. On May 11, many of the emigrants with their wagons crossed the bridge over Wolf Creek near the mission, but that night heavy rains sent the stream out of its bank and early the next morning washed away the bridge. To ferry the remaining people and their wagons across the creek, two canoes and a platform were built. On May 15, once everyone had crossed, the emigrants organized their company. Gilliam was chosen as general, or commander-in-chief. He immediately organized the company in a military fashion and began drilling the men, ostensibly to prepare them for Indian attacks. He divided the wagon train into three divisions, captained by Robert W. Morrison, William Shaw, and Richard Woodcock. Willard H. Rees was named adjutant. A court of equity with a judge and two associate justices was also established, but it did not function because Gilliam had declared martial law to maintain military discipline for the journey. A day or two later the wagon train continued its journey west toward the Blue River. Gilliam has the distinction of having led the first party of emigrants to use St. Joseph, Missouri, as a jumping-off point for Oregon Country.

Not too much was then known about the country to the west of the Presbyterian mission, but Gilliam was certain he could blaze a new trail west to a point where it would intersect Sublette's Trace, the trail to Oregon used by emigrants in 1843. In camp on the night of May 20, in what is now Brown County, Kansas, Martin Gilliam, one of Cornelius's sons, and Elizabeth Asabill were married by Rev. Edward E. Parris, an emigrant also bound for Oregon. The next day the wagons pushed westward and crossed the Nemaha River and then followed the south bank of the Black Vermillion River until they came to the trail used by emigrants the previous year. Frequent heavy rains slowed the company's travel as did a woman in "delicate health"—an emigrant term for pregnancy—who gave birth to a baby. Then in early June a young man named Clarke Eades was accused of shooting at another man. Since the company was still under martial law declared by "General" Gilliam, he had Eades arrested for violating a general order and held court on the evening of June 4. Although Eades's father paid his bail, Gilliam ordered that for punishment Eades be tied and staked out in the hot sun the following day from 11 a.m. until the sun went down. This was done, but instead of baking in a hot sun, Eades was showered by torrents of rain most of the day. Gilliam's reaction is not recorded. After nearly a month the company had traveled only a hundred miles.

When the wagons reached the Black Vermillion River, the company was delayed for seventeen days because of high water and was able to cross the stream only after building two canoes, or hollowed-out logs, to serve as pontoons. One emigrant, B. F. Nichols, recalled how mothers went splashing through the mud and slime to reach the pontoons that had started across. "One I remember carrying a small child on one arm and leading or pulling another, scarcely larger, through the mud [who called] 'Mamma, my shoe has come off.' The mother turned and fished it out, and then went forward again, the children squalling, until at last she reaches a wagon fastened on the two canoes, into which she climbs with her children and is pulled across the muddy waters, is landed and finally stands on solid ground, safe with her little brood."[3]

After traversing the Black Vermillion River, they continued until they crossed the Blue River near modern Marysville, Kansas, and then traveled northwest along the Little Blue until they reached the Platte on July 7 near modern-day Grand Island, Nebraska. There they traveled west along the

This is the crossing on the Little Blue River in northeast Kansas Territory in the spring of 1859. The photo was made by Albert Bierstadt after he left St. Joseph, Missouri, and started up the Oregon Trail. (Courtesy Kansas State Historical Society)

south bank of the Platte. When they reached the South Platte, Gilliam resigned as "general" and the companies reorganized. Why Gilliam resigned is unclear, but by then many emigrants were objecting to his military discipline.

Of many emigrants who kept diaries or journals or later wrote their recollections of going to Oregon Country in 1844, perhaps the most moving is that of Catherine Sager, who described her father as "one of the restless ones who are not content to remain in one place long at a time." Her father was a farmer and blacksmith who moved to Missouri from Ohio. Late in 1843 he sold his property and prepared to join Gilliam's company to move to Oregon.

We had one wagon, two steady yoke of old cattle, and several of young and not well-broken ones. Father was no ox driver, and had trouble with these until one day he called on Captain William Shaw for assistance. It was furnished by the good captain pelting the refractory steers with stones until they were glad to come to terms.

Reaching the buffalo country [on the Platte River], our father would get some one to drive his team and start on the hunt, for he was enthusiastic in his love of such sport. He not only killed the great bison, but often brought home on his shoulder the timid antelope that had fallen at his unerring aim, and that are not often shot by ordinary marksmen. Soon after crossing South Platte the unwieldy oxen ran on a bank and overturned the wagon, greatly injuring our mother. She lay long insensible in the tent put up for the occasion.

August 1st we nooned in a beautiful grove on the north side of the Platte. We had by this time got used to climbing in and out of the wagon when in motion. When performing this feat that afternoon my dress caught on an axle helve and I was thrown under the wagon wheel, which passed over and badly crushed my limb before father could stop the team. He picked me up and saw the extent of the injury when the injured limb hung dangling in the air.

In a broken voice he exclaimed: "My dear child, your leg is broken all to pieces!" The news soon spread along the train and a halt was called. A surgeon was found and the limb set; then we pushed on the same night to Laramie, where we arrived soon after dark. This accident confined me to the wagon the remainder of the long journey.

After Laramie we entered the great American desert, which was hard on the teams. Sickness became common. Father and the boys were all sick, and we were dependent for a driver on the Dutch doctor who set my leg. He offered his services and was employed, but though an excellent surgeon, he knew little about driving oxen. Some of them [her father and brothers] often had to rise from their sick beds to wade streams and get the oxen safely across. One day four buffalo ran between our wagon and the one behind. Though feeble, father seized his gun and gave chase to them. This imprudent act prostrated him again, and it soon became apparent that his days were numbered. He was fully conscious of the fact, but could not be reconciled to the thought of leaving his large and helpless family in such precarious circumstances.

The evening before his death we crossed Green River and camped on the bank. Looking where I lay helpless, he said: "Poor child! What will become of you?!" Captain Shaw found him weeping bitterly. He said his last hour had come, and his heart was filled with anguish for his family. His wife was ill, the children small, and one likely to be a cripple. They had no relatives near, and a long journey lay before them. In piteous tones he begged the Captain to take charge of them and see them through. This he [Shaw] stoutly promised. Father was buried the next day on the banks of the Green River. His coffin was made of two troughs dug out of the body of a tree, but next year [1845] emigrants found his bleaching bones, as the Indians had disinterred the remains.

We hired a young man to drive, as mother was afraid to trust the doctor, but the kind-hearted German would not leave her, and declared his intention to see her safe in the Willamette. At Fort Bridger the stream was full of fish, and we made nets of wagon sheets to catch them. That evening the new driver told mother he would hunt for game if she would let him use the gun. He took it, and we never saw him again. He made for the train in advance, where he had a sweetheart. We found the gun waiting our arrival at Whitman's. Then we got along as best we could with the doctor's help.

Mother planned to get to Whitman's [mission] and winter there, but she was rapidly failing under her sorrows. The night and mornings were very cold, and she took cold from the exposure unavoidably. With camp fever and a sore mouth, she fought bravely against fate for the sake of her children, but she was taken delirious soon after reaching Fort Bridger, and was bed-fast. Traveling in this condition over a road clouded with dust, she suffered intensely. She talked to her husband, addressing him as though present, beseeching him in piteous tones to relieve her sufferings, until at last she became unconscious. Her babe was cared for by the women of the train. Those kind-hearted women would also come in at night and wash the dust from the mother's face and otherwise make her comfortable. We traveled a rough road the day she died, and she moaned fearfully all the time. At night one of the women came in as usual, but she made no reply to questions, so she thought her asleep, and washed her face, then took her hand and discovered the pulse was nearly gone. She lived but a few moments, and her last words were, "Oh, Henry! If you only knew how we have suffered." The tent was set up, the corpse laid out, and the next morning we took the last look at our mother's face. The grave was near the road; willow brush was laid in the bottom and covered the body, the earth filled in—then the train moved on.

Her name was cut on a head-board, and that was all that could be done. So in twenty-six days we became orphans. Seven children of us, the oldest fourteen and the youngest a babe. A few days before her death, finding herself in possession of her faculties and fully aware of the coming end, she had taken an affectionate farewell of her children and charged the doctor to take care of us. She made the same request of Captain Shaw. The baby was taken by a woman in the train, and all were literally adopted by the company. No one there but was ready to do us any possible favor. This was especially true of Captain Shaw and his wife. Their kindness will ever be cherished in grateful remembrance by us all.[4]

The Sager children were left by Captain Shaw with Marcus and Narcissa Whitman at their Waiilatpu mission as the emigrants continued toward the Willamette Valley.

Many of the emigrants who traveled with Cornelius Gilliam's company were farmers, but the remainder represented a wide range of occupations. There was a minister, a lawyer, a millwright, a gunsmith, a weaver, a tailor, a ship carpenter, a cooper, and a merchant. There were also three millers, four wheelwrights, two shoemakers, two cabinetmakers, five carpenters, and two blacksmiths. All were white except for George Washington Bush, who was born in Pennsylvania about 1790. He was half Irish and half black, and was considered a free black. Almost nothing is known about his life before 1812 when he fought in the Battle of New Orleans under Andrew Jackson. After the war he went to St. Louis, where he worked for a French fur trader. By the 1820s he was employed by the Hudson's Bay Company, and by 1844, Bush had married a woman named Isabel and they had five sons. When Gilliam announced his plans to go to Oregon Country, Bush's friend Michael T. Simmons probably encouraged Bush to join him and take their families west. Bush agreed, and when the Gilliam company was organized, Simmons was elected colonel, or second in command, of General Gilliam's company.

Apparently, neither Bush nor Simmons kept a journal or diary of the journey west, but John Minto, another emigrant, wrote in his recollections that Bush was "always watchful." When the emigrants reached what is now eastern Oregon, Bush cautioned Minto and others about the country ahead and said, "Boys, you are going through hard country.... Take my advice; anything you see as big as a blackbird, kill it and eat it." When Bush and his family reached The Dalles, on the Columbia River, they learned that the provisional legislature had just revised the rules on land claims, banning slaves as well as free blacks from settling in Oregon Country. Bush and his family remained at The Dalles during the winter of 1844. By spring Bush decided to take his family and settle north of the Columbia River. Michael T. Simmons also took his family to settle with the Bush family near modern Olympia, Washington, in a place now known as Bush Prairie. Bush's decision to settle north of the Columbia River would later give weight to the United States' claims against the British that the region north of the Columbia River was already settled by Americans.[5]

THE EMIGRANTS who headed to Oregon Country in the spring of 1844 were not viewed kindly by many people in St. Louis. The daily *Missouri*

Republican, published in St. Louis on May 30, 1844, reported on the emigrants' departure, but added:

> The poor devils who start for Oregon, generally spend all they have to scrape together a wagon, some cattle, and a small outfit of provisions. They will spend the summer in the severest toil in getting there. How they will spend the winter is not known even to themselves; for they are as ignorant as they are poor, and know nothing whatever of the country they are going to. In truth, no man of information, in his right mind, would think of leaving such a country as this, to wander over a thousand miles of desert and five hundred of mountain to reach such as that.... It is wrong in the people of St. Louis to encourage this spirit of emigration. The settlement of Oregon will not result in any advantage to your city. Your share of its limited trade will be but small. Trade cannot cross the Rocky Mountains; it must come by way of the isthmus of Panama. You can do better for your city by settling the vacant lands in your own State.

An unidentified eastern artist produced this drawing showing one party of emigrants camped along the Oregon Trail while others continued westward. The illustration appeared in Samuel Bowles's Our New West: Records of Travel Between the Mississippi River and the Pacific Ocean, *published in 1869. Although the wagons in this illustration are horse-drawn, most emigrants used oxen because of their staying power.* (Courtesy Kansas State Historical Society)

From all indications none of the emigrants who set out for Oregon Country in the spring of 1844 paid any attention to such views. They had made up their minds that they were leaving Missouri. On May 14, five days after Gilliam's wagon train started for Oregon, another party of emigrants set out west from Lone Elm. The *Western Expositor*, published at Independence, Missouri, reported the company consisted of 358 persons—55 married men with their wives (110), 80 single men, 168 children—with 54 wagons, 500 head of cattle, 60 horses, and 28 mules. The newspaper added that another 125 people with 10 wagons were about to join them. Moses "Black" Harris, an experienced mountain man, was hired to guide them. Harris, a man of dark complexion of medium height with black hair and whiskers, and dark brown eyes, had been over the trail before. A few days after leaving Lone Elm, the emigrants elected Nathaniel Ford of Howard County, Missouri, as their commander, but like Gilliam he attempted to turn the male emigrants into an army. Ford's company was also slowed in their travels by the heavy spring rains and experienced many of the same difficulties as Gilliam's company. When the company reached the crossing on the Black Vermillion in modern Marshall County, Kansas, they learned that Gilliam's company had crossed the river only four days earlier. By July 20, Ford had communicated

This realistic painting by an unknown artist shows two yoke of oxen pulling each wagon, an emigrant walking with his son and a dog, and presumably the man's wife riding in the wagon. Likewise the cattle following the leading wagon (left of center) are typical of emigrant travel. Broken and abandoned wagons such as the one shown at left were commonplace, especially to the west of new Fort Kearny. The river behind the wagons could be the North Platte, the Sweetwater, or the Snake. (Courtesy Kansas State Historical Society)

with some of the emigrants in Gilliam's company and reached an agreement to travel in the vicinity of each other. Former mountain man James Clyman, traveling with Ford's train, wrote of this in his journal and noted that both trains would camp no farther apart than necessary for the good of their stock.

Clyman, who had been one of William Ashley's mountain men, knew the West well. In 1824, with fellow mountain man Thomas Fitzpatrick, he had discovered the Platte River–Sweetwater route across modern Nebraska and Wyoming, which became a large portion of the trail to Oregon Country. During the winter of 1843–44, Clyman had developed a cough while in the East. By spring he headed west to find a cure and joined Ford's wagon train led by another mountain man, Clyman's old friend Moses Harris.

When Ford's wagon train reached Independence Rock on August 16, 1844, Clyman wrote in his journal: "Saw the notable rock Independence with the names of its numerous visitors most of which are nearly obliterated by the weather & ravages of time amongst which I observed the names of two of my old friends the notable mountaineers Thos. Fitzpatrick & W. L. Sublette...." After Ford's train reached the Sweetwater River, Clyman wrote on August 21: "Mr. [J. M.] Barnette who has been confined 5 or 6 days with a fever has the appearance of being quite dangerous and has been delirious during the whole of the night." On August 24, Clyman noted in his journal: "All rolled out except ourselves who remain to take care of Mr. Barnette whose prospects for living seem a little better than yesterday although yet quite small. Every preparation seemed dull & melancholy & many bid the sick man their last farewell look. A spade was thrown out and left which looked rather ominous. The ravens came croaking around us and the shaggy wolf was seen peeping from the hills...." Then, late on the evening of August 26, Clyman wrote: "He [Barnette] departed this life very easy... & all his troubles were in silent death. Having nothing better we cut a bed of green willows and laid him out on the cold ground & all of us seated ourselves around our camp fire & listened to the hair breadth escapes of Mr. Harris & other mountaineers." The next morning the body was buried nearby. Clyman inscribed the headstone and stuck it in the ground before leaving to catch up with the main body of wagons. The grave site can still be seen today on a lonely ranch in Fremont County, Wyoming, but the headstone placed on it by James Clyman has disappeared.[6]

A THIRD COMPANY that set out across the prairie and plains in 1844 left from Westport, now part of Kansas City, Missouri. The company consisted of Catholics led by an unidentified Jesuit priest from St. Louis, and the group has the distinction of being the first party of emigrants to go to the Mountain West for their health. Perhaps half were invalids. In comparison to the other companies of emigrants, this group was small, numbering perhaps twenty. Their guide was Andrew Sublette, who had himself developed a bad cough that he hoped to lose in the dry climate of the mountains. Andrew was paid $75 a month to take the party to Fort Laramie.

Unfortunately, no one in the company left a journal or diary that has been found, but from scattered bits of information in records left by other emigrants in other wagon trains, including Rev. Edward E. Parrish, who was traveling with the Gilliam company, some details of the small party of Catholics are known. On July 13, 1844, Parrish wrote in his journal that "Mr. Sublette came up this afternoon with a company of sick folks going to the mountains for their health. They have had four deaths in this company since they left St. Louis." The four deaths all occurred after the small company left Westport. The first to die was James H. Marshall, who was buried on the bluffs northwest of the Black Vermillion crossing. The second man to die was named Ketchum, and he was buried somewhere west of the Blue River. The exact location of his grave is not known. On June 29, I. P. W. Chutheson was the third man to die. The exact location of his grave is not known. And the fourth to die was named Browning, on July 6, on the Little Blue River about fifty-eight miles beyond Rock Creek in modern Nebraska. Andrew Sublette delivered the party to Fort Laramie as he had been hired to do. Sublette next traveled south to Bent's Fort in what is now eastern Colorado and then to Taos, where he spent the winter, but what happened to the Jesuit priest and his Catholic parishioners is not known.[7]

THE YEAR 1844 saw a fourth company of Americans gather on the east bank of the Missouri River in the vicinity of what is today Council Bluffs, Iowa, an area named by Lewis and Clark in 1804 when they held a council with local Indian tribes on one of many nearby bluffs. Some historians call this fourth company the Stephens-Murphy-Townsend party, so named for Elisha Stephens of Holt County, Missouri, traveling with his two older sons; Dr. John Townsend; and Martin Murphy, Sr., with seven grown sons and daughters. They were heading for California. Most of the other people in the party were going to Oregon Country. On May 22, 1844, the first contingent of the company crossed the Missouri River in a boat belonging to the Pottawatomie Indian chief. The chief and his people were meeting with Otoe Indians on the west bank of the Missouri at what is today Belleview, Nebraska. It was several days before all of the emigrants were able to cross the river.

One of the emigrants in the party was twenty-eight-year-old Jacob Hammer, a Quaker, who kept a daily journal primarily for his in-laws, who disapproved of him taking his wife and children to Oregon. Four years earlier Jacob had married Hannah Cox in Noblesville, Indiana. About a year later his wife gave birth to a son, and a few months later the family moved to Missouri. There, early in 1843, Hannah gave birth to a daughter, and early in 1844 she gave birth to a second son, who was only eleven weeks old when the Hammers set out for Oregon.

Three days after the first emigrants crossed the Missouri River, Hammer and his family did so. In his journal he wrote: "Today the wind is still and the river calm. We crossed the river in safety and all the cattle were taken to the river and swam over in a little while and without any danger." The following morning he paid the Pottawatomie chief for transporting his family across the river and started westward, traveling six miles before camping for the night. Hammer described the country, which belonged to Otoe Indians, as "rich as far as we have traveled and three-fourths prairie."[8]

The following day they crossed two creeks and traveled eight miles and camped when rain began to fall. The next day the emigrants remained in camp because the rain continued. The following day, May 29, Hammer wrote in his journal:

Last night A. C. R. Shaw, getting into a passion at the captain [Elisha Stephens] (because he gave orders contrary to our regulations) and coming into camp in haste, took up his gun and fired it off and then reloaded his gun, at the same time swearing he would kill the captain.

But some others, not liking the movements of the captain, immediately caused a new election to be held. But Elisha Stephens was elected captain the second time. Those that supported him at first supported now the same man for nothing but contrariness, as they supposed Shaw would be elected captain. Shaw was not so much as nominated. J[ohn] Thorp was nominated, and we voted for him. Those that voted for Elisha Stephens acknowledged that they did not want him in office and by their own doings spited themselves. Our getting along seems to be dull, as the captain does not act with good judgment.[9]

On June 21, the emigrants came to the Platte River a few miles above Grand Island. Hammer described the Platte as very wide and shallow, with low banks about two to four feet in height. At this point the wagon train pushed westward along the north bank of the river, the same route followed from the west by the Astorians in 1813. This company has the distinction of having been the first emigrants to use this route, but they did not realize there was more sand along the north bank than the south bank of the Platte River. The sand made wagon travel more difficult. The next day, Hammer wrote in his journal:

We traveled all day in a town of the prairie dogs. Many buffalow bones are to be found here. Thomas Vance very sick and has been for several days. Some others not very well. Traveled five miles up the Platte. This afternoon we crossed Unknown Creek [where it flows into the Platte].

[June 23] We found Blue grass and herd grass. Salt found on the grass and also on the ground. Vanity grass also found here. Crossed gravelly run about noon. T. Vance very sick yet. Distance traveled is twenty miles.

[June 24] Stay in camp today for Vance to get better.

[June 25] Vance is no better. Traveled sixteen miles today. At noon we saw Mackinaw boats on the south side of the Platte which were loaded with furs and so forth. Some few of the men came over to us in one of their boats. Several letters were sent to the states from our company by them.

We made a division in the company and elected Harmon Higgins captain of our company. We let the contrary party go, for when we undertook to elect a captain the old captain denied throwing up his commission by being put up to it by other others. The division was very unexpected to them for they thought we would not leave them. We had better left them at the start.

[June 26] Vance is not better. Distance traveled is twenty miles.

[June 27] Our sick man is no better. Some buffalo occasionally brought in. Distance traveled, twenty miles today.

[June 28] Traveled twenty miles. Thomas Vance died this evening about sunset. This man is a member of the Baptist society, the regular Baptists. But notwithstanding his belief in this hard doctrine, I believe this young man is a Christian. His faith appeared to be good. He seemed to be sincere. He said to my wife one day that if he did die, that he supposed that he would go as well as here as if [he] was in the states, to which she answered [that] she thought there would be no difference.

This evening, as I discovered he was about to depart this life, I prayed the Lord if it was consistent with his divine will that this young man might pass from this veil of tears without a struggle, and that he might be taken into the heavenly kingdom, and be able to sing praises unto him that sitteth on the throne of mercy for ever and ever.

My prayer, I believe, is answered this evening, for the young man as he departed sighed one sigh and departed without a struggle. And as he departed he opened his eyes and looked up as if he was looking into heaven.... He was decently laid out. Now the people ... thought best to bury him as quick as the grave could be dug, for mortification had taken place. Some thought to wait till morning the smell would be so great that they could not endure it very well.... We had no coffin for him. We dug the grave deep and dug a very neat vault and placed in it some dry grass. And putting a quilt around the corpse, we placed it in the vault and laid some pieces of planks on the vault. This formed his coffin. We then filled the grave with lose earth and then putting sod on the top so that it might not be noticed by the savages, though no danger of being robbed that we know of by them. All this was done before midnight. I believe it was doctor Townsend's medicine that caused this mortification to take place. We buried this young man about ten miles up the North fork of the Platte river [on] the North side of the river in the bottom a few rods from the river.[10]

The emigrants moved on the next day and a few days later, on July 6, camped in view of Scotts Bluff, which they visited the following day. On July 10, 1844, they reached the vicinity of Fort Platte and camped. A band of Sioux Indians approached the emigrants' camp with a flag of peace and presented the travelers with buffalo meat that had been fried in buffalo marrow. The emigrants gave the Indians tobacco, some powder, some lead, and pieces of bread and meat. Two days later, after the party had moved their camp across the Platte River, another band of Sioux Indians approached. On the evening of July 13, the Indians on horseback rode around the camp singing a song in their own language. "This showed that they were friendly," wrote Hammer.[11]

The party reached Independence Rock on July 29, and Hammer noted in his journal: "The rock is about one mile in circumference and probably is two hundred feet high. Many people have put their name on this rock and the year that they visited this place. I put my name on this rock near a small spring in the side of the rock, though in the rock a little distance. The rock is gray granite with a few small crevices in it that contain earth. And in this dirt are Pine currents growing." The emigrants remained in camp for two days to give their oxen time to rest and to welcome a new member of the company. Mrs. Thomas Murphy gave birth to a baby girl and she was named Ellen Independence. Meanwhile, some of the men killed and butchered buffalo and many of the women dried the meat.[12]

After passing Devil's Gate on the Sweetwater River on August 1, the emigrants continued to travel through the Sweetwater Valley, with mountains on either side. On the morning of August 8 they left the Sweetwater, and that night Hammer wrote in his journal:

> We seem to rise very gradual as we traveled along this morning for about six miles. And then to descend as gradual for about six miles till we come to the quag[mire] spring. This is passing over the Rocky Mountains and at the same time not know it if we are not told that this is that tremendous mountain of the west that we have heard so much talk about and thinking it almost impossible to cross it with wagons.
>
> This is called the South Pass. Here is about as good road as any that we have yet traveled on. This pass is many miles in width. To the right the mountains rise very high and are covered with perpetual snow. But to the left hand, the mountains. I could not see them. This spring is nearly the top of the mountain I may say, and I can say that it is the first water of the west that I have seen. Here we took dinner on the headwater of the waters of the Pacific Ocean. But this morning we took breakfast at the headwaters of the waters of the Atlantick Ocean.
>
> We traveled this evening and camped on a creek which is called Sand Spring. Distance traveled is twenty-five miles. This is fast traveling in a mountainous country.[13]

Sixteen days after crossing South Pass, the company reached Fort Bridger, where, Hammer wrote, there were many Indians "who will steal everything they can lay their hands on." Jim Bridger, they learned, was away on a hunting trip. Still in camp the following day, the emigrants met a party of men traveling east from Oregon. The emigrants sent several letters to relatives with the men before resuming their journey. On August 29 they reached Fort Hall, but for some reason Hammer made only passing reference to the Hudson's Bay Company trading post, even though it was a major stop on the road to Oregon. His August 29 entry simply reads: "Traveled twenty miles and reached Fort Hall on [the] Snake River. Very rich land yet." The emigrants remained in camp at Fort Hall an extra day before continuing their journey.[14]

Not far from Fort Hall, at the mouth of the Raft River, the majority of the wagon train continued on to Oregon Country, but more than fifty emigrants with thirteen wagons turned southwest for California. They included Elisha Stevens, Martin Murphy, Edmund Bray, Moses Schallenberger, old mountain man Caleb Greenwood with his two sons, and perhaps others in addi-

This is a photo of Jim Bridger, whose trading post, or fort, located in what is now southeastern Wyoming, became a prominent stopping point for travelers. (Courtesy Western History Collection, University of Oklahoma)

tion to the families of those mentioned. When the party reached the Humboldt River, they hired Chief Truckee of the Paiute Nation as a guide. The going was rough. At times they had to haul their wagons up and down cliffs and use rafts to cross the Humboldt, Truckee, and Yuba rivers. When snow began falling, some in the party built a cabin and made camp while others, including Bray, went ahead to find help. It came from Sutter's Fort, on the Sacramento River, which the rest of the party finally reached in late December 1844. They had blazed what became known as the Truckee Route, named for the Paiute chief who had guided the party. In addition to more than fifty emigrants who reached California, in all nearly 1,500 emigrants traveled overland to Oregon in 1844. The rush was only beginning.[15]

CHAPTER EIGHT

FIFTY-FOUR FORTY
OR FIGHT

Good company in a journey makes the way to seem the shorter.

Izaac Walton

A S 1845 BEGAN, the boundary dispute between Great Britain and the United States was still unresolved, but voters in the presidential election late in 1844 had made it clear they wanted Oregon Country as a territory of the United States. The Whig Party nominee, the celebrated Henry Clay, kept quiet during the campaign on the issue of western expansion, as did James G. Birney of the antislavery Liberty Party, but the Democratic Party nominee, forty-nine-year-old James K. Polk, favored westward expansion and said so. He knew the British wanted Oregon Country, and they also were making overtures about obtaining Texas. Polk favored getting both for the United States. While the political campaign was under way during the summer of 1845, negotiations over Oregon Country began between the United States and Great Britain. The initial American proposal called for the boundary to be drawn along the 49th parallel, running through Vancouver Island. But Polk took the bold position that the boundary be along latitude 54°40′. He wanted the United States to control all of Oregon Country from California northward to modern Alaska. He also called for the joint-occupancy agreement to be terminated within a year. "Fifty-four Forty or Fight" became his campaign slogan. When the presidential election was held, Polk won and was inaugurated as the eleventh president on March 4, 1845.[1]

When he took office, the joint-occupation agreement was still in effect. Neither the United States nor Great Britain could legally extend its jurisdiction over the settlers in Oregon Country, who had established their own Provisional Government much like American pioneers had done years before in the East by creating the Watauga and the Cumberland compacts for self-rule. Dr. John McLoughlin of the Hudson's Bay Company at Fort

Vancouver believed that the region north of the Columbia River would eventually belong to Great Britain, and he continued to encourage American emigrants to settle to the south of the Columbia. McLoughlin treated the settlers with kindness, but they realized that the Hudson's Bay Company still had a strong hold on its retired employees who had settled among the Americans. The American settlers also realized the Company's trading system kept the Indians in the region loyal to the British. Many of the Americans felt like second-class citizens, and some feared a clash between themselves and those loyal to the British, but this began to change after the arrival in 1844 of the emigrants.

Some of the new emigrants were responsible leaders who helped to bring both sides together. In July 1845, as more American emigrants were traveling overland toward Oregon Country, the settlers revised the Organic Act, changing the dates of elections and the meeting dates of the legislature. The somewhat unwieldy ruling executive committee was changed to a single governor, and they created a unicameral legislature to replace the legislative committee. They dropped voluntary contributions as a method of raising revenue and introduced optional taxation. Persons who did not pay taxes had no vote and no recourse to the law for any purpose. George Abernethy, a miller at the Oregon City Methodist Mission, was elected Oregon's first governor. Settlers with loyalties to the Hudson's Bay Company became more tolerant toward the American ones, especially after a census showed that 1,900 of the 2,109 people in Oregon early in 1845 were Americans. In an election, Frank Ermatinger, who worked for the Hudson's Bay Company, was elected treasurer of the Provisional Government. Then in August 1845, McLoughlin, on behalf of the Hudson's Bay Company, recognized the Provisional Government and formally joined it for the security of the Company's property and the protection of its rights. Within six months Hudson's Bay demoted McLoughlin to associate chief factor, and soon he retired to Oregon City, where in time he would become an American citizen and serve as mayor in what was designated the capital of Oregon Territory in August 1848.

As changes were being made in their Provisional Government, the residents of Oregon Country were unaware that more than two thousand emigrants had already crossed the Missouri River and were heading their way. Once there, the new settlers would almost double the population of Oregon Country. Unlike in earlier years, the emigrants of 1845 leaving from St. Joseph, Missouri, a town of 650 inhabitants, were not traveling as one large group, but in four or more companies. W. P. Richardson, at the Great Nemaha Indian agency, recorded the companies that had crossed at

St. Joseph. He counted a total of 954 persons with 545 firearms, plus 9,425 cattle and 108 horses and mules.[2]

The largest of these companies had about 275 persons traveling in 61 wagons. After crossing the Missouri River, the emigrants elected as captain William G. T'Vault from Kosciusko County, Indiana. They also elected John Waymire lieutenant, and hired John Clark (sometimes spelled "Clarke") to pilot them to the place in modern Kansas where they would strike the Oregon Trail after leaving St. Joseph.

The second group to leave St. Joseph was called the Savannah Oregon Emigrating Society Company. It had been organized in Andrew County, Missouri, by two ministers, William Helm and Lewis Thompson. This company crossed the Missouri River on a recently constructed ferry and a few days later camped on Wolf Creek. There, Solomon Tetherow was elected captain, and Hardin D. Martin, lieutenant. This company had 287 persons (63 females over the age of fourteen, 56 females under age fourteen, 100 armed men over the age of sixteen, and 68 males under sixteen years of age). They had 66 wagons, with 1,022 head of cattle and 74 mules and horses. Richardson counted 170 rifles and pistols among the men. Captain Tetherow's journal has survived, along with the company's constitution, in which are recorded the officers and their duties, the rules of travel, and other matters relating to the journey. At the end the Executive Committee added the following under the heading "BY LAWS &c":

MURDERS—

Anyone guilty of willful murder shall be punished by death and shall not be forced into trial before three days.

Anyone guilty of manslaughter shall be delivered to the authorities in Oregon.

Any one guilty of Rape or attempt at it shall receive thirty nine lashes for three successive days—

Any one guilty of open adultery, or fornication shall receive 39 lashes on their bare back.

Any one guilty to Larceny shall be fined double the amount, and receive 39 lashes on his bare back.

Any one guilty of indecent language shall be fined at the discretion of the Ex. Counsel.

Every Dog found running about Camp at large shall be shot at the discretion of the Capt.—

There shall be a driver of every 33 head of lose Cattle and every one shall
drive in proportion to the lose cattle he may have.[3]

The third company leaving from St. Joseph had fewer than 200 emigrants
and about 48 wagons. Samuel Parker, who came from Winchester, Iowa, was
elected captain once the company reached the Great Nemaha Subagency,
established by the government in about 1837 to serve the Sac and Fox tribes.
It was located about seven miles south of where the Missouri River flows
northwest around the modern northeast corner of Kansas.

The fourth company of some 214 persons with about 50 wagons and 666
head of cattle was the last group of emigrants to leave St. Joseph in 1845.
They called themselves the New London Emigrating Company, and about
twenty-five miles west of St. Joseph in what is now Kansas, Abraham Hack-
leman was elected captain.[4]

In 1845, emigrant companies also left for Oregon from points south. The
editor of the weekly newspaper at Weston, Missouri, about twenty-five
miles south of St. Joseph, told his readers that spring that two or three thousand people were gathering to start west from Independence with as many
as 200 wagons in two or more companies. After they crossed the Missouri
River, the editor got his horse, crossed the river, and rode about a hundred
miles west from Independence to view the emigrants firsthand. Before he
returned to Missouri, the editor counted 421 males, 138 females, and 412 children (204 boys and 208 girls) for a total of 971 people. He also counted 223
wagons, 3,261 cattle, and 182 horses among the emigrants.[5]

Exactly how many emigrants left Independence and other jumping-off
points south of St. Joseph, Missouri, in 1845 is not known, but there were
large and small companies. One small company of perhaps 150 emigrants
traveled in 38 wagons with about 1,000 head of loose cattle. It was led by John
Henry Brown, who had in 1840 gone to live with the Cherokee Indians and
then in 1843 traveled overland to California with a party of Cherokees. After
returning east in 1844, Brown decided to return to California and helped to
organize the party he led. While details are lacking, it is known that his
party traveled to Fort Hall over the Oregon Trail and then followed a route
via the Humboldt and Truckee rivers and arrived at Sutter's Fort in California during the month of October.[6]

A great deal is known about the larger company that left from Independence, because one of the emigrants traveling with it was thirty-five-year-
old Joel Palmer, a Canadian by birth who made his home in Laurel, Indiana.
Palmer kept a journal of each day's happenings and produced what remains

today the most complete firsthand description of travel over the Oregon Trail during the 1840s. He not only described the route, where his company camped each night, the rivers, springs, and grassy oases, but he also noted events that occurred, usually in some detail.

Palmer arrived at Independence a few days after a large company had left, but he caught up with them on May 8, 1845. Five days later, after the company crossed the Kansas River and reached Soldier Creek near modern Topeka, Kansas, the emigrants camped to elect permanent officers to replace the temporary ones chosen at Independence. Palmer wrote:

> The most important officers to be elected were the pilot and captain of the company. There were two candidates for the office of pilot.—one, a Mr. Adams, from Independence,—the other a Mr. Meek, from the same place. Mr. Adams had once been as far west as Fort Laramie, had in his possession Gilpin's Notes, had engaged a Spaniard, who had traveled over the whole route, to accompany him, and moreover had been conspicuously instrumental in producing the "Oregon fever." In case the company would elect him pilot, and pay him five hundred dollars, *in advance*, he would bind himself to pilot them to Fort Vancouver.
>
> Mr. Meek, an old mountaineer, had spent several years as a trader and trapper, among the mountains, and had once been through to Fort Vancouver; he proposed to pilot us through for two hundred and fifty dollars, *thirty* of which were to be paid in advance, and the balance when we arrived at Fort Vancouver. A motion was then made to postpone the election to the next day. While we were considering the motion, Meek came running into the camp, and informed us that the Indians were driving away our cattle. This intelligence caused the utmost confusion: motion and propositions, candidates and their special friends, were alike disregarded; *rifles* were grasped, and *horses* were hastily mounted, and away we all galloped in pursuit. Our two thousand head of cattle were now scattered over the prairie, at a distance of four or five miles from camp.
>
> About two miles from camp, in full view, up the prairie, was a small Indian village; the greater part of our enraged people, with the hope of hearing from our lost cattle, drove rapidly forward to this place. As they approached the village, the poor Indians were seen running to and fro, in great dismay—their women and children skulking but then hiding themselves,—while the chief came forward, greeted our party kindly, and by signs offered to smoke the pipe of peace, and engage with them in trade. On being charged with the theft of our cattle, they firmly asserted their innocence; and such was their conduct, that the majority of the party was

convinced they had been wrongfully accused: but one poor fellow, who had just returned to the village, and manifested great alarm upon seeing so many "pale faces," was taken away; and failing to prove his innocence, was hurried away to camp and placed under guard. Meanwhile, after the greater part of the company had returned to camp, and the captain had assembled the judges, the prisoner was arraigned at the bar for trial, and the solemn interrogatory, "Are you guilty or not guilty," was propounded to him: but to this, his only answer was—a grunt, the import of which the honorable court not being able clearly to comprehend, his trial was formally commenced and duly carried through. The evidence brought forward against him not being sufficient to sustain the charge, he was fully acquitted; and, when released, "split" for his wigwam in the village. After the excitement had in some degree subsided, and the affair was calmly considered, it was believed by most of us that the false alarm in regard to the Indians had been raised with the design of breaking up or postponing the election. If such was the design, it succeeded admirably.

May 14. Immediately after breakfast, the camp was assembled, and proceeded to the election of officers and the business of organization. The election resulted in the choice of S. L. Meek, as pilot, and Doctor P. Welch, formerly of Indiana, as captain, with a host of subalterns; such as lieutenants, judges, sergeants, &c.[7]

After the election the emigrants harnessed up their teams and resumed their journey. A few days later, on May 17, they climbed to the high, rolling prairie. Late in the afternoon they camped and had supper, and as Palmer noted in his journal, "a wedding was attended to with peculiar interest." Palmer does not mention the bride and groom, but they were none other than the company guide, forty-year-old Stephen Hall L. Meek, the younger brother of mountain man Joseph Meek, and seventeen-year-old Elizabeth Schoonover, a Canadian by birth. The company celebrated the wedding with a dance. But the following day Palmer wrote in his journal:

May 19. This day our camp did not rise. A growing spirit of dissatisfaction had prevailed since the election; there were a great number of disappointed candidates, who were unwilling to submit to the will of the majority; and to such a degree had a disorderly spirit been manifested, that it was deemed expedient to divide the company. Accordingly, it was mutually agreed upon, to form, from the whole body, three companies; and that, while each company should select its own officers and manage its internal affairs, the pilot, and Capt. Welsh, who had been elected by the whole company, should retain their posts, and travel with the company in advance. It was also arranged that each company should take its turn in traveling in advance, for one week at a time. A proposition was then made and acceded to, which provided that a collection of funds, with which to pay the pilot, should be made previous to the separation, and placed in the hands of some person to be chosen by the *whole*, as treasurer, who should give bonds, with approved security, for the fulfillment of his duty.

A treasurer was accordingly chosen, who after giving the necessary bond, collected about one hundred and ninety dollars of the money promised; some refused to pay, and others had no money in their possession. All these and similar matters having been satisfactorily arranged, the separation took place, and the companies proceeded to the election of the necessary officers. The company to which I had attached myself, consisting of thirty wagons, insisted that I should officiate as their captain, and with some reluctance I consented. We dispensed with many of the officers and formalities which existed in the former company, and after adopting certain regulations respecting the government of the company, and settling other necessary preliminaries, we retired to rest for the night.[8]

The dispute having been resolved to the satisfaction of nearly all of the emigrants, the three companies on May 20 continued their journey and covered fifteen miles. They traveled another thirteen miles on May 21 to the Big Vermillion River, and camped on its west bank. The next day they crossed the Big Blue River. On May 25, Palmer noted in his journal: "Early this morning we were passed by Col. Kearney and about three hundred dragoons. They have with them nineteen wagons drawn by mules, and drive fifty head of cattle and twenty-five head of sheep. They go to the south Pass of the Rocky Mountains."[9]

Colonel Stephen Watts Kearny had been ordered on April 7, 1845, to travel from Fort Leavenworth, located on the Missouri River in modern northeast Kansas, as far west as South Pass. At Fort Laramie, Kearny arrived with five companies of the First Dragoons and camped on the grassy Laramie River bottoms. There, the colonel held a formal council with the Sioux Indians and warned them against drinking "Taos Lightning," a home brew brought north by traders to sell to Indians, and also warned the Indians not to molest the peaceful emigrants traveling the Oregon Trail. Kearny duly impressed the Indians with his power by putting on a display of fireworks using his howitzer and rockets. He assured the Indians of the love and solicitude of the Great White Father in Washington. Guided by Thomas Fitzpatrick, Kearny reached South Pass in late June and then returned to Fort Laramie. From there he and his men traveled south past Long's Peak and Pike's Peak to the Arkansas River, where they turned east to Bent's Fort and followed the Santa Fe Trail east. Ninety-nine days after leaving, they returned to Fort Leavenworth.

Two days after watching Kearny and his dragoons pass his company, Joel Palmer on May 27 wrote in his journal: "As it was now the turn of our company to travel in advance, we were joined by Capt. Welsh and our pilot. The country is of the same character with that we passed through on yesterday, and is highly adopted to the purpose of settlement, having a good soil and streams well lined with timber." Five days later the company reached the Platte River and followed the south bank for about nine or ten miles and made camp on the Republican Fork.[10]

Two days later, Palmer wrote in his journal:

June 2. Our week of advance traveling being expired, we resolved to make a short drive, select a suitable spot, and lay by for washing. We accordingly encamped about six miles up the Platte River. As I had been elected captain but for two weeks, and my term was now expired, a new election was held, which resulted in the choice of the same person. The captain, Welsh, who was originally elected by all the companies, had been with us one week, and some dissatisfaction was felt, by our company, at the degree of authority he seemed disposed to exercise. We found, too, that it was bad policy to require the several companies to wait for each other;—our supply of provision was considered barely sufficient for the journey, and it behooved us to make the best use of our time. At present one of the companies was supposed to be two or three days travel in the rear. We adopted a resolution desiring the several companies to abandon the arrangement that required each to delay for the others; and that each company should have the use of the pilot according to its turn. Our proposition was not, for the present, accepted by the other companies. While we were at our washing encampment one of the companies passed us, the other still remaining in the rear.[11]

Failing to get the other companies to agree to let each company travel as it saw fit, Palmer and his company continued on the next day but camped early to wait for the last company to pass. It did not appear, but Palmer's group met about eighty Pawnee Indians returning east from their spring hunt. The next day, June 5, Palmer's company traveled twelve miles and passed the company leading the way, captained by H. L. Stephens. Palmer encouraged Stephens's company to pass and resume the lead, but at noon an axletree on one of the wagons in Stephens's company broke, causing the company to stop. Palmer's company again passed Stephens's company, much to the objection of Captain Stephens. Then and there, Palmer's company dissolved its connection with the other companies and went on their way. A few days later Stephens's company took the same action and each of the three companies then traveled on their own.[12]

On June 7, Palmer's company found their oxen growing lame and began to treat the animals. Palmer described the problem and the solution in his journal: "The prairie having been burnt, dry, sharp stubs of clotted grass remain, which are very hard, and wear and irritate the feet of the cattle. The foot becomes dry and feverish, and cracks in the opening of the hoof. In this opening the rough blades of grass and dirt collect, and the feet generally festers, and swells very much. Our mode of treating it was, to wash the foot with strong soap suds, scrape or cut away all the diseased flesh, and then pour boiling pitch or tar upon the sore. If applied early this remedy will cure. Should the heel become worn out, apply tar or pitch, and singe with a hot iron."[13]

Palmer also described human problems. The day after the company stopped to treat the cattle, Palmer wrote: "In the evening a young man, named Foster, was wounded by the accidental discharge of a gun. The loaded weapon, from which its owner had neglected to remove the cap, was placed at the tail of a wagon; as some one was taking out a tent-cloth, the gun was knocked down, and went off. The ball passed through a spoke of the wagon-wheel, struck the felloe, and glanced. Foster was walking some two rods from the wagon, when the half spent ball struck him in the back, near the spine; and, entering between the skin and the ribs, came out about three inches from where it entered, making merely a flesh wound. A small fragment of the ball had lodged in his arm."[14]

Palmer also captured the flavor of camp life. On June 15 a herd of buffalo was spotted near camp. Some of the men went buffalo hunting and returned at noon "overloaded with buffalo meat." The emigrants then commenced drying, or jerking, the meat.

> This is a process resorted to for want of time or means to cure meat by salting. The meat is sliced thin, and a scaffold prepared, by setting forks in the ground, about three feet high, and laying small poles or sticks

This is an unidentified eastern artist's depiction of emigrants grieving following the death of a man in their wagon train, about 1845. (Courtesy Kansas State Historical Society)

crosswise upon them. The meat is laid upon those pieces, and a slow fire built beneath; the heat and smoke completes the process in half a day; and with an occasional sunning the meat will keep for months.

An unoccupied spectator, who could have beheld our camp to-day, would think it a singular spectacle. The hunters returning with the spoil; some erecting scaffolds, and others drying meat. Of the women, some were washing, some ironing, some baking. At two of the tents the fiddle was employed in uttering its unaccustomed voice among the solitudes of the Platte; at one tent I heard singing; at others the occupants were engaged in reading, some the Bible, others poring over novels. While all this was going on, that nothing might be wanting to complete the harmony of the scene, a Carmelite preacher, named Foster, was reading a hymn, preparatory to religious worship. The fiddles were silenced, and those who had been occupied with the amusements, betook themselves to cards. Such is but a miniature of the great world we had left behind us, when we crossed the line that separates civilized man from the wilder-

This illustration drawn by A. R. Waud appeared in Harper's Weekly, *on December 23, 1871. One of the men in the picture may have been the guide for the wagon train. It was not uncommon for the first arrivals to set up camp, settle in, and cook the evening meal even before the last wagons, seen in the distance, were arriving. Notice the man to the left of the campfire playing his violin.* (Author's collection)

ness. But even here the variety of occupation, the active exercise of body and mind, either in labor or pleasure, the coming of evil and good, show that the likeness is a true one.[15]

Palmer's company reached Fort Laramie on June 24 and went into camp. Some of the men shoed their horses and oxen. Others went to trade with the Indians, and still others went into the fort. Palmer noted in his journal that "flour, sugar, coffee, tea, tobacco, powder and lead, sell readily, at high prices." During the afternoon the emigrants gave the Sioux Indians at the fort a feast. Each emigrant family, as they could spare it, contributed a portion of bread, meat, coffee, or sugar for the meal. While the meal was being cooked, buffalo skins were laid upon the ground and the provisions placed on top. Palmer described what happened next:

> Around this attractive board, the Indian chiefs and their principal men seated themselves, occupying one forth of the circle; the remainder of the male Indians made out the semi-circle; the rest of the circle was completed by whites. The squaws and younger Indians formed an outer

semi-circular row immediately behind their dusky lords and fathers. Two stout young warriors were now designated as waiters, and all the preparations being completed, the Indian chiefs and principal men shook hands, and at a signal the white chief performed the same ceremony, commencing with the principal chief, and saluting him and those of his followers who composed the first division of the circle; the others being considered inferiors, were not thus noticed.... The two Indian servants began their services by placing a tin cup before each of the guests, always waiting first upon the chiefs; they then distributed the bread and cakes, until each person had as much as it was supposed he would eat; the remainder being delivered to two squaws, who in like manner served the squaws and children. The waiters then distributed the meat and coffee. All was order. No one touched the food before him until all were served, when at a signal from the chief, the eating began.

Having filled themselves, the Indians retired, taking with them all that they were unable to eat.[16]

After leaving Fort Laramie on June 26, Palmer's company reached Independence Rock on July 12, and South Pass on July 19. That day Palmer wrote in his journal: "This day we passed over the dividing ridge which separates the waters flowing into the Atlantic from those which find their way into the Pacific Ocean. WE HAD REACHED THE SUMMIT OF THE ROCKY MOUNTAINS. Six miles brought us to a spring, the waters of which run into Green River, or the great Colorado of the west.—Here, then, we hailed Oregon."[17]

Before Palmer's journal was published in 1848 as a guide to emigrants, he took time to include a description of what they should take with them. He wrote:

For burthen wagons, light four horse or heavy two horse wagons are the size commonly used. They should be made of the best material, well seasoned, and should in all cases have falling tongues. The tire should not be less than one and three fourth inches wide, but may be advantageously used three inches; two inches, however, is the most common width. In fastening on the tire, bolts should be used instead of nails; it should be at least ⅝ or ¾ inches thick. Hub boxes for the hubs should be about four inches. The skeins should be well steeled. The Mormon fashioned wagon bed is the best. They are usually made straight, with side boards about 16 inches wide, and a projection outward of four inches on each side, and then another side board of ten or twelve inches; in this last, set the bows for covers, which should always be double. Boxes for carrying effects should be so constructed as to correspond in height with the offset in the wagon bed, as this gives a smooth surface to sleep upon.

Ox teams are more extensively used than any others. Oxen stand the trip much better, and are not so liable to be stolen by the Indians, and are much less trouble. Cattle are generally allowed to go at large, when not hitched to the wagons; whilst horses and mules must always be staked up at night. Oxen can procure food in many places where horses cannot, and in much less time. Cattle that have been raised in Illinois or Missouri, stand the trip better than those raised in Indiana or Ohio; as they have been accustomed to eating the prairie grass upon which they must wholly rely while on the road. Great care should be taken in selecting cattle; they should be from four to six years old, tight and heavy made.

For those who fit out but one wagon, it is not safe to start with less than four yoke of oxen, as they are liable to get lame, have sore necks, or to stray away. One team thus fitted up may start from Missouri with twenty-five hundred pounds and as each day's rations make the load that much lighter, before they reach any rough road, their loading is much reduced. Persons should recollect that every thing in the outfit should be as light as the required strength will permit; no useless trumpery should be taken. The loading should consist of provisions and apparel, a necessary supply of cooking fixtures, a few tools, &c. No great speculation can be made in buying cattle and driving them through to sell; but as the prices of oxen and cows are much higher in Oregon than in the States, nothing is lost in having a good supply of them, which will enable the emigrant to wagon through many articles that are difficult to be obtained in Oregon. Each family should have a few cows, as the milk can be used the entire route, and they are often convenient to put to the wagon to relieve oxen. They should be so selected that portions of them would come in fresh upon the road. Sheep can also be advantageously driven. American horses and mares always command high prices, and with careful usage can be taken through; but if used to [pull] wagons or carriages, their loading should be light. Each family should be provided with a sheet-iron store, with boiler; a platform can easily be constructed for carrying it at the hind end of the wagon; and as it is frequently quite windy, and there is often a scarcity of wood, the stove is very convenient. Each family should also be provided with a tent, and to it should be attached good strong cords to fasten it down.

The cooking fixtures generally used are of sheet iron; a Dutch oven and skillet of cast metal are very essential. Plates, cups, &c., should be of tin ware, as queens-ware is much heavier and liable to break, and consumes much time in packing up. A reflector is sometimes very useful. Families should each have two churns, one for carrying sweet and one for sour milk. They should also have one eight or ten gallon keg for carrying water, one axe, one shovel, two or three augers, one hand saw, and if a farmer he should be provided with one cross-cut saw and a few plough moulds, as it is difficult getting such articles. When I left the country, ploughs cost from twenty-five to forty dollars each. A good supply of ropes for tying up horses and catching cattle, should also be taken. Every person should be well equipped with boots and shoes and in fact with every kind of clothing. It is also well to be equipped with at least one feather bed, and a good assortment of bedding. There are no tame geese in the country, but an abundance of wild ones; yet it is difficult procuring a sufficient quantity of feathers for a bed. The Muscovy is the only tame duck in the country.

Each male person should have at least one rifle gun, and a shot gun is also very useful for wild fowl and small game, of which there is an abundance. The best sized caliber for the mountains is from thirty-two to fifty-six to the pound; but one of from sixty to eighty, or even less, is best when in the lower settlements. The buffalo seldom range beyond the South Pass, and never west of the Green River. The larger game are elk, deer, antelope, mountain sheep or bighorn, and bear. The small game are hare, rabbit, grouse, sage hen, pheasant, quail, &c. A good supply of ammunition is essential.

In laying in a supply of provisions for the journey, persons will doubtless be governed, in some degree, by their means; but there are a few essentials that all will require. For each adult, there should be two hundred pounds of flour, thirty pounds of pilot bread, seventy-five pounds of bacon, ten pounds of rice, five pounds coffee, two pounds of tea, twenty-five pounds of sugar, half a bushel of dried beans, one bushel of dried fruit, two pounds of Saleratus [sodium bicarbonate], ten pounds of salt, half a bushel of corn meal; and it is well to have a half bushel of corn, parched or ground; a small keg of vinegar should also be taken. To the above may be added as many good things as the means of the person will enable him to carry; for whatever is good at home, is none the less so on the road. The above will be ample for the journey; but should an additional quantity be taken, it can readily be disposed of in the mountains and at good prices, not for cash, but for robes, dressed skins, buckskin pants, moccasins, &c. It is also well for families to be provided with medicines. It is seldom however, the emigrants are sick; but sometimes eating too freely of fresh buffalo meat causes diarrhea, and unless it be checked soon prostates the individual, and leaves him a fit subject for disease.[18]

THE FOUR EMIGRANT COMPANIES that left St. Joseph, Missouri, that spring of 1845 traveled the same route. The first company, captained by T'Vault, apparently was ahead of Joel Palmer and the other emigrants who left from Independence, Missouri. James Field, who traveled with T'Vault's company, kept a diary in which he noted their arrival at Fort Laramie on June 20, a few days before Palmer. Field noted that along the Platte River he saw Indian travois trails as well as deep wheel ruts left by the wagons of emigrants in 1844. He also wrote that a child was run over by a wagon, but the ground was so soft the little boy was not killed.[19]

The New London Emigrating Company, the last to leave St. Joseph, Missouri, did not reach Fort Laramie until July 10. One of the emigrants in this company was Rev. Ezra Fisher, who had been preaching in the Davenport, Iowa, area when he received a call from the American Baptist Home Mission Society to go to Oregon. He put together an outfit and with Rev. Hezekiah Johnson and his family left St. Joseph with the company on May 14. In a letter sent east from Fort Laramie, Reverend Fisher reported he had reached the fort and told the reader, "I am now writing seated on a buffalo robe under a scorching sun, with the bottom of a wash tub for a table." He added, "You must therefore tax your patience in deciphering my hieroglyphics. Our wagons now undergoing repair, having become shrunk by protracted heat, sun, and sand."[20]

Somewhere between the T'Vault and New London Emigrating companies traveled the third company to leave St. Joseph. Captain Samuel Parker kept a diary of his journey in which he mentions his company having caught up with the second party leaving from St. Joseph, the Savannah Oregon Emigrating Society, captained by Solomon Tetherow. By the time emigrant companies reached the Columbia River, their members began intermingling. Parker's family was one of about two hundred who accepted Stephen Meek's offer to guide them with their wagons over a route to The Dalles that he said was 150 miles shorter than the route most emigrants followed. Parker was to regret the decision to follow Meek, who had trapped in the region with Captain Benjamin L. E. Bonneville in 1834. Meek remembered the route they had followed along the Malheur River across what is today central Oregon. At first all went well. There was plenty of grass, fuel, and water, but as Meek led them over some rough mountainous country, there was little vegetation or water. What water they found was in stagnant pools and unfit even for the cattle, but the emigrants had no choice but to use it. Joel Palmer picks up the story:

> The result was, that it made many of them sick; many of the cattle died, and the majority were unfit for labor. A disease termed camp fever, broke out among the different companies, of which many became victims.
>
> They at length arrived at a marshy lake, which they attempted to cross, but found it impracticable; and as the marsh appeared to bear south, and many of them were nearly out of provisions, they came to a determination to pursue a northern course, and strike the Columbia. Meek, however, wished to go south of the lake, but they would not follow him. They turned north, and after a few days' travel arrived at Deshutes or Falls River. They traveled up and down this river, endeavoring to find a passage, but as it ran through rocky canyons it was impossible to cross.
>
> Their sufferings were daily increasing, their stock of provisions was rapidly wasting away, their cattle were becoming exhausted, and many attached to the company were laboring under severe attacks of sickness;— at length Meek informed them that they were not more than two days' ride from The Dalles. Ten men started on horseback for the Methodist stations, with the view of procuring provisions; they took with them a scanty supply of provisions, intended for the two days' journey. After riding faithfully for ten days, they at last arrived at The Dalles. On their way they encountered an Indian who furnished them with a fish and a rabbit; this with the provisions they had started with, was their only food for the ten days' travel. Upon their arrival at The Dalles they were so exhausted in strength, as to render them unable to dismount without assistance.[21]

Nearly fifty emigrants died, including Samuel Parker's wife and one of his five children. Eventually, Parker, his four children, and other survivors were rescued. Later it was learned that Stephen Meek had easily traveled the route with Bonneville in 1834, but it had been a very wet year. The year 1845 was very dry, lacking the water and grass Meek thought the emigrants would find to successfully traverse the route. Everyone blamed Meek, who with his wife settled in Oregon Country, where a daughter, Spicy Jane, was born October 16, 1846. Meek remained something of an outcast among the settlers for several years.[22]

One of the men who refused to follow Meek was William Barlow, from Farmington, Illinois. Barlow with his family and his father, S. K. Barlow, traveled with four oxen-drawn wagons. William's father captained a company that left Independence, and when it reached Fort Hall, some of the emigrants turned toward California. The remaining thirteen wagons, including those belonging to the Barlows, continued along the Snake River. When they reached the Malheur, the Barlows refused to accept Meek's offer to follow what became known as his "famous cutoff." The Barlows continued to the Columbia River and reached The Dalles six weeks before the survivors of Meek's party arrived. At The Dalles, however, Barlow learned he would have to wait many days for a Hudson's Bay Company bateau, a flat-bottomed boat with raked bow and stern and flaring sides, to take his wagons and party down the Columbia River where it cuts through the Cascade Mountains. Nearly out of money, food, and patience, Barlow decided to find a route around Mount Hood to the Willamette Valley.

On September 24, 1845, Barlow, with seven wagons and nineteen people including his wife, Susannah, and their six children, left The Dalles and headed southwest toward Mount Hood. They camped on Five Mile Creek while Barlow and a few other men scouted the area. Meantime, Joel Palmer arrived with twenty-three wagons and families and joined Barlow's company. While they waited in camp for Barlow to return, some of the men returned to The Dalles to purchase wheat and beef. Barlow and his small party returned to the camp on October 6. The following day Barlow, Palmer, and other men began to build a road at the end of an Indian trail around the south side of Mount Hood. The eastern slope did not have as many trees on it as the western slope did and the men cleared three to six miles a day. At one point Palmer and others could see the Willamette Valley in the distance from Mount Hood, but it soon became evident that they could not finish the road before winter weather arrived. They decided to leave their wagons under guard in a mountain cache while the women and children were placed on horseback and the men walked toward the Willamette Valley.

When the emigrants reached the western slopes of the mountains, travel through the heavier timber was more difficult and food supplies were almost gone. Two men went ahead for provisions, and after many more difficulties the emigrants reached Oregon City on November 1, 1845. Joel Palmer wrote in his journal:

> Passing through the timber that lies to the east of the city, we beheld Oregon and the Falls of the Willamette at the same moment. We were so filled with gratitude that we had reached the settlements of the white man, and with admiration at the appearance of the large sheet of water rolling over the Fall, that we stopped, and in this moment of happiness

recounted our toils, in thought, with more rapidity than tongue can express or pen write.[23]

Palmer is best remembered for having written a simple factual narrative of each day's happenings, taking special care to describe the route, where his company camped each night, the possible cutoffs that supposedly would save time, rivers, springs, grassy oases, and whatever else he believed would be valuable information for future travelers. Because of this, Palmer's narrative, published in Cincinnati after he returned east, went through many editions and was used by later emigrants going west.

According to figures kept at Fort Laramie, more than 3,000 emigrants passed that post in 1845. Perhaps 260 of them went to California, the rest to Oregon. A newspaper correspondent traveling with Kearny's military expedition noted that the emigrants were divided into companies of 100 to 200, a day's march between them. The correspondent added that the emigrants seemed to be a good class of people, "possessing many of the conveniences, and some even of the luxuries of life."[24]

Not all travelers going up the Oregon Trail left Missouri in the spring of 1845. At least two small parties are known to have left late in the year. In mid-August 1845, Lansford W. Hastings and a small party of ten men on horseback, with pack animals, left a camp west of Independence, Missouri, and set out for California by way of the Oregon Trail. Originally, twenty-three men said they wanted to go with him, but thirteen backed out. Hastings had first gone to Oregon in 1842. Unimpressed by what he found there, he went south in 1843 to California. After several months in what was then part of the Republic of Mexico, Hastings returned east and completed a manuscript for a 152-page book published in Cincinnati in 1845 titled *The Emigrants' Guide to Oregon and California*. This guide contains narratives of his trip to Oregon and California, a discussion of the different routes, and his recommendations for emigrant conduct on the trail, equipment and supplies needed, and methods of travel. It is unclear if Hastings had copies of his guide when he left Independence in mid-August for California. Regardless, he and his party arrived at Sutter's Fort safely on December 25, 1845.

In mid-September 1845, about a month after Hastings's party left Independence, mountain man Miles Morris Goodyear, twenty-eight, with a few companions, set out from Independence with a pack train for Fort Bridger. Goodyear, born in Connecticut in 1817, was orphaned at age four. He was bound to a family at age ten and obligated to work until he was sixteen years old. When his indenture ended, Goodyear left Connecticut for the west, joining Marcus Whitman's party of missionaries traveling with Thomas

Fitzpatrick and other mountain men and traders heading to the rendezvous of 1836 on the Green River, near the site of present-day Daniel, Wyoming. For the first time Goodyear had the opportunity to see and talk with mountain men whom he had only heard about. From the rendezvous, Whitman, Goodyear, and the rest of the party traveled to Fort Hall, but it was there Goodyear left the missionaries and apparently got a job trapping and hunting for the Hudson's Bay Company, which operated the fort. During the years that followed, he lived among the Indians, marrying a Ute woman. By 1842, Goodyear was living in the Uintah Mountains of modern Utah; then in 1843 he was invited to join Sir William Drummond Stewart's party of pleasure-seekers in the Green River Valley. Goodyear accepted and, at what is now Fremont Lake, a few miles northwest of South Pass, Goodyear and other mountain men invited by Stewart spent "great days of exploring and fishing and story-telling and drinking, culminating in three days of Rocky Mountain Racing."[25]

While engaged in trading horses at Fort Bridger in what is now southwest Wyoming, Goodyear heard about a new route being promoted by Lansford Hastings called Hastings Cutoff. Knowing the route went through the Great Basin of what is now Utah, which was uninhabited, Goodyear realized having a trading post there might be profitable. In the summer of 1845 he headed east to obtain supplies for his venture. In September 1845, the *Western Expositor,* published weekly in Independence, Missouri, reported that Miles Goodyear had been in town and was returning west to the mountains to build a trading post or what he called "a sort of half-way house" between Independence and Oregon and California, where emigrants could stop, refresh themselves, and obtain supplies. Goodyear and his small party left Independence by mid-September, and by the following summer he had constructed a trading post on the Weber River about two miles above its junction with the Ogden River. It consisted of about half an acre enclosed with pickets, with a log house at each corner of the enclosure and nearby corrals for horses, cattle, sheep, and goats. Goodyear named his post Fort Buenaventura. It was the first permanent Anglo settlement in the Great Basin.[26]

CHAPTER NINE

THE YEAR
OF DECISION

Men are seldom blessed with good fortune
and good sense at the same time.

Titus Livy

THE YEAR 1846 marked a decisive turn in American history. A few days before the year began, Texas became the twenty-eighth state in the Union, but because of its unresolved border disputes, President James Polk declared war against Mexico on May 13, 1846. Before the year ended, the United States acquired a vast amount of land, including the parts of California previously claimed by Mexico. The Oregon boundary question was also resolved in June, when the Senate, otherwise preoccupied with the Mexican War, approved the Oregon Treaty with Great Britain. But Polk did not get his boundary at latitude 54°40'. The treaty set the boundary at the 49th parallel. Southern senators had made it clear that they did not want to risk war with Britain over Oregon. At the same time, British leaders did not want war because it would jeopardize their growing economic relationship with the United States.

The shape of the United States was changing dramatically, driven by "Manifest Destiny," a vague catchall phrase used to describe the great nationalizing movement of western expansion. The phrase was apparently coined by editor John L. O'Sullivan in the *Democratic Review* in July 1845 to describe the desire of Americans to expand the size of their nation westward. Some citizens believed the United States had a natural right to occupy all of the land between the Atlantic and the Pacific. Other Americans believed it was predestination and simply an extension of the freedoms enjoyed in a nation that was only seventy years old. Others accepted their government's actions as testimony that God had granted the United States title to the vast region west and southwest of the Louisiana Purchase.

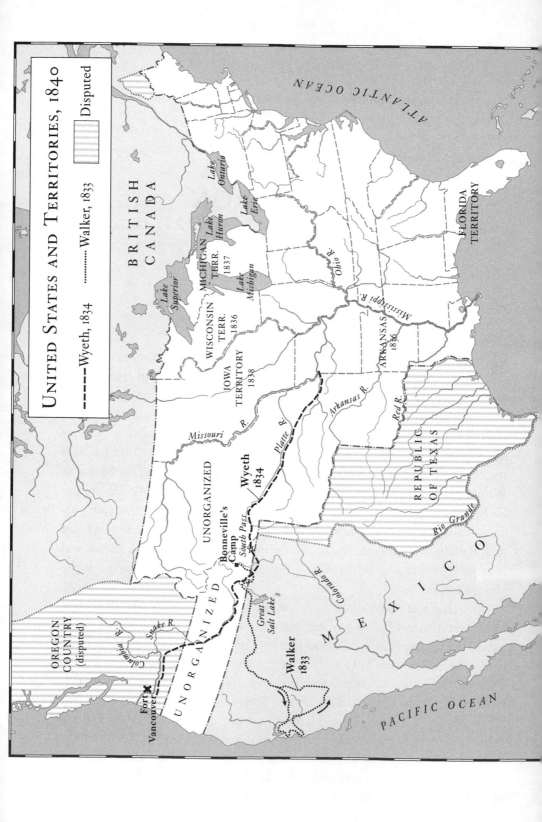

UNITED STATES AND TERRITORIES, 1840

----- Wyeth, 1834
········· Walker, 1833

Disputed

BRITISH CANADA

ATLANTIC OCEAN

Lake Ontario

Lake Erie

Lake Huron

MICHIGAN TERR. 1837

Lake Michigan

Lake Superior

WISCONSIN TERR. 1836

IOWA TERRITORY 1838

Ohio R.

Mississippi R.

ARKANSAS 1836

FLORIDA TERRITORY

Missouri R.

Platte R.

Wyeth 1834

Arkansas R.

Red R.

UNORGANIZED

Bonneville's Camp

South Pass

Great Salt Lake

Colorado R.

REPUBLIC OF TEXAS

Rio Grande

M E X I C O

OREGON COUNTRY (disputed)

Snake R.

Columbia R.

Fort Vancouver

UNORGANIZED

Walker 1833

PACIFIC OCEAN

When 1846 began, American settlers in Oregon Country were not aware of the far-reaching changes that would occur before the year ended. They did expect more emigrants to arrive in Oregon Country, perhaps even more than the previous year. In anticipation, some settlers in Oregon set about to improve the last leg of travel from The Dalles, on the Columbia River, to the Willamette Valley. One of them was fifty-three-year-old Samuel Barlow, who arrived the previous year. Barlow decided to complete the road around the south side of Mount Hood that he and others had started to build in 1845. He obtained a charter from the Provisional Government to finish it and to operate it as a toll road. He entered into a partnership with Philip Foster and hired forty men who soon opened a road from the Willamette Valley east to where his 1845 party had cached the wagons in the mountains. The Barlow Road was almost ninety miles long, with sixty-five of the miles cut through forests and canyons. Before 1846 ended, 145 wagons, 1,059 horses, mules, and cattle, and one herd of sheep reportedly traveled over it. When the construction began, Barlow tried to gather subscriptions from settlers in the Willamette Valley to pay the cost, but after a year he had raised only $30.[1]

The second effort to improve the last leg of travel to Oregon was the establishment of a new route by Lindsay, Jesse, and Charles Applegate. On

William Henry Jackson's painting shows emigrants following the Barlow Road, a cutoff around the south side of Mount Hood in Oregon. The wagon to the right is bogged down on the muddy road. (Courtesy Scotts Bluff National Monument)

the last part of their journey to Oregon in 1843, two Applegate children drowned as the families floated down the Columbia River in boats. The brothers resolved that if they remained in Oregon Country, they would find a better way for other emigrants to reach the Willamette Valley. On June 20, 1846, Lindsay and Jesse Applegate, along with Levi Scott and ten other men, set out from La Creole Creek near what is now Dallas, about thirteen miles from modern Salem, to blaze a new route. They traveled south through the areas where the cities of Corvallis, Eugene, and Ashland, Oregon, now stand, and then turned east toward what is today northwest Nevada. There they traveled northeast toward Fort Hall in modern Idaho. This new southern route to the Willamette Valley became known as the Applegate Trail. Although initially poorly marked, it connected with the trail to California at Humboldt.

Until the Barlow Road and the Applegate Trail were opened, taking wagons overland beyond The Dalles was almost impossible because the Columbia River was hemmed in by steep slopes and cliffs of hard volcanic rock. The emigrants either abandoned their wagons at The Dalles or floated them down the Columbia River on flatboats rented from the Hudson's Bay Company, rafts bought or traded from Indians, or rafts they themselves took time to build from pine logs. For those floating down the Columbia, the scenery was beautiful. Below The Dalles were the Memaloose Islands, so named by Upper Chinookan Indians, probably Wascos, Wishrams, White Salmons, and Watlalas (Cascades) living on the river's banks. Memaloose is a Chinook word meaning "the dead." Rafting around the islands, the emigrants could see where Indians had left their dead. Skeletons on racks and mats surrounded by baskets containing the belongings of those who died were clearly visible. Floating down the Columbia River may have been beautiful, but it was hazardous because high winds would often overturn a raft, and then there were two points where the river was so violent the travelers had to portage.

Emigrant families wanting to take their cattle and other livestock to the Willamette Valley had to separate at The Dalles. The men would drive the animals over one of two trails as their wives and children floated down the river. One route followed an Indian trail over Lolo Pass around Mount Hood to Eagle Creek and Oregon City. To follow the other route the men had to drive their livestock across the Columbia River near The Dalles and follow the treacherous northern bank of the river to Fort Vancouver and then recross the Columbia to reach the Willamette Valley. Until the Barlow Road and the Applegate Trail were opened in 1846, perhaps a fourth of the emigrants arriving at The Dalles traveled down the Columbia River. The

Lewis and Clark saw the Memaloose Islands as they traveled down the Columbia River in April 1806. For centuries the islands had been used for Indian burials. Bodies were wrapped in a blankets and placed in shallow pits, often in sitting positions. Over the pits protective covers were constructed of poles, slabs of wood, and bark, but they were not maintained and collapsed after years of weathering and rain. Other bodies were simply placed on the rocky top of a portion of the large island similar to the tree burials of the Sioux. These photos were made in the late nineteenth century. Many bones were washed away during a flood in 1894. When a dam was being constructed in the 1950s at The Dalles that would raise the level of the Columbia River, the remaining bones were removed and interred in an Indian cemetery at The Dalles. (David C. Herrin photo)

families not wanting to separate usually abandoned their wagons and tied their belongings to the backs of oxen or packhorses and, with the women and children riding the other animals or walking, followed the trail they had chosen to the Willamette Valley.

IN THE EAST, the War Department in Washington, D.C., responded to the growth of overland emigration by deciding to establish a chain of military posts across the West to protect travelers. On May 15, 1846, Colonel Stephen W. Kearny, in the company of Brigadier General George M. Brooke, other officers, and two companies of soldiers, left Fort Leavenworth on the steamboat *Amaranth*. The ship also carried lumber, flooring, stoves, and other materials. Kearny was under orders to construct the first military post along the Oregon Trail. It was to be located on the Missouri River near the mouth of Table Creek on the site of present-day Nebraska City, Nebraska. Meantime, another detachment of troops was sent overland to assist. Kearny, Brooke, and the others traveling by steamboat arrived about May 21, while the troops moving overland got there the following day. Kearny and Brooke decided on a location for what was to be called Camp Kearny, later Fort Kearny, and a log blockhouse was constructed. Kearny and Brooke then returned to Fort Leavenworth by steamboat. The log blockhouse was nearly completed when the soldiers were ordered to abandon the post. A handful of soldiers finished the task and a civilian, a man named William R. English, was hired to care for it. Under orders the soldiers returned to Fort Leavenworth because on May 13, President Polk had declared war on Mexico. The troops were needed for Kearny's Army of the West, which would march to what is now New Mexico.

Even if more than a log blockhouse had been constructed that spring, few emigrants would have passed by it. Most left from points south. Emigrants began gathering in western Missouri in April 1846 to prepare for the long overland journey. It was the first year that more settlers went to California than to Oregon. By late April and early May, the emigrants with their wagons began crossing the Missouri River at St. Joseph and at other points north of Weston, Missouri. Still other emigrants left from the vicinity of Independence and followed the Santa Fe Trail southwest to near modern Gardner, Kansas, where they turned northwest, passed over the site of modern Lawrence, Kansas, before crossing the Kansas River. One unidentified resident of Independence wrote on May 11, 1846: "Our town for the last few weeks, has presented a scene of business equal to a crowded city. Emigrants have been pouring in from all quarters. There are, this spring [in contrast to previous years], two distinct companies [groups], one to Oregon, and the other to California."[2]

Exactly how many emigrants headed west from Missouri in 1846 is not known, but from Weston, Missouri, northward it is known that about 1,350 emigrants probably crossed the Missouri River at different points, including St. Joseph, Elizabethtown, and Iowa Point, all in Missouri. From Independence, it is estimated that 267 wagons headed west, but how many emigrants were with the wagons is not known. If one wagon carried an average of five persons, one can calculate that another 1,335 emigrants left the Independence area. Thus, the best estimate is that about 2,685 emigrants headed west from Missouri in 1846. Of that total, perhaps 1,200 went to Oregon, while slightly fewer than 1,500 souls headed for California.[3]

The last emigrant known to have departed from Missouri that year was Joel M. Ware, who was bound for Oregon. He left Independence on June 2 and soon caught up with a company of twenty-five wagons captained by William Crosby. Among his company were nineteen wagons of Mormons, most from the South, who called themselves "Mississippi Saints," members of the Church of Jesus Christ of Latter-Day Saints officially founded by Joseph Smith. As a young farm boy in western New York, Smith claimed he had experienced a series of visions and was visited by an angel named Moroni, who led him to the hiding place of certain gold tablets on which were inscribed *The Book of Mormon*. In 1830, Smith, who saw himself as the agent and prophet of the Lord, reestablished a form of communal Christianity that he said existed at the time of the Apostles. Eventually, Smith and his followers were driven from New York, Ohio, and Missouri. They then moved to Illinois and established their own town called Nauvoo on the Mississippi River. There they began to prosper, but soon they were persecuted for their beliefs, which included the practice of polygamy. On June 24, 1844, Joseph Smith and his brother Hyrum were arrested on a treason charge and jailed in Carthage, Illinois. Three days later they were shot to death by an angry mob.

At Nauvoo, Brigham Young was elected president of the church and decided the only safety for the Mormons lay in leaving Illinois, and in the spring of 1846 he led his people west to find a new home. While the bulk of the Mormons headed across what is now Iowa toward the Missouri River, Young sent the "Mississippi Saints" west across Missouri with vague instructions to meet the other Mormons on the plains. They were among the emigrants who left Independence in early June with Crosby's company, which included six wagons of families bound for Oregon. One of the Mormons in the company was John Brown, who later recalled that when the wagons reached Indian country, the Oregon-bound emigrants learned they were traveling with Mormons and became "a little uneasy and somewhat frightened."[4]

The Oregon-bound group had heard rumors that "five thousand Mormons were crossing, or had crossed, the Kansas River; that they marched with ten brass fieldpieces, and that every man of the party was armed with a rifle, a bowie knife, and a brace of large revolving pistols. It was declared that they were inveterately hostile to the emigrant parties; and when the latter came up to the Mormons, they intended to attack and murder them, and appropriate to themselves their property."[5] The rumors caused groups to ask for protection by U.S. troops, but the requests were denied. Because it was too late in the year to journey westward, the large Mormon exodus did not occur until 1847.

Meanwhile, before the first wagons of Mormons reached the Missouri River in the spring of 1846, Captain James Allen approached the Mormons seeking five hundred volunteers to join the U.S. Army to fight Mexico. The volunteers would be called the Mormon Battalion. Brigham Young approved. In correspondence a year earlier with Jesse C. Little, the presiding elder of the church in New England and the middle states, Young had asked Little to seek aid for the migrating Latter-Day Saints then in Iowa. Little arrived in Washington a few days after war was declared on Mexico. President Polk offered to aid the Mormons by permitting them to raise a battalion of men to fight with Colonel Stephen W. Kearny's Army of the West. Little accepted the offer. When Captain Allen began meeting with the Mormons, some suspected it was a plot against them. But Brigham Young supported the action, and by July 1846 about 543 Mormons had enlisted. The battalion marched from the site of modern Council Bluffs, Iowa, to Fort Leavenworth, where they were given arms, accoutrements, and a clothing allowance of $42 each. Since the Mormon soldiers did not have to wear military uniforms, many of them sent the money to their families in Iowa. The Mormon Battalion marched to Santa Fe, arriving there in early October 1846 and then continued to Tucson and on to California, arriving there in early January after the longest sustained march in U.S. history.

WE KNOW SOMETHING of the experiences of the emigrants following the Oregon Trail in 1846 because some of them later wrote their recollections. More than a dozen wrote letters along the way that have survived and contain bits and pieces of information. At least six emigrants kept diaries and a few kept journals. One of the better diaries was kept by thirty-year-old Nicholas Carriger, who had been born and raised on a farm in Carter County, Tennessee. He served in the First Tennessee Mounted Volunteers in 1835 and 1836 during the Seminole War and then returned home to work in milling and distilling, and later joined his father in manufacturing iron and hardware. In 1840, Carriger moved to Missouri, where in 1842 he married Mary Ann Wardlow, a native of Highland County, Ohio. He and his wife had two children but decided to leave Missouri for Mississippi, where Carriger purchased 160 acres of land, built a house, fenced his land, and began raising hemp, tobacco, and cereals. Soon he heard talk about the fertility of California. Displeased with his farm and without consulting anyone, Carriger sold his farm for only $500, less than what he had spent building his house. In April 1846, Carriger, his wife, and their two children left Mississippi and returned to Missouri, determined to go west.

Carriger and family joined a company of emigrants that began crossing the Missouri River near Oregon, Missouri, in early May. It took several days for all of the wagons to be ferried across. Beginning on May 11, Carriger's diary reads:

> 11th set out across the bluffs into the Prairie about 3 miles where we again encamped and lay by the 12th.
>
> 12th our members have increased to 31 Waggons and are still Waiting for more to Cross.
>
> 13th and 14th this day Joseph Blanton died and his family went bak [back] set out with fifty Waggons from our Camp on Honey Creek and Travelled about 12 miles to a Water of the big Ome Haw [Great Nemaha River].
>
> 15th Travelled about 5 miles and encamped on Water of the Big Ome haw [Great Nemaha River].[6]

It is obvious that Carriger spent little time making his diary entries, but they reflect the flavor and tempo of overland travel. Carriger's company blazed a new trail along the ridge between the Big and Little Nemaha rivers to a junction with the road from Independence and St. Joseph, where they met another company of emigrants with nine wagons belonging to the Reed and Donner families from Illinois. They traveled together, arriving at the Big Blue River only to find the stream swollen. That was on May 26 and the emigrants went into camp to wait for the water level to recede. The women took advantage of the break and washed clothes while some of the men went fishing. One man caught a catfish three feet long. That evening the leaders of the company held a meeting with everyone to discuss the preparation of a system of law so that order could be preserved. As the sun set, a new moon appeared above the treetops, and soon nearly everyone but the guards went to sleep. During the night there was a rainstorm, but at dawn the sky was clear and blue. A few men went in search of bee trees and eventually returned with several baskets of honey. The emigrants were still waiting for the river to recede on the morning of May 29. The day was beautiful, but there was a feeling of gloom throughout the camp. Early that morning Mrs. Sarah Keyes, age seventy, the mother-in-law of J. H. Reed from Illinois, died. She had been in poor health. Her son had emigrated to Oregon two or three years earlier, and she expected to meet him at Fort Hall. At two o'clock that afternoon Rev. Josephus Adamson Cornwall, a forty-eight-year-old Presbyterian minister from Georgia, performed the funeral service, and Sarah Keyes's body was laid to rest in a grave not far from Marysville, Kansas.

Two days later the company was able to cross the Blue River and move northwest toward the Platte River. When they reached a Pawnee Indian village on the Platte, the emigrants gave the Indians presents and an ox, which the Indians killed, cooked, and ate. In his diary, Carriger mentions that a woman fell under the wheel of a wagon and was badly hurt. Two days later, June 6, Carriger noted: "One boy [seven-year-old Enoch Garrison] fell and two wheels run over one leg and the other foot and ancle near cutting the leg off breaking the bone." The company went into camp and some of the emigrants did what they could for the boy. Two days later the company resumed travel with the injured boy carried in his family's wagon.

Within a few days the boy's condition worsened and three men were sent to locate a doctor in one of the other emigrant companies. They traveled back along the trail and apparently stopped at each emigrant company and asked if they had a doctor. After traveling about thirty miles without finding one, they came upon a large company in camp, captained by William H. Russell. When asked if they had a doctor, someone pointed to Edwin Bryant, who with two friends was heading for California. Bryant, former editor of the *Louisville* (Kentucky) *Courier,* was well educated and had treated some emigrants in his company as a "good Samaritian," but he was not a doctor. He told this to the three men, but they insisted he accompany them back to where their company was camped. What happened next is told in Bryant's own words:

> After a most fatiguing and exhausting ride, we reached the encampment to which I had been called about five o'clock, p.m.... When I reached the tent of the unfortunate family to which the boy belonged, I found him stretched out upon a bench made of planks, ready for the operation which I would perform. I soon learned, from the mother, that the accident had occurred nine days previously. That a person professing to be a "doctor," had wrapped some linen loosely about the leg, and made a sort of trough or plank box, in which it had been confined. In this condition the child had remained, without any dressing of his wounded limb, until last night, when he called to his mother, and told her that he *could feel worms crawling in his leg!* This, at first, she supposed to be absurd; but an examination of the wound for the first time was made, and it was discovered that gangrene had taken place, and the limb of the child was swarming with maggots! They then immediately dispatched their messengers for me. I made an examination of the fractured limb, and ascertained that what the mother had stated was correct. The limb had been badly fractured, and had never been bandaged; and from neglect gangrene had supervened, and the child's leg, from his foot to the knee, was in a state of putrefaction. He was so much enfeebled by his sufferings that death was

stamped upon his countenance, and I was satisfied that he could not live twenty-four hours, much less survive an operation. I so informed the mother, stating to her that to amputate the limb would only hasten the boy's death, and add to his pains while living; declining at the same time, peremptorily, all participation in a proceeding so useless and barbarous under the circumstances. She implored me, with tears and moans, not thus to give up her child without an effort. I told her again, that all efforts to save him would be useless, and only add to the anguish of which he was now dying.

But this could not satisfy a mother's affection. She could not thus yield her offspring to the cold embrace of death, and a tomb in the wilderness. A Canadian Frenchman, who belonged to this emigrating party, was present, and stated that he had formerly been an assistant to a surgeon in some hospital, and had seen many operations of this nature performed, and that he would amputate the child's limb, if I declined doing it, and the mother desired it. I could not repress an involuntary shudder when I heard this proposition, the consent of the weeping woman, and saw the preparations made for the butchery of the little boy. The instruments to be used were a common butcher-knife, a carpenter's handsaw, and a shoemaker's awl to take up the arteries. The man commenced by gashing the flesh to the bone around the calf of the leg, which was in a state of putrescence. He then made an incision just below the knee and commenced sawing; but before he had completed that amputation of the bone, he concluded that the operation should be performed above the knee. During these demonstrations the boy never uttered a groan or a complaint, but I saw from the change in his countenance, that he was dying. The operator, without noticing this, proceeded to sever the leg above the knee. A cord was drawn round the limb, above the spot where it was intended to sever it, so tight that it cut through the skin into the flesh. The knife and saw were then applied and the limb amputated. A few drops of blood only oozed from the stump; the child was dead—his miseries were over. The scene of weeping and distress which succeeded this tragedy cannot be described. The mother was frantic, and the brothers and sisters of the deceased boy were infected by the intense grief of their parent.[7]

Bryant was then asked to visit the father of the dead child, who was lying prostrate in his tent suffering from inflammatory rheumatism. The man had been devouring his medicines like food, believing large quantities would produce a fast cure. Bryant advised him to cut back on the amount of medicine. Bryant was then invited to attend a wedding in the camp. It was performed by Rev. Josephus Cornwall of Russell's company, in the tent of the bride's father. Bryant recalled: "The wedding-cake was not frosted with sugar, nor illustrated with matrimonial devices, after the manner of confectioners in the 'settlements,' but cake was handed round to the whole party present. There was no music or dancing on the occasion. The company separated soon after the ceremony was performed, leaving the happy pair to the enjoyment of their connubial felicities."

It was dark when Bryant left the wedding. In the distance he saw the torches and lanterns of a funeral procession. From the wedding Reverend Cornwall had gone to the wagon of the dead boy to conduct a funeral service. Now the boy's remains were being taken to the spot where a grave had been dug near the trail. While watching the funeral procession, a man approached Bryant and told him that a woman in a nearby emigrant company had just given birth to a baby and both mother and child were doing well. Bryant walked away and later wrote: "I could not but reflect upon the singular concurrence of the events of the day. A death and funeral, a wedding and a birth, had occurred in this wilderness, within a diameter of two miles, and within two hours' time; and tomorrow, the places where these events had taken place, would be deserted and unmarked, except by the grave of the unfortunate boy deceased!"[8]

The company Edwin Bryant was going with was the largest one traveling westward in 1846. It was led by Colonel William Henry Russell, a harddrinking Kentuckian born in 1802. He became a lawyer and represented Nicholas County in the Kentucky legislature in 1830 and married Zanette Freeland of Baltimore, Maryland. Russell, who was a large man, boastful and bombastic in speech but with many substantial and endearing qualities, came to the attention of Henry Clay. For a time, Russell served as Clay's secretary. Russell moved to Missouri in 1831, served in the Black Hawk War, and in 1841 was appointed U.S. marshal for the District of Missouri. At some point he was given the courtesy title of "Colonel." The story goes that Russell one evening supposedly mistook a chorus of "tu-whoo's" from some owls as a challenge of "Who are you?" He supposedly thundered back, "Colonel William H. Russell, of Kentucky—a bosom friend of Henry Clay." Thereafter he was known as "Owl" Russell. Like Bryant, Russell was heading for California and was elected captain of the company of about 250 people that included Bryant; former Missouri Governor Liburn Boggs and his wife Panthea Grant Boone, a granddaughter of Daniel Boone; and another Boone relative, probably Albert G. Boone, a nephew. Some days later the nine wagons carrying thirty-one members of the

James F. Reed and George and Jacob Donner families and their hired hands joined the company.

Colonel Russell had managed to keep cohesion among the emigrants as their company moved across what is now Nebraska, but disputes over firewood and water, petty grievances, and complaints about almost anything the mind can conceive, made it difficult for Russell to keep everyone happy. Near Fort Laramie, Russell resigned as captain. He said he was suffering from an attack of "bilious fever," something many other captains had complained about. Liburn Boggs was elected captain as the emigrants rested in the vicinity of Fort Laramie. On June 29, a twenty-two-year-old man from Boston visited the post and saw Colonel Russell "drunk as a pigeon." The Bostonian also saw emigrants purchasing supplies. The young man from Boston was none other than Francis Parkman, who had also traveled the trail from Missouri.[9]

Parkman, the son of a well-known Unitarian minister in Boston, finished his education at Harvard and headed west in 1845 to find Indians and adventure and to regain his health after his studies. Parkman and a cousin, Quincy A. Shaw, had arrived in the town of Kansas (now Kansas City, Missouri) in very early May aboard the steamboat *Radnor* from St. Louis. They stayed with Colonel William M. Chick in his log home while buying horses, mules, and supplies for their journey westward to the Rocky Mountains. Parkman visited Independence and Westport and even went across the western border of Missouri into Indian country to visit Wyandotte Indians. On May 9, Parkman, Shaw, and two other men—a guide and hunter named Henry Chatillon, and a man named Delorier, who drove a two-wheeled cart carrying supplies—left the town of Kansas and traveled to Fort Leavenworth, where they were to meet a small British hunting party. With them Parkman's party traveled up the Oregon Trail to where the Platte River forks. The hunting party went into the Rocky Mountains, while Parkman and his party continued on to Fort Laramie to spend several weeks. He went only about fifty miles farther up the trail, visited with Sioux Indians around Fort Laramie, and observed and talked with a few emigrants arriving and departing the fort, including members of the Reed and Donner party. Parkman, after purchasing more than $100 worth of supplies, wrote in his journal on June 16: "Prices are most exorbitant. Sugar, two dollars a cup—5-cent tobacco at $1.50—bullets at $.75 a pound, etc. American Fur Cmp'y. exceedingly disliked in this country—it suppresses all opposition, and keeping up these enormous prices, pays its men in necessaries on these terms."[10]

In early August, Parkman's party headed south from Fort Laramie along the eastern side of the Rocky Mountains until they reached what is now

William Henry Jackson's painting of Westport Landing, now part of Kansas City, Missouri. It was the jumping-off point for Francis Parkman when he started his journey up the Oregon Trail to Fort Laramie in 1845. (Courtesy Scotts Bluff National Monument)

Pueblo, Colorado, located on the upper Arkansas River. There they followed the river east to Bent's Fort. Four other men joined them there, and they followed the Santa Fe Trail east to Westport, where they sold their horses and gear before boarding a steamboat for St. Louis. Returning east, Parkman wrote an account of his four-month journey, which was published serially in *Knickerbocker* magazine between February 1847 and February 1849, and then was published as a book in 1849 titled *The California and Oregon Trail*. It became a classic and was reprinted many times and through the twentieth century was a perennial favorite of high school students.

From the beginning Edwin Bryant was bound for California. So were a few others in the party, including William H. Russell, whose company Bryant joined at Independence. By the time Russell resigned as captain, Russell, Bryant, and a few other men in the company were dissatisfied with the slow pace of the travel. In the vicinity of Fort Laramie, Bryant traded his wagon and oxen for mules with packsaddles and associated trappings. Others in the company apparently did the same, and the following day, June 28, a small party of nine men including Bryant and Russell set out. Some days later, on July 17, Bryant and the others arrived at Fort Bridger. Several emigrant companies arrived at the trading post with whom they could travel northwest to Fort Hall. The following day Bryant's party decided to go with Benoni M. Hudspeth, who earlier in the summer had returned from California with Lansford W. Hastings to explore a new desert route.

Bryant wrote:

Mr. Hudspeth—who with a small party...will start in advance of the emigrant companies which intend traveling by this route, for the purpose of making further explorations—has volunteered to guide us as far as the Salt Plain, a day's journey west of the [Salt] Lake. Although such was my own determination, I wrote several letters to my friends among the emigrant parties in the rear, advising them *not* to take this route, but to keep on the old trail, via Fort Hall. Our situation was different from theirs. We were mounted on mules, had no families, and could afford to hazard experiments, and make explorations. They could not.[11]

Bryant and the eight other men in his party along with Hudspeth and three men from the emigrant parties set out on July 20. That same day Lansford Hastings, who had been waiting for late California-bound companies to arrive, decided to move on and took those who had gotten there and left. Bryant's group, led by Hudspeth, made better time since they had no wagons, but soon unseasonably cold weather set in, and a few days later Bryant and the others could see forest fires in the mountains. In late July they reached the Great Salt Lake, where Hudspeth and his party left to explore the area. Bryant's party made preparations to cross the Salt Desert, to the west of the Great Salt Lake. Early in August they started and soon

entered upon the hard smooth plain... composed of bluish clay, incrusted in wavy lines, with a white saline substance, the first representing the body of the water, and the last the crests and froth of the mimic waves and surges. Beyond this we crossed what appeared to have been beds of several small lakes, the waters of which have evaporated, thickly incrusted with salt, and separated from each other by small mound-shaped elevations of a white, sandy, or ashy earth, so imponderous that it has been driven by the action of the winds into these heaps, which are constantly changing their positions and their shapes. Our mules waded through these ashy undulations, sometimes sinking to their knees, at others to their bellies, creating dust that rose above and hung over us like a dense fog.[12]

Bryant's party pushed on as rapidly as they could, but travel became more difficult. The mules became so fatigued that Bryant and the others dismounted and walked, leading their animals. It took them about two days to cross the Salt Plain, which Bryant estimated was seventy-five miles across. Later, it was measured as sixty-five miles and not the forty miles Hastings had estimated. As they followed Hastings's directions, they soon reached the Humboldt River, where the party met one or both Applegate brothers and some other men from Oregon working out a new route between the Humboldt and the headwaters of the Willamette River in Oregon Country. From the Humboldt, Bryant and the others followed the Truckee River over the Sierra Nevada and reached Johnson's Ranch on August 31 and Sutter's Fort the following day.

Bryant later calculated the following table of distances from Independence to Sutter's Fort by the route he traveled:

From Independence, Mo., to Fort Laramie	672 miles
From Fort Laramie to "Pacific Springs," (South Pass,)	311 "
From the "South Pass," (Pacific Springs,) to Fort Bridger	133 "
From Fort Bridger to Salt Lake,	106 "
From Salt Lake to Mary's river [Humboldt River],	315 "
Down Mary's river to the "Sink,"	274 "
From the "Sink" to Truckee Lake, [Donner Lake]	134 "
From Truckee Lake to Johnson's,	111 "
From Johnson's to Sutter's Fort,	35 "
Total distance from Independence, Mo., to Sutter's Fort in California,	2091 "
The distance from Sutter's Fort by land, to the town of San Francisco, (via the Pueblo of San Jose,) near the mouth of the Bay of S. F., and five miles from the Pacific Ocean, is	200 "
Total	2291 miles[13]

Before leaving Fort Bridger, Bryant had sent letters to emigrant friends advising them not to follow the same route for the reasons already stated, but about eighty wagons of emigrants set out from Fort Bridger to follow

Lansford Hastings's route. Before arriving at the fort, they and other emigrants met Wales B. Bonney, who was carrying an open letter from Hastings, whose *Emigrants' Guide to Oregon and California* was published in 1845. The *Guide* had inspired many of the emigrants to go west. Hastings's letter advised emigrants bound for California that he would wait for them at Fort Bridger to lead them over a newly explored cutoff route south of the Great Salt Lake. Hastings claimed the new route would reduce the distance by as much as three hundred miles, and cut the time it would take to reach California.

Exactly how many emigrants traveled by way of Fort Bridger is not known. Many who did continued on to Fort Hall and Oregon. But there were those who followed Lansford Hastings over his cutoff. By the time the Donner company arrived at Fort Bridger, Hastings had already left, leading those emigrants who had gotten there earlier. The eighty-seven emigrants now in the Donner company debated whether to follow the Hastings cutoff. After discussion they decided they would and apparently were given some directions by Jim Bridger or Louis Vasquez. The Donner company set out southwest, the last emigrants that summer to leave Fort Bridger for California. For several days they traveled without much difficulty. When they reached the Weber River near the head of Weber Canyon, they found a letter from Hastings stuck in the split of a stick addressed to any emigrants who might be following. Hastings wrote that the road down Weber Canyon was in terrible condition, and he indicated it was doubtful if wagons would be able to reach the plain below. Hastings urged all emigrants to avoid the canyon road, and to go over the mountains. In his letter he faintly outlined the directions emigrants should follow.

Virginia Reed, the twelve-year-old stepdaughter of James F. Reed, later recalled that Hastings's directions

> were so vague that C. T. Stanton, William Pike, and my father rode on in advance and overtook Hastings and tried to induce him to return and guide our party. He refused, but came back over a portion of the road, and from a high mountain endeavored to point out the general course. Over this road my father traveled alone, taking notes, and blazing trees, to assist him in retracing his course, and reaching camp after an absence of four days. Learning of the hardships of the advance train, the party decided to cross towards the lake. Only those who have passed through this country on horseback can appreciate the situation. There was absolutely no road, not even a trail. The canyon wound around among the hills. Heavy underbrush had to be cut away and used for making a road bed. While

cutting our way step by step through the "Hastings Cut-off" we were
overtaken and joined by the Graves family, consisting of W. F. Graves, his
wife and eight children, his son-in-law Jay Fosdick, and a young man by
the name of John Snyder. Finally we reached the end of the canyon
where it looked as though our wagons would have to be abandoned. It
seemed impossible for the oxen to pull them up the steep hill and the
bluffs beyond, but we doubled teams and the work was, at last, accomplished, almost every yoke in the train being required to pull up each
wagon.[14]

It had taken the Donner company a month, instead of a week, to cover
the distance from Fort Bridger to the Great Salt Lake. The emigrants and
their oxen were fatigued and camped in a valley called Twenty Wells, where
they found wells of pure and cold water. There they prepared for their journey across the Salt Plain. Once the party was ready, they started in the
evening, traveled all night, all the next day, and the next night, suffering
from piercing cold at night and thirst and heat during the day. Some families
lost their oxen and had to leave their wagons. Some of their possessions were
loaded on the remaining wagons and the rest were buried near their abandoned transport. When the company neared the end of the Salt Plain desert,
the emigrants took an inventory of their provisions and realized they were
not sufficient to reach California. That night there was a storm, and by
morning the hilltops were covered with snow. Two members of the party,
C. T. Stanton and William McCutchen, offered to go ahead to Sutter's Fort
and get provisions. The two men left, and the rest of the party soon resumed
its journey. Days later it reached Gravelly Ford on the Humboldt River and
afterward the Truckee River. The spirits of the emigrants were raised when
C. T. Stanton, returning with two Indian vaqueros sent to help by Captain
Sutter, met the emigrants along the Truckee River. Stanton brought seven
mules loaded with provisions. McCutchen had taken ill and remained at
Sutter's Fort.

As the Donner company climbed the Sierra Nevada in late October,
snow began falling. Winter was beginning a month early. Virginia Reed
recalled:

When it was seen that the wagons could not be dragged through the snow,
their goods and provisions were packed on oxen and another start was
made, men and women walking in the snow up to their waists, carrying
their children in their arms and trying to drive their cattle. The Indians
said they could find no road, so a halt was called, and Stanton went ahead

with the guides, and came back and reported that we could get across if we kept right on, but that it would be impossible if snow fell. He was in favor of a forced march until the other side of the summit should be reached, but some of our party were so tired and exhausted with the day's labor that they declared they could not take another step; so the few who knew the danger that the night might bring yielded to the many, and we camped within three miles of the summit. That night came the dreaded snow. Around the campfires under the trees great feathery flakes came whirling down. The air was so full of them that one could see objects only a few feet away.... We children slept soundly on our cold bed of snow with a soft white mantle falling over us so thickly that every few moments my mother would have to shake the shawl—our only covering—to keep us from being buried alive. In the morning the snow lay deep on mountain and valley. With heavy hearts we turned back to a cabin that had been built by the Murphy-Schallenberger party two years before.[15]

Some emigrants constructed tents out of wagon canvas and others built cabins. Many books have since been written about what happened to the stranded emigrants during the weeks that followed. There was cold, starvation, and death, and some of those who survived did so by living off the flesh of those who died. On February 19, 1847, the first of several rescue parties reached the area where the emigrants were located and began to take survivors to Johnson's Ranch. William O. Fallon, an old mountain man and member of the fourth relief party, kept a journal. He described what he found:

Left Johnson's on the evening of April 13th, and arrived at the lower end of the Bear Valley on the 15th. Hung our saddles upon the trees, and sent the horses back, to be returned again in ten days, to bring us in again. Started on foot, with provisions for ten days, and traveled to the head of the valley and camped for the night, snow from 2 to 3 feet deep.

15th. Started early in the morning and traveled 23 miles, snow 10 feet deep.

April, 17th. Reached the Cabins between 12 and 1 o'clock. Expected to find some of the sufferers alive, Mrs. Donner and Kiesburg in particular. Entered the cabins and a horrible scene presented itself,—human bodies terribly mutilated, legs, arms, and skulls scattered in every direction. One body, supposed to be that of Mrs. Eddy, lay near the entrance, the limbs severed off and a frightful gash in the skull. The flesh from the bones was nearly consumed and a painful stillness pervaded the place. The supposition was that all were dead, when a sudden shout revived our hopes, and we flew in the direction of the sound, three Indians [who] were hitherto concealed, started from the ground and fled at our approach, leaving behind their bows and arrows. We delayed two hours in searching the cabins, during which we were obliged to witness sights from which we would have fain turned away, and which are too dreadful to put on record.—We next started for "Donner's camp" 8 miles distant over the mountains. After traveling about half way, we came upon a track in the snow, which excited our suspicion, and we determined to pursue it. It brought us to the camp of Jacob Donner, where it had evidently been left that morning. There we found property of every description, books, calicoes, tea, coffee, shoes, percussion caps, household and kitchen furniture scattered in every direction, and mostly in the water. At the mouth of the tent stood a large iron kettle, filled with human flesh cut up, it was the body of Geo. Donner, the head had been split open and the brains extracted therefrom, and to the appearance, he had not been long dead, not over three or four days at the most. Near by the kettle stood a chair, and thereupon three legs of a bullock that had been shot down in the early part of the winter, and snowed under before it could be dressed. The meat was found sound and good, and with the exception of a small piece out of the shoulder, wholly untouched. We gathered up some property and camped for the night.

April, 18. Commenced gathering the most valuable property, suitable for our packs, the greater portion requiring to be dried. We then made them up and camped for the night.

April 19. This morning, [William] Foster, [John] Rhodes, and J. Foster [Joseph Sels] started with small packs for the first cabins intending from thence to follow the trail of the person that had left the morning previous. The other three remained behind to cache and secure the goods necessarily left there. Knowing the Donners had a considerable sum of money, we search diligently but were unsuccessful. The party for the cabins were unable to keep the trail of the mysterious personage owing to the rapid melting of the snow, they therefore went direct for the cabins, and upon entering discovered Kiesburg lying down amidst the human bones and beside him a large pan full of fresh liver and lights. They asked him what had become of his companions, whether they were alive, and what had become of Mrs. Donner. He answered them by stating they were all dead; Mrs. Donner, he said, had in attempting to cross from one cabin to another, missing the trail, and slept out one night; that she came to his camp the next night very much fatigued, he made her a cup of coffee, placed her in bed and rolled her well in the blankets, but the next morning found her dead; he eat her body and found her flesh the best he had ever tasted! He further stated that he obtained from her body at least four pounds of fat! No traces of her person could be found, nor the body of Mrs. Murphy either.—[16]

Of eighty-nine emigrants who had set out to follow the Hastings Cutoff from Fort Bridger, only forty-five survived. Lansford Warren Hastings was a factor in the Donner tragedy, having touted his shorter route to California. When his guide was published the previous year, he included reference to the route almost as an afterthought. He wrote: "The most direct route, for the California emigrants, would be to leave the Oregon route, about two hundred miles east from Fort Hall; thence bearing west south west, to the Salt Lake; and thence continuing down to the bay of St. Francisco." It is doubtful that Hastings traveled the route before his *Guide* was published. The *Guide*, however, may have been responsible for the Donners deciding to go west. The *Guide* was published late in 1845, and early in 1846 the following notice appeared in the *Sangamo Journal* in Springfield, Illinois:

WHO WANTS TO GO TO CALIFORNIA WITHOUT COSTING THEM ANYTHING?

As many as eight young men, of good character, who can drive an ox team, will be accommodated by gentlemen who will leave this vicinity about the first of April. Come, Boys! You can have as much land as you want without costing you anything. The Government of California gives large tracts of land to persons who have to move there.

G. Donner and Others[17]

Hastings's *Guide* probably was responsible for many of the emigrants going west in 1846, because he said settlers going to California could get as much land as they wanted. Emigrants who might otherwise have gone to Oregon, where the homestead laws limited the amount of land an individual could obtain, were attracted to California instead.

While the experience of the Donner party is only one page in the history of the Oregon Trail, the horrors of the cannibalism that occurred often make it seem more significant than it really was in the trail's broader history. Of far more importance is the fact that about 1,200 emigrants successfully reached Oregon and more than 1,400 reached California that year. As the late Bernard De Voto wrote in his classic book *The Year of Decision, 1846*, that year "best dramatizes personal experience as national experience. Most of the characters are ordinary people, unremarkable commoners of the young democracy."[18]

CHAPTER TEN

NEW ZION,
MORE EMIGRANTS,
AND A MASSACRE

Where there is no vision, the people perish.

Proverbs 39:18

NEWS OF THE DONNER TRAGEDY did not reach Missouri before emigrants began moving west in the spring of 1847. The weekly *St. Joseph Gazette* carried the first reports of what had happened to the Donner party in July, and the stories provided vivid details. If emigrants heading west that year had heard the news before they left, some might not have gone. Apparently none learned about the Donners' fate until later, because the 1847 emigration to Oregon and California was greater than the previous years. The *Gazette* reported in June that 867 wagons had crossed the Missouri River at St. Joseph, while only 433 had departed from Independence, for a total of 1,300 wagons. Figuring there were four emigrants per wagon, the editor concluded that 5,200 emigrants, along with about 13,000 cattle, 1,200 horses, 700 sheep, and 90 mules, had started west by early June.[1]

Most of the 1847 emigrants who were bound for Oregon were encouraged by the news that the boundary dispute between the United States and Great Britain had been resolved. California, however, was not as attractive because the Mexican War was still being fought. No more than five hundred settlers left Missouri for California in 1847, since because of slow communication few knew that the United States had gained control of Mexican California at San Gabriel on January 8, 1847, well before the start of spring emigration. On that day, Americans won a battle with a large force of Mexican troops after Robert F. Stockton, the U.S. naval commander, sent a relief column to aid General Stephen Watts Kearny with his small force of only a hundred dragoons.

In 1847, for the first time, more emigrants chose to cross the Missouri River in the vicinity of St. Joseph than to follow the earlier established Santa Fe Trail west from Independence, which avoided the Missouri River. West of modern Gardner, Kansas, they left the Santa Fe Trail and joined the Oregon Trail, which led to the Kansas River in the vicinity of present-day Topeka, Kansas. About two-thirds of the emigrants probably chose to jump off from the St. Joseph area to avoid having to cross the Kansas River, considered by some emigrants a more difficult crossing than the Missouri. Another factor may have been that since Independence was also the eastern terminal of the Santa Fe Trail, trading and military activity over that route increased considerably in 1847 because of the Mexican War.

By 1847, emigrants had learned that if they could reach specific points along the Oregon Trail by specific times, they would avoid early winter storms toward the end of their journeys. Although not all emigrants used this schedule, many did. Those who did knew that if an emigrant train crossed the Missouri River and started up the trail by about April 15, they could reach Fort Kearny by May 15, Fort Laramie by about June 15, and then arrive at South Pass in early July. If they were able to meet this schedule, they would reach Oregon in early September.

A THIRD MAJOR destination in the West developed in 1847 for emigrants following the established corridor of travel along the Platte River. On April 16, Brigham Young set out west from what is now eastern Nebraska to find a new home for the Mormons. He led a "pioneer band" of 148 persons that included two children and three women, with seventy-one wagons plus a cannon, a boat, nine cows, and seventeen dogs. The previous year, as we have seen, the Mormons left Nauvoo, Illinois, and headed west, establishing a winter camp on the site of modern Omaha, Nebraska. The forty-three-year-old Young was now heading west in search of a new home for the Mormons. His advance party followed the north bank of the Platte River and a few days later met some fur traders who suggested the Mormons cross the Platte and follow the established trail along the south bank. After some discussion the Mormons voted to stay on the north side and away from the other travelers on the south bank because, as William Clayton noted in his journal, "We are making a road for thousands of Saints to follow."[2]

The Mormons followed the north bank of the Platte River and its North Fork to Fort Laramie along what they called the Mormon Trail. English-born thirty-year-old Thomas Bullock, who joined the church in 1841, kept a diary as the pioneer band headed west that became something of the official record of the trek. Two days after starting, Bullock recorded in the daily routine for travel established by Brigham Young:

> At 5 a.m. the Horn should be blown & every man then arise & pray, attend to their cattle, & have every thing done, in order that all may start by seven o'clock. That each extra man should travel on the off side [left] of his team, with his gun loaded over his Shoulder; that each driver shall have his gun so placed that he can lay his hand on it in a moment; that every gun shall have a piece of leather over the nipple, or in the pan of his gun, having their caps & Powder Flasks ready for a moment's warning. The brethren will halt for an hour to have dinner [midday meal], which must be ready cooked. When the Camp comes to halt for the night, the front of every Wagon shall be outward where the fires shall be built; the horses to be secured inside the circle. At ½ past 8 the Horn will be blown when every man must retire to their wagons & pray, & be in bed by 9'clock, except the night guard; all fires to be put out at bed time. All the Camp to travel in close order.[3]

Will Bagley, who edited Bullock's diary for publication, relates that the Mormons in the party started each day with coffee, and later, as some of the Mormons returned east, Young would distribute a canteen of spirits among the brethren. Neither is a modern LDS practice, but in the introduction to his book, *The Pioneer Camp of the Saints,* Bagley wrote: "The 1833 revelation in *Doctrine and Covenants,* Section 89, called the Word of Wisdom, which proscribes hot drinks, tobacco, and alcohol, 'was given as counsel or advice rather than as a binding commandment' and until the early twentieth century observance of this scripture was 'sporadic' among Latter-day Saints. Especially among pioneers and Brigham Young's clerks, the sage advice of the Word of Wisdom was more honored in the breach than in the observance."[4]

As the Mormons pushed westward, Heber C. Kimball, one of the Twelve (Mormon) Apostles, second only to Young, would often go ahead of the main party in his carriage to select the best route. The pioneer band followed on the north side of the Platte River to its confluence with the Laramie River, crossed near the ruins of Fort Platte, and paused there on June 1 and made camp. For a few days the Mormons repaired their wagons and visited nearby Fort Laramie, where James Bordeaux was in charge. There they made a survey of the facilities available for the Mormons who would follow. Bullock visited the store at Fort Laramie and recorded the following prices in his diary: "Sheeting, Shirting, Calicoes & Cottons are [$]1.00 per yard; Butcher Knife 1.00; Robes from 3 to 5.00; buck skins 2 to 5.00;

Mocassins 1.00; Cows from 15 to 25; Horses & Ponies 40; Flour 25 [cents]." At Fort Laramie, Young and the others learned that the "Mississippi Saints," who had come west the previous year and wintered in the vicinity of modern Pueblo, Colorado, were moving north to join their brethren heading west from Fort Laramie.[5]

From Fort Laramie the Mormons started for Fort Bridger, about 350 miles away. They crossed South Pass on June 26 and 27, and then met Jim Bridger at the Little Sandy River traveling east. Bridger stopped to visit with Young and others in authority. When asked about the Great Salt Lake Valley, he praised the country but recommended that the Mormons should settle far to the south in what is now Arizona. Bridger apparently did not want the Mormons settling near him. On Wednesday, July 7, Young and his party reached Fort Bridger, with its two ramshackle log houses and large horse pen. There some of the Mormons traded with French trappers and Indians. After resting for two days, the pioneer band left and traveled in a southwesterly direction. Later, on July 21, Young and the first contingent of Mormons entered the Great Salt Lake Valley. There, Brigham Young declared, "This is the place!" He had decided the Mormons would concentrate on irrigation agriculture and not engage in fur trading, mining, or other endeavors that might lead to rough competition with "Gentiles."

The men began at once to plow and plant corn, beans, wheat, and potatoes and to dig irrigation ditches. A town site was laid out, log buildings were constructed, and a community began to take shape. On Sunday afternoon, August 22, 1847, the Mormons gathered and among other things Brigham Young proposed, "I move that we call this place 'the Great Salt Lake City' of the Great Basin, North America." The name was approved. So was a motion to fence areas under cultivation with adobe walls. The following Thursday, Brigham Young and about a hundred Mormons, wishing to return east to get their families, left the Great Salt Lake Valley and headed back toward Fort Bridger.[6]

In the meantime, about 1,500 Mormons with 566 wagons left their winter quarters and followed the same route traveled by Young's "pioneer band." In the vicinity of South Pass, Young and his returning party met the lead party of the second group of Mormons heading west. Young directed them toward the Great Salt Lake Valley and told them what had been decided. The information was also given to other Mormon parties met along the trail. Isaac Chauncey Haight, one westbound Mormon who met Young's party returning east, noted that while following the Platte River those in authority tried to have the wagons travel five abreast to minimize the dust, but they found it impractical and resumed travel in a single file. Another Mormon, Thomas

Bullock, did something no other traveler going west is known to have done. He tried to plant a hill of corn near each camp, believing those Mormons who later traveled the route might benefit. In contrast, overland emigrants bound for Oregon or California showed little concern for those who would follow them.

On the journey west some of the Mormons in the main body devised a way to measure the distance traveled by their wagons. William Clayton discussed the problem with Orson Pratt and suggested they fix a set of wooden cog wheels to the hub of a wagon wheel in order to record the number of miles the wagon traveled each day. While Pratt was thinking about this, Clayton tied a piece of red flannel to a wheel, counted the 4,070 rotations it made in one day and calculated that since a wheel made exactly 360 rotations for each mile, they had traveled just over eleven and a quarter miles. Meanwhile, at Brigham Young's request, Pratt designed a double endless screw. Then, with the help of Appleton Harmon, they constructed a "roadometer" and attached it to a wagon wheel. Although not a new invention, it counted off the distance like a clock keeping time.[7]

BY 1847, travel along the Platte River and beyond was becoming rather routine. Wagons moving over the route had left a well-marked road in many areas, and emigrant guides provided a great deal of information on where to camp, where to find water, and a host of other details. Based upon the experiences of others who had gone before them, the emigrants knew it might take six months to reach Oregon or California. Of course, the number of days required depended upon the weather, the season of the year, the number of days travelers remained in camp, and the routes that were followed once they reached what is now western Wyoming. It appears that emigrants also felt more confident to start out for Oregon or California without the benefit of an old mountain man or frontiersman to guide them west, although some companies still used guides. Almost anyone who had once traveled the trail was usually thought suitable to serve as a guide. One such company left St. Joseph in late May 1847 with forty-eight wagons and was captained by William Vaughan of Platte County, Missouri. He had gone to Oregon earlier, returned east to get his family, and was taking them back to settle. Three of the wagons belonged to Vaughan, who also took along some cattle and 258 sheep. One hundred of the sheep survived the journey and reportedly were the first blooded sheep to reach Oregon overland.

Another emigrant going to Oregon in 1847 made his mark in a different way. Nurseryman Henderson Luelling, a Quaker from Salem, Iowa, brought his wife and eight children west with an extra wagon loaded with about 700 young plants, including apple, peach, cherry, plum, and pear trees, plus shrubs of all kinds and grape and raspberry vines. Emigrant Ralph Geer later wrote: "That load of living trees and shrubs brought more wealth to Oregon than any ship that ever entered the Columbia River."[8] Perhaps half of his plants survived the journey, and Henderson settled at Milwaukie, near Oregon City, and started a nursery, where he began grafting trees. One of Henderson's daughters married William Meek, who joined the business. In 1850, Luelling's brother Seth came west and joined as well, and by 1853 they had 100,000 trees for sale, selling them for $1.00 to $1.50 each. The Luellings are credited with introducing the Gravenstein apple to Oregon and the famous sweet cherry variety known as the Bing cherry, named for one of Luelling's Chinese workmen.[9]

The only contributions made by many other emigrants was in getting to Oregon, building their homes, raising their families, and contributing to the growth of the future state, but considering the hardships they endured, their contributions were significant. One company of emigrants apparently thought that if they were highly organized the journey would be easier. Captained by Lot Whitcomb, the party left Jackson County, Iowa, heading west, and crossed the Missouri River on May 20, near St. Joseph. Albert Briggs, a member of the company, recalled that they had lieutenants and sergeants and everything in military style, but it took too long to sort out the cattle each morning. So the company split into three divisions and traveled much easier, with fewer problems. The most serious difficulty occurred along the Platte River, when Indians drove off forty head of cattle, but most were recovered.[10]

Hugh Cosgrove, another emigrant traveling in the same company, recalled that it was Pawnee Indians who attempted to stampede the cattle in the vicinity of Castle Rock. Cosgrove recalled that the Indians fled when they saw the emigrants. A little later two men out hunting were surprised by the Indians and forced to disrobe. But they were more embarrassed than injured. Cosgrove remembered that when the company reached Independence Rock, a young girl clambering among the crevices was bitten by a rattlesnake. Large doses of whiskey were administered and, according to Cosgrove, they "neutralized the venom." All of the emigrants in the company made it safely to Oregon.[11]

One insightful account was left by Dr. Benjamin Cory, a physician, who joined a company bound for Oregon. He recalled that one of its members, Wesley Tustin from Illinois, was swept off his horse and killed while crossing the swift upper Platte. Dr. Cory recalled treating emigrants mangled by accidental gunshots, children run over by wagon wheels, and cases of what he described as "prostrate fever" and "bilious remitting fever." He wrote in his journal, "I pull teeth and deal out a pill occasionally free." Near Courthouse Rock he delivered a baby girl in a moving wagon, and as the company followed the Platte River across what is now Nebraska, Dr. Cory noted that the buffalo left enough manure "to fill a bushel basket in two minutes." The manure, often called "buffalo chips," was used to build camp fires when there was no wood. It produced a hot fire. When the company reached Fort Laramie on June 8, Cory said they were treated decently by the agent in charge, but the rest of the crew were "scamps, cheats, and liars." When they got to the Columbia River, they followed the Barlow Road and arrived at the site of modern Portland on October 21.[12]

At least six women either kept diaries or journals or later wrote their recollections of traveling to Oregon in 1847. Elizabeth Dixon Smith left La Porte, Indiana, in early April with her husband and eight children. They reached St. Joseph, Missouri, crossing the Missouri River on June 4, in a company of 140 persons. She remembered that on June 29 the company's work oxen were discovered to be missing, apparently stolen by Indians. When several men went looking for the animals, one man accidentally shot himself to death. He left a widow and six children. With most of their work oxen gone, the emigrants had to hire, borrow, or buy what oxen they could get. They gave begging Indians at Fort Laramie meat, flour, and beans, which the emigrants later found they themselves needed. Another man, the father of six children, drowned as the emigrants crossed the Snake River. A little later a woman in the company broke under the strain of travel and went berserk. Smith said the woman calmed down after "a good flogging." The Smiths left the company at Fort Hall. When she, her husband, and their children reached The Dalles, they and two other families disassembled their wagons to build a large raft to float down the Columbia River. The weather was cold and their food had run out, but the three families reached what is now Portland. Mrs. Smith's husband, however, was very sick. She wrote in her diary: "Ran about trying to get a house to get into with my sick husband. At last found a small leaky concern. He was never out of that shed until he was carried out in his coffin."[13]

One company of emigrants, most bound for California, elected William Wiggins as their captain as they left Missouri. They started with seventy-six wagons, some bound for California, the others for Oregon. When they crossed the Kansas River near present-day Topeka, the wagons were ferried across at a cost of a dollar each. A few days later the emigrants decided to divide into two companies, according to destination. The California-bound company consisted of thirty wagons and forty-five men plus a guide, who was probably Charles Hopper. One emigrant claimed Hopper had made the journey eight times. While this is doubtful, it is known he first went to California in 1841 and returned to Missouri in 1842. Captain Wiggins, who was returning to California himself, took charge of the company. What happened next is not clear, but after the California-bound company reached the Platte River and followed its south bank west, several families took their wagons and left the company. The remaining emigrants began quarreling, and on June 17, Wiggins resigned as captain and left. Later, Wiggins returned, and organized eighteen of the wagons headed for California. But when he decided to follow a cutoff in what is now Idaho, he found the route impassable and turned north, leading the company into Oregon. In time, Wiggins and many of the emigrants with him sailed for California by ship from Oregon. The other California-bound emigrants left the Oregon Trail at either Fort Bridger or Fort Hall and headed southwest. Most appear to have followed the Raft, Humboldt, Truckee, and Yuba rivers to Johnson's Ranch in California, located about forty miles east of Sutter's Fort.[14]

IN LATE SUMMER 1847 the government resumed its plans to establish military posts along the Oregon Trail, and on August 9 a force of mounted volunteers from Missouri gathered at Fort Leavenworth. The year before, Camp Kearny (Fort Kearny) had been established on the Missouri River near modern Nebraska City, but only a log blockhouse had been built before the troops were called to fight with Colonel Kearny's Army of the West. Since then its location had been deemed a poor choice, because military posts were needed farther to the west. Dr. Ludwell E. Powell of St. Charles, Missouri, was elected lieutenant colonel of the new force, which was called the Oregon Battalion. Toward the end of August 1847, the battalion of 477 men, including 25 officers, started northwest for the Platte River to select the site for a new military post along the river. On September 3, however, Powell received orders to send the bulk of the battalion east to Camp Kearny, with instructions that the volunteers were to construct cabins and winter at the post. The remaining seventy men, led by Lieutenant Daniel P. Woodbury and escorted by Andrew Sublette, continued west along the Platte and selected a site west of modern Grand Island, Nebraska. The new post, to be built in 1848, was first called Fort Childs, but when it was constructed the following year, it was renamed Fort Kearny in honor of Colonel Stephen Watts Kearny for his service in the Mexican War.

Some emigrants going west in 1847 made note in their diaries and journals of having seen members of the Oregon Battalion preparing the site for Fort Kearny. Others also reported seeing Kearny, now a brigadier general, along with Lieutenant Colonel John C. Frémont and more than eighty other men, traveling east on the Oregon Trail that summer. Kearny, Frémont, and the others were returning from California to Fort Leavenworth and then east to Washington. After the United States gained control of Mexican California, Frémont was appointed civil governor by Robert F. Stockton, U.S. naval commander in California. Frémont immediately refused to obey General Kearny until orders came from Washington sustaining Kearny. When the two men arrived at Fort Leavenworth, Frémont was arrested and ordered to Washington, where he was court-martialed for insubordination. Kearny went on to become civil governor in Vera Cruz and then Mexico City, but his health was soon shattered by tropical disease. Kearny, who had married Mary Radford, stepdaughter of the explorer William Clark, died on October 31, 1848, at the Clark home in St. Louis. Frémont, convicted of mutiny and disobedience of orders, resigned his military commission and led two more exploratory expeditions to the West between 1848 and 1853, then served briefly as a U.S. Senator from California, and was nominated for president by the Republican Party in 1856, but lost to Democrat James Buchanan.

Kearny and Frémont's party was not the only eastbound group on the Oregon Trail in 1847. Some emigrants who started west from Independence in early May met Pierre D. Papan, Charles Beaumont, and seven other fur traders. They were traveling from Fort Laramie to Westport, Missouri, with three wagons loaded with more than a thousand packs of buffalo robes. Farther up the trail some emigrants ran into Colonel William Henry Russell and a party of eighteen men traveling to Independence. This was the same "Owl" Russell who was captain of an emigrant train in 1846 that went to California. There, Russell had served as secretary of the Territory of California in John C. Frémont's brief administration. Later, other westbound pioneers ran into a party of about fifteen men led by R. H. Holder, who had gone to Oregon the previous year. Some of the men were returning east to get their families. Holder's party made the journey from Oregon to St. Joseph, Missouri, in eighty-three days.

JAMES JORY, bound for Oregon in 1847, was an English immigrant who first settled in New Brunswick, Canada. Finding the land poor, he moved to Missouri, where the land was better, but he soon found he disliked slavery. He then moved to Illinois, where he got married, but since there was a great deal of sickness among the residents, he took his young bride and left Pike County, determined to find better conditions in Oregon. Before departing Illinois, Jory constructed a special wagon that would double as a boat. At Independence, Jory and his wife joined a company of emigrants bound for Oregon captained by Joseph Magone, a young bachelor. Years later Jory would recall that five times Magone had to order the company to stop for twenty-four hours for the birth of a child. At one of the stops Jory became a father. Toward the end of their journey, the party stopped at Marcus Whitman's mission about twenty-three miles east of Fort Walla Walla, the Hudson's Bay Company trading post. Jory recalled that Whitman was "a plain man of medium size and direct manner and speech." Afterward, they followed the Columbia River to The Dalles, where they took a flatboat down the river to the Willamette Valley.[15]

When Jory and the other settlers in the company reached the Whitman mission, they learned there was an outbreak of measles apparently brought by emigrants in an earlier wagon train that had stopped at the mission to have the doctor examine the sick children. Dr. Whitman diagnosed their sickness as black measles and told the parents the disease was relatively harmless, but to keep the children quiet and clean and give them a light diet

This William Henry Jackson painting shows the Whitman mission a few years after it was established by Rev. Marcus Whitman. (Courtesy Scotts Bluff National Monument)

with plenty of water, and they would recover. Whitman's treatment was fine for white children born with natural immunities to it, but black measles was deadly for the Cayuse Indians. The Whitmans had established their mission on Cayuse land in 1836. The Cayuse tribe was small and lived in three nearby villages in lodges constructed of mats. Dr. Whitman treated whites and Indians alike for all sorts of ailments and gradually the mission grew. By late 1847 there were more than seventy persons living at the mission, including the Sager children, orphaned coming west with their parents and left in the care of the Whitmans in 1844 by Captain William Shaw.

When the measles outbreak spread to the Indians, Dr. Whitman was away from home surveying a new trail from Fort Vancouver. When he heard the news, he hurried back and learned that about half of the small Cayuse tribe had died from measles and accompanying dysentery in a matter of weeks. From his arrival more than a decade earlier, Dr. Whitman had been very careful in treating the Cayuses. He learned early it was their custom "to reward a successful medicine man, or *tewat*, with honor and riches, and to kill an unsuccessful *tewat* in justified revenge."[16]

Artist David Manuel of Joseph, Oregon, used historical evidence to accurately paint the Whitman mission as it appeared in about 1846. Today, Manuel's painting hangs in the lobby of the visitors' center at the Whitman Mission National Historic Site, near Walla Walla, Washington. (Courtesy National Park Service, Whitman Mission National Historic Site)

Dr. Whitman's position was made worse by an unprincipled scoundrel named Joe Lewis, a half-breed who claimed to have been born in Canada, grown up in Maine, and to have fought with Frémont in California during the Mexican War. Lewis, who had joined a wagon train at Fort Hall, was left at the mission by emigrants who refused to take him any farther. Although he was described as a troublemaker, Dr. Whitman took him in. Now Lewis saw the possibility of personal gain by spreading discontent among the Cayuses. Lewis believed that if the Indians drove Whitman away, he could plunder the mission. Toward this goal he went among the villages and pointed out that the Indians the doctor had treated were dying, but that the white children at the mission were recovering. Lewis suggested that Dr. Whitman was giving medicine to the whites but spreading poison among the Indians. Some accounts suggest that the Cayuses recalled a story told by Indians along the coast about an Astorian trader, Duncan McDougal, who years earlier had showed them a corked bottle containing what he claimed was deadly smallpox. McDougal supposedly told the Indians they would die if he removed the stopper. The Cayuses knew Dr. Whitman had bottles with stoppers. The Cayuses believed Lewis and began planning how to kill the doctor.

On Saturday, November 27, Dr. Whitman and Henry Spalding rode south from the mission to the Cayuse village on the Umatilla River to treat the Indians. The following day both men visited the lodge of an Indian named Stickus, who had proven to be a friend of the Whitmans. Stickus warned Whitman that his life was in danger and urged the doctor to leave the area until conditions improved. Dr. Whitman took the warning seriously. Because Spalding's horse had fallen on him the day before, he remained in Stickus's lodge, while Dr. Whitman got on his horse and returned to his mission, arriving about ten o'clock that night. He examined the sick children and then had a long conversation with his wife, Narcissa, telling her about Stickus's warning and that he had decided not to leave.

The next morning, Monday, November 29, the weather was cold and foggy as the the daily routine at the mission began. Narcissa, who had not slept well during the night, remained in her bedroom during the morning. Dr. Whitman treated the sick and at one point performed a funeral service for an Indian child whose mother brought the body to the mission for burial. By noon Narcissa was up and helping to prepare dinner, after which she bathed two of the younger Sager children in the living room. Dr. Whitman remained in the house following the noon meal. Too weary to visit the Cayuse lodges, the doctor sat in a corner of the living room, resting and reading. At about two o'clock in the afternoon, two Cayuse leaders,

Tiloukaikt and Tomahas, entered the kitchen. This was unusual. That morning several Indians had been in and out of the kitchen, but now the two Indians walked through the kitchen into the living room and loudly demanded medicine.

Dr. Whitman sprang to his feet and firmly told the Indians not to enter. He said he would get them medicine, but for them to wait in the kitchen. He forced the door closed, bolted it, and then went to a storage cabinet under the stairway where he kept medical supplies. Telling Narcissa to lock the door behind him, he went into the kitchen as his wife bolted the door. The doctor gave the medicine to the Indians and told them how to use it. Tiloukaikt then deliberately got into an argument with the doctor while Tomahas moved behind Whitman, pulled out a tomahawk hidden in his blanket, and struck the doctor from behind. Mary Ann Bridger, who was in the kitchen at the time, ran outside and around to the front door of the living room. Meanwhile, John Sager, who was also in the kitchen, reached for a pistol lying on a shelf. Before he could grasp it, one of the Indians shot him dead.

In a matter of a few minutes the Cayuses killed thirteen of the roughly seventy persons at the mission. In addition to seventeen-year-old John Sager, Francis Sager, two years younger than John, was killed in a schoolroom as he tried to comfort his terrified sisters. Others who died included Joseph Smith, who helped to operate the mission sawmill, and Judge L. W. Saunders, the teacher at the mission school, who was stabbed by a Cayuse as he ran from the school to save his wife at their home. Others killed were James Young, as he drove a wagonload of lumber toward the mission, and Jacob Hoffman, who, with Nathan S. Kimball, was butchering a beef. Hoffman was killed as he tried to defend himself with an ax. Kimball was only wounded, but later, when he disguised himself as an Indian to get water from the river for the children, he was discovered by a Cayuse and killed.

Another victim was Walter Marsh, who operated the mission gristmill. He was shot as he tried to evade the Indians. Isaac Gilliland, a tailor hired to make a new Sunday suit for Dr. Whitman, was killed as he sat sewing. Andrew Rodgers, who was studying for the ministry, was wounded by a Cayuse while near the river. He ran to the mission house and stayed with Narcissa Whitman on the second floor. The Cayuses threatened to burn the house and persuaded them to come outside. Rodgers and Narcissa Whitman slowly walked down the stairs. It was then that Narcissa caught sight of her dead husband. She collapsed. Rodgers lifted her body and placed it on a settee. Joe Lewis, who was in the house, picked up one end of the settee and ordered Rodgers to take the other. Both men carried Narcissa through the kitchen and into the yard, but just outside the door, Lewis dropped his end of the settee and moved away. Indians standing there shot Narcissa and Andrew Rodgers. A Cayuse then grabbed Narcissa's hair, raised her head, and whipped the face of the dead woman over and over with his riding quirt. Rodgers, mortally wounded, lay in the mud for hours before he died. Eighteen-year-old Crockett Bewley and a man named Amos Sales, both ill with the measles, were beaten to death with slats from their beds several days after the massacre.

The Cayuses decided to hold as captives fifty-four women and children, including Catherine, Elizabeth, Matilda, and Henriette Sager, who had survived along with eleven-year-old Mary Ann Bridger, daughter of Jim Bridger, who sent her to the mission school. Like others, she was recovering from the measles. One of the survivors, Mary Mash, whose father was killed at the gristmill, later wrote:

> I was washing the dishes when I heard the report of a gun. It was the gun that killed Gillion [Gilliland], the tailor. He was doing some sewing... when an Indian stood in the door and shot him. At the same time the horrible work was going on outside. I and some others went upstairs where we could look from a window and see a part of the conflict near the doctor's house.... Meanwhile Mrs. Whitman had barred the doors and windows to keep them out of the house—but they broke in anyway. I saw them break into the house, led by Joe Lewis, the instigator of the trouble. There they finished their bloody work for that day.
>
> After the horrible work was done there were nearly 50 widows and orphans in captivity—expecting any time to share the fare of the others, but we were spared—only to endure the fear, suspense and cruel treatment that an Indian is capable of inflicting. For one month the prisoners were kept well guarded and made to work. One old fellow put me to knitting for him a pair of long-legged socks. I got one nearly made when Governor Ogden of the Hudson's Bay Company came to our relief....[17]

After word of the massacre reached Fort Walla Walla, twenty-three miles away, factor William McBean sent a courier with an urgent message to Peter Skene Ogden, who had John McLoughlin's job as factor at Fort Vancouver. Ogden was the only man McBean knew who was capable of negotiating the release of the captives. Ogden sent a note to the governor of Oregon asking that he do nothing to jeopardize ransom negotiations and then took two flatboats loaded with trade goods up the Columbia River. Sixteen French Canadians paddled the bateaux upstream. In early January 1848,

The ruts of the Oregon Trail can still be seen at the Whitman mission, near Walla Walla, Washington. The wagon is a replica. (Author's collection)

Ogden succeeded in negotiating a ransom for the fifty-four captives and then escorted them to safety downriver. The Hudson's Bay Company never billed the Americans for the goods, nor did the Americans ever offer payment. Governor George Abernethy did write Ogden a note of thanks.

The Provisional Government of Oregon declared war against the Indians and sought help from the federal government. Although the treaty signed with Great Britain the year before made Oregon a territory of the United States, officials in Washington had provided no money to organize the Oregon Territory, nor had it accepted the Provisional Government's Code of Laws. The Provisional Government agreed to send a messenger to Washington seeking help. Former mountain man Joseph Meek, who had settled in Oregon about 1841, was chosen unanimously. Meek had been a close friend to the Whitmans, and he had left his daughter Helen Mar Meek with them to be educated in the mission school. Ten-year-old Helen died several days after the Whitman massacre from illness. It happened that Meek was a distant relative by marriage to President James Polk. Meek assured everyone that when he reached Washington City, Polk would listen to what he had to say about Oregon.

With a friend, George Ebbert, an experienced express rider and former employee of the Hudson's Bay Company, Meek left the Willamette Valley

Fort Walla Walla, first named Fort Nez Percé, was built by Donald McKenzie of the North West Company in 1818 near the fork of the Walla Walla and Columbia rivers.
(Courtesy Bill Gulick)

on January 4, 1848, for Washington. Governor George Abernathy intended for Meek to travel by way of California, but Meek and Ebbert knew the Oregon Trail through the Rocky Mountains. The two men, along with a few others, traveled up the Columbia River to The Dalles and on to Fort Walla Walla, which they reached in late February. There they found Colonel Cornelius Gilliam, the highest-ranking military officer in Oregon, and his militia protecting the peace commission that was trying to get the Cayuses to surrender the guilty Indians. At one point Gilliam and his men engaged some Cayuses in battle, killing one chief and wounding another. Gilliam and his volunteer army, along with Meek's party, reached the Whitman mission in very early March. It was a scene of desolation. The houses had been looted, some burned. Bodies and belongings were lying at random. Meek found his daughter's little body dug up by wolves, and with a heavy heart buried it again. He also buried what was left of the remains of Narcissa Whitman but cut a few locks of her hair as memorials for her friends. Meek believed Narcissa was one of the finest women he had ever met.

Some of Gilliam's soldiers escorted Meek's party as far as the Blue Mountains. From there Meek, Ebbert, and a few others made their way to Fort Hall, where they rested a few hours and then pushed on through falling snow. Soon snow was deep and made it impossible for the group to find any

The Great Grave Memorial is the Whitman burial site, located on a rise above the site of the Whitman mission, near Walla Walla, Washington. (Courtesy Bill Gulick)

feed for their animals, which were abandoned. Close to starving, Meek and Ebbert killed a horse, butchered the animal, and ate it in front of a campfire, although the three other men in the party did not like horseflesh and refused to eat it. The travelers then constructed snowshoes of willow sticks and rawhide thongs and continued down the trail. In time, they reached Fort Bridger, where Meek had the sad mission of informing the old mountain man that his daughter Mary Ann had survived the Whitman massacre and had been taken to Oregon City, but several weeks later died from the measles. Jim Bridger gave Meek four good mules and supplies, and the five men in the party took turns riding the mules as they went through South Pass. Near Independence Rock, Meek thought he saw Indian signs, and his party hid in the brush, but they were out of food. At Red Buttes they killed a lone buffalo and again feasted. They began to make better time. At Fort Laramie, the agent in charge gave Meek's party five fresh mules, and they continued their journey. On May 11, Meek, Ebbert, and the others reached St. Joseph, Missouri. In spite of their difficulties, they had covered the Oregon Trail in half the time a company of emigrants would have taken in good weather.

Meek traveled by steamboat to St. Louis, where he met an old friend, Robert Campbell, an Indian trader. After Meek related what had happened in Oregon, Campbell told the local newspapers, and the stories that were published made Meek a personality overnight. From St. Louis, Meek traveled by steamboat up the Ohio River to Pittsburgh, then rode the train to Washington, where he managed to see President Polk soon after arriving because the president's private secretary was also a relative. Meek told the president why he had come. In short order, Polk sent a message to Congress asking for prompt action on Oregon, but politics was slow. It was not until August 1848 that a bill was passed making Oregon a formal territory of the United States; it included what is now Oregon, Washington, and parts of Montana and Wyoming. President Polk appointed Joseph Lane of Indiana as governor. Lane had served as a brigadier general in the Mexican War. Polk also signed a commission appointing Meek as U.S. marshal of Oregon Territory in accord with a petition Meek had carried east signed by 250 persons expressly asking for that appointment.

Meek and Lane headed west. On September 10, both men left Fort Leavenworth with an escort of twenty-four mounted riflemen and a wagon train and set out over the Santa Fe Trail. While the soldiers went no farther than Santa Fe, Meek and Lane continued west following the Gila River across the desert. The journey was difficult, but they reached southern California, made their way north to San Francisco, and took passage on a slow sailing ship, the *Jeanette*, which was packed with miners heading for the Columbia River. It took the ship eighteen days to reach Astoria. When they docked, the new governor and Meek traveled by canoe to Oregon City, arriving on March 2, 1849, only two days before President Polk's term expired. The following day Lane was sworn in as governor, and from the balcony of William Holmes's farmhouse just outside Oregon City, Lane proclaimed that Oregon was now part of the United States.

While Meek had been away, the Cayuse Indians were persuaded to turn over the five Indians responsible for the Whitman massacre. They were brought to Oregon City and kept under guard on an island at the Falls of the Willamette that was connected to the shore by a wooden bridge. A grand jury found true bills against the five Indians and they were arraigned for trial, which did not begin until May 22, 1850. Kintzing Prithett, secretary of Oregon Territory, was chief counsel for the defense, and Amory Holbrook represented the prosecution. Prithett held that the court had no jurisdiction in the case because at the time of the murders, the laws of the United States were not in force in Oregon. Holbrook, however, made the prosecution's case so plain and simple that the jury was convinced of what they had to do before they left the jury box. The Indians were found guilty. Judge Orville C. Pratt then passed a sentence of death on the five Indians, set June 3, 1850, as the date of their execution, and told U.S. Marshall Joe Meek to officiate at their hanging in Oregon City. Hundreds of people came to watch.

Of what happened that day, Meek later remembered: "I brought out the five prisoners and placed them on the drop. Then the chief, Kiamsumpkin, who always had declared his innocence, begged me to kill him with my knife—for an Indian fears to be hanged. But I soon put an end to his entreaties by cutting the rope which held the drop with my tomahawk. As I said, 'The Lord have mercy on your souls,' the trap fell, and the five Cayuses hung in the air. Three of them died instantly. The other two struggled for several minutes—the little chief, Tamahas, the longest. It was he who was cruel to my little girl at the time of the massacre; so I just put my foot on the knot to tighten it, and he got quiet. After thirty-five minutes they were taken down and buried."[18]

While most of the crowd began to move away from the scaffold, a few remained to watch as the five hooded bodies hanging in the sun were removed and taken up Abernethy Road and across the bridge some distance to where they were buried. Weeks later, on July 27, 1850, the *Oregon Spectator* noted in its pages: "The five Indians, whose trial and condemnation we recorded in our last paper, were hung in the 3d inst., according to the sentence of the court. The execution was witnessed by a large concourse of people.... This closes another act in the sad and terrible tragedy."

As for Joe Lewis, the half-breed who had spread discontent among the Cayuses, he was never punished, nor was he ever found. From what is known, he slipped away from the mission with two Cayuses and disappeared. There are many stories about what happened to him. Although unconfirmed, it is believed Lewis later killed his two companions in their sleep and fled with their horses and belongings. Sometime later Lewis supposedly was shot and killed by an express man along a trail in Idaho after he failed to stop and identify himself.

CHAPTER ELEVEN

A LULL BEFORE
THE RUSH

Gold will be slave or master.

Horace

IT WAS LATE JANUARY 1848, when gold was discovered in the American River about thirty miles northeast of John Sutter's fort in northern California. Sutter, who had arrived in California in 1839, built the fort in the Sacramento Valley, amassed thousands of head of cattle, and was building an empire. Several months before the gold discovery, Sutter hired James W. Marshall to supervise the construction of a sawmill on the South Fork of the American River. On January 24, Sutter was sitting at a table in his fort writing a letter when Marshall hurried into the room and put a white cotton rag on the table and opened it, revealing nearly two ounces of gold. Marshall said the gold came from the river the sawmill was on. Sutter took a copy of *American Cyclopedia* from a nearby shelf and looked up gold. He then tested it with aqua fortis, which he had in his apothecary shop, and declared it to be of the finest quality. The next morning Sutter gathered his workers together and asked them to keep the discovery a secret for six weeks so that a large flour mill being constructed nearby could be finished. The workers agreed, but about two weeks later word leaked out and soon made it to San Francisco, where the *Californian*, on March 15, 1848, published the first printed notice of the discovery:

GOLD MINE FOUND: In the newly made raceway of the Saw Mill recently erected by Captain Sutter, on the American Fork, gold has been found in considerable quantities. One person brought thirty dollars worth to New Helvetia, gathered there in a short time. California, no doubt, is rich in mineral wealth, great chances here for scientific capitalists. Gold has been found in almost every part of the country.

The small newspaper story apparently attracted little attention. It was the Mormon Samuel Brannan, publisher of the *Californian*, who made the news come alive. He returned from the Sacramento Valley with a small bottle full of gold, which he waved in the air on the streets of San Francisco, shouting, "Gold! Gold! Gold from the American River!" The small town of San Francisco was soon nearly empty as residents hurried to what soon came to be called the "goldfields." The gold rush had started.[1]

Distance was so great and communications so slow that none of the emigrants preparing to migrate west in April 1848 knew anything about the gold discovery. The first word of the gold did not reach Missouri until October, when the *St. Joseph Gazette* and other Missouri papers printed reports from eastern newspapers of the find. The *Gazette* quoted one account from a Washington, D.C., newspaper that noted, "An immense bed of gold, 100 miles in extent, has been discovered in California." A New Orleans paper described the arrival of a U.S. naval officer carrying dispatches to Washington from Colonel Richard B. Mason, military governor in California. The naval officer was Lieutenant Lucien Loeser, who also carried a Chinese tea caddy containing about 230 ounces of gold. After telegraphing the War Department of his arrival in New Orleans, Loeser lost no time in setting out for Washington. In the meantime, another newspaper story told of B. F. Chouteau's arrival at Santa Fe from California, confirming the discovery of gold and telling how one man had found two pieces of virgin gold worth $2,000. As the news spread over the eastern half of the continent, gold fever began to build. But in St. Joseph and other Missouri towns, many people believed the reports were "make-believe" on the part of the U.S. government to get the newly acquired land in the west "quickly populated." This attitude changed in November when a party from California reached St. Joseph carrying gold. The party included Jacob Wittmer, an employee of John Sutter, who had been sent east to escort Sutter's wife and daughter to California. They were coming to America from Switzerland. The *St. Joseph Gazette*, on November 24, 1848, reported the arrival of Wittmer and others and noted they carried large quantities of "the Feather River gold dust." A chemist in St. Joseph, then a town of more than 1,500, assayed a portion of the dust and declared it "pure gold." As the news spread, the skeptics went quiet.[2]

Exactly how many emigrants left St. Joseph, Independence, and other jumping-off points in the spring of 1848 for Oregon and California is not known, but the total number was significantly fewer than the previous year. The unsettled conditions in the West caused by the Mexican War and word of the Whitman massacre in Oregon Country probably contributed to a waning interest in migrating to Oregon or California.

Thomas Fitzpatrick, who had been appointed head of the Upper Platte and Arkansas Indian Agency two years earlier, returned east over the Oregon Trail early that spring. Three days after passing the forks of the Platte River, he began meeting emigrants coming west. Between that point and Westport, Missouri, Fitzpatrick counted 364 wagons moving quietly in small companies of twelve to thirty. It was still common for emigrants bound for Oregon and California to travel in the same companies. Fitzpatrick figured that if each wagon carried an average of five emigrants, he must have passed 1,820 persons; 1,670 bound for Oregon and 150 going to California.

In retrospect, Fitzpatrick's estimate of five emigrants per wagon was high. From what is known today, a more accurate estimate would be four emigrants per wagon, and using that figure Fitzpatrick probably saw only 1,456 emigrants; 1,340 going to Oregon and 120 heading for California. The *St. Joseph Gazette* which quoted Fitzpatrick's figures, also reported that at least 210 wagons had crossed the Missouri River in the vicinity of the town by May 5, and that another 40 or 50 wagons were waiting to cross on ferries. If correct, about 1,000 emigrants jumped off from St. Joseph and vicinity. The *Gazette* also reported that mountain man Moses Harris, who was guiding one company west, had returned briefly to St. Joseph and reported that all of the companies were doing well except for one still camped about thirty-five miles beyond the Missouri River in what is now Kansas. They had no leader, their oxen had either strayed or had been stolen by Indians, and, according to Harris, the company was in "utter confusion."[3]

In 1848, as in the previous year, more emigrants chose to cross the Missouri River in the vicinity of St. Joseph than to follow the trail from Independence, apparently for the same reasons as the year before, but merchants in St. Joseph were also trying harder to attract the emigrant trade by stressing the town's advantages as an embarkation point. Even men who had gone to Oregon earlier from Independence were now leaving from St. Joseph. These men liked what they found in Oregon, returned east to get their families, and were now going back. But others who had never been to Oregon also chose to depart from St. Joseph. One such emigrant who had heard stories about the rich Willamette Valley was thirty-one-year-old George Belknap, a farmer from Allen County, Ohio. He married twenty-nine-year-old Keturah Penton, also from Allen County, in 1839, and moved to Van Buren County, Iowa, which they apparently did not find to their liking. Between the time of their marriage and 1848, they had four children, but three died. One son, named Jessie, born in 1845, survived. In 1847, George, his parents, Jesse and Jane Belknap, and a few other relatives and friends decided to move to Oregon. George and Keturah began to make plans, and by the spring of 1848 their preparations were under way. In a vivid description of how she loaded their farm wagon for the journey, Keturah wrote in her journal on April 8, 1848:

I am the first one up; breakfast is over; our wagon is backed up to the steps; we will load at the hind end and shove the things in front. The first thing is a big box that will just fit in the wagon bed. That will have the bacon salt and various other things; then it will be covered with a cover made of light boards nailed on two pieces of inch plank about 3 inches wide. This will serve us for a table, there is a hole in each corner and we have sticks sharpened at one end so they will stick in the ground; then we put the box cover on, slip the legs in the holes and we have a nice table, then when it is on the box George will sit on it and let his feet hang over and drive the team. It is just as high as the wagon bed. Now we will put in the old chest that is packed with our clothes and things we will want to wear and use on the way. The till is the medicine chest; then there will be cleats fastened to the bottom of the wagon bed to keep things from slipping out of place.

Now there is a vacant place clear across that will be large enough to set a chair; will set it with the back against the side of wagon bed; there I will ride. On the other side will be a vacancy where little Jessie can play. He has a few toys and some marbles and some sticks for whip stocks, some blocks for oxen and I tie a string on the stick and he used my work basket for a covered wagon and plays going to Oregon. He never seems to get tired to cross.... The next thing is a box as high as the chest that is packed with a few dishes and things we won't need till we get thru. And now we will put in the long sacks of flour and other things. The sacks are made of home made linen and will hold 125 pounds; 4 sacks of flour and one of corn meal. Now comes the groceries. We will make a wall of small sacks stood on end; dried apples and peaches, beans, rice, sugar and coffee, the latter being in the green state. We will brown it in a skillet as we want to use it. Everything must be put in strong bags; no paper wrappings for the trip. There is a corner left for the wash-tub and the lunch basket will just fit in the tub. The dishes we want to use will all be in the basket. I am going to start with good earthen dishes and if they get broken have tin ones to take their place. Have made 4 nice little table cloths so am going to live just like I was at home. Now we will fill the other corner with pick-ups. The iron-ware that I will want to use every day will go in a box on the hind end of the wagon like a feed box.

Now we are loaded all but the bed. I wanted to put it in and sleep out

but George said I wouldn't rest any so I will level up the sacks with some
extra bedding, then there is a side of sole leather that will go on first, then
two comforts and we have a good enough bed for anyone to sleep on. At
night I will turn my chair down and make the bed a little longer so now
all we will have to do in the morning is put in the bed and make some
coffee and roll out.

The wagon looks so nice, the nice white cover drawn down tight to
the side boards with a good ridge to keep from sagging. Its high enough
for me to stand straight under the roof with a curtain to put down in front
and one at the back end. Now it is all done and I get in out of the tumult.[4]

Jesse Belknap, George's father, captained a nine-wagon company of
friends and relatives including his son, daughter-in-law, and grandson Jessie.
They crossed the Missouri River at St. Joseph on a rope ferry apparently on
April 25, leaving earlier than most other emigrants. The Belknaps took three
milch cows. Keturah wrote in her journal what happened with the animals
when they crossed the Missouri River:

The cattle that go as they are in a dry lot without anything to eat. When
they get the cattle on the boat they found one of our cows was sick; she
had got poisoned by eating the Jimpson weeds. She staggered when
walked onto the ferry and in the crowd she was knocked overboard and
went under but when she came up the boat man had his rope ready and
throwed it out and lassoed her and they hauled her to land but she was
too far gone to travel so the boat man said he would take our wagon and
stock over for the chance of her [no ferry toll in exchange for the cow] so
they hauled her up to the house and the last we saw of her a woman had
her wrapped in a warm blanket and had a fire and was bathing her and
pouring milk and lard down her. She could stand alone the next morning
so we bade farewell to the Missouri River and old Brock.[5]

The Belknaps continued their journey with the remaining two milch
cows, which had to be milked each morning and evening. After the evening
milking Keturah would strain the milk in little buckets, cover them, and set
them under the wagon. The next morning she would take off the thick
cream and put it in a churn and place it in the wagon. After riding all day, she
would have a nice roll of butter the next morning, provided the cows had
plenty of grass and water.

The Belknap family appears to have had a mostly uneventful journey,
although they had a little trouble with Pawnee Indians and some white

renegades who tried to steal horses. While at Ash Hollow, Joseph Meek and his party rode into the Belknap camp and told of the Whitman massacre and asked for a meal. Keturah wrote in her journal: "The captain divided them [Meek's party] up so all could help feed them. Father B. [Belknap] was captain so he and George took three so they made way with most all of my stuff I had cooked up; on the whole we are having quite a time; some want to turn back and others are telling what they would do in case of an attack." Before they reached Fort Hall, they joined a large wagon train for protection. At Fort Hall they rested for several days before continuing over the Blue Mountains. They followed the Columbia River down to The Dalles, where the men took the livestock overland and the women, children, and household goods were transported down the river in Indian canoes and floating wagon beds. It was October when they arrived at what became Portland, Oregon, then only a tiny settlement of a few houses and a trading post. They settled on 640 acres in what is now Benton County, Oregon, and built a log house for shelter before winter.[6]

Another Oregon-bound emigrant was William Wright Anderson from Indiana. He joined a company of thirty-five wagons and crossed the Missouri River at St. Joseph. Most of the emigrants in the party were, like Anderson, going to Oregon, but a few had chosen California. The company crossed the Blue River on May 8, and then turned west along the south bank of the Platte River. On June 8, they arrived at Fort Laramie, and thirteen days later camped at Independence Rock. They made good time and several days later reached South Pass. From there they continued on to Fort Hall. Near there the California-bound emigrants left the company. Anderson and the remaining emigrants continued on and took time to stop and pay tribute at Whitman mission on August 28. The emigrants had learned of the massacre when they, too, met Joseph Meek and his party heading over the Oregon Trail. From the Whitman mission they traveled down the Columbia River to The Dalles and then followed the Barlow Road to the Willamette Valley, arriving on September 10.[7]

James D. Miller, who was encouraged to go to Oregon by Joel Palmer, left Fort Wayne, Indiana, with his family in April 1848 and traveled by steamboat to St. Louis. They went overland to Weston and then St. Joseph, Missouri, and organized a company of thirteen wagons with thirty-one men, most with their families, plus two Catholic priests, including Honoré-Timothée Lempfrit, a French Catholic missionary. When they crossed the Missouri River at St. Joseph on May 11, they met Joseph Meek and his party from Oregon and learned of the Whitman massacre. Miller's company was the last emigrant company to leave Missouri that spring. Not too much about their journey is known, but Father Lempfrit wrote in his journal that the charm of Fort Hall "evaporates upon our approach," and he added that the post could be leveled by a bombardment of "baked apples." When the company crossed the Green River on a ferry built and operated by Mormons, the emigrants were told that gold had been discovered in California, but, as Miller wrote, "We did not believe them."[8]

Probably the largest company of emigrants bound for California in 1848 was led by Joseph Chiles, a veteran of the Seminole Wars. Chiles had farmed in Missouri for several years. In 1841 he tired of farming and traveled to California. "Colonel" Chiles, as he was called, returned east in 1842 via the southern route, which included the Santa Fe Trail, and organized a new company with former mountain man Joseph Walker. They headed west in 1843, carrying mill irons and other accoutrements to construct a mill. When the company reached Fort Hall, they were running out of food. While Walker remained with the main body, Chiles took twelve men, left most of the food for the women and children, and set off on horseback. He took a new route around the north end of the Sierra and down past snow-covered Mount Shasta to Sutter's Fort. Meanwhile, Walker took the remainder of the company into California via Walker Pass, which he had discovered in 1834 in modern Kern County, California.

Now, in 1848, Chiles was again going west with a company of emigrants. He left Independence on May 12, and, having heard that Richard May's company wanted to join him, Chiles traveled slowly until May's wagons caught up. May had left his home in Ohio in early April, traveled by steamboat to Independence, and organized a company of 18 wagons with 112 men, women, and children. From one emigrant's journal and the recollections of another, we know something of their overland journey. The company was troubled by Pawnee Indians along the Platte River, and at one point they feared Indian attack when they saw a large party of horsemen in the distance. But the mounted riders turned out to be not Indians but Kit Carson and a party of traders who camped one night with the emigrants. Carson had been in California and was now headed east carrying dispatches to Washington, D.C.

As they traveled west, the emigrants in Chiles's company probably passed twenty-nine government wagons, twelve of which were loaded with artillery and fixtures for Fort Childs. When the emigrants reached Grand Island on the Platte River, they saw volunteers of the Missouri Battalion constructing a sod stable and a storehouse on the site selected the year before for Fort Childs, which was soon renamed Fort Kearny. By late September, troops of the regular army began replacing the Missouri volunteers, who were mustered out of service by November. Chiles's company stopped at Fort Laramie, operated by the American Fur Company, and noticed that nearby Fort Platte, deserted in 1847, was once again in operation. The company continued west to South Pass, where they met mountain men, one with cattle to trade. In the Bear River Mountains of modern southeast Idaho, they ran into Chiles's old friend Joseph Walker at Peg-Leg Smith's crude little trading post. Thomas L. Smith, better known as "Peg-Leg," had established the post in Bear Lake Valley, with horses to trade or sell. Smith, a former mountain man, gained the nickname in 1827 along the headwaters of the Platte River after an Indian shot him in his left leg, shattering the bones above the ankle. Mountain man Milton Sublette, brother of William and Andrew, took his knife and severed the foot.

Chiles's company continued on to Fort Hall. A few families had planned to go on to Oregon, but now, after hearing rumors at Fort Hall that Snake Indians had gone on the war path, they changed their minds. The rumors turned out to be untrue. One Oregon-bound emigrant in Chiles's company was Thomas Stock Bayley, traveling with his young boys to give them "good practical schooling." Before leaving Missouri, the postmaster at Independence asked Bayley if he would carry a pouch of United States mail addressed to people from Independence known to have gone to Oregon. In exchange for delivering the mail, the postmaster said Bayley could collect 40 cents for each piece delivered. Regardless, Bayley and his family joined the others following Chiles and headed for California. On this trip Captain Chiles helped to firm up the alignment of the Humboldt-Carson Route, which the following year would be the principal path followed by gold-seekers to California. As for Thomas Bayley and the mail, he found about half of the able-bodied men from Oregon looking for gold in California. Bayley let it be known that he had Oregon mail in his tent. He collected two dollars per letter from those Oregon men to whom the letters were addressed. The letters not claimed were kept by Bayley for a year and then burned.[9]

While the migration of 1848 was under way, many men in Oregon had rushed south to the California goldfields. Some days after the five Cayuse Indians were hung for their crimes at the Whitman mission, the brig *Honolulu* dropped anchor in the Columbia River, and those on board tried to buy out the Hudson's Bay Company supply of mining equipment at Fort Vancouver. Word had leaked out that gold had been discovered in California. In a matter of weeks, Oregon men said good-bye to their families and headed south to strike it rich. It has been estimated that three-quarters of the male population of Oregon went south looking for gold. Most stayed through the winter and returned to Oregon by midsummer 1849, some successful, some not.

The year 1848 was not unlike earlier years when emigrants moving overland would change their destination, often on a rumor or whim. But this year a new and compelling reason for going to California was to find gold. Pierre Barlow Cornwall, age twenty-four, and his brother Arthur, age sixteen, started out for Oregon. At St. Joseph they became friends with Tom Fallon, who had once worked for the Hudson's Bay Company and in 1843 had been recruited by Charles A. Warfield for the little army of mountain men he raised to fight Mexico. When that enterprise did not work out, Fallon went to Missouri. With Fallon, the Cornwall brothers traveled north to Council Bluffs, joined up with four others going to Oregon, and started west by crossing the Missouri River. At some point along the Platte River, the party of seven men stumbled into a camp of 2,000 Pawnee Indians and were immediately taken prisoner, but after being warned of what would happen to them if any harm came to the white men, the Indians let them go. Later the seven were threatened by Sioux warriors, but the Indians backed off when the chief recognized Fallon as his son-in-law. Fallon had married the chief's daughter the previous fall.

At the Green River crossing they apparently learned of the gold discovery in California, and by the time they reached the Raft River, the Cornwalls, Fallon, and the other men had decided to head for California. Pierre Cornwall, however, had a problem. He carried with him a Masonic charter from the Grand Lodge of Missouri for the newly established Multnomah Lodge in Oregon City, a document he had promised to deliver. Happily he found an Oregon-bound emigrant who gave his word to deliver the charter. It is known that Cornwall also carried with him a Bible, a dictionary, and a copy of *Irish Eloquence,* a book containing the speeches of the celebrated Irish orators Charles Phillips, John Curran, and Henry Grattan, first published in 1833, and a few other books. The Cornwall brothers and the five other men began following the trail to California, but near the modern Idaho-Nevada border, Tom Fallon was killed by Indians. Fortunately, the Cornwalls had a copy of a map published with one of Frémont's reports, which they used to follow the Humboldt and Carson rivers to reach the Sierra Nevada. Going over the mountains through snow was tough. At one point while traversing the Sierra Nevada, they took the wagons apart and carried them. Once they reached a lower elevation on the other side, they put their wagons back together and continued the last leg of their journey. From all indications the remaining six men quickly became gold-seekers, but whether they found gold is not known.[10]

WHILE THE NUMBER of emigrants bound for Oregon and California in 1848 was far smaller than in 1847, the Mormons heading west to the Great Salt Lake Valley more than made up the difference. Brigham Young, with help, organized the emigrants into companies at their winter quarters on Indian land in what is now Omaha, Nebraska, but in response to governmental pressure to leave Indian lands, the Mormons laid out a new town in 1847 called Kanesville, in a hollow below the bluffs on the east bank of the Missouri. The temporary town was named in honor of a gentile friend named Thomas Leiper Kane. Although some accounts suggest 4,000 Mormons made the journey from the Missouri River to the Great Salt Lake Valley in 1848, a more accurate figure seems to be 2,400, with about 700 wagons. As the pioneer band had learned firsthand in 1847, Fort Laramie provided them with a great way station. As with emigrants going to Oregon or California, Fort Laramie provided a break in travel where men could engage in blacksmithing and general repair of their wagons and equipment, conduct trade at the fort, or go fishing. The women could catch up on chores and maybe gather chokecherries in season.

When the Mormon pioneer band stopped at Fort Laramie in 1847, they apparently conceived a plan whereby ox-drawn-wagon supply trains from Salt Lake would meet new arrivals at Fort Laramie. The oxen from Salt Lake had acclimatized to mountain travel. At the fort the arriving teams of oxen were exchanged for those brought from Salt Lake. As a result, the Mormons avoided any serious loss of low-country oxen when they continued on over South Pass and the rugged mountain trails leading to the Great Salt Lake Valley.

Anson Call, a Mormon who left the winter quarters on June 27, later recalled that his company did not travel on Saturdays or Sundays. The only accident he witnessed was when Elisha Grove's wife broke her leg under a wagon wheel; the leg was set by Brigham Young and Call. The accident only delayed the company for about thirty minutes. Another Mormon, Joseph Holbrook, who was traveling with Young's company, had been in business with Anson Call in Missouri. Holbrook recollected that another woman cut her knee with a penknife and died from infection along the Sweetwater River. They carried the woman's body all the way to the Great Salt Lake Valley to be buried.[11]

Another Mormon traveling in Brigham Young's company was Louisa Barnes Pratt, who described herself as the "grass widow" wife of Elder Addison Pratt. He had gone off with the Mormon Battalion during the Mexican War to fight in California. While many Mormons simply abandoned their cabins at winter quarters, she was able to sell hers for $11. Quite depressed when she left camp, her mood improved as the company moved west along the north side of the Platte River. To her the scenery was fascinating. Frequently when the wagons stopped, she would climb steep hills to get a better view of the landscape. When they came in sight of large herds of buffalo, she thought they looked like a company of soldiers moving along.[12]

Peter Wilson Conover was one Mormon who was especially happy to leave the winter quarters. There a fire had destroyed his house, and then his wife had died, leaving him with ten small children. He and his children traveled in a company led by Heber Kimball. Along the Platte River, Indians tried to steal some of the Mormons' cattle. When the men exchanged gunfire with the Indians, a Mormon named Thomas Ricks was shot and fell to the ground. Conover later recalled that he rescued Ricks, placed the wounded man on a buffalo robe, and, with the others, started for their wagons. Several times they had to stop and stand off charges by the Indians.[13]

Another Mormon traveling with Kimball's company was Charles Emerson Griffin, who had one yoke of oxen, at least one cow, and provisions that he hoped would last until he could raise a crop in the Great Salt Lake Valley. Griffin's wagon was colorful but not fancy. Its cover was made of a few strips of carpet and old quilts. In his recollections, Griffin recalled that they kept alive mainly on cornbread because flour for white bread was a rarity.[14]

Among the Mormons leaving winter quarters in 1848 was fifteen-year-old John Smith, the son of Joseph Smith, who had been killed in 1846 by a mob at Carthage, Illinois. John Smith later recalled that the company he traveled with had a great shortage of work cattle. He remembered there were many wolves along the Oregon Trail and his company took extra precautions to guard their oxen. Several times, he recalled, gangs of wolves would howl and fight over the carcasses of emigrant animals that had died. His company traveled down the mountains into the Great Salt Lake Valley on September 23, 1848.[15]

ASIDE FROM THOSE already mentioned, there were other eastbound travelers on the Oregon Trail in 1848, including a company of thirty-six men who arrived at St. Joseph on August 1. They had left Oregon in early May. At about the same time, four men arrived at St. Joseph and then continued to Independence carrying private mail from California, including more than 2,000 copies of a special edition of the *California Star* published on April 1, 1848. On their journey down the Oregon Trail the men had distributed copies to westbound emigrants they met. The paper contained a six-column article on the advantages and disadvantages of California, probably the first mass effort to promote California. The article contained a brief mention of the gold discovery, but perhaps by design its significance was underplayed. Samuel Brannan, a native of Maine and a Mormon, had started the *California Star* early in 1847. From what is known, Brannan encouraged the merchants and property owners in San Francisco, then a town of about 800 people, to purchase copies of the special edition and send them east to attract new residents. Many did, and Brannan hired men to carry the papers east. Probably to defray some of the cost, Brannan said the "California Star Express," as it was called, would carry letters east for 50 cents each and newspapers at 12½ cents each. As many as ten men apparently were hired for the service. Four of them are known to have arrived at St. Joseph and Independence, while two others, both Mormons, went through to Mormon headquarters at Council Bluffs, across the Missouri River, with mail and newspapers. How many letters were sent east with the express is not recorded, but it is known that packets of the *California Star's* special edition were addressed to nearly all areas east of the Mississippi River. One large packet was sent to the National Library, now the Library of Congress, in Washington, D.C.[16]

On November 3, Miles Goodyear, his brother Andrew, and eight other men with 120 horses and packs of pelts arrived at St. Joseph, Missouri. Winter had arrived early on the plains, and Goodyear and the others had suffered from the cold temperatures. About three years earlier, Goodyear had established Fort Buenaventura on the Weber River about two miles above its junction with the Ogden River in what is now Utah. The fort consisted of a log cabin, sheds, corrals, and a garden inside its log walls. Goodyear hoped to capture the trade of emigrants traveling between Fort Bridger and California, but about a year after he established the trading post and before it became a profitable venture, the Mormons settled in the Great Salt Lake Valley. In July 1847, Goodyear tried to entice them to settle on the Weber River but was unsuccessful. Then, in November 1847, James Brown was authorized by the Mormon High Council in Salt Lake City to purchase Goodyear's fort. The two men agreed on a price of just under $2,000 for everything but Goodyear's horses. The Mormons renamed it Brown's Fort. The settlement soon became known as Brownsville and is today Ogden, Utah. As for Goodyear, he then went to California and engaged in horse trading and gold mining, making a rich discovery of gold on the Yuba River at what was called "Goodyear's Bar." Late in 1848 he traveled to Missouri but returned to California the following spring. Later that year he became ill and died in the Sierra Nevada on November 12, 1849, at the age of thirty-two. He was buried at Benecia, California.

By November 1848, merchants at St. Joseph, Independence, and other jumping-off points in western Missouri were hopeful that the migration the following year would be greater than that of the year ending. They became even more optimistic after President James Polk delivered his last message to Congress on December 5, 1848. By then Polk had received the dispatches carried by Lieutenant Loeser and the gold that accompanied them, and he made reference to the gold discovery in his message, saying: "The accounts of the abundance of gold in that territory are of such an extraordinary character, as would scarcely command belief, were they not corroborated by the authentic reports of officers in the public service, who have visited the mineral district and derived the facts which they detail, from personal observations."[17]

When newspapers reported Polk's words, the gold fever increased across the nation, and along the western border of Missouri merchants began to prepare for what they believed would be a rush of gold-seekers heading for California.

CHAPTER TWELVE

THE GOLD RUSH
OF 1849

To get rich, mine the miners!

Anonymous

THE WEATHER WAS COLD as 1849 began in St. Joseph, Missouri. Founded six years earlier, the town already claimed a population of 1,800 and was the fourth-largest in Missouri. It boasted flourishing businesses that included nineteen stores, two steam flour mills, two steam sawmills, nine blacksmith shops, four wagon factories, two tin and sheet ironware factories, two large saddleries and harness-making firms, plus at least three churches. The town's residents were surprised in late January when two rich New York merchants arrived in a horse-drawn sleigh to buy supplies for a winter journey over the Oregon Trail, something the locals would not even attempt. The winter was severe. The Missouri River was frozen, blocking all steamboat travel. To the west and north of St. Joseph, bitter arctic cold and snow were sweeping across the prairie and plains, making travel over the Oregon Trail next to impossible. The arrival of the New Yorkers was noted in the journal of Swiss artist Rudolph F. Kurz, who was then living in St. Joseph. Kurz did not identify the two men, but he noted that they wanted to be the first easterners to arrive in California that year. Whether or not they reached California in their sleigh is not known, but their arrival reflected the intensity of the gold fever that was sweeping the nation.[1]

About two weeks later, copies of the February 7 issue of the *St. Louis Daily Union* reached St. Joseph, Independence, and other towns in western Missouri, and residents read an advertisement placed by the firm of Turner, Allen & Company in St. Louis announcing a "Pioneer Passenger Train for California! Overland by the South Pass." At a date to be announced, the firm would take its train from Independence, Missouri, using covered, elliptic-spring wagons, each seating six persons. The fare would be $200 and include one hundred pounds of baggage per person, and rations for one hundred days.

When residents of Independence read the advertisement, they were already thinking that advertising might help them capture more emigrant trade in the spring. There was a growing rivalry between Independence and St. Joseph. Independence residents knew St. Joseph the previous year had captured much of the trade from Oregon-bound emigrants because of the town's strategic location, and that Independence offered a starting point to California over either the Oregon or Santa Fe trails. William Gilpin and a few others in Independence took out an advertisement in the March 21 issue of the *St. Louis Daily Union* emphasizing their town's advantages for gold-seekers. Gilpin, who had traveled with Frémont in 1843, also had a small circular printed and distributed that described the routes to California.

Meanwhile, from St. Louis to the east coast, publishers were scrambling to print California guidebooks. By March several had been printed and were being sold by booksellers in St. Louis. One St. Louis bookman, John Halsell, advertised Joseph E. Ware's new *Emigrants' Guide to California* for 60 cents in paper and 75 cents in cloth. Ware, who had never traveled to California, compiled the guide by taking material from dated reports published about John C. Frémont's western expedition. Unlike the wordy government reports, Ware summarized the information in easy-to-read prose. Other new guides included Samuel A. Mitchell's *A New Map of Texas, Oregon, and California*, published in Philadelphia; Charles Foster's 106-page *The Gold Placers of California*, published in February 1849 in Akron, Ohio, with a map from Frémont's government reports; Jessy Quinn Thornton's 379-page *Oregon and California in 1848*, which included a map and was published in New York; T. H. Jefferson's *Accompaniment to the Map of the Emigrant Road from Independence, Mo. to St. Francisco, California*, also published in New York, with a summary of the author's overland experiences of 1846; and Ephraim Sandford Seymour's *Emigrant's Guide to the Gold Mines of Upper California*, published in Chicago with a not very accurate map. Seymour had compiled his 104-page guide with material taken from Bryant's book and Frémont's government reports.

Booksellers obtained other books about California printed before the discovery of gold and offered them for sale in newspaper advertisements. Such books included Lieutenant William H. Emory's *Overland Journey from Fort Leavenworth to San Diego*, first published in 1847, describing his 1846 travels. Copies were priced at 25 cents each. Copies of Edwin Bryant's *What I Saw in California*, published late in 1848 and describing his travels in 1846 and

1847, were sold for $1.25 a copy. Some booksellers were able to offer copies of William Clayton's *The Latter-Day Saints' Emigrants' Guide: Being a Table of Distances, Showing All the Springs, Creeks, Rivers, Hills, Mountains, Camping Places, and All Other Notable Places, from Council Bluffs, to the Valley of the Great Salt Lake,* which had been published in St. Louis in March 1848. Clayton's 24-page booklet was to be one of the most valuable guides for emigrants. As many gold-seekers would later write in their diaries and journals, other guides were not of much value once they were on the Oregon Trail.

In New York, publisher George P. Putnam hurried into publication in March 1849 a book containing Francis Parkman's articles published earlier in *Knickerbocker* magazine about the author's travels over part of the Oregon Trail. The book was titled *The California and Oregon Trail;* the word "California" was added to the title to capture the gold-seekers' trade. Parkman had gone only as far as Fort Laramie and had not been to California. Parkman even returned east following the Santa Fe Trail and not the Oregon Trail. Historian W. J. Ghent, in the introduction to his 1929 book *The Road to Oregon,* was critical of Parkman's work, noting that it gives little information on the trail itself:

> Parkman was ill; he was young, and he had not yet developed that first essential of a historian—the spirit of inquiry. On matters that especially interested him he writes with an engaging charm; on all other matters he seems to show the incuriousness of an Indian. He disliked and shunned the emigrants; that constantly renewing company of pioneers that...he found uncouth, intrusive, dour, and unfriendly; and those who invaded Fort Laramie, shortly after his arrival, "totally devoid of any sense of delicacy or propriety." He seems, moreover, not to have had the slightest notion of the significance of the emigration movement.[2]

By the time the ice on the Missouri River began to break up in late March and steamboat travel resumed, copies of many guides were being sold in Independence and St. Joseph, where merchants, mechanics, artisans, and operators of hotels, boardinghouses, and saloons were getting rich as more and more gold-seekers crowded into these towns waiting for the grass to grow on the prairie. Without grass, their oxen, mules, and horses might starve. In letters from the western border of Missouri to the *St. Louis Republican,* a correspondent reported that Independence was the main jumping-off point for easterners and for people from St. Louis, who for the most part arrived there by steamboat. St. Joseph was favored by those coming overland from Missouri and other states. The reporter also noted that the wagons of most emigrants were overloaded and their oxen unseasoned. He wrote that veterans of "mountain service" were predicting disaster for these emigrants, especially "the fools who are drinking, gambling, and whoring, instead of training for the hardships to come." He also reported that there had been several deaths at Independence from various causes, such as falling overboard from steamboats, overdrinking, and street fighting.[3]

The migration got under way on April 16, when Captain G. W. Paul of St. Louis led the first group of gold-seekers west from Independence. The company was made up of ten Missourians and easterners, plus a party from Upper Sandusky, Ohio. The party had to stop fifty miles beyond the Kansas River crossing because the spring grasses were not yet sufficient to feed the oxen. Captain Paul sent someone back to the Kansas River to buy corn for the animals. The country had greened up by the time the company reached the Platte River and the new Fort Kearny. Other companies of gold-seekers had caught up and were just behind them, including a company of men from southern states, and several from Pittsburgh that had left from St. Joseph.[4]

Three days after Captain Paul's company left Independence, Colonel Vital Jarrot of St. Louis led the first company west from St. Joseph with thirteen wagons, most of the emigrants having come from St. Clair County, Illinois. The company called itself the "St. Clair Mining Company." Within a week about 3,000 emigrants were ready to leave St. Joseph. The *Gazette* observed that

> roads in every direction were lined with wagons from the lower counties of Missouri, and from Iowa, Wisconsin, Michigan, and Illinois. A majority of these intend moving leisurely as far as [old] Fort Kearny and Council Bluffs and there make their final start. Roads from Independence, St. Joseph, [old] Fort Kearny, and Council Bluffs connect at Grand Island." At Independence, about 1,000 emigrants were in town from every state in the Union except Delaware and Texas, the most from Ohio. "There were fifty-one in a party from Cincinnati, with ten wagons, twenty tents for sleeping and five large tents to provide shelter while eating. Two of the wagon bodies were made of sheet iron for occasional use as boats; 200 lbs of bread and 28 lbs of bacon for each man and provisions for twelve months after their arrival, had been shipped via Cape Horn.[5]

Sailing around Cape Horn, at the tip of South America, was one way to reach the California goldfields, but it took nearly twice as long as going overland, and the price of a ticket was too costly for most gold-seekers, especially those in the middle of the country who would have had to travel to the east or Gulf coasts to make connections. Another way was to sail to the Isthmus of Panama, go overland to the Pacific, and then hope to catch a ship sailing up the coast to California. This route was both costly and chancy. Following the Santa Fe Trail from Independence to Santa Fe and then continuing westward to southern California was cheaper than going by ship but also chancy because of hostile Indians on the southern plains and the mostly uninhabited desert country in what is now Arizona. While some lesser number of gold-seekers did travel these routes, the cheaper and seemingly the best route followed by most gold-rushers was the Oregon Trail.

By late April, ferryboats in the St. Joseph area were running day and night to transport gold-seekers across the Missouri River. The ferryboat owners took full advantage of the situation and charged $5 to $10 to transport a single wagon and its ox team across the river. The demand for ferry service became so great that the steamboats *Sacramento* and *Highland,* which had come up the Missouri River from St. Louis, even served as ferries while at St. Joseph. Some gold-seekers became impatient waiting and crossed at other places up the river, including Savannah Landing and Iatan, Missouri, and opposite old Fort Kearny above Weston, Missouri. Some gold-seekers gave up and returned east, but exactly how many turned back is not known.[6]

By late April the towns of Independence and St. Joseph were three or four times their normal population. Gold-seekers were everywhere. The steamboats that kept coming up the Missouri River from St. Louis were also packed with "forty-niners," as they were being called. It was inevitable that the crowded conditions and poor sanitation in the towns and aboard the steamboats would result in sickness and disease, and a cholera epidemic that began on some steamboats reached the town of Kansas (now Kansas City, Missouri) on April 25. Dr. Charles Robinson, a thirty-year-old gold-seeker from Fitchburg, Massachusetts, who would later become governor of Kansas, traveling with the Congress and California Mutual Protective Association organized in Boston, was at the town of Kansas when the cholera struck. His services were in great demand, but in one night ten persons died. The town of Kansas had ten stores, several blacksmith's shops, a gunsmith's store, wagonmaker's factories, and three hotels, which were soon deserted after more people died of cholera. The disease quickly spread to nearby Independence and Westport, located three miles south of the town of Kansas, and it soon moved up the Missouri River to St. Joseph and beyond and westward into the Kansas River valley. The cause of cholera was then uncertain, but we now know that it is caused by drinking water or eating food contaminated by the feces of an infected person. Cholera is an acute, diarrheal illness caused by infection of the intestine by the bacterium *Vibrio cholerae*. The infection is often mild or without symptoms, but it can be severe, causing diarrhea, vomiting, and leg cramps. The rapid loss of body fluids leads to dehydration and shock. Unless treated, death can occur within hours.[7]

In early May the *St. Joseph Gazette* reported that six persons who arrived aboard a steamboat had died, and then it reported that cholera had struck Fort Leavenworth, across the Missouri River to the southwest, where twenty-five people died in one day. Business at the fort was suspended. In St. Joseph, and perhaps elsewhere, many gold-seekers who went on drinking sprees and ended up sleeping it off in the streets came down with cholera and died. Down the Missouri River from St. Joseph other gold-seekers died aboard steamboats coming up the river. In one instance thirty-five persons aboard the steamboat *Mary* died before it docked above the town of Kansas. Many Mormon emigrants from England, who had arrived in New Orleans and then traveled by steamboat to Council Bluffs, also died before reaching there. It became a common sight to see a steamboat tied up along the Missouri River and a party of passengers burying one or more victims of cholera. The epidemic was devastating. While it appears that many of the gold-seekers who started west along the Oregon Trail in April may have escaped cholera, others did not. Exactly how many people died of cholera that spring and summer is not known, but the total was at least 5,000 persons. Cholera was found as far west as Fort Laramie on the Oregon Trail, but beyond that point there were few victims. A correspondent for the *St. Louis Republican* figured that there must have been one death for every one and a half miles traveled by the gold-seekers between the Missouri River and Fort Laramie. Few companies of gold-seekers escaped without having one or more members die from cholera before reaching Fort Laramie.[8]

TWO HUNDRED MILES WEST of the Missouri River along the south side of the Platte River was the new Fort Kearny. Situated in the wide Platte Valley with plenty of space around the post for wagons and emigrants to camp, new Fort Kearny was not a fort in the usual sense. There was no wall around it. Some of the buildings were constructed of sod, the rest of wood with dirt floors. They were built around a four-acre square that served as the parade ground. In the center a flagstaff was erected. Cottonwood trees were planted around the parade ground.

Following the discovery of gold in California, the U.S. Army hurriedly made plans to reinforce new Fort Kearny and to establish another post to the west along the Oregon Trail. In early May the Regiment of Mounted Rifle-men and the Sixth U.S. Regiment of Infantry left Fort Leavenworth and started up the trail to Fort Kearny, which was located where the various trails from the Missouri River converged. The first California-bound gold-seekers reached new Fort Kearny on May 6, 1849, and by the end of May nearly 4,000 wagons had passed the fort. By June 23, the number reached 5,516 wagons, not including those that had followed the north bank of the Platte River coming from Council Bluffs. The average number of persons per wagon had declined in 1849, since more men and fewer families headed for California. Several authorities suggest there was an average of only three and a half persons per wagon. If so, at least 19,306 persons would have passed Fort Kearny between May 6 and June 23, 1849. A more accurate estimate of westbound travelers during this period may be at least 25,000. The late Mer-rill J. Mattes, an authority on overland travel, believed that during 1849 per-haps 40,000 people may have traveled the Oregon Trail.[9]

Not surprisingly, most people traveling the route were headed for the goldfields in California. Not more than five hundred chose Oregon in 1849. Gold was a larger attraction than the prospects of life in Oregon. Then, too, the Whitman massacre and a declining interest among people in the East

This painting by William Henry Jackson shows new Fort Kearny, located on the south side of the Platte River about two hundred miles west of the Missouri River. Here, emi-grants are talking to two army officers. (Courtesy Scotts Bluff National Monument)

probably contributed to the drop in the year's migration to Oregon. By mid-October only fifty-five wagons had arrived in Oregon City, and another twenty-seven wagons were reported to be nearby. Farther down the trail a few more wagons were coming up from Fort Hall.

Unlike the gold-seekers who hurried west, most of the emigrants bound for Oregon progressed in a more leisurely fashion. One such emigrant was William J. Watson, who crossed the Missouri River at St. Joseph on May 8. Five days later one man in his company, G. Butler, died of cholera, and he was buried the next day. On May 19, Watson's company traveled with mounted U.S. soldiers heading for Fort Laramie. They reached Fort Kearny on the Platte River on May 26, and Watson wrote in his journal: "The fort is a considerable place: the houses are made of sod and covered with plank. Some garden spots are enclosed with a sod fence. It has a store at which some of our men bought some necessaries very reasonably: Flour $3.50 per bbl.; sugar 61-4 cents per lb. and other things in proportion." They continued up the trail, reaching Fort Laramie on June 14. "It has a store, a blacksmith shop, and a grocery. Five dollars and a half for shoeing a mule, and other work in proportion," wrote Watson, who made little mention of the gold-seekers on the trail. Watson and the other emigrants he was traveling with reached Oregon City on September 13. In his last journal entry Watson wrote that its population was about 1,400 and that the town had nine stores, two churches, two sawmills, two gristmills, two groceries, and two boardinghouses. He described the population as a "mixed multitude; Sandwich Islanders, Indians of several tribes, Mexicans, and Spaniards."[10]

Virginia Watson Applegate and her family also traveled to Oregon. They left Springfield, Illinois, and traveled to St. Joseph, planning a six months' trip to Oregon City. They had four wagons and hired three single men to help with the driving. At St. Joseph they joined a company of fifty-two wagons. Most of the emigrants in it were heading to California. Virginia was only nine years old at the time, but in her recollections recorded much later, she remembered one man who rode horseback while letting his wife yoke up the oxen and then drive them by walking alongside. Virginia wrote, "I had never seen women doing men's work." Virginia and her family reached Oregon safely.[11]

Another emigrant who ended up in Oregon was John McWilliams, leaving from Pike County, Illinois. He traveled with a company of twenty wagons of gold-seekers who waited three days before they could cross the Missouri River at St. Joseph. McWilliams recalled that every gold-seeker seemed to have a butcher knife in his belt and carried bacon, coffee, calomel, quinine, and gold pans. McWilliams had planned to go to Califor-

This painting by William Henry Jackson depicts Mormon wagon trains on the east bank of the Missouri River at Kanesville (Council Bluffs) approaching a river ferry. (Courtesy Scotts Bluff National Monument)

nia and find gold, but when the company reached Fort Hall, six of the nine wagons he was traveling with decided to go to Oregon. He joined them.[12]

The year also saw more Mormons heading for their promised land in what would become Utah. From their new headquarters at Kanesville, Iowa, on the east bank of the Missouri River, about 1,500 Mormons in five units, or wagon trains, went west in 1849, but those who started early soon found they did not have the route along the north bank of the Platte River to themselves. More than 3,000 gold-seekers were also traveling that route. While the Mormons still referred to the route as the Mormon Trail, others began calling it the Council Bluffs Road. While many Mormons died of cholera coming up the Missouri River to Kanesville on crowded steamboats that came to be called death ships, William I. Appleby and his wife somehow avoided the disease. The Appleby family came from Philadelphia, and as they traveled up the river, William's wife gave birth to a daughter. All three arrived safely at Kanesville, where Appleby became clerk of Ezra Taft Benson's company of Saints bound for Salt Lake City. The company, largely made up of Welsh and Norwegian converts, headed west on July 14, the last of the five Mormon emigrant trains to head for Salt Lake City that year. They crossed the Missouri River at what was called the Upper Ferry, a simple rope ferry with a flatboat large enough to carry two wagons, located about ten miles above Kanesville. They reached Fort Laramie on September 15. At Independence Rock they were met by a relief train from Salt Lake City carrying provisions and with fresh oxen. Because it was late in the year to be traveling, they were caught by snow and suffered from the cold, but they safely reached Salt Lake City on October 27.[13]

THE WINTER OF 1848–49 had been severe, and many Pawnee Indians on the plains had died from starvation. They abandoned their village located about seventy-five miles east of new Fort Kearny on the Platte River because of frequent raids by the Sioux, their enemy. The Pawnees established a new village at the mouth of the Saline River, about eighty miles west of the Missouri River, but by spring had resumed their roaming to the west along the Oregon Trail. While some of the Pawnees were helpful to the gold-seekers, the diaries and journals of the travelers leave no doubt that not all were. In fact, some gold-seekers described Pawnees as masters of horse stealing. The Indians would also often beg or try to trade with the whites along the trail. In 1849, guidebooks warned the gold-seekers that Indians would steal. Travelers were encouraged to guard their animals and camps every night. They were also warned not to wander away from their camps alone because they might be robbed. Many guidebooks also emphasized that most Indian attacks came not along the Platte, but toward the end of the journey in Oregon or California.

Many gold-seekers became annoyed when Indians came up and begged or tried to trade. Many whites, inexperienced with Indians, thought their begging and trading were nothing more than attempts to steal something. There are several accounts of gold-seekers writing on paper a message to a pestering Indian that supposedly attested to his good character. The Indian, who could not read, would smile and proudly take the paper and leave. But in truth these "begging papers," as they became known, were not what the Indian thought. When he showed the paper to the next gold-seeker he met, that person would read something different. One such paper read, "This is a bad Indian; he will steal anything he can lay his hands on. Look out for him." Another had the simple message "Give this old devil hell if he comes around you he is an old thief." While there were many rumors of Indian massacres in 1849, they were nothing more than rumors. Although one study indicates that thirty-three gold-seekers were killed that year, nearly twice as many Indians were killed when attempting to steal horses or other possessions of the gold-rushers.[14]

One gold-seeker, in a letter written on May 18 and later published in the *St. Louis Republican,* related that his company, while traveling along the trail, watched as a small band of Pawnees, fleeing from a larger party of Sioux Indians, tried to find refuge with the emigrants. He told how they watched the Sioux kill and scalp all of the Pawnees except for one squaw who escaped with her son. The son was taken prisoner but was rescued by men from one of the emigrant companies.[15]

Exactly how many forty-niners kept diaries, journals, or sent letters home recounting their experiences up the Oregon Trail is not known. More than two hundred diaries and journals are known to exist, not counting those persons who later wrote recollections of their journeys. A majority of the diaries and journals provide scant details, but many gold-seekers recorded the names of their companies, names that often indicated where they were from. One such company was the Battle Creek Mining Company from Michigan. When the fifty-seven men in the company left Battle Creek, a brass band escorted them out of town. They traveled by steamboat from St. Louis to St. Joseph, where they outfitted their company and then crossed the Missouri River. Some days later a violent storm wrecked their tents and wagon covers. One member of the company, George P. Burrall, wrote in his diary that "the elephant is in the neighborhood," meaning they had nearly had enough and almost returned home. The phrase "seeing the elephant" became closely associated with the gold rush, but its use went back to at least 1834. It was best defined by George Wilkins Kendall in his *Narrative of the Texan Santa Fé Expedition,* published in 1844: "When a man is disappointed in anything he undertakes, when he has seen enough, when he gets sick and tired of any job he may have set himself about, he has seen the elephant." When the Battle Creek Mining Company reached the new Fort Kearny, Burrall noted in his diary that about fifty government wagons were preparing to take supplies up the Oregon Trail to Fort Hall. The company reached Sacramento safely in mid-October, but whether any of the members struck it rich is not known.[16]

Another company with an interesting name was the Washington City and California Mining Association. They assembled in the nation's capital on Lafayette Square, just across the street from the White House. Before they left, President Zachary Taylor gave them his blessing. The company consisted of ninety-two men and two ladies. Leaving Washington on April 2, they traveled by railroad to Pittsburgh, where they took a steamboat to St. Louis and then St. Joseph, Missouri, arriving there on April 27. Because the St. Joseph crossing was jammed with emigrants waiting to cross the Missouri River by ferry, the company headed north and crossed north of

St. Joseph, about eight miles below old Fort Kearny, and then pushed westward along the Platte River. The Washington City and California Mining Association had been organized by J. Goldsborough Bruff, who had been a civilian topographical engineer with the U.S. Treasury Department. Bruff had taken leave to go to California. The company passed the deserted Pawnee Indian village and then came to new Fort Kearny. They apparently had no difficulties traveling along the Platte River to Fort Laramie. On the Sweetwater River, they observed U.S. troops searching for deserters from Fort Laramie who apparently had taken off for California to find gold. It took Bruff's company twenty days to travel from Fort Laramie to South Pass. There, Bruff and others saw the debris that emigrants had thrown away to lighten their loads. Bruff wrote in his diary on July 2, 1849:

> In this extensive bottom are the vestiges of camps—clothes, boots, shoes, hats, lead, iron, tin-ware, trucks, meat, wheels, axles, wagon beds, mining tools, etc. A few hundred yards from my camp I saw an object, which reaching proved to be a very handsome and new Gothic bookcase! It was soon dismembered to boil our coffee kettles.[17]

Since the company had not found any buffalo chips in the vicinity of South Pass, the wood from the bookcase provided them with needed fuel for their fire.

When Bruff led the company over Lassen's Cutoff, early winter snows trapped their wagons in drifts on a ridge above the Feather River. Bruff volunteered to remain with the wagons while the others promised to send help and continued on. Later Bruff reached the gold fields in California. Nearly one year and a half after arriving, Bruff returned to his government job in Washington, D.C. The Lassen Cutoff followed by Captain Bruff was blazed in 1848 by Peter Lassen, who had received a 26,000 acre Mexican land grant. He established Lassen's Rancho in the upper Sacramento Valley. The route included a rough and perilous three-mile canyon through which the rocky-bottomed Pit River flows, and it required emigrants to cross the river many times. One of the men who started out with Captain Bruff's company was Henry Austin, a physician, who like most doctors going overland spent a great deal of time treating emigrants for illnesses. Two other doctors traveled with another company that left St. Louis. One was named Caldwell, the other Allen McLane. They apparently had been partners in a St. Louis practice. Little is known about them, but Captain Bruff found Caldwell's diary in an abandoned wagon in his winter camp. One entry indicates that Caldwell sold opium, then widely used, to an emigrant near Devil's Gate. In another entry Dr. Caldwell wrote that he was "too busy with teams to tend much to sickness." Still another physician known to have traveled the Oregon Trail in 1849 was Dr. Charles R. Parke, Jr., who went with eight other men in three wagons from Como, Illinois. The Como Pioneer Company, as they called themselves, traveled overland to St. Joseph, crossed the Missouri River north of there, and followed the Platte River west. Dr. Parke tried to help four dying Indians at the Pawnee village on the Platte and treated many emigrants for smallpox and cholera. Like Dr. Caldwell, Dr. Parke used opium to treat many patients. The company stayed on the old and better-known route along the Humboldt River to the sink, and then to California over the Sierra Nevada.[18]

Another California-bound physician who kept a diary was Charles E. Boyle, who joined another party of gold-seekers and left Columbus, Ohio, in early April 1849. Called the Columbus and California Industrial Association, they traveled by steamboat from Cincinnati to Missouri. They reached Independence, Missouri, aboard the *John Hancock* on April 15. Boyle wrote in his diary:

> The village of Independence is situated three miles from the river. Along the landing there are a few log and frame houses and [a] short distance back of these there is a steep hill.... After breakfast Decker [a friend from Ohio] and I started for town and found the road hilly and not very good.... We passed several encampments of California emigrants, mostly from the Buckeye state. When we reached the town I was well pleased with the location and apparent thrift and neatness of the place....
>
> In the vicinity of the town there were, according to the most authentic accounts, from 1,500 to 2,000 Californians encamped.
>
> Independence would be a pleasant place of residence and were it not for the institution of slavery I might at some future day make this or some other place in Missouri my home. After an hour's stay in town we returned to the boat.

The next morning the *John Hancock* left Independence and continued up the Missouri River, passing Fort Leavenworth. At noon the steamboat stopped at Weston, Missouri, which Boyle described as "a flourishing and neat village." Boyle noted in his diary that when the steamboat moved up the river, "sometimes the passengers would whoop at the Indians we saw on

This view of gold-seekers working a stream in California was painted by William Henry Jackson. (Courtesy Scotts Bluff National Monument)

the river bank. One old Indian saw a man looking at him with a telescope and probably mistaking it for a gun, hid himself in double-quick time, but of course no shooting was done. We occasionally fired our guns at geese, ducks, and pelicans, but as the boat jarred very much and we were at a great distance, we did nothing much more than scare them some."

At dusk the *John Hancock* came in sight of St. Joseph, Missouri. By then it was raining. Boyle and others went into town to find lodging, but the town was full and they returned to the steamboat for the night. Boyle was then called upon to treat a man who had been kicked by a mule. It was a few days before Boyle and the others organized their party and were heading northwest across what is now Kansas by late April. A few days later Dr. Boyle and others in his Ohio party joined a company from Illinois, expanding their group to fifteen wagons, ten belonging to the gold-seekers from Ohio.

On May 7 they passed the intersection of the Independence route and moved toward the Platte River, reaching Fort Kearny on May 14. In his diary

Dr. Boyle noted that he met "a Negro interpreter, who was born in St. Louis but had been raised among the Indians. He spoke English, French, and several other Indian languages, and had been to Paris, France. He told me that he received a pension from the government for the share he had in perpetrating an Indian treaty and was also appointed interpreter at a salary of $300 per year. After this who dares say that Republicans are ungrateful! From this man I learned a great many curious things about the trading customs and superstitions of the Indians."

Dr. Boyle and others in the company met Indians and did some trading as they pushed westward along the south bank of the Platte River. When they reached buffalo country, Dr. Boyle tasted the meat of that animal for the first time. "Some of the buffalo meat I ate raw, it was good and sweet, and when cooked looked much like beef and tasted so nearly like it that it would be difficult to distinguish between buffalo and tough beef." On the afternoon of May 27, about thirty days after leaving St. Joseph, Dr. Boyle wrote that there was nothing but grass and prairie flowers on the level or rolling prairie. He then observed that as they crossed a small stream they spotted a solitary tree some distance from the trail. Dr. Boyle wrote:

> After we had passed this stream four or five hundred yards, Tommy Davis, who was behind the rest of the company, fired his gun, swung his hat, etc. Several of us started back running, supposing he had got into trouble, but when we came back he informed us that all the rumpus had been made to call our attention to a bale of buffalo robes in the tree top.
>
> This we decided to be the final resting place of a defunct Indian, but he could not be convinced until we had found a similar bale in the hollow of the tree, which we unrolled and found to be the remains of a papoose, dressed in a suit of grave clothes made of fine buffalo and deer skin, elaborately ornamented with beads and other trinkets, and thus kept they slept—the child in the hollow of the tree and the brave on the branches.

By June 2 the company reached the junction of the Platte and Laramie rivers. Some of the men crossed the Laramie River to visit Fort Laramie. But, as Dr. Boyle wrote, "No trading could be done here as they of the fort had all they wanted and nothing more." Near where the company camped, they found things abandoned by other gold-seekers. Dr. Boyle noted: "Some of them were abandoning their wagons and everything else except the most absolutely necessary articles of provisions and clothing." Fourteen days later they reached South Pass, where the doctor wrote in his diary that some members of the company were sick with "Mountain Fever." He added, "I indeed began to feel the effects of the attenuation of the atmosphere producing difficulty in respiration as far back as Fort Laramie, and many of the other boys have felt its inconveniences as well as myself. The feeling is of want of a sufficient amount of air."

When they reached Fort Hall on June 29, they stopped for a few hours "to regale ourselves on bread and milk as these articles could be had here in great abundance. A Mormon family had moved hither from Salt Lake City for the purpose of supplying emigrants with articles of this kind and had brought a very large number of cows. Butter was very scarce as they sold it as far as they could make it. Cheese brought 25 cents per pound, milk 12½ cents per quarter." A few days later Dr. Boyle and the others left the Oregon Trail and reached California in mid-August. The doctor spent a little time searching for gold, with scant success. He decided it was more profitable to practice medicine. Later he and several friends constructed a sailboat, launched it in San Francisco, and spent two years exploring the Pacific coast. They went south, came around Cape Horn, and eventually sailed up the Atlantic coast to Norfolk, Virginia. From there he returned to Columbus, Ohio, and resumed the practice of medicine. He served as surgeon of the Ninth Ohio Regiment during the Civil War before his death in 1868.[19]

WHEN GOLD-SEEKERS became ill on the trail, they could only hope their friends would take care of them. William E. Chamberlain and five other men started for California riding mules and carrying their belongings on the backs of other mules. They made good time, especially along the Platte River, where they covered up to forty miles a day, passing at least a thousand wagons before reaching the South Fork of the Platte River. But along the trail four men in the party either deserted or died, leaving Chamberlain and one other young man to go it alone. At Fort Laramie, Chamberlain began suffering from exhaustion, exposure, and a cankerous mouth. At the upper Platte crossing, he came down with severe diarrhea that knocked him flat. His lone partner abandoned him to his fate, but another gold-seeker from Virginia traveling in a horse-drawn buggy took pity on him and took him to find a doctor in one of the many companies on the trail. The doctor put Chamberlain on a diet of laudanum (opium), brandy, and Sappington pills, concocted by Dr. John Sappington, a Missouri country doctor. Each Sappington antifever pill contained one grain of quinine, three-fourths of a grain of licorice, and one-fourth grain of myrrh and the oil of sassafras to give it an agreeable odor. By the time the Good Samaritan's buggy reached Independence Rock, Chamberlain could walk again. He continued to improve and successfully reached Sacramento on August 19, after following the Humboldt-Truckee Route.[20]

Edwin Bryant, who had gone to California in 1846 and returned east to write the book *What I Saw in California,* was among the gold-seekers heading west in 1849. He led a pack-mule train of Indians and some Kentuckians that left from Independence on May 8. There were about sixty men in his company, which apparently was not given a name by its members. But another group of men from Michigan, each having paid $85, created a stock company with the name Wolverine Rangers. Judge James D. Potts was their captain when they left Independence. They reached California.

Then there were the Colony Guards, a group of men from New York City, who arrived at Independence aboard the steamboat *Alice* and then organized their company. Each man was reportedly armed with a government rifle, a bowie knife, and a Colt revolver, and unlike many other gold-seekers, they took wagons pulled by mules and each man rode a mule. J. W. Berrien, a gold-seeker from Indiana, described the New Yorkers as "green as a pumpkin vine," but on the trail beyond Fort Kearny, Captain J. Goldsborough Bruff ate a meal with them and described them in his journal as "a very clever set of adventurers."[21]

Although there is no record of exactly how many California-bound gold-rushers gave up and turned back, most who did were either discouraged by the hardship or fell ill. One man who turned back for a different reason was Almarin B. Paul, apparently a wealthy merchant who had traveled from New York to St. Louis. There, as an investment, he purchased $10,000 worth of hardware and gave orders to have it shipped via New Orleans, apparently to New York. Paul then went by steamboat up the Missouri River to St. Joseph. There he joined another gold-seeker, a Dr. White, who had a "commodious buggy, several ladies, and three black servants" for what Paul believed would be a "jolly time crossing the plains." The small party got as far as the Blue River in modern northeast Kansas when a messenger from St. Louis caught up with Paul and told him the business in St. Louis from whom he had purchased the hardware had failed. Paul left Dr. White and returned to St. Louis hopeful of salvaging his investment. A little later Paul returned to St. Joseph by steamboat, only to find cholera killing two hundred people a day. He later recalled that everyone on one steamboat from St. Louis that he had seen had died from cholera. Instead of trying to go overland to California, he returned east as quickly as he could and later went to California by way of Panama.[22]

Not all gold-seekers were as lucky as Almarin B. Paul. A man identified only as Frank traveled with fifteen other men from Painesville, Ohio, in what they called the Ashtabula Company. They reached St. Joseph and organized their outfit, crossed the Missouri River, and followed the trail to where it joined the trail from Independence. There, Frank died following an attack of bilious fever. His grave is today about four miles west of the trails' junction. Others in the company wrote letters to Frank's relatives in Ohio advising them of his death and asking that they auction his belongings and send the proceeds to them in California. It is not known what happened.[23]

WHEN THE GOVERNMENT sent troops from Fort Leavenworth to rein-force Fort Kearny, some of them were ordered to establish a second post to protect emigrants at or near Fort Laramie. If necessary, Lieutenant Daniel P. Woodbury of the Corps of Engineers was authorized to purchase the build-ings of Fort Laramie, about 670 miles west of the Missouri River. Woodbury traveled as far west as Big Sandy Creek, a few miles from modern Farson, Wyoming, before he and Major W. F. Sanderson, commander of the Mounted Rifles, concluded that Fort Laramie was the best site for a military post. First called Fort John, it was soon named after the nearby Laramie River. The river, in turn, was named for an early fur trader named Jacques Laramee, a French Canadian, who was killed by Indians about 1820. The fort, indirectly named for him, marked the end of the High Plains for westbound travelers and the beginning of the climb to the Rocky Mountains. The traders at the fort in 1849 soon realized that it was also an appropriate place for gold-seekers who were sick or tired and ready to return home and end their west-ward journey. For those continuing, Fort Laramie was also the place to lighten their loads and prepare for the mountain journey ahead. Sanderson and Woodbury came to an agreement with Bruce Husband, an agent of the American Fur Company, to purchase the post. Elijah Bryan Farnham, a gold-seeker from Ohio, happened to approach Fort Laramie on June 16 as Major Sanderson and his troops were arriving. Farnham wrote in his journal:

> Started at sunrise. Came to Laramie creek [river], one mile from the fort, that we had to ford.... Other trains that had gotten there earlier had to take their turn, and there was quite a number. Our hearts were high in anticipation of getting to the fort. Here among this multitude all was excitement to get across. Something was ahead, it seemed like a gala day, as a convention.... Then the sound of the cannon, that was fired to greet the arrival of Major Sanderson, came booming from the fort.... We

found [Fort Laramie] to be a place of no very imposing structure and appearance.... The inhabitants of this fort consist at this time of about 18 to 20 traders and trappers, regular old "hosses" as they term themselves. Some of these have squaw wives living here at the fort and are a rough, outlandish, whisky drinking, looking set.... Major Sanderson is to take possession.[24]

Ten days later, on June 26, 1849, the papers were signed and the government formally purchased Fort Laramie for $4,000. Major Sanderson soon garrisoned the fort with two companies of mounted riflemen and one company of Sixth Infantry troops plus eight heavy 12-pound howitzers and ammunition. The walls around Fort Laramie were twenty feet high and constructed of sun-baked adobe bricks with bastions on two diagonally opposite corners. Inside the walls were several adobe buildings. The soldiers soon began to make improvements.

From all indications the American Fur Company was pleased to sell Fort Laramie to the government. While they had conducted a moderately brisk business with emigrants and more recently with gold-seekers, fur trading at the fort had declined since the early 1840s. The American Fur Company, however, moved about fifty miles east of Fort Laramie and established a new trading post at Scotts Bluff.

Exactly how many gold-seekers reached Fort Laramie in 1849 before the government took possession is not known, but those who came afterward were undoubtedly pleased to see the Stars and Stripes waving in the breeze over the fort. They were also pleased to find the fort's sutler, John S. Tutt, selling goods, and to see that set up around the fort were numerous retired mountain men turned traders to sell and barter. Many gold-seekers took time at the fort to write letters and send them east. In July one traveler identified only as "Joaquin" sent a letter to the *St. Louis Republican* advising that between St. Joseph and Fort Laramie he had counted fifty-eight graves. He wrote that the wagon trains had to leave the regular road and travel two or three miles for grass to feed their animals, and that he had seen many graves far off the trail. He specifically mentioned four graves at the upper crossing of the South Platte River, and he noted that he accidentally discovered eighteen more graves in the vicinity. He said the bodies had been buried together. Joaquin added: "The greatest fatality was among Missourians and western people generally. The epidemic [cholera] was scarcely felt at all among the people from the eastern states, because they were well equipped and had all kinds of medicines."[25]

Joaquin made it safely to California and on August 19, 1849, sent another letter east describing what he had seen between Fort Laramie and California:

From Laramie grass began to fail for our stock, and the utmost diligence had to be used to sustain them. From thence after the first fifty miles, dead cattle and fragments of wagons come in sight, and as far as here [Green River, California Territory], I have counted about one thousand wagons that have been burnt or otherwise disposed of on the road. Destruction seems to have been the prevailing emotion of everybody who had to leave anything on the trip. Wagons have been wantonly sacrificed without occasion by hundreds, being fired for the apparent purpose of preventing them from being serviceable to any body else, while hundreds have been used by piecemeal for fuel at nearly every camping ground by each successive train.

From Dee Creek to the summit [South Pass], the greatest amount of property has been thrown away. Along the banks of the North Platte to where the Sweetwater road turns off, the amount of valuable property thrown away is astonishing—iron, trunks, clothing, &c., lying strewed about to the value of at least fifty thousand dollars in about twenty miles. I have counted about five hundred dead oxen along the road, and only *three* mules. The reason of so many wagons having been disposed of, was the apparent necessity of *packing*, in order to insure a quick and certain transit to the mines; and people did not care for the loss of any personal goods, so they reached *there*.

Many of the St. Louis boys have left their names and respects to any of their friends behind, on the smooth trees and rocks along the road, and it is sometimes cheering to see a well known name penciled at a crossing or watering place.

Death seems to have followed the emigration out thus far, although in a mitigated degree as to numbers. Eight or ten of those below are buried in the Pass, and there are some others also who have no identity on their graves.[26]

From one of Joaquin's letters and accounts of other gold-seekers, we know something of Turner, Allen's "Pioneer Passenger Train," the commercial venture that was advertised about six months earlier in a St. Louis newspaper. While no diary or journal from anyone who traveled with the train has been found, the firm's covered, elliptic-spring wagons pulled by mules were delayed in leaving the Lone Elm campground southwest of Independence because several passengers died of cholera. Twenty passengers, no more than six persons to a wagon, finally left on May 13. Two passengers who were ill remained behind only to die from cholera a few days later. Moses "Black" Harris, who came down the trail from the Fort Laramie area with a load of furs in April and was now going back, was hired to guide them to California. Initially progress was slow because of rainy weather and more sickness. When the wagons reached the Black Vermillion River on about May 29, another passenger, C. M. Sinclair, died of bilious fever and was buried. On June 8 the wagons reached Fort Kearny, where someone traveling in the train reported that eleven passengers had died of cholera up until that time. They reached Fort Laramie on June 27, apparently without any other passengers dying, and the wagons reached California on October 12. Newspaper stories indicate that the firm sent a second "Pioneer Train" west from Independence on about June 18 with seventy-five passengers. The second train, with less heavily loaded wagons, arrived at Fort Kearny in about two weeks, reached Fort Laramie on August 17, and crossed into California late in October. From all indications, Turner, Allen & Company was the first commercial venture to carry passengers across the plains and mountains in the West over much of the Oregon Trail.[27]

CHAPTER THIRTEEN

THE HECTIC YEAR
OF 1850

*The use of traveling is to regulate imagination by reality, and instead
of thinking how things may be, to see them as they are.*

Samuel Johnson

W HEN EMIGRANTS first started west over the Oregon Trail, they
could not ignore the vast distances they had to traverse, the breadth
of the land with its broad horizons, and the time required to cross the
prairies, plains, and mountains to reach Oregon or California or Utah. The
emigrants talked in terms of taking months to complete their journeys,
unlike today, when we talk of covering the same distances in a matter of
hours by air, or in days by auto. In 1850 the pace of travel over the Oregon
Trail was slower than that of steamboats plying the Missouri River or the
railroads that were beginning to crisscross many areas of the East. That year,
however, the closest railroad to Missouri was in Illinois, where only III miles
of track ran west from Springfield.

Lawmakers in Congress wanted to improve communication in the West
and had discussed building a railroad linking the Atlantic to the Pacific
before the California gold rush, and even before the Oregon boundary question was settled in 1846. In fact, Dr. Hartwell Carver first proposed a
transcontinental railroad in 1832, as did George Wilkes in his 127-page book
The History of Oregon, published in New York in 1845. That year Asa Whitney,
a New York merchant active in the China trade and a distant cousin of Eli
Whitney, inventor of the cotton gin, petitioned Congress for a charter and
grant of a sixty-mile strip through the public domain to help finance the
construction of a transcontinental railroad.

Whitney wanted the line to run from Prairie du Chien, Wisconsin, westward across the Rocky Mountains north of South Pass. In 1849 he published
a report titled *Project for a Railroad to the Pacific with Reports and Other Facts*

Relating Thereto. At the same time, others expressed their own ideas about where a Pacific railroad should run, including Missouri Senator Thomas Hart Benton, who wanted the line to start at St. Louis. Congress did not act on Whitney's proposal, but he and others succeeded in making the Pacific railroad one of the great public issues of the day. Everyone seemed to agree that such a railroad was needed, but there was no agreement on where it should start and where it should end. All of the talk offered no consolation to the emigrants who in the spring of 1850 were gathering at various jumping-off points for their long and tedious journeys west.

Many emigrants were consumed with gold fever, which continued to sweep the nation. In fact, some people thought there might be gold in what is now Kansas. A Missourian named Smallwood Noland organized a party of men and traveled about 160 miles west of Independence to see if rumors of gold along the Kansas River were true. They found none and returned to Independence in May 1850. One Missourian then observed: "The grand bubble of the gold mines on the Caw River, or Kansas, is exploded at last. Those who went out there some weeks ago to dig for the 'dust' have returned with their 'pockets full of rock,' but they happen to be not of the right sort."[1]

People in the East who did not go west in search of gold were anxious for news of those who did. Horace Greeley, editor and publisher of the *New York Weekly Tribune,* had correspondent Ralph Ringwood report on the year's westward migration. From St. Joseph, Missouri, on January 18, Ringwood wrote Greeley: "From present appearances, it is likely that the overland emigration for California will commence here at least a month earlier than last season. The Missouri River opposite this town has never once been closed over since Winter set in, and we have every indication of an early Spring."[2]

A little more than a month later the *St. Ange,* the first of 226 steamboats that would arrive at Weston, Missouri, in 1850, brought emigrants bound for the California goldfields. Weston was twenty-five miles south of St. Joseph and across the Missouri River just northeast of Fort Leavenworth. It was founded after two young dragoons from the fort went up the river in a canoe in 1837 to explore the river. They found a bay and went ashore. They decided the spot would be an excellent place for a steamboat landing or a ferry. Soon they bought a little property in the area and then sold some lots, establishing the town of Weston, Missouri. It grew rapidly and by 1850 had about 1,400 residents and had become of some importance as a jumping-off point for emigrants, but its ferryboats—flatboats propelled with oars—were slow. In March, nearly three weeks after the first steamboat arrived at Weston, two steamboats, the *Haydee* and the *Cora,* arrived at St. Joseph, the first of many to dock there that year. Their captains reported the river was in "good boating condition."[3]

Writing from St. Joseph on March 19, Ralph Ringwood reported to the *New York Weekly Tribune:* "With the opening of steamboat navigation they [the California-bound emigrants] have been pouring in upon us, and a few of them are now ready for their long tramp.... As yet the arrivals are confined chiefly to those who have come from our ground [Missouri].... Some will leave as early as the 1st of April, taking along corn enough to last their cattle and mules [until there is grass to sustain them]."[4] Emigrants from more distant places began arriving by steamboat in late March. For instance, the steamboat *El Paso* carried more than two hundred on her first trip up the river, and the *Melodeon* carried about three hundred passengers, most bound for California. It was described as "one of the roomiest boats on the river."[5]

While Ringwood simply sent straight news reports to Greeley's *Weekly Tribune,* another newspaper correspondent sought to promote Independence over St. Joseph. Identified only as "California," he wrote in the March 7 issue of the *St. Louis Missouri Republican* that Independence was the best place to leave from. Independence merchants then distributed printed circulars encouraging California emigrants to depart from their town. To alleviate concerns about delays in crossing the Kansas River, the circular emphasized that twelve new ferryboats would be operating at the river crossing by the time the first emigrants arrived.[6]

Merchants in St. Joseph apparently were not overly concerned about losing the emigrant trade. Their town continued to grow and a second newspaper, called *Adventure,* was started. The new paper and the older weekly *Gazette,* started in 1845, continued to promote the town as the best jumping-off point for California and Oregon. Because gold-seekers had experienced delays the previous year in crossing the Missouri River because there were not enough ferries, St. Joseph businessmen took steps to enlarge the ferry service. In its March 24 issue, the *Gazette* reported: "There are now at this land three large flat boats, and a new and excellent horse boat, and a steam ferry boat will be here in April next. In addition to the above, there are two new flat boats at the ferry a few miles above St. Joseph."

As might be expected, new emigrant guidebooks appeared early in 1850. One was written by Major John Stemmons of Rocheport, Missouri, and published in St. Louis. Titled *A Journey to California* and containing the author's account of a trip to California in 1849, it sold for 35 cents and was being sold along the western border of Missouri. It undoubtedly contained Stemmons's description of the route traveled, his experiences, and information on what emigrants should take with them. But no copy is known to have survived.

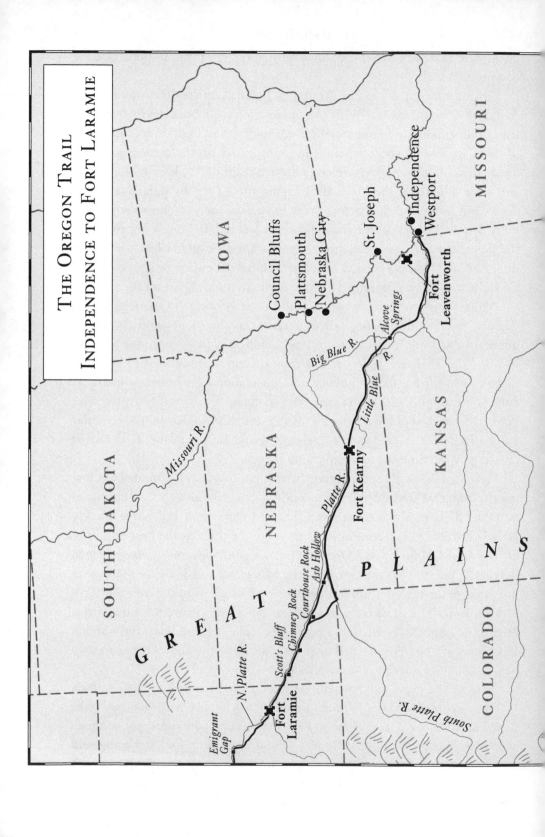

THE OREGON TRAIL
INDEPENDENCE TO FORT LARAMIE

Another book was G. S. Isham's *Guide to California, and the Mines, and Return by the Isthmus,* published in New York. The author, whose home was in Michigan, had traveled from St. Joseph to California in 1849 and kept a journal that was used as the basis for his guide. Still another book that many emigrants apparently used was Riley Root's *Journal of Travels from St. Joseph to Oregon . . . Together with a Description of California,* published at Galesburg, Illinois. The 143-page book related details of Root's journey to Oregon in 1848 and a trip to California in the spring of 1849.

Most of the guidebooks, including those published in the spring of 1850, provided advice on the equipment and provisions emigrants would need on their journey west. The publishers of these books were not the only entrepreneurs seeking to take advantage of the thousands of emigrants heading west over the Oregon Trail. In addition to government-operated stores at Fort Kearny and Fort Laramie, private entrepreneurs established trading posts along the trail. For emigrants leaving from Independence, the first place where they could purchase a few provisions was Union Town, located on a hill one mile south of the Kansas River about fifteen miles west of modern Topeka, Kansas. The settlement had grown up around a government trading post established there in 1848 for the Pottawatomie Indians. Located at what became known as the upper crossing of the Kansas River, a ferry was soon established there, and by 1850 it was a popular crossing point. The rush of 1849 naturally attracted more traders, and by the spring of 1850, Union Town had perhaps half a dozen. The settlement itself had a population of about 300 people, mostly Indians. There were fifty log houses, and the government station there had a physician, two blacksmiths, a wagonmaker, two gunsmiths, and a circular sawmill.

There appears to have been much less trading activity at the lower crossing, located about fifteen miles to the east of the site of present-day Topeka, where the Papan ferry was located. Union Town, however, was a better stop for emigrants, since provisions could be purchased there. Between Union Town and Fort Kearny on the Platte River, there were no established trading posts in 1850. From Fort Kearny they had to travel three hundred miles before finding another trading post. The first was Fort John, operated by Andrew Drips for Chouteau & Company and located about four miles off the Oregon Trail in Helvas Canyon. Many emigrants did not take time to travel the extra distance to Fort John unless they definitely needed supplies or repairs, but those who stopped there found a blacksmith and a few log cabins where some goods were sold, plus nearby Indians who often traded with the emigrants. Eight miles to the west on the trail at what was called Robidoux Pass, near Scotts Bluff, was a trading post established by Joseph E.

This painting by William Henry Jackson shows the road through Mitchell Pass in Nebraska, in the vicinity of Scotts Bluff. (Courtesy Scotts Bluff National Monument)

Robidoux that captured much business from the emigrants. It had cabins, a blacksmith shop, and a store. After the trail shifted from Robidoux Pass to Mitchell Pass in 1852, the Robidoux trading post was relocated there.

The next post was thirty miles west at Ash Point. It had only one building with a small stock of provisions offered for sale by John Richard. It was sometimes referred to as Fort John. Richard did not capture much emigrant trade. The same is true of another trading spot farther west built on the site of old Fort Bernard and operated by Joseph Bissonette and James Bordeaux. Few emigrants stopped there because the post was only eight miles from Fort Laramie. The next post west of Fort Laramie was Fort Bridger in what is now southwest Wyoming, which supplied mostly California-bound emigrants. If emigrants went south from there, they could also find provisions and make repairs in Salt Lake City. Emigrants following the Sublette Cutoff, west of South Pass, were able to turn south and go to Fort Bridger or turn northwest toward Fort Hall, where provisions and wagon repairs could be found. Beyond Fort Hall, emigrants bound for Oregon could stop at Fort Boise, constructed in 1834 by Thomas McKay and in 1850 controlled by the Hudson's Bay Company. Between Fort Boise and the Willamette Valley there was only Fort Walla Walla and a new U.S. Army outpost called Fort Dalles, both located on the Columbia River, where supplies could be obtained. For those going to California following either the Hudspeth Cutoff from Fort Hall or the Hastings Cutoff west from Salt Lake City, there were no trading posts before California unless emigrants took the Carson Route. After crossing the Humboldt desert and striking the Carson River, they found Ragtown, the first water stop. From all accounts Ragtown was not a town but a rest stop before the emigrants started over the Sierra Nevada. Occasionally a trader would have provisions to sell, but in 1850, Asa Kenyon had not yet built his trading post in the vicinity. That came four years later. A little farther west, Mormon Station would be established in 1852 where Genoa, Nevada, now stands. John and Enoch Reese, Salt Lake City merchants, established a trading post and began planting wheat, corn, barley, watermelons, and turnips nearby, giving rise to agricultural production in the area.

Exactly how many emigrants headed west over the Oregon Trail in 1850 is not known, but from the daily counts made by soldiers at Fort Laramie, at least 50,000 or more men, women, and children followed the trail that year, or at least twice as many as in 1849. A majority headed for California, but at least 6,000 headed for Oregon, a substantial increase over the 500 emigrants of 1849 bound for the Willamette Valley. The following newspaper reports give some sense of the numbers:

April 5—Several hundred emigrants have arrived at this place during the past week. The season's first ox train with 10 wagons captained by D. Burroughs of Kendall County, Ill. is scheduled to leave St. Joseph. Burroughs and 19 men arrived here March 17. (*St. Joseph Gazette*)

April 12—This place is all bustle at this time with emigrants for California. From the best estimate that can be had, there have been 8,200 arrivals at this place, and a great many of them have crossed over the river and started on their journey.... There are in this place and across the river encamped, about five thousand. None of the Missouri boys have gotten here yet, except some five or six from Ralls County. (*St. Joseph Gazette*)

April 19—During the past week upwards of three thousand California emigrants have arrived at this place by land and water. From the best estimate we can make, we supposed upwards of eight thousand have arrived at this place, during the present spring. (*St. Joseph Gazette*)

April 23—The larger portion of the emigration go this year with American horses. How the experiment will succeed is doubtful. (Ralph Ringwood, *New York Weekly Tribune*)

April 23—The Californians still continue to pour into this place in one constant stream.... A few days since I crossed the Missouri to visit them at their encampments, I found it impossible to make out a list of the companies.... From the river bank out to the bluff, a distance of some five-miles, their camps are strung all along.... As near as it can be computed there are now 1,000 wagons between this point and Grand Island [Fort Kearny]. Most of them carry with them corn sufficient to feed their cattle on for three weeks. Over 5,000 persons have already rendezvoused at this point alone. One of our papers sets it down at 8,000.... Among those now here are a few from the western part of New York. The Eastern emigration overland is small in comparison with that from the Western States. (Ralph Ringwood, *New York Weekly Tribune*)

April 26—From the best estimate we have been able to make, 15,000 emigrants have made this place a point of departure for California... and about 3,000 teams are reported to be at Council Bluffs.... It is estimated that at least 15,000 will leave this state [Missouri] alone and we think the balance of the states will swell the number of 50,000. (*St. Joseph Gazette*)

May 3—Since our last paper [April 26] went to press some 8,000 emigrants have arrived at this place—mostly emigrants from Missouri. More than half, who have crossed [the Missouri River], are going across the plains with horse teams. This we presume is owing to the scarcity of mules and oxen in Michigan, Iowa, Wisconsin, Illinois and Indiana, where a large majority of the emigrants are from. From the best information we can obtain there are about 1,500 emigrants at Independence, 1000 at [the Town of] Kansas, 3 or 400 at Weston and about 10,000 at Council Bluffs. Up to the present time some 20,000 emigrants have arrived at this place by land and water and they will still continue to arrive in large numbers. (*St. Joseph Gazette*)

May 6—The great rush of emigration appears now to be over; yet still they are pouring in by thousands.... During the two weeks last past there were more arrivals than in any proceeding ones.... Just across the Missouri—almost within stone's throw of us—there is now in the midst of the [Kansas] wilderness the hum and bustle of a great city. Not less than 10,000 emigrants are encamped in the woods on the opposite bank. The poor Kickapoos and Pottawatomies [a band of that nation living with the Kickapoos]... gaze upon the crowd and their doings with wonderment.... Since this letter was commenced, several hundred emigrants who had got out as far as 300 miles (beyond Grand Island), have returned, and are now recrossing with their teams. They report that they saw the 'Elephant,'—head, tail and all—large enough to satisfy them. To-morrow their teams will be sold at auction [and they will return home]. (Ralph Ringwood, *New York Weekly Tribune*)

May 13—From Independence to St. Joseph, the country was full of emi-grants. Hundreds left from every starting point, anxious to be on their winding way, though the grass is scarcely above the ground. Vehicles of almost every size and shape, from a wheelbarrow to an old hackney coach, have been put in requisition, with animals from the diminutive Indian poney, with a pack-saddle, to the spirited gelding.... The num-ber of emigrants are variously estimated at from 20 to 40,000. (*St. Louis Intelligencer*)

May 17—California emigrants continue to arrive overland with teams in great numbers. Those starting from St. Joseph may be set down at thirty thousand persons, from points above, to Council Bluffs, about ten thou-sand. The number of animals will average more than two to each person, say from one hundred thousand to one hundred and twenty-thousand horses, mules, and oxen, will be taken on the plains from the States this spring. Those arriving now cross the river immediately, three ferries—one steam ferry boat and four flats—have been constantly employed for the last four weeks. (*St. Joseph Adventure*)

May 29—Our town [Independence] is yet quite crowded with emigrants, the numbers passing through greatly exceed our anticipation, and from every enumeration we can make we are firmly of the opinion that they are more in number by one-third than passed through here last spring. (*New York Weekly Tribune*)

July 11—The last company of California emigrants numbering near thirty men and some 50 or 60 horses left the Missouri River at this place [Council Bluffs] the latter part of last week [about June 12].... This brings up the rear of about 4,000 wagons, ten or twelve thousand persons and eighteen or twenty thousand head of horses, cattle, &c.... [All of them] have crossed within a scope of twenty-five miles of this place, numbering nearly six times as much as the emigration of last year.... [The Mormons have taken] some 500 or 600 wagons and teams, besides large quantities of cattle, sheep, hogs, poultry, &c. (*St. Louis Intelligencer*)

The hardships, the mass of humanity pushing westward, the congested trail conditions, or maybe homesickness caused many emigrants to turn back. How many turned around and headed for wherever they came from is not known, but these "gobacks" or "turnarounds," as many emigrants called them, often complained that there was either little or no grass for their animals or that there was too much cholera or that the Indian threat was too great. The grass did come late in 1850, and cholera became a serious problem once the weather warmed, but the Indian threat was less than in 1849 because most Indians had moved away from the trail for fear of cholera. The Cheyennes went to the South Fork region for the summer, while the Sioux moved into the Sand Hills of what is now northern Nebraska. Many of the "gobacks" were probably simply ashamed that they had given up and embellished their reasons for returning east in an attempt to explain their actions to emigrants still heading west.

Late winter storms struck the jumping-off points of St. Joseph, Independence, and Council Bluffs in 1850. Ralph Ringwood wrote in the *New York Weekly Tribune* on May 6 that "ice to the thickness of an inch formed in the Missouri, and in the vicinity of Council Bluffs boats experienced considerable difficulty in navigating, owing to the large masses of it floating in the river." The following day, May 7, Eleazar S. Ingalls, an Illinois lawyer heading to California, wrote in his journal, while camped on the Missouri River bluffs about six miles west of St. Joseph, that he experienced "a bad night last night, it rained and snowed nearly all night. Had about two inches of snow on the ground this morning."[7]

As in 1849, cholera did take a heavy toll among the emigrants in 1850, but because spring was late in arriving in northwest Missouri, the starting towns were spared serious outbreaks. The worst cholera outbreak occurred among emigrants as the weather warmed after they were on the trail. In a letter written from a camp about 110 miles west of Fort Kearny on June 9, one emigrant wrote of cholera breaking out following a "terrific thunder storm on the afternoon of June 3. Rain fell all night." He went on to say that cholera appeared in every train in Plum Creek valley (a popular campground thirty-five miles from Fort Kearny) from June 1 to June 7; he had counted forty graves in sixty miles. On June 7, about fifteen miles west of Plum Creek, he saw three wagons, with only one man able to sit up. That man was one of twelve persons in a small company from Missouri. Six of the party had already died and been buried; four others were dying of cholera, one had measles, and the man in question was well but could scarcely stand from fatigue. After traveling another 130 miles up the trail, the same emigrant wrote on June 16 that sixteen out of seventeen persons in one company were sick, and another seven had already died and been buried. He noted that he saw five graves beside one tent that was still standing and another tent that had been struck. He wrote that he believed 250 persons had died between Plum Creek and where he finished his letter.[8]

Another emigrant, identified only by the initials R.H.D., in a letter written from ten miles west of Fort Laramie on June 25, observed that his company had traveled on the north side of the Platte River "where emigration was less and water better" and not a single case of cholera occurred. He added:

> Most physicians along the road believe the disease which has prevailed among emigrants with such fatality, to be epidemic cholera. Of this I am somewhat incredulous. Certainly, local causes sufficient exist on the Platte to produce, if not the most violent forms of darrhoea [diarrhea], to incite, at least, the most latent predisposition to cholera into unrestrained action. The entire Platte bottom is covered with saline matter, such as salt-petre, Salaratus, &c. The springs are also strongly impregnated with sulphur, copper, &c., (I have used no analysis but that of

The restored soldiers' bar at Fort Laramie is today a favorite stop for visitors, but only soft drinks can be purchased. Tending bar in period dress is Dean Herschberger. (Author's collection)

taste). Add to this the first emigration-sunk wells in the bottom. Into these had accumulated the filth and scum which 30,000 persons had left along the road. The use of this filthy water, together with exposure and unwholesome diet, are sufficient, in my opinion, to account for all the sickness which has occurred.[9]

R.H.D. may have been a physician. When his company crossed the Laramie Fork, he was called to see a sick man who had been traveling with his wife and seven children. "His case I considered then almost desperate, but by close attention might have been saved. Several days after, I chanced to see him again. As I sat by his side with my finger on his sinking pulse, and heard in his throat the death-rattle, that most ominous sign to the physician of approaching dissolution, his wife, with a smothered groan, asked me to tell her precisely his condition, saying she wished to know the worst. I told her she should not flatter herself any longer with hope, but be prepared for the worst. I arose to leave the tent, and as I did so returned the fee I had received on a former occasion, and I let drop a tear in sympathy for her desolate and bereaved condition. God grant I may not, on this trip, be called upon to perform such another duty."[10]

Dr. Samuel Matthias Ayres, who is identified as a physician, provided another account in a series of letters written to his wife in Pettis County, Missouri. Dr. Ayres left Independence in a small company of eighteen men with five wagons. He reported that cholera was at its worst along the four hundred miles between Fort Kearny and Fort Laramie, where it began to decline. Dr. Ayres wrote to his wife that "some doctors charge more than at home but not me" because money was scarce. While one man in his company died from cholera and was buried near the South Platte crossing, Dr. Ayres informed his wife that the first casualty he saw was a young man who had been shot while in camp. The boy had crept into the sleeping quarters of a young woman, and when he was discovered, her father shot him. Dr. Ayres reached California safely in mid-September.[11]

Parties of Mormons who jumped off from Kanesville (Council Bluffs) also experienced the horror of cholera. Sopia Lois Goodridge was traveling with her parents and five sisters and a brother to Salt Lake. They had traveled west from their home in Lunenberg, Massachusetts, and departed Kanesville on June 7. Sopia kept a diary, which included these matter-of-fact entries:

June 25. Crossed the creek this morning. Passed 5 graves. They died the 15th of June. They all had grave tablets made of wood rudely hewn, and the name engraved with a knife. A verse was written on the grave of

M. Dona, which was very touching. We crossed three more creeks today without accident. Went ten miles and camped at Weeping Water Creek.

June 26. We traveled ten miles today. Passed three graves. No names on them. Came up with a Government Company. One man sick with cholera. Died and was buried in the forenoon. In the afternoon, passed three more graves, no names, died June 22nd. One of our company took sick with the cholera. Camped at Salt Creek.

June 27. Sister Green [Mary Ann Gibson Green] died of cholera this morning. Brother Blazerd taken sick. Crossed the creek and went on to the bluff and camped for the night. The first fifty caught up with us today. They are on the other side of the creek. One man sick with the cholera among them.

June 28. We started about noon and traveled six miles and camped on the open prairie without wood or water. Found water about one-half mile from camp. Passed the grave of a child.

June 29. Our company all in good spirits this morning and I feel grateful of my Heavenly Father for his kindness in preserving us from accidents and dangers of all kinds. We traveled eight miles and camped on the open prairie without wood or water, except what we brought with us. There is nothing to see but one boundless sea of grass, waving like the waves of the sea, and now and then a tree. We had a very heavy thunder-shower this morning.

June 30 [Sunday]. Jane Green [daughter of Mary Ann] died of cholera this morning. She was 18 years old. Our fifty came up with us this morn-ing. They had buried Brother Smith this morning. The rest of the camp all well. We went four miles and camped where there was wood and water. We killed a rattlesnake.

July 1. Joseph Green died this morning, age 19 months, making three out of one family that have died within five days. Came up with our first fifty. Found Brother [Joseph] Hall dead with cholera. Our camp allicted and distressed. We felt like humbling ourselves before the Lord and pray that he might turn from us the sickness and distress. We therefore met together, the speakers exhorint us to be diligent in our devotions and united. A vote was taken to that effect. They then called upon the Lord in prayer that He would bless and preserve us on our journey to the valley [Salt Lake]. We then started on our journey rejoicing. We met the mail from the Valley. Brother Crosby and seven other missionaries on their way to England. We were very glad to see them. They brought cheering news from Salt Lake which caused us to rejoice. We traveled six miles and camped on the prairie.[12]

Compared to 1849, 1850 was much worse in terms of emigrant deaths along the Oregon Trail. Merrill J. Mattes wrote, "An estimate of 5,000 trailside deaths, or one out of every ten or twelve emigrants, seems to be a conservative one."[13]

The year 1850 saw a significant change in the pattern of travel to the west of Fort Laramie. Until then nearly all emigrants traveling along the north bank of the Platte River crossed to the south bank at Fort Laramie, believing that further progress along the north side was dangerous and not possible. This notion was encouraged by traders and a few of the soldiers at Fort Laramie to ensure that emigrants would patronize the ferry over the Laramie River. Some emigrants believed that some of the soldiers at Fort Laramie were silent partners in the ferry business. But in June 1850 emigrants Byron N. McKinstry, Vance L. Davidson, Andrew Child, and a few others bound for California left their Upper Mississippi Ox Company and continued on their own along the north bank of the Platte, proving the rumors wrong. Child, who kept a journal, sent a copy home to his brother in Wisconsin, where it was published in Milwaukee in the spring of 1852 under the title *Overland Route to California; Description of the Route, Via Council Bluffs, Iowa: Keeping the North Side of the Platte River, for the Whole Distance*. In his guide Child wrote at what he listed was mile 515¾ of his journey:

RIVER OPPOSITE FORT LARAMIE. The Fort is a mile and a half west of the river, on Laramie Fork, a beautiful and clear stream that flows into the north fork of the Platte, from the south-west. The Platte is here sometimes fordable, but more often otherwise, and owing to the great rapidity of its current, it is unsafe to ford, except in very low stages of water. The route we followed from this point, was still upon the *north side* of the river, which route was then [June 1850] untraveled and unknown. We, however, encountered no serious obstacle, and gained two days in time upon those who here crossed to the south side, as nearly all of the emigration did. By this route we avoided twice crossing the Platte, and also the dreaded Black Hills of the south side. It must be added, however, that in very wet seasons, this route would be impracticable, on account of deep creeks, which we found dry.[14]

Even before Child's guidebook was published, word spread, and other emigrants began following the north bank of the Platte River beyond Fort Laramie.

ONE CAN IMAGINE the romantic scene of long rows of wagons with emigrants riding and walking westward over the Oregon Trail, but it is more difficult to picture their hardships or to grasp their individual experiences without reading individual accounts. For instance, when a California-bound emigrant named Orange Gaylord from Illinois reached Fort Kearny on May 20, he was impressed by two tame yearling buffalo kept at the post. In another account written in June along the Platte River, an unidentified observer wrote: "You very seldom see a person on the road with a defensive weapon about him. My rifle and pistols have not been loaded for a month. As to game, there is none near enough the road to hunt. In fact, our fire arms are dead weight—you can buy a good rifle for three or four dollars. Hundreds are broken up and thrown away...." On June 25 an emigrant traveling along the Platte River wrote: "The most detestable thing in creation is the buffalo gnat, a very small diminutive insect that, before you are conscious of its presence, has bitten your face, ears, and neck in ten thousand places. My face at one time, had the appearance of one with small pox, my eyes were swollen up so much that I could hardly see, and my ears as thick as my hand." A correspondent at Fort Laramie writing under the name "Cheyenne," perhaps a military officer, observed that many emigrants were stealing from other emigrants. And he reported that a boy of twelve years was picked up near Laramie, trudging along with an outfit of five biscuits and a bundle. He had been turned adrift "by a gentleman whose name I forbear to mention." Cheyenne described the character of the emigrants in 1850 as being "inferior" to those of 1849. He added that of the seven hundred emigrants "who now lie buried between here and the Missouri, nine-tenths died of carelessness, lack of experience, and cleanliness." At Fort Kearny a correspondent writing under the name "Observer" reported: "A Scotchman passed along with a wheelbarrow. 'Na, na, mum, I ken ye'll all brak doon in the mountains, sa I'll gang along myself.' He was thirty-five years old and showed no signs of fatigue."[15]

There are at least three other reports of California-bound travelers pushing their supplies and belongings in wheelbarrows, but none of them apparently used this mode of transportation all the way to California. Eventually they abandoned their wheelbarrows and joined other emigrants traveling in wagons. Perhaps the most complete early account of an emigrant walking and pushing a two-wheeled handcart over the Oregon Trail concerns James Gordon Brookmire, a thirty-nine-year-old man who left his wife and two teenage sons to run the family farm in Warren County, Pennsylvania, and headed for California. Before leaving, he sold 50 of his farm's 280 acres to finance his journey. Brookmire traveled by steamboat down the Ohio River to the Mississippi and then up the Missouri River to the town of Kansas. At nearby Westport he joined a company of Kentuckians and made a late start west on June 27, 1850. By the time the company reached Fort Kearny, Brookmire had a falling-out with the Kentuckians and they parted company. The Kentuckians refunded Brookmire's money. He purchased a handcart and became the first handcart emigrant to be identified by name. Twenty-five days later Brookmire reached Fort Laramie. He then continued over South Pass to Fort Bridger and through the Wasatch Mountains, but when he was crossing the Weber River near Salt Lake City, he lost his wheelbarrow in a ferryboat accident and nearly drowned. In Salt Lake City he got new supplies and continued his journey to California, where he soon struck it rich. Within eighteen months he had saved $15,000 worth of gold dust. A letter from home told him his wife had inherited $10,000 from her father's estate. Brookmire soon took a ship to Nicaragua, crossed the Isthmus, caught another ship for New York and returned to his wife and family in Pennsylvania in the spring of 1852.[16]

JUST AFTER THE START of the Mexican War, the government tried to freight supplies from Fort Leavenworth to New Mexico for Brigadier General Stephen Watts Kearny's Army of the West. The government did such a poor job that it decided it would be more effective to hire private freighters to transport supplies to military posts in the West. The establishment of Fort Kearny, the purchase of Fort Laramie, and the manning of a small military garrison in the vicinity of Fort Hall—all on the Oregon Trail—meant these places had to be kept supplied. In 1849, two Missouri freighting firms were given contracts to transport government stores up the Oregon Trail to Fort Kearny and Fort Laramie. More supplies were shipped to the two posts in 1850, but a third freighting company was needed to supply the troops stationed near Fort Hall. Two Missourians, James Brown and John S. Jones, received the government contract to deliver the supplies. They were to be paid $14.15 for each hundred pounds delivered. At the same time, Jones apparently planned to use the opportunity to go to California. On March 15, 1850, the *St. Joseph Gazette* reported that Jones had advertised in the *Boonville* (Missouri) *Democrat* for eighty men to drive his wagons to Fort Hall. If the men volunteered to drive his teams, Jones promised he would guide them to California with the empty wagons. Once they arrived "at the mines," Jones promised to provide each man with one month's provisions. Whether Jones found volunteers is not known, but on May 21 his wagon train, loaded with government stores, left Fort Leavenworth accompanied by a mounted escort of soldiers. When they reached Fort Laramie in early July, Jones was informed that the U.S. troops near Fort Hall had been withdrawn and the temporary post abandoned. Jones was ordered to leave the government stores at Fort Laramie. From what is known, Jones never succeeded in getting any teamsters to volunteer to drive his wagons in exchange for being guided to California and given a grubstake. Jones left Fort Laramie on July 20 and arrived on August 1 at Independence, Missouri, making one of the quickest trips made by wagons up until that time between those two points. He averaged more than 50 miles a day on the 650-mile journey down the Oregon Trail.

Meanwhile, after Jones paid off his teamsters at Fort Laramie, some of them headed for California on their own. One of them was William Grinstead of Pettis County, Missouri. We know about Grinstead because his account book of the journey has survived. He reached California safely in mid-October.[17]

ONE OF THE MORE interesting stories of California-bound emigrants in 1850 concerns Walter Crow of Pike County, Missouri, who had already been to California with two of his seven sons in 1849. They apparently found gold, and Crow talked of settling there. Crow observed that cattle were being sold at premium prices to the miners, who liked beefsteak. Crow apparently left his two sons in California and returned to Missouri via the Isthmus of Panama late in 1849. In late February 1850, Crow and four of his sons who had stayed behind in Missouri, along with Cyrus C. Loveland, who also had been to California and struck it rich, purchased Durham cattle in Cooper County, Missouri. The Durhams were a better quality than the Spanish cattle found in California. In May 1850, Crow, his four sons, and Loveland started driving 785 cattle, including 64 work steers, across the western border of Missouri southwest of Independence and soon struck the Oregon Trail west of modern Gardner, Kansas.

Details of this 1850 cattle drive over the Oregon Trail are recorded in the diary of Cyrus Loveland, which is preserved in the California State Library in Sacramento. On May 23, Crow, Loveland, and the others herded the cattle across the Big Blue River southeast of the site of modern Waterville,

Kansas. Loveland wrote in his diary: "Last night we lost no cattle but have nearly every other night." Once across the Big Blue, Loveland recorded that one of the men "found a human skeleton with a pair of shoes on it." Three days later he noted: "Began to see signs of buffalo." These California-bound cattle herders were soon using buffalo chips to fuel their evening campfires. By May 29 they reached the South Platte and then passed Fort Kearny, where they learned that 4,500 teams and 21,287 emigrants were ahead of them on the trail. In early July they drove their cattle past Devil's Gate and on July 4 rested and quietly celebrated Independence Day. "We killed a beef and had a fine spot of soup, which was the best of anything that we have had on the trip. We also had a dessert of peach pie which really reminded me of home," wrote Loveland. On the last day of July, Crow, Loveland, and the others reached Fort Hall on the Snake River and found plenty of good grass for their cattle in the vicinity. Crossing the Portneuf River and Bannock Creek, they drove their cattle past American Falls on the Snake River. Travel was often difficult and grass was not always plentiful for the cattle. The men drove the herd past Thousand Springs and on August 13 reached the North Fork of the Humboldt River in what is now north-central Nevada. Eighteen days later they arrived at the Humboldt Sink and killed two beeves for hungry emigrants they met who had run out of provisions.

633 — THOUSAND SPRINGS, IDAHO.

This photograph of the Thousand Springs gushing from the side of a canyon wall was made early in the twentieth century during a wet year. (Author's collection)

That day Loveland wrote in his diary: "Provisions are very scarce. Our mess has just ate the last of our breadstuff and fruit. We have one mess of beans and then beef is our only show." Travel during the next three days was very difficult as they passed through country that was mostly desert, keeping the cattle moving day and night.

On September 5, 1850, they drove the cattle up along the Truckee River and stopped. Loveland wrote: "Never was this party so completely used up as when we came in from the desert. We were so wore out with fatigue and for want of sleep that like many of the old crows it might have been said of us that we were give out, for we had been without sleep two days and nearly all of two nights and on the go constantly. The last night on the desert we were so overcome with sleep that we were obliged to get off our horses and walk for fear of falling off. As we were walking along after the cattle it certainly would have been very amusing to anyone who could see us staggering along against each other, first on one side of the road, then the other, like a company of drunken men, but no human eyes were there to see, for all alike were sleeping while walking. Thanks to the Almighty Ruler above, we overcame all difficulty thus far on our long journey."

Three days later the herd was near the site of modern Reno, Nevada, and five days later they had climbed more than 9,200 feet above sea level and were crossing the area where four years earlier the Donner tragedy had occurred. Crow, Loveland, and the others made it safely over the mountains by late summer and reached California, where the last entry in Loveland's diary is dated September 30. On that day the herd was driven across the Sacramento River and set to graze, while Loveland and some of the others made camp. It had taken the little party about five months to drive the cattle from western Missouri to California. Their cattle losses were not great; about five hundred head survived the journey.

THE NUMBER of commercial passenger wagon trains bound for California increased in 1850. Originating at St. Louis but starting their journeys from St. Joseph or Weston, Missouri, at least six groups of entrepreneurs advertised that they would carry passengers through to the goldfields. John M. McPike and E. J. Strother of Ashley in Pike County, Missouri, promoted their passenger train, which consisted of twenty hacks, each pulled by four mules with backup mules and horses in reserve. The two men promised that a doctor would travel with their train, which would leave Independence on about May 1. Each of the passengers paid $200, and they included men from Iowa, Ohio, Kentucky, Pennsylvania, and Ireland. Each man could take fifty pounds of baggage, and McPike and Strother furnished every passenger with a weapon and ammunition as well as provisions and cooking utensils. From all accounts they got through safely to California by September, but the train lost twenty-five mules and horses on the South Fork of the Platte River and the men were forced to leave most of their hacks on the desert and walk over the Sierra Nevada.[18]

Another group, called the Mississippi and Pacific Line, operated by three men named Jerome, Hanson, and Smith, left from St. Joseph in early May. They used a train of spring wagons and carried about 120 passengers, both men and women. They arrived at Fort Kearny on about May 17 and apparently reached Sacramento in late September. The passenger train of Wiles & Bennett was organized at St. Louis, and its forty passengers, twelve wagons, and "their 'entire fixens' " traveled up the Missouri River aboard the steamboat *St. Paul* to Weston. They set out in May on the Oregon Trail and succeeded in crossing the desert west of Salt Lake City with their wagons. But they lost some of them crossing the Sierra Nevada and only got a few over the mountains to California. Some of the passengers on the fourth passenger train, operated by G. C. Alexander of Edwardsville, Illinois, and a Captain Hall of St. Louis, failed to reach California. Their train, consisting of spring wagons, crossed the Missouri River at Weston in late May. By the time they reached Chimney Rocky on June 13, four passengers had died of cholera. Another member came down with smallpox. The remainder of the passengers reached Sacramento in late September.[19]

The fifth passenger train, operated by Glenn & Company, started in late May from Independence and consisted of 124 passengers and their baggage in 39 wagons plus 200 mules and horses. They were delayed by the flooding Big Blue River but reached Fort Kearny on June 17. What happened next is not clear, but two passengers and a teamster died, perhaps from cholera, before they reached Salt Lake City in early July. There the passenger train broke up. The fate of the sixth passenger train, operated by J. C. Faine & Company and called the Southwestern Company, is not known.[20]

WITH SO MANY AMERICANS in California, Oregon, and Utah, both the government and private entrepreneurs sought to meet the demand for mail service. James M. Estill of Weston, Missouri, and James W. Denver, for whom Denver, Colorado, was later named, formed a company to take mail to California emigrants. They charged 50 cents each to carry letters with U.S. postage on them. The firm purchased three spring carriages and twenty-four fine horses. They sent ahead, carried by emigrants who preceded them, five-pound sacks of oats to be left for the mail wagons at Forts Kearny and Laramie and other points along the Oregon Trail. The mail carriages held twenty-four mailbags, each stamped with a letter of the alphabet. Traveling ahead were riders who distributed printed alphabetical lists of the letters in the mailbags to the emigrants they met. As the mail wagons reached the emigrants who had found their names on the lists, the wagons would stop and the appropriate mailbag would be opened and the mail given out. One of the wagons went through to California to bring back mail to the East. After the others distributed all the mail they carried, the wagons returned east.[21]

Meanwhile, Brown, Woodson & Company obtained a government contract worth $19,500 to carry the mail up the Oregon Trail from Independence to Salt Lake City once each month using stagecoaches drawn by four or six mules. The contract called for the mail to leave Independence on the first day of each month and arrive at Salt Lake City on the last day of the month. The firm had difficulties. At one point in September 1850, the mules gave out and the driver had to walk into Salt Lake City with the mail. The October mail from Independence got only as far as the South Fork of the Platte River, where early winter snow made the road impassable. The stage had to return to Fort Kearny until it could get through. The December mail run got through to Fort Kearny in seventeen days, but west of there winter weather made travel impossible. The two hundred pounds of mail did not reach Salt Lake City until the following March.[22]

Of the 6,000 people who traveled to Oregon in 1850, some of them planned to visit California the following summer. Whether all of the new arrivals were counted in the census of 1850 is not known, but the count gave Oregon a population of 11,873. When President Zachary Taylor died in Washington, D.C., on July 9 of an acute intestinal infection, the residents of Oregon and the emigrants on the trail during that summer of 1850 did not learn they had a new president for weeks, if not months. Taylor had participated in Independence Day ceremonies in extremely hot temperatures at the Washington Monument on July 4, and he died five days later. Vice President Millard Fillmore became the thirteenth president, as the nation was rapidly becoming an industrial power. As president, Zachary Taylor was prepared to hold the Union together by armed force rather than by compromise over the issue of whether new territories would be slave or free, but Fillmore chose compromise and states' rights. For example, on the one hand Congress passed the Fugitive Slave Act, which set up strict procedures under federal control for the capture and return of escaped slaves. On the other, slavery was banned in the District of Columbia, and because of the gold discovery and the thousands of emigrants who followed the Oregon Trail, California was admitted as the thirty-first state in the Union and as a free state.

CHAPTER FOURTEEN

THE CHANGING ROAD

Oxen that rattle the yoke and chain, or halt in the leafy shade!
What is that you express in your eyes?
It seems to me more than all the print I have read in my life.

Walt Whitman

O N A COOL SPRING MORNING in early May 1851, six mounted men leading pack animals crossed the Missouri River at St. Joseph, Missouri, and struck the branch road to the Oregon Trail. Four of the men were from La Porte, Indiana, the other two from Joliet, Illinois, and they were bound for the goldfields of California. Their departure was not noted in the news columns of St. Joseph's two weekly newspapers, but seventy-seven days later, on July 17, the *El Dorado News* of Placerville, California, reported their arrival. They were the first overland emigrants to reach Placerville that year.

The six emigrants who arrived at Placerville were a small group of the 1,100 or so persons who set out for California in 1851. Once they started west, however, some of the 1,100 decided to go to Oregon instead of California. The number of California-bound emigrants had dropped considerably because the gold fever had subsided and because the cholera epidemic of the previous year had killed thousands of travelers. Many who might have gone stayed home. The decline in the number of emigrants was a disappointment to the merchants in the jumping-off towns along the Missouri River. At St. Joseph the *Gazette* reported on March 26: "From best information few persons will emigrate to California or Oregon this year. This time last year our town literally was crowded but now very few are in the place. A few Oregon emigrants have passed through, who will camp a short distance from town to wait for grass." By late April, however, the number of emigrants gathering at St. Joseph had increased, and the *Gazette* reported on April 23: "Quite a number of Oregon and California emigrants are now here. Several wagons have crossed the ferry here and we learn that the ferries above have crossed upwards of 200 wagons."

The emigrants bound for Oregon included a company of forty persons from Vermilion County, Illinois, and a small group of five men, two women, and eight children from Kaskaskia, Illinois. One California-bound group was called the Mohican Gold Company, and it ferried across the Missouri River at St. Joseph on April 23. There were forty men from Delaware and Ashland counties in Ohio in the company. Another small party consisted of Rev. Neill Johnson and his family from Mt. Pleasant, Iowa. They had three wagons and after leaving St. Joseph joined other Oregon-bound emigrants at Wolf Creek in what is now northeast Kansas, where an outbreak of smallpox was occurring. About a fifth of the Sac and Fox Indians living in the area died of smallpox that spring. Fortunately their Indian agent hired a doctor to vaccinate other Indians, thereby stopping the epidemic from spreading.

In early May another Oregon-bound company, made up mostly of people from Ohio and some from Pennsylvania, outfitted at Weston, Missouri, and then crossed the Missouri River at Fort Leavenworth. The company had 40 men, 8 women with their children, 18 wagons, and about 150 cattle. After Quincy A. Brooks from Pennsylvania reached Oregon, he sent a letter home advising any future emigrants coming west not to try to stop a stampede if their oxen decide to run. Rounding them up would be easier. Brooks wrote: "Let them rip. If you do not attempt to control them they will run in a straight line, but if you attempt to stop or control them, they will take a short turn when at full speed."[1]

By mid-May fewer than 10,000 emigrants had headed west from the jumping-off towns along the Missouri River. Aside from the 1,100 who started for California, Andrew Jensen, assistant historian of the Church of Latter-Day Saints, estimated that 5,000 Mormons set out for Salt Lake City in 1851. Because migration was much reduced from the previous year, the Mormons began leaving earlier then usual from Kanesville, which in 1853 was renamed Council Bluffs. In earlier years they had left later in the season to avoid possible conflicts with an increased number of non-Mormons who had chosen to travel along the north bank of the Platte River, but now they pretty much dominated that trail. In fact, the Mormons outnumbered an estimated 3,600 emigrants bound for Oregon who chose to follow the south bank of the Platte.

Most of the Oregon-bound emigrants were motivated by the passage in Congress of the Donation Land Act, also known as the Oregon Land Law, which President Fillmore signed on September 27, 1850. Under the law, settlers in Oregon could select claims on unsurveyed land in the Willamette Valley. Each settler could have 320 acres of land, and a married couple could claim 640 acres, or one square mile, provided they cultivated and lived on the land for four consecutive years, at which time they would be given final title. A land office was opened at Oregon City to handle land claims for what the law said was a "free gift of a generous nation." Interestingly, the law gave a wedded woman the right to hold property, which was rare at the time anywhere in the United States.

There were scattered reports of cholera in 1851 but no epidemic. More than sixty diaries, letters, recollections, and narratives of travelers over the road that are known to exist reflect this, and most relate experiences similar to those already mentioned by earlier emigrants. But a letter written by Lucia Loraine Williams, uncovered a few years ago by historian Kenneth Holmes, stands out. Born Lucia Bigelow in Vermont in 1816, she married Elijah Williams in Ohio, where he had farmed and read law in Hancock County after his first wife had died, leaving his two boys motherless. Lucia and Elijah then had two children, John and Helen, who were ten and three when their parents decided in 1851 to make a new home in Oregon. They crossed the Missouri River at Council Bluffs in early May 1851 and reached the town of Milwaukie, Oregon, in September. There on September 16, 1851, Lucia wrote a letter to her mother in the East:

Dear Mother:

We have been living in Oregon about 2 weeks, all of us except little John, and him we left 12 miles this side of Green River. He was killed instantly by falling from a wagon and the wheels running over his head. After leaving the desert and Green River, we came to a good place of feed and laid by a day for the purpose of recruiting our teams. On the morning of the 20th of June we started on. John rode on the wagon driven by Edwin Fellows. We had not proceeded more than 2 miles before word came for us to turn back. We did so but found him dead. The oxen had taken fright from a horse that had been tied behind the wagon preceding this, owned by a young man that Mr. Williams had told a few minutes to turn out of the road. Two other teams ran also. John was sitting in back of the wagon but as soon as the cattle commenced to run he went to the front and caught hold of the driver who held him as long as he could but he was frightened and did not possess presence of mind enough to give him a little send, which would have saved him. Poor little fellow, we could do nothing for him He was beyond our reach and Oh, how suddenly, one half hour before we had left him in health as lively as a lark, and then to find him breathless so soon was awful. I cannot describe to you our feelings. We buried him there by the road side, by the right side of the road, about one-half mile before we crossed the Fononelle, a little stream. We had his grave covered with stones to protect it from wild beasts and a board with his name and age and if any of our friends come through I wish they would find his grave and if it needs, repair it.[2]

IN 1851, fairly regular mail service between Independence and Salt Lake City continued over the road, as did the flow of military troops and the freighting of supplies to military posts along the Oregon Trail. Then, too, traders went back and forth over the road, taking furs east and carrying supplies west to their trading posts. Early in 1851, Ben Holladay of Weston, Missouri, received a two-year contract to transport supplies from Fort Leavenworth to Fort Kearny at $3.80 per 100 pounds and to Fort Laramie for $6.80 per 100 pounds. Holladay's firm carried nearly 140,000 pounds of government freight to Fort Laramie and more than 71,000 pounds to Fort Kearny before the year ended. The supplies were valued at $100,000.[3]

The increased travel over the Oregon Trail, especially during 1849 and 1850, due to the California gold rush, caused officials in Washington to realize that some sort of understanding was needed between the Indians along the road and the government. Aside from Indians often begging from travelers and occasionally stealing stock, things had been peaceful, but the increased number of travelers was alarming the Sioux and other tribes. Then, too, the policy makers in Washington realized that having one big reservation in the West for Indians was not going to work. They decided to follow a policy of moving Indians into restricted areas. Early in 1851, Congress authorized holding a great treaty council with the Indians to try to maintain peace along the Oregon Trail. In late July 1851, Colonel David D. Mitchell, the superintendent of Indian affairs, left St. Louis and traveled up the Missouri River by steamboat to Fort Leavenworth. Mitchell, a fur trader on the upper Missouri River and a master of the art of Indian diplomacy, was in charge of a succession of trading posts and in 1835 became a partner in the Upper Missouri Outfit, formerly the Columbia Fur Company, within the American Fur Company. In 1841, he took up the post of superintendent of Indian affairs at St. Louis. From Fort Leavenworth, Mitchell and his party started up the military road toward the Platte River. Dragoons from Fort Kearny met them on the Little Blue River and escorted them to Fort Laramie, where the council would be held. Months earlier, Indian agents in the West were told of the grand peace council meeting and had sent runners to all the tribes from the Missouri River to Fort Bridger and from Canada to

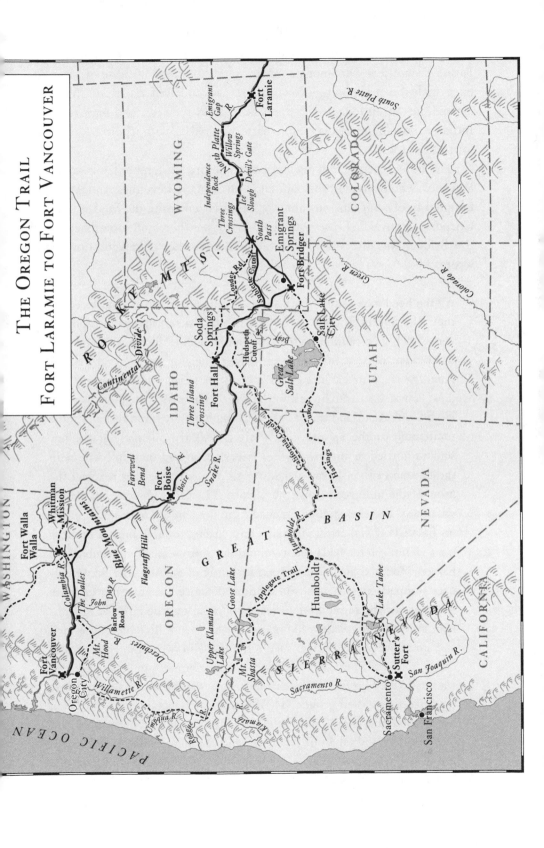

the Arkansas River, inviting them to come to Fort Laramie on September 1. Father Pierre-Jean De Smet was also invited to attend because of his influence with the Assiniboin, Crow, Minnetara, and Arikara tribes. When he arrived, he set up lodges of buffalo hide, held services, and baptized 1,586 Indian children. Jim Bridger came with the Snakes, with whom he had lived for two decades.

The Indians began arriving many days before September 1, all except the Pawnees, who boycotted the council. The Sioux, Cheyennes, and Arapahos mingled freely, but tensions mounted as their enemies, the Snakes, arrived. Corporal Percival G. Lowe of the U.S. Army was there and remembered that Jim Bridger was directed to lead the Snakes to their campsite. Lowe later wrote:

> All the head men of the Sioux and Cheyennes had given assurance that they [the Snakes] should not be molested, so down they came, moving very slowly and cautiously, the chief alone a short distance in advance. They were dressed in their best, riding fine war horses, and made a grandly savage appearance.... Lieutenant Hastings had "boots and saddles" sounded so as to be ready whatever happened. Just below us was a large Sioux camp, and the people were showing great interest and some excitement at the approach of their hereditary enemies, and a few squaws howled in anguish for lost friends who had died in battle with these same cautiously moving warriors. When the Snakes reached the brow of the hill overlooking the beautiful Laramie [River], less than a mile away, and the chief commenced the descent, a Sioux sprang upon his horse, bow and arrows in hand, and rushed towards him. A Frenchman, an interpreter, had been watching the Sioux, expecting trouble, and he, too, mounted his horse and was instantly in pursuit. The Snake column stopped and sent up a wild shout of defiance, the chief moved a few steps farther and raised his gun ready to fire just as the intrepid Frenchman reached the reckless Sioux, pulled him from his horse, disarmed and stood over him. Then ensued a harangue between interpreters and chiefs. The wild Sioux, who sought to revenge himself on the Snake chief who had killed his father some time before, was led back to camp while the Snakes held their ground. Their position was a good one; every man had a good gun, plenty of ammunition, besides bows and arrows. Not one out of a hundred Sioux had guns, and the Snakes, though not one to five of the Sioux, would have defended themselves successfully, and the battle would have been the most bloody ever known amongst the wild tribes.[4]

But violence was averted and Corporal Lowe was then given the task of showing Bridger and the Snakes where to establish their camp, some distance from the Sioux.

Meanwhile, the military learned that a wagon train carrying gifts for the Indians would be late in arriving, and it soon became evident there was not sufficient grass in the area around Fort Laramie for the thousands of Indian ponies. The animals required so much forage that the council site was moved about thirty miles east of Fort Laramie to the meadows at the mouth of Horse Creek, just west of Scotts Bluff. It took a few days for everyone to relocate their camps.

In a dispatch to the *Missouri Republican*, correspondent B. Gratz Brown reported: "In moving camp, as in all drudgery, everything in the way of labor is performed by the women and female children. The men and boys do nothing; they regard it as a disgrace to do any kind of work." The Indian women put their lodges, camp equipment, children, and sometimes their dogs on the poles dragged along behind the horses. The soldiers called them "Prairie Buggies." At the new location soldiers put up Superintendent Mitchell's tent at the point where Horse Creek and the Platte River meet. The military erected their tents on higher ground, while Superintendent Mitchell and Thomas Fitzpatrick had their tents higher up along the creek. Fitzpatrick, a veteran mountain man who had been appointed Indian agent for the upper Platte and Arkansas rivers, had been instrumental in organizing the great council. The Cheyenne made their camp up the Platte beyond the creek. Some of the Sioux made camp on both sides of the Platte while the Arapahos, Apaches, Snakes, and other tribes scattered their camps over the area. Once all participants were settled, the Oglala Sioux, who were camped on the opposite side of the Platte River, gave two dog feasts to the Snakes, Arapahos, and Cheyennes. Afterward, the Indians danced all night. The next day there was a great all-nations procession to the common center of the camps when the council began. The *Missouri Republican* reported:

They came out this morning, not armed or painted for war, but decked out in all their best regalia, pomp, paint, and display for peace. The Chiefs and Braves were dressed with punctilious attention to imposing effect. The "Bucks" [young men] were out on horse-back or afoot, in all the foppery and display of prairie 'dandies.' In their efforts to be elegant, fashionable, and exquisite, it must be confessed that the Prairie Dandy, after his manner, displays quite as much sense and taste as his city prototype, with this advantage. The Indian does not conceal his features with abundance of hair. In their bearings, and effort to show pride of dress and tinsel, they are on a par.

The squaws were out in all the richness and embellishments of their 'toggery.' Their displays, according to their stations and the wealth of their husbands or fathers, marked their ability to dress and their *distingué* in genteel Indian society. The 'belles' (there are Indian as well as civilized belles) were out in all they could raise of finery and costume, and the way they flaunted, tittered, talked and made efforts to show off to the best advantage before the Bucks, justly entitled them to the civilized appellation we have given them. We concluded that coquetry was not of foreign origin. Even more than ordinary care had been bestowed on the dress of the children. They were entirely on their best behavior. With those little ones it was easy to decide upon the thrift, the cleanliness and industry of the mothers.... Some were decked out in all the variety of finery that skins of wild animals, beads, porcupine quills, and various colored cloths could suggest. Others were in more simple costume, a string of beads around the neck, and a string round the loins. It is due to the Indian women to say, that whilst the male children, even to an advanced age, are often permitted to go naked, or nearly so, we saw but one female child so exposed.[5]

The Arapahos, Cheyennes, Sioux, Assiniboins, Snakes, Arikaras, Gros Ventres, and Crows were then informed that only the principal chiefs were expected within the circle prepared for the council. When the Sioux could not agree on who their principal chief was, Superintendent Mitchell nominated Frightening Bear. He placed the Indian in a circle of twenty-four tribal representatives selected by the several bands in proportion to the number of their lodges. Each representative was provided with a little stick or twig, which the voter placed in the hand of the nominee if he favored his election. Frightening Bear was nominated. The chiefs took their places in the council circle and the proceedings began.

The pipe of peace was smoked. Areas for tribal limits were discussed. Many speeches followed. Father De Smet and Jim Bridger gave the benefit of their great knowledge in defining boundaries of the territories of the various Indian tribes. But the Indians did not grasp the government's new policy of putting Indians in designated areas. By September 17 it was agreed that peace should reign among the Indians and between them and the whites, who were free to travel the roads and retain their scattered forts. In exchange, the government promised to provide the Indians annually with $50,000 in annuity goods to be divided among the tribes. Three days later the wagon train carrying gifts for the Indians arrived and the presents were distributed. Two days after that, the Indians departed as did Mitchell, Fitzpatrick, and others. Everyone seemed to agree that the council was a success and that it gave promise of a lasting peace on the western plains.

But the government representatives who arranged the treaty failed to anticipate what would happen to the document when it reached Washington. The signed treaty was ratified by the Senate on May 24, 1852, but it was amended, changing the annuity from fifty years to ten years, with an additional five years at the discretion of the president, provided all of the tribes agreed. By September 1854 all of the tribes had agreed to the amendment, but the Interior Department apparently forgot to have the State Department certify the treaty and it therefore was not sent to the president for his signature. It was not until the 1920s that someone in the Indian Office in Washington wrote a memorandum admitting that through oversight or design the Indian Service and the Department of the Interior neglected to formally advise the secretary of state that all of the tribes had ratified the amended treaty. The treaty was never published in the *United States Statutes at Large* and remains in limbo today. The government, however, did fulfill the provisions of the treaty, and peace did prevail for a time among the Indians and between the Indians and whites along the Oregon Trail.[6]

AT THE BEGINNING OF 1851, the population of Oregon was slightly more than 12,000 people. Unmarried women were scarce. Since the Donation Land Act set forth that married men could claim 640 acres of land, or 320 acres if unmarried, a few men resorted to marrying young girls, some as young as ten, to claim more land. If the parents gave their consent, the marriage would take place, but the bride would often remain with her parents for a few years, enabling her husband to claim and work a full section of land. At the time, marriage licenses were not required in Oregon.

George W. Bush, who brought his family west over the Oregon Trail in 1844, had a problem of a different sort. Bush was half Irish, half black, but he was listed on the census as Negro. Just before he arrived, residents had voted to exclude blacks. Bush took his family north across the Columbia River and settled in what is now the state of Washington. A year later in 1845, the Oregon provisional legislature repealed the law. By 1850, the year the Donation Land Act became law, Bush had become a prosperous farmer near modern Olympia. But the law gave land ownership only to white citizens and half-breeds. The issue was finally resolved after Washington Territory was created from part of Oregon Territory in 1853. Isaac Stevens, Washington's first territorial governor, then asked the territorial legislature to persuade Congress to declare Bush eligible under the Donation Land Law. Congress did, but the territorial legislature turned down Bush's request for full citizenship and the right to vote.

Before that, another exclusion law had been passed in Oregon Territory in 1849 prohibiting blacks from settling in the new territory. In August 1851, a black businessman named Jacob Vanderpool was arrested and jailed on a complaint by Theophilus Magruder. Vanderpool owned a saloon, restaurant, and boardinghouse in Salem. Five days later he was brought to trial, charged with illegally residing in Oregon. Vanderpool's lawyer argued that the law was unconstitutional since it had not been approved by the legislature, but the next day after all of the arguments and witnesses had been heard, Judge Thomas Nelson ordered Vanderpool to leave Oregon.

By then the land office at Oregon City was crowded almost daily with settlers and emigrants who wanted to file their claims to land they had selected. The Donation Land Act meant non-Indians could claim land even if Indians claimed it or were living on it. The Indians had been ignored in the act. Many Indians did not object to being paid for land they lived on or claimed, but payments were not always made and hard feelings developed. Good relations might have returned in time, but in December 1851 gold was discovered in the Rogue River valley in what is now southwest Oregon. Later, in 1852, gold was also found along the Umpqua River in west-central Oregon near the settlement of Scottsburg. The new claims attracted gold-seekers from the Willamette Valley, while to the south hardened miners from California crossed the Siskiyou Mountains or took ships north to Crescent City, Umpqua City, or Port Orford. The gold-seekers, unlike the settlers who came to Oregon with their families to farm, were mostly single men. In the mining areas new towns sprang up overnight.

Although relations between whites and Indians in northern Oregon were tense, they were not fraught as were those between the two groups in southern Oregon, through which the Applegate Trail passed. The Takelmas, Shastas, Chetcos, Mikonotunnes, Cow Creeks, and others resisted the miners, who thought nothing of forcing the Indians from their villages, many of which were located on old stream terraces, prime locations for placer deposits. Indians were often killed by whites, some of whom were irregular volunteers operating independently of the regular army and all established authority. These volunteers were not great in number and often planned their raids while influenced by drink. Finally war erupted in July 1855 along Humburg Creek and spread. Many Indians and whites died. U.S. troops tried to keep the peace, but in the spring of 1856 a band of Indians killed twenty-three whites. In time, three of the Indian chiefs promised to surrender at a place called Big Meadows. Fifty dragoons and thirty infantrymen waited for the Indians to arrive. Then two Indian women came to the soldiers' camp and warned them that Indian bands were going to attack the next day. The U.S. troops moved to a nearby hill and dug in, and the Indians attacked the next morning. A third of the troops were killed or wounded before a company of regulars arrived and helped to rout the Indians.[7]

WHEN SPRING ARRIVED in 1852 in the jumping-off towns along the Missouri, merchants were pleased that many more emigrants had arrived than had by the same time the previous year. The merchants took this as a sign that the spring migration would be great, and in anticipation that many more people would go west, Charles A. and Elias H. Perry, merchants at St. Joseph and Weston, began advertising on March 10 in the *St. Joseph Gazette* that their passenger wagon train would take people to California beginning April 15. Tickets were $150 per person, cash in advance, and they promised "provisions plus good, new tents and double wagon sheets." Customers, however, would have to bring their own bedding. Within a few weeks, at least four other passenger wagon trains were advertised in the *Missouri Republican.* One of them, organized by George Hughes and John Duffy, planned to leave St. Louis on about April 20 and to depart from St. Joseph between May 1 and 10. They promised to transport paying customers in sixteen light wagons drawn by six to eight head of oxen. Tickets were $100 per person, and they set a limit of no more than thirty customers.

Emigrant Gilbert L. Cole chose to travel with a party of twenty-four men and one woman from his hometown of Monroe, Michigan. Bound for California, they traveled in eight wagons and had forty-four head of horses and mules to pull their wagons. They left Michigan on March 16 and arrived at St. Joseph, Missouri, on May 1. In his recollections, Cole wrote that St. Joseph "was a collection of one-story, cheap, wooden buildings, located along the [Missouri] river and Black Snake Hollow. The inhabitants appeared to be chiefly French and half-breed Indians. The principal business was selling outfits to immigrants and trading horses, mules, and cattle. There was one steam ferryboat, which had several days' crossing registered ahead."[8]

By late April, Independence, St. Joseph, and other Missouri River towns were buzzing with activity. Someone with the initials R.B.L. wrote a letter to a newspaper from St. Joseph on April 29. He noted: "The influx of emigrants gives our thriving city a very animated appearance.... The emigrants are generally men of moral character, and have so far manifested but little of that spirit of recklessness and lack of restraint, that characterized so many of them in 1850 and 1851.... Many of the emigrants are preparing to start in a few days, others have already gone, taking with them extra wagons, with feed.... The spring is unusually backward—vegetation is at least fifteen days behind that of last year or the year preceding.... There seems to be a very large proportion of the gentle sex among the emigrants, and to diversify the matter, a few of those latterly assigned to an extra gender, Bloomers."[9]

Two years earlier, Amelia Bloomer, editor and publisher of a temperance paper published in Seneca Falls, New York, commented on the short dresses and knee-length undergarments being worn by a few ladies. She was pleased with the trend and adopted the clothing in place of the long, heavy skirt that ladies commonly wore. Bloomer also defended the attire in *Lily,* her temperance paper. She believed its use would promote the comfort and health of females everywhere. Her articles were picked up by the *New York Weekly Tribune,* and soon the outfit became known as "the Bloomer Costume," which consisted of trousers like those worn by Turkish women. She favored the baggy bloomer trousers that reached to the ankle and which were frill-cuffed and worn with a simple knee-length skirt and bodice. Interest in the costume spread. Women dressed in bloomers first appeared in California in 1851. The outfit initially appeared among westbound emigrants on the Oregon Trail in 1852, and when the wearers reached Oregon, the *Oregonian,* on October 8, 1852, reported: "Quite a number of Bloomers—just over the Plains—have made their appearance in Oregon City, and being the first specimens of the genuine Bloomer costume ever seen here, of course attracted much attention."

While most emigrants waited until April to leave the Missouri River towns, a few started much earlier. Three Michigan men on foot reached Fort Kearny during a snowstorm on March 1. From where and when they departed is not known, but one of the men apparently had seen the elephant and enlisted in the U.S. Army at the post. The two others continued west after the snowstorm stopped, only to be robbed by Cheyenne Indians. Learning of this, an officer at Fort Kearny sent a wagon with supplies to the two men. One returned to the post while the other continued west. On April 1, two more men from Michigan arrived at Fort Kearny on foot. Hearing what had happened to those who had arrived earlier, the pair decided to wait until the first emigrant company arrived and join them.

When one emigrant got to Fort Kearny on May 24, he reported in a letter to the *Missouri Republican* that regions of the Little Blue and Big Sandy were almost destitute of grass but that with grain and a light load a company could do well. The emigrant, whose initials were S.M.B., said he favored Westport as the starting point. He said Westport was better than St. Joseph because provisions were as cheap there as at St. Louis. For instance, he reported corn and oats selling for 30 cents a bushel, and mules were 20 percent cheaper than in St. Louis. The emigrant noted that it was difficult to cross the Missouri River at St. Joseph with fresh, unbroken teams, and the river bottom was terrible. He believed the emigration would equal that of 1849.[10]

Andrew Goodyear, on his third trip overland to California, reached Fort Kearny on June 10. By then 30,000 people, 7,000 wagons, 100,000 cattle, 5,000 mules, and 8,000 sheep had passed the post following the south bank of the Platte River. Later, after Goodyear had reached California, the *Sacramento Union,* on August 28, reported that he believed an equal number of emigrants had followed the north bank of the Platte River. If correct, 60,000 emigrants would have been moving westward during May and early June. Goodyear told the Sacramento newspaper that much sickness existed among the emigrants. Although the cholera epidemic of 1850 had subsided, Goodyear said he met four hundred wagons returning east on account of sickness. One company of seventy-two men with nine wagons had lost twenty-four mem-

The identity of these emigrants is not known, but they appear to be nooning somewhere along the road. This photograph probably was made during the late 1850s or early 1860s. They may have been Mormons bound for Salt Lake City. (Author's collection)

bers and had buried five men on June 19. Whether they died from cholera is not known. Goodyear said the company had scarcely enough men in good health to drive their ox teams.

A California-bound man from Illinois reportedly left Independence, Missouri, in May with a large flock of turkeys. If the following letter published by the *St. Joseph Gazette*, on October 19, 1852, is to be believed, the man accomplished what otherwise would be thought impossible because of the nature of turkeys. The *Gazette* reported that the August mail from California included a letter that read: "A man from Illinois has just arrived from Independence having driven the entire distance two thousand turkeys, all hale and heavy. They cost him about fifty cents apiece in the States.... He has been offered eight dollars apiece."

On August 6, 1852, Corporal F. Longfield, of Company I, Sixth Infantry, wrote in a letter from Fort Kearny: "The great emigration of the present season is past and gone. The mighty throng that crowded the roads from east to west is no longer seen, the murmuring of voices, the rattling of chains and wagons, the lowing of thirsty oxen, that daily passed our garrison, are heard no more." Although Longfield believed more than 28,000 emigrants had passed Fort Kearny following the south bank of the Platte River, John D. Unruh, Jr., in his book *The Plains Across* suggests that at least 60,000 persons traveled the Oregon Trail in 1852. Of those about 10,000 were bound for Oregon, perhaps 10,000 were Mormons heading for Salt Lake, and the remaining 40,000 went to California.[11]

As the migration season began in the spring of 1853, merchants along the Missouri River were optimistic that the year would be good for sales. On April 13, the *St. Joseph Gazette* reported: "Emigrants for the plains, still continue to come, though they are not as numerous here as they were this time last year." On April 20 the newspaper noted: "Many of the emigrants now here, are destined for Oregon, and still they come. They are mostly persons well fixed who are going there to settle permanently." St. Joseph's other weekly newspaper, the *Adventure*, reported on May 25: "The emigration this spring, so far, is much greater at this point than was anticipated. Great numbers arrive daily, make their purchases and cross the river on the way to the plains. Not a day passes but large droves of stock are driven thro' our streets—the amount on the plains, if equal at each of the other starting points...will be immense. Emigrants are encamped in every direction in and around the city; the streets are thronged, and business brisk."

During the early 1850s, entrepreneurs would take wagons filled with merchandise and set up shop along the road. By 1853, emigrants reported that in the vicinity of Fort Laramie and Fort Hall they were hardly out of sight of these traders. Other entrepreneurs sought to make money in other ways. On May 4, Seth E. Ward and William Guerrier ran an advertisement in the *St. Joseph Gazette* announcing that they and some experienced plainsmen had established a ferry across the North Fork of the Platte River nine miles above Fort Laramie. The location was four miles below an established ferry at what was known as Mormon Crossing. Ward and Guerrier said they would charge $5 to ferry each wagon across the North Fork. By then relatively few streams along the Oregon Trail lacked ferries for emigrants to use. In at least one case ferry owners discouraged emigrants from trying to ford the streams by digging large holes in the river bottom, forcing travelers to use the ferry. In several locations bridges were constructed by entrepreneurs who charged tolls. At one such bridge, emigrants who refused to pay the toll and forded the stream were told by the bridge owner that they still must pay. The emigrants got their guns, refused to pay, and continued on their journey. It seems the bridge owner had tried this ploy on other travelers with only occasional success.

The more than one hundred diaries, recollections, journals, and accounts left by emigrants from the 1853 migration reflect many of the experiences and hardships already related. But a sampling reflects events that were not routine. Oregon-bound Henry Allyn started out from Fulton County, Illinois, and traveled to the Council Bluffs area. There he saw a teenager hanged in an emigrant camp by a drumhead court for allegedly committing an ax murder.[12] Count Leonetto Cipriani, an Italian aristocrat who had visited California ranchos in 1852, returned east and in the spring of 1853 hired 24 hands to take 500 cattle, 600 oxen, 60 horses, 40 mules, and more than 20,000 pounds of cargo to California. The party left St. Louis in May 1853. In his diary Cipriani tells of cattle stampedes and of finding a French naval deserter trading in a little cabin at Ash Hollow. At South Pass, the tired and disgusted Cipriani turned over his cattle drive to Herman Reinke, a companion, noting in his diary, "I am leaving the company, tired of leading an ignoble life among beasts with the wretched aim of amassing a fortune."[13]

California-bound Harriett Sherrill Ward, who came from Dartford, Wisconsin, followed the north bank of the Platte River in a company of ten horse-drawn wagons. After crossing the Missouri River at Council Bluffs, she wrote: "Nebraska is a miserable, unpleasant place indeed, and can never be inhabited except by Red men." But days later as the weather improved she wrote in her journal that "the soil is fine and it will be inhabited by a civilized race of beings in time."[14]

Another emigrant heading for California was Judge T. H. Cann, who observed that the Sioux and the Pawnees were at war and that this saved the lives of emigrants. The Sioux, he wrote, were "along the line of the emigrant road and kept the hostile Pawnee back." Cann also reported that because many emigrants were overloaded, "hundreds of wagons had to be left by the wayside...and stacks of costly furniture were piled along the way." He described the migration as "a wonderful procession." He noted that the sun had burned and browned the emigrants.[15] By August the year's migration totaled 27,500, less than the previous year; 2,603 of the travelers were Mormons.[16]

By the summer of 1853, the Sioux were becoming alarmed at the great numbers of whites going over the Oregon Trail. More of the buffalo and wild game on which the Indians relied were being killed by the whites, and the Indians were very much aware of the new diseases carried by the whites. On June 15, a party of Sioux seized the ferryboat at Fort Laramie. One of the Indians fired on an army sergeant, who then gained control of the boat. A party of twenty-four soldiers was sent to the Sioux village to arrest the man who had shot at the sergeant. The Indians, however, refused to turn over the Indian. Shooting followed and three Indians were killed, another three wounded, and two taken prisoner. The Sioux were incensed by what the soldiers had done, but after Captain R. Garnett, commander of the fort, explained to the chiefs what had happened, the Indians accepted their annu-

Emigrants moving westward over the Oregon Trail with their heavily loaded wagons. Many ignored the advice of those who had gone before them and tried to carry too many belongings west. After weeks on the road many emigrants were forced to discard unneeded items to lighten their loads. (Courtesy Kansas State Historical Society)

ities from the Indian agent and peace was restored, save for isolated incidents of thievery and begging by the Indians.

THERE WAS MUCH DEBATE in Congress before California was admitted to the Union in 1850. The emigrants who had gone overland to California and others who had traveled by sea had given the territory sufficient population to seek admission as a state. But southern lawmakers wanted California to be a slave state. In a compromise Kentucky Senator Henry Clay proposed that California be admitted as a free state and that New Mexico and Utah be organized into territories where residents could later decide on slavery. In September 1850, Congress approved the measure. Proponents on both sides of the slavery question were pacified until early in 1854, when Illinois Senator Stephen A. Douglas introduced to the Senate Committee on Territories a bill that would organize a territory called Nebraska, located in part of the Louisiana Territory, in which slavery would be prohibited, renewing the debate in Congress over slavery.

In its final form the bill created two territories—Kansas and Nebraska—and declared the Missouri Compromise of 1820 void. That compromise, which admitted Missouri as a slave state and Maine as a free state, provided for an equal number of free and slave states in the Union. The Kansas-Nebraska Act, which would admit Nebraska Territory as free and left it up to the voters to determine whether Kansas Territory would be free or slave, was passed by Congress in late May 1854 and signed on May 30 by President Franklin Pierce, whose presidency began in 1853. The act gave rise to the new Republican Party in the North and aroused fears in the South.

Historians disagree about Douglas's complex motives for introducing the bill, but certainly one reason was his interest in removing Indians from the region west of the Missouri River and encouraging a continuous line of settlements to the Pacific Ocean.

As the migration of 1854 began that spring, settlers poured into eastern portions of the new territories, both of which stretched west to the summit of the Rocky Mountains, while Nebraska Territory stretched from the northern border of Kansas to the Canadian border. New towns were founded, including Omaha, N.T., and Leavenworth and Atchison, K.T., among others.

That year, 1854, the number of emigrants traveling the Oregon Trail dropped. Only 18,000 people went west, about 6,000 to Oregon, 3,167 to Salt Lake City, and the remaining 9,000 to California. As usual, the emigrants left the Missouri River in late April or May, and the migration was routine until

August 18, when a company of Mormons were passing a Brulé Sioux Indian camp about eight miles east of Fort Laramie. What happened next is told by James Bordeaux, who operated a nearby trading post, in a letter written by Samuel Smith:

A lame cow ran into the camp which the Indians, who were waiting for payment and were out of provisions, shot and ate. The Mormons reported their loss at the fort, whereupon, August 19, about two o'clock in the afternoon, Lieutenant Grattan, with twenty-seven soldiers and Auguste Lucien, interpreter, went to arrest the thief. Bordeaux sent for the chiefs to go with the lieutenant to make the arrest. They went, but the Indian refused to give himself up. Then, while Bear Chief of the Wazhazha, and three other chiefs, Little Thunder, Big Pratizan [Partisan], and the Man Who Is Afraid of his Horses, were among the soldiers, Grattan ordered [his men] to fire. They did so, wounding Bear Chief and his brother. They fired only one round. The Indians charged and killed all the soldiers except one private who is not expected to recover. Grattan and two men were killed while standing by their cannon, the lieutenant receiving twenty-four arrows, one through his head. The Oglala camp was about a mile off and Sefroy Iott, white, a Sioux interpreter, was there, at the request of the chiefs, to prevent the young Indian from charging on the soldiers, but he could not succeed, and barely escaped with his life. The Indians then took all the goods from Bordeaux's store, worth $2,000, and threatened to go to the fort and kill the rest of the soldiers. They broke the cannon to pieces. Bordeaux buried the dead soldiers. Second Lieutenant Hugh B. Fleming, Sixth Infantry, commanding at the fort, instructed Bordeaux, in a letter, to protect himself as well as possible, evidently being afraid to leave the fort with his command. About a thousand Indians were in the battle, Bordeaux said. Six men attest the correctness of Bordeaux's account: Antonine Reynal, Tofiel Groph, Peter Pew, Samuel Smith, Paul Vial, Antonio Lahone.[17]

After ransacking Bordeaux's trading post, the Indians helped themselves to both annuity goods and other property at the American Fur Company's trading post three miles up the river from Fort Laramie. The Sioux then left the area, while the Cheyenne and Arapahos, who were not involved in the attack, waited only until they received their annuity goods and then moved away. The soldiers and neighboring traders went inside a large adobe building at Fort Laramie for safety. There were not enough soldiers at the fort to pursue the Indians. As for emigrants traveling the Oregon Trail, none apparently were harmed by the Sioux.

An investigation concluded that Lieutenant Grattan was arrogant and that the interpreter was drunk. The military called it the Grattan Massacre. But on September 5, the *Missouri Republican* in St. Louis published an editorial signed by the initials D.D.M., probably David D. Mitchell, superintendent of Indian affairs, who wrote: "The miserably mistaken policy which the Government has pursued in establishing petty little Forts, along the Arkansas and Platte, for the purpose of protecting traders and travelers, and at the same time overawing the Indians, has been worse than a useless waste of the public money. These little Forts were generally garrisoned by the fragments of a company of *infantry,* a force that could be of no more use in protecting travelers, or chasing Indians, than so many head of sheep. The Indians being well mounted, could at any time come within sight of a fort and commit any murders or outrages that chance might throw in their way, and laugh with scorn at any impotent attempts that might be made to punish them. To my own knowledge, the Indians look upon these feeble establishments with sovereign contempt, and consider themselves abundantly able at any time to 'wipe them out.' They in fact have no other effect than to impress the Indians very unfavorably as to our military strength and prowess." Mitchell then called for three new regiments of mounted men for this service.

Before 1854 ended, another tragedy occurred. A party of emigrants led by Alexander Ward and consisting of nineteen other persons, including his family, had stopped for noon on the south bank of the Boise River about twenty-five miles above Fort Boise. About sixty Indians soon appeared in the emigrants' camp. At first, they seemed to be friendly, but an Indian climbed on one of Ward's two horses and rode off a distance before returning. He then got off the horse and got on his own animal. A member of Ward's party, standing nearby, saw the Indian point his gun at him. Apparently believing he was going to be shot, the white man pulled his revolver and shot the Indian. A fight began and Ward's party was being attacked by the Indians when a small party of emigrants looking for a lost cow came on the scene. They fired at the Indians, who fled and began firing back at the white men. When one of the men in the rescue party was shot and killed, the rest of the men retreated to Fort Boise for safety and to seek help. When an armed party from the fort returned to the scene two days later, the wagons had been burned and all but two persons in Ward's party had been killed. The Indians had also fled with about $2,000 in gold carried by the emigrants, and had driven off about sixty head of cattle.

When news spread east about the massacres of 1854, it had the expected effect on migration. In the spring of 1855 only about 2,000 emigrants headed west over the Oregon Trail—1,500 for California, and 500 for Oregon. They believed the western part of the trail would be unsafe without a military escort. One emigrant bound for California, James Bardin, left Independence on April 28, reached Fort Kearny on May 19, and soon joined with another company, giving the party nearly sixty men with twenty wagons. Bardin noted in his diary that there were rumors the Sioux wanted white women and scalps, but when the company met a rider carrying the mail east from Fort Laramie, the carrier assured the emigrants that there was no danger from Indians except their stealing of stock.[18] Another emigrant, Loring Samuel Comstock, helped drive 250 head of cattle to California. In his journal, Comstock said that along the Platte River the company he was with conducted some brisk trade with Indians for horses that turned out to have been stolen from other emigrant companies. When his company was west of Fort Laramie, he related how some Sioux Indians blocked the road, spread a blanket, and demanded tribute. It was paid, and everyone took a turn at the peace pipe.[19]

By the spring of 1855, officials in Washington had decided the Indians responsible for the massacres had to be punished. A force of six hundred soldiers under General W. S. Harney left Fort Leavenworth in late May and marched toward Fort Kearny, but rain and swollen streams delayed their progress. Once Harney and his soldiers reached Fort Kearny, they remained there until August 24, when he and his units of the Fourth Artillery, the Second Dragoons, and the Sixth and Tenth Infantry regiments started west on the road toward Fort Laramie. As they crossed Ash Hollow, teamsters with a large wagon train informed Harney that he would find Little Thunder's band of Brulé Sioux camped about six miles north near the mouth of Ash Hollow. General Harney and his soldiers camped for the night on the North Platte River. From a nearby bluff the soldiers could see the Indian camp perhaps five miles away. Harney decided to attack them the next morning. A correspondent for the *Missouri Republican* traveling with the soldiers recalled what happened next:

> The plan was for the Dragoons, consisting of four companies, to cross the river at three o'clock in the morning, and endeavor to get into position behind them; the Infantry to march at 4 o'clock under the command of Major Cady, immediately upon the camp; General Harney and staff to march at half-past 4; Major Cady to wait for the General before crossing the river. Our plans, being formed the night before, were executed with

promptness in the morning. Monday, the 3d of September, will long be remembered by everyone engaged in the attack, and who was on the field.... The Dragoons were commanded by Col. [Phillip St. George] Cooke.... We had four companies of Infantry. The Infantry move up in beautiful style upon the village. As we moved up the Indians showed signs of parley; but, as we had come for war and not for peace, we paid no attention to them. As soon as they saw that, signal was given to their lodges, and they began to move beautifully in the very direction of the Dragoons; that is, in the position *we thought* they would be. The Indians, being well mounted, were about to escape us, as we thought, when we determined to talk a while with them, so as to give the Dragoons time to show themselves. We gave the signal and the Chief, Little Thunder, came up to us. We had a long talk with him and discovered that this was the band which had attacked the Mail Train. While talking with the chief, we perceived a great commotion among the Indians, which showed us plainly that the Dragoons were near. The conference was broken up and the Infantry were ordered to place their rifles at long range of from six hundred to a thousand yards, and advance rapidly. The Indians ran, of course, to the hills, and were in a fine position to repel an attack of Infantry when the Dragoons showed themselves, then, I can assure you ... the fun commenced in reality. I never saw a more beautiful thing in my life. When the Infantry saw the Dragoons coming down in such beautiful style, they gave a yell, which resounded far and wide. The Indians threw away everything they had in the world. We suppose we killed about seventy [eighty-six were killed].... We lost four men killed, four wounded and one missing. We, of necessity, killed a great many women and children. We took forty women and children prisoners, a good many horses, buffalo meat enough to supply a whole company for some time. I do not suppose the Indians in this country ever had such a perfect clearing out as upon this occasion. They will have cause to remember General Harney for some time.[20]

When the battle occurred, all of the year's westbound emigrants had passed Ash Hollow and had either reached their destinations or were close. Most did not learn what had happened for many weeks or months, but as many would learn, the Battle of Blue Water, as it came to be called, signaled more change along the Oregon Trail. It marked the beginning of troubled times between the whites and the Indians.

CHAPTER FIFTEEN

MORE CHANGE AND CIVIL WAR

We cross the prairie as of old
Our fathers crossed the sea,
To make the West as they the East
The homestead of the free.

John Greenleaf Whittier

B Y 1855 THE OREGON TRAIL had become a well-established road over which thousands of people had traveled. Aside from occasional problems with Indians, early winter storms, and spring thunderstorms with torrents of rain and lightning, the journey had become pretty routine. Travelers could obtain provisions and assistance at Fort Kearny, Fort Laramie, Fort Hall, and at an increasing number of small private trading posts, or ranches, as they were called, situated along the road. By 1855 the impact of those who traveled the Oregon Trail was obvious. California had become a state and Oregon and Washington were territories. The jumping-off towns along the Missouri River had grown and were prosperous, and after the territories of Kansas and Nebraska were opened to settlement in 1854, the Missouri border towns contributed to the rapid growth of their new towns. At the same time, some Missourians contributed to the violent struggle that erupted to make Kansas free or slave. The struggle reverberated in the North and the South and set the stage for the Civil War that followed.

The winter of 1855–56 had been terrible along much of the Oregon Trail. Between October and May, snow was on the ground, but when spring finally arrived, the rivers and creeks were full and the route of the trail was bright green. The trees were rich with foliage, and flowers burst forth seemingly more colorful than ever. Military troops, freight wagons—government and private—and men carrying the mail resumed travel, while about 12,000 emigrants gathered and departed from the Missouri River jumping-off towns.

Exactly how many emigrants were struck by lightning during spring thunderstorms is not known, but in this painting by William Henry Jackson, emigrants appear to be trying to save the life of someone the lightning had hit. (Courtesy Scotts Bluff National Monument)

At least 1,000 emigrants headed for Oregon, 8,000 to California, and a minimum of 3,000 Mormons to Utah, many with handcarts. Constructed of wood with either rawhide or light metal tires on the wheels, each handcart weighed about sixty pounds. Some were crudely made, but others were purchased in Iowa or at the town of Florence, Nebraska. Handcarts were less expensive than wagons and oxen. Many handcart companies also included one or more wagons to carry heavy belongings. Even so, handcarts were about three weeks faster in travel than going by wagon train. Records suggest that most handcart companies also experienced fewer deaths on the road than the trains. Walking instead of riding may have kept those with the handcarts in better physical shape. One exception in 1856 occurred when two Mormon handcart companies did not leave the Missouri River until late August. Mormon James Sherlock Cantwell, traveling with James Willie's handcart company consisting of seventy-five handcarts and ten supply wagons, wrote that two days after leaving Fort Laramie, Cantwell's and another handcart company ran into hail and an early winter blizzard. Nearly 230 Mormons died. Cantwell survived and eventually made it safely to Salt Lake after having had to dig through snowdrifts up to eighteen feet deep.

William Henry Jackson depicts a Mormon handcart brigade fording a stream near Fort Bridger in southwest Wyoming. (Courtesy Scotts Bluff National Monument)

Brigham Young spelled out how to construct a handcart in a letter written in 1855. Young's letter, now in the church archives at Salt Lake City, reads, in part:

> I will give you my plan of building the carts, take Iron Wood or Hard Hack for Hubs, turn them out about six inches long and five or six inches in the diameter at the shoulder, and one and a quarter at the point, and about, four and a half, feet from point-to-point, the hubs should be lined for boxes, with sole leather. The spokes should be turned or shaved out of hickory, long enough so as to make the wheel about four and a half, or five feet high. The spokes should be set bracing in the hub and seasoned. It will draw much easier built high than low so that the shafts may draw level; split out rims from good hickory, something like spinning wheel rims only thicker, and fasten them through and through with green hide and cover them also with the same when it can be done, the beds should be made out of one half inch stuff in order to be light, as possible. You will not need a particle of Iron and the brethren can come along with no trouble or perplexity of teams and save a great deal of expense.[1]

The Mormons used handcarts extensively until 1860, when a new breed of mountain oxen was used to transport emigrants from eastern Nebraska Territory to Salt Lake City. The oxen pulled empty wagons from Salt Lake City to eastern Nebraska and returned carrying settlers. This mode of transporting emigrants was used until the arrival of the railroad.

William Audley Maxwell, a California-bound emigrant in 1857, traveled in a company of eight wagons and thirty-seven people over the road. He was surprised when he met a non-Mormon with a pushcart on the Oregon Trail just before reaching Fort Laramie. In his recollections, Maxwell wrote:

> One evening when we were going into camp we were overtaken by a man trundling a push-cart. This vehicle had between its wheels a box containing the man's supplies of food and camp articles, with the blankets, which were in a roll, placed on top; all strapped down under an oilcloth cover. With this simple outfit, pushed in front of him, this man was making his way from one of the Eastern States to California, a distance of more than three thousand miles. He was of medium size, athletic appearance, with a cheerful face. He visited us overnight. The next morning he was invited to ride with us. He replied that he would be pleased to do so, but was anxious to make all possible speed, and felt that he could not wait on the progress of our train, which was somewhat slower than the pace he maintained.[2]

Maxwell provided one of the better descriptions of the emigrants' communication system, called "bone-writing." After passing through Salt Lake City, he noted:

> There were along the line of travel many bare, bleached bones of animals that had died in previous years, many of them doubtless the animals of earlier emigrants. Some of these, as for example, the frontal or the jaw-bone, whitened by the elements, and having some plain, smooth surface, were excellent tablets for pencil writing. An emigrant desiring to communicate with another, or with a company, to the rear, would write the message on one of these bones and place the relic on a heap of stones by the roadside, or suspend it in the branches of a sage bush, so conspicuously displayed that all coming after would see it and read. Those for general information, intended for all comers, were allowed to remain; others, after being read by the person addressed, were usually removed. Sometimes where passing such messages, placed by those ahead of us, we

added postscripts to the bulletins, giving names and dates, for the edifica-
tion of whomever might care to read them. It was in this way that some of
the developments regarding the Indian situation were made known by
one train to another.[3]

Another California-bound traveler, J. Robert Brown, had signed on to
work for merchants bound for Salt Lake City before continuing on to the
goldfields. Brown wrote in his journal that he met a group of Mormons
heading east on the trail "escaping from captivity," and he added that they
gave "Salt Lake a bad name." After Brown reached Fort Kearny, he learned
that Cheyenne Indians had attacked a wagon train, and he later met U.S.
dragoons who were pursuing them.[4] The wagon train that had been attacked
had been sent west from eastern Nebraska with supplies for Salt Lake City
by Almon W. Babbitt, a prominent Mormon leader. Because he had business
to conduct in St. Louis, Babbitt did not travel with the train, but followed it
later, only to learn along the Platte River that his wagons had been attacked
by Indians and destroyed. All but one of his teamsters were killed, and a
woman traveling with the wagons was kidnapped by the Indians. When Babbitt reached Fort Kearny, he refused a military escort and left with two other
Mormons for Salt Lake. About a hundred miles west of Fort Kearny and east
of Ash Hollow, Babbitt and his party were attacked by Indians and killed.

Babbitt had first gone to Salt Lake in 1848, a year after Brigham Young
had arrived. The land that is now Utah then belonged to Mexico, but when
the United States won the Mexican War and the Treaty of Guadalupe-
Hidalgo was signed, the territory became part of the United States. From
their arrival in Utah the Mormons were ruled only by the laws of their
church and by their leader, but the California gold rush brought many non-
Mormons through Salt Lake, and some of them stayed. The Mormons soon
realized a legal structure was needed to govern the growing population. A
constitutional convention met in 1849 and proposed the State of Deseret,
which would include not only modern Utah and Nevada but parts of southern California, Wyoming, Colorado, New Mexico, Oregon, and Idaho. Babbitt was sent to Washington as its delegate to Congress, but lawmakers
refused to let him take his seat. Instead of granting statehood, Congress
shrank the size of the proposed state and created the Territory of Utah in
1850, named after the Ute Indian tribe. As a compromise, Brigham Young
was appointed territorial governor, and two years later Babbitt became secretary of the territory. Only four of the newly appointed territorial officials
were non-Mormons.

Federal officials sent to Utah did not stay long. Some charged that Young and other Mormon leaders refused to recognize the power of the federal government. There also were charges that the Mormons had a secret organization to take the lives and property of anyone who questioned the church's power. Mormons were accused of burning the papers of the territorial supreme court and of being responsible for Indian attacks on some officials. Acting on these reports and sensitive to Republican charges that the Democratic Party favored the "twin relics of barbarism—polygamy and slavery," President James Buchanan sought a non-Mormon governor for Utah and selected a Georgian, Alfred Cumming, who was the great-grandson-in-law of Samuel Adams. Hearing rumors that the Mormons might resist the ouster of Brigham Young, Buchanan ordered 2,500 U.S. troops to accompany Cumming to Salt Lake City.

When Brigham Young heard the news, he declared martial law and deployed Mormons to delay the "Utah Expedition" of federal troops. Meanwhile, the first soldiers began leaving Fort Leavenworth in mid-July for Salt Lake, following the Oregon Trail. On August 7, 1857, a newspaper correspondent for the *Missouri Republican* at Fort Kearny reported that Cheyenne Indians had "made a pretty clean sweep of the beef cattle for the expedition, within a few miles of the fort."[5] The expedition was soon strung out over three hundred miles of the Oregon Trail, with the dragoons on horseback and a string of mule-drawn wagons carrying provisions bringing up the rear. The dragoons were commanded by Lieutenant Colonel Philip St. George Cooke, who in his official report noted that Fort Kearny was unable to supply his command with corn. He added that about 60,000 emigrant cattle had depleted the grass along the route. By the time they left Fort Laramie in late October, the weather was cold. The dragoons blanketed their horses and had them led and mounted alternately. Snow fell between Devil's Gate and South Pass, where the temperature dropped to 25 degrees below zero. Animals collapsed and men were frostbitten.[6]

Meanwhile, in July the first detachment of the expedition had reached what is now southwest Wyoming and established Camp Winfield on Ham's Fork about thirty miles to the northwest of Fort Bridger. Soon afterward, Mormons began to annoy and harass the federal soldiers and succeeded in burning three wagon trains of their supplies before retreating to Fort Bridger. In early November, Colonel Albert Sidney Johnston, the expedition's commander, arrived at Camp Winfield. After learning the Mormons had committed an act of war, he ordered an advance on Fort Bridger. When they arrived there several days later, after marching through cold, snow, and sleet, Johnston found the Mormons had burned Fort Bridger to the ground. They had also burned Fort Supply, about twelve miles to the south, a farm established to grow food. Aside from the farmland, the Mormons had built a stockade fence around several buildings where the workers lived. Meanwhile, Lieutenant Colonel Cooke arrived with the dragoons, along with the new territorial governor and other officers. Colonel Johnston ordered the establishment of what became Camp Scott, about two miles south of Fort Bridger, where the soldiers dug in for the winter in tents, rude huts, lean-tos, dugouts, and anything else they could construct for shelter. Later, Fort Bridger was rebuilt and became a U.S. military post.

While the Utah Expedition was following the Oregon Trail to Fort Bridger, a man named Thomas Kane met with President Buchanan in Washington. Kane was friends with Buchanan and Brigham Young. Kane offered to try and settle the dispute. Buchanan accepted the offer, and Kane started for Salt Lake City as the president's private envoy to serve as mediator. He arrived early in 1858 and found that the Mormons had decided not to fight but were preparing to search for a new home, perhaps in Mexico or in the South Pacific. Kane traveled to Camp Scott, where he persuaded Alfred Cumming, the new territorial governor, to go with him back to Salt Lake City. When the two men rode into Salt Lake City on horseback on April 5 and met Brigham Young, the Mormon leader did not challenge Cumming and accepted him as the governor of Utah Territory. Two months later, two commissioners appointed by President Buchanan arrived carrying an amnesty proclamation to the Mormons. Johnston's army marched through a deserted Salt Lake City on June 26, 1858, and established Camp Floyd forty miles to the southwest. The war was over.

Because of the threat of war, no more than 200 Mormons, some using handcarts, made the journey from Council Bluffs to Utah in 1857. The threat, however, did not reduce the number of emigrants bound for Oregon and California. The war had ended by late spring, and 6,000 people headed for California and 1,500 went to Oregon. The Oregon migration was about the same as 1857, but the migration to California in 1858 was one-third higher than the previous year.[7] By the summer of 1858, word was rapidly spreading across the plains that gold had been discovered at Cherry Creek in far western Kansas Territory near what is now Denver, Colorado. When some emigrants heading west along the Platte River heard the news, gold fever struck and they left the Oregon Trail and followed the South Platte south to what people were beginning to call the Kansas goldfields. Exactly how many people intending to go to Oregon or California decided instead to go to Cherry Creek is not known, but the gold fever was strong, and even soldiers at Fort Kearny deserted to look for gold. One Mormon, Richard Thomas Ackley, wrote in his journal that he had learned of the gold discovery just before reaching Courthouse Rock. Ackley, however, continued to Salt Lake.[8]

When news of the new gold find reached eastern Nebraska Territory, Anselm Holcomb Barker and a group of men hurriedly organized a party and with six wagons left Plattsmouth on the Missouri River in late summer for Cherry Creek, following the Oregon Trail to the west. Near the ruins of an old Indian village near Grand Island along the Platte River, Barker and the others met a former trader from Fort Laramie traveling with several wagons and his Indian squaw. They were returning east from Cherry Creek, and the trader showed Barker specimens of gold he had found. Barker later met fourteen men returning east to Lawrence, Kansas Territory, with more gold.[9]

As with the California gold rush, numerous guidebooks to the Kansas goldfields suddenly appeared. Some urged gold-seekers to follow the Santa Fe Trail and then to travel north to the goldfields. Others favored a new central route across Kansas Territory. Others favored the Oregon Trail. Two Nebraska Territory men, William N. Byers, a former government surveyor,

This illustration appeared in Harper's Weekly, *August 13, 1859, and shows gold-seekers following the Oregon Trail to the goldfields in far western Kansas Territory, now Colorado.* (Courtesy Kansas State Historical Society)

This photo by Albert Bierstadt shows a party of gold-seekers
about to leave St. Joseph, Missouri, in the spring of 1859,
bound for the Kansas goldfields in what is now Colorado.
(Courtesy Kansas State Historical Society)

and John N. Kellom, then the new territorial superintendent of public instruction, produced *A Handbook to the Gold Fields,* published in Chicago in 1859. They favored the Oregon Trail and wrote: "There is no feasible route south of the Platte Valley—no good starting point south of Leavenworth; and all the passable roads converge and unite in the Platte Valley, at Fort Kearny, 189 miles from Omaha." They included not only a detailed guide to travel along the north bank of the Platte River, but an extensive list of what they described as the "most complete outfit" for gold-seekers:

TEAM, WAGON, AND FIXTURES.

	PRICE
3 yoke of oxen, at $75 per yoke,	$225.00
1 wagon (wooden or wrought iron axle),	85.00
Wagon sheet, chains, and yokes,	15.00
Total,	$325.00

CAMP FIXTURES AND FURNITURE.

	WEIGHT	PRICE
1 Tent and poles—the latter ironed,	40	$15.00
10 pairs blankets, at $4 per pair,	60	40.00
1 Dutch oven, for baking bread,	12	1.25
3 Camp kettles, for tea, coffee, soap, etc.	10	3.00
1 Frying pan, for meat,	2	.75
1 Coffee mill,	1	.50
6 tin plates,	1	.50
6 tin cups	1	.50
1 set knives and forks,	1	.75
1 set spoons,	1	.50
2 butcher knives,	1	.50
1 large pan, for mixing bread,	2	.75
1 Lard can, to hold forty pounds,	5	1.50
1 wooden bucket,	2	.25
Totals,	140	$66.75

TOOLS

	WEIGHT	PRICE
4 steel picks, best quality, with handles,	26	$9.50
4 steel shovels, best quality, Ames' make,	18	6.00
1 Crow bar,	12	1.50
4 Gold pans, largest size,	8	4.00
Sheet iron for Long Tom,	12	.75
Pair of gold scales,		2.00
4 Axes, and handles,	20	6.00
1 hand saw,	2	1.50
1 drawing knife,	1	.75
3 Augurs, ½ in., 1 in., and 1½ in., and handles	4	1.30
1 Chisel, 1 inch,	1	.35

1 twelve inch file,		.40
1 Hatchet,	2	.75
2 small gimlets,		.15
Totals,	106	$34.95

PROVISIONS

	WEIGHT	PRICE
Flour, at $3.50 per 100 lbs,	1,200	$42.00
Bacon, at 10c. per lb.,	400	40.00
Dried Beef, at 12½c. per lb.	100	12.50
Lard, at 10c. per lb.,	40	4.00
Corn Meal,	200	2.00
Beans,	150	5.25
Dried Fruit,	60	4.00
Salt,	100	1.50
Sugar—dry brown, at 9c. per lb.	200	18.00
Coffee,	75	11.50
Tea, at 65c.,	8	5.20
Rice, at 8c.,	30	2.40
Pepper, in the grain,	6	1.20
Soda,	3	.30
Cream Tartar,	6	3.00
Box of Pickles, in jars,	40	4.00
Totals,	2618	$156.85

SUNDRIES

	WEIGHT	PRICE
3 gallons Brandy,	24	$12.00
Soap,	25	2.00
Gunpowder,	8	3.20

Lead,	25	2.50
Shot,	10	1.00
2000 Gun Caps,	1	1.20
2 dozen boxes matches,	5	1.00
10 yards drilling, for sluice	2	1.25
Wrought nails,	4	.50
Cut nails,	6	.35
Candles,	15	3.75
Whetstone,	1	.20
75 feet of ⅝ or ¼ inch manila rope,	7	1.60
5 gallon water keg,	5	1.25
Totals,	138	$31.80

GIVING TOTAL WEIGHT AND COST OF COMPLETE OUTFIT AS FOLLOWS:

	WEIGHT	PRICE
Team, wagon and fixtures,		$325.00
Camp fixtures and furniture,	140 lbs.	65.75
Tools,	106 "	34.95
Provisions,	2618 "	156.85
Sundries,	138 "	31.80
Grand Totals,	3002 lbs.	$614.35[10]

Since this outfit was organized for four men, a trip to the goldfields of far western Kansas would have cost each man about $153. But many made the journey for far less.

In the small settlement of Oskaloosa in northeast Kansas Territory, Samuel Peppard, a millwright by trade, got the gold fever, as did several of his friends. Peppard suggested that they build a windwagon—a wagon with sails that was pushed along by the wind—and follow the Oregon Trail to the goldfields. His friends laughed at first, but the more they thought about it, the better the idea sounded. The idea of a windwagon was not new. When Captain Meriwether Lewis and William Clark crossed the plains early in the nineteenth century, one of their boats on wheels with its sails set was blown along. Whether or not Peppard got his idea from reading the journals of Lewis and Clark is not known, but he probably had heard about a Missouri man named Thomas who in 1846 started to build a windwagon with the intent of sailing down the Santa Fe Trail, although it was not completed until 1853 at Westport, Missouri. Thomas managed to sail about a hundred miles to the southwest over the Santa Fe Trail before returning to Missouri, but the idea of using windwagons went nowhere.

By early 1860, Peppard began to build his windwagon of rough lumber and shaped it like a skiff. It was eight feet long, three feet across midships, and two feet deep. It was placed on a running gear with axles six feet apart and equipped with wheels about the size of those on a buggy. He fastened a ten-foot mast to the front axle, which came up through the bottom. To this he rigged two sails. The larger was eleven feet by eight, the smaller seven by five feet. Both were worked by a rope through a pulley located at the top of the mast. Peppard concluded that if the wind was high the smaller sail would be used. If the wind was low, the larger sail could be employed. His windwagon weighed about 350 pounds. It carried a crew of four men, a cargo of 500 pounds, plus a camping outfit and provisions that served as ballast.

In early May 1860, after testing his windwagon south of Oskaloosa, Peppard and his crew headed northwest until they struck the Independence Trail near modern Marysville, Kansas, traveling on the open prairie parallel to the trail ruts. Soon they came to the Platte River near Fort Kearny and followed the road along the south bank. A correspondent for *Leslie's Illustrated Weekly* was at Fort Kearny and saw the windwagon arrive about May 26. He sent a report to his magazine describing the vehicle and crew, and added: "I timed her going two miles and with the moderate breeze at the time, she made it in little less than 14 minutes (about 8 miles an hour)." Peppard added:

> Our best time was two miles in four minutes. We could not run faster than that rate as the boxing would have heated. One day we went fifty miles in three hours, and in doing so passed 625 teams. There were, you know, a great many people enroute to the gold fields.... If we went ninety miles a day it was considered a good day's travel.

Peppard's windwagon followed the Oregon Trail to near modern North Platte, Nebraska, and then traveled southwest following the South Fork of the Platte before crossing into Kansas Territory. It continued toward the goldfields until it reached a point about fifty miles north-northeast of Den-

This illustration of Samuel Peppard's windwagon as it was departing new Fort Kearny on May 26, 1860, appeared in Leslie's Illustrated Weekly *on July 7 of that year.* (Courtesy Kansas State Historical Society)

ver, where Peppard and his crew spotted a dust devil. Before they could lower their sails, it struck the windwagon and tossed it twenty feet into the air, and it broke up when it hit the ground. Fortunately, Peppard and his crew were not injured. They gathered their belongings together and caught a ride into Denver with a passing wagon train. Peppard's party had traveled more than five hundred miles in the windwagon, much of it over the Oregon Trail.[11]

How many gold-seekers used the Oregon Trail in 1859 and 1860 to reach the Kansas goldfields is not known, but in 1859 at least 30,000 persons traveled the trail, including 1,000 or more Mormons bound for Salt Lake, 1,000 emigrants going to Oregon, and about 17,000 to California. As many as 10,000 other people may have followed the trail to the Kansas goldfields and to Nevada, where silver had been discovered. The following year, 1860, between 10,000 and 15,000 traveled the trail, but their destinations, like their number, can only be guessed at, since by then many people were moving west to escape the threat of the impending Civil War.

SINCE 1855 the freighting of government supplies to all military posts in the West and Southwest from Fort Leavenworth was monopolized by the firm of Russell, Majors & Waddell. William H. Russell and William B. Waddell of Lexington, Missouri, and Alexander Majors of Westport, Missouri,

formed their company to obtain two-year contracts with the government.
The firm made money until the government asked it to freight supplies west
over the Oregon Trail for the Utah Expedition. Three of the company's supply trains were destroyed by Mormons, causing the company to go into debt.
While Waddell and Majors tried to save the firm from financial ruin,
William H. Russell started a new venture in 1860 with John S. Jones. They
established the Pony Express to carry the mail from St. Joseph, Missouri, to
Sacramento, California. Russell and Jones wanted to obtain the $600,000
mail contract then held by John Butterfield's Overland Mail Company,
whose southern route had been chosen over a more northerly route following much of the Oregon Trail and going through Salt Lake City. Even
though the southern route from St. Louis across Arkansas, Texas, and modern New Mexico and Arizona was longer than the central route, the Post
Office Department in Washington favored it, believing winter weather
would delay the mail. Russell wanted to prove that overland travel to California over a central route was practical during the winter months.

Russell and Jones gave their employees only sixty-five days to prepare the
Pony Express service. Rapidly the company purchased horses, hired station
keepers, stock tenders, and eighty riders, and established 190 relay stations,
each about ten miles apart. More than a third of the stations were located
along the Oregon Trail from northeast Kansas Territory to the Platte River
and west into what is now southwest Wyoming. There the route went southwest to Salt Lake City and west across the modern state of Nevada and into
California to Sacramento. On April 3, 1860, at 7:15 p.m., the first rider set out
with mail from St. Joseph. At about the same time, another rider left from
San Francisco for St. Joseph, a distance of 1,966 miles. The Pony Express
proved to be efficient, with riders changing horses about every ten miles and
turning the mail over to a new rider every seventy-five to a hundred miles.
They averaged about ten miles an hour, carrying the mail east and west
between Sacramento, the official western terminus, and St. Joseph in thirteen days. Travelers along the Oregon Trail often watched as riders passed
their wagon trains. C. M. Clark, M.D., heading for the Kansas goldfields, said
of one rider "the pony [was] on the full run and wet with perspiration."[12]

The Pony Express did not last. It went out of business about eighteen
months after it began—when the transcontinental telegraph was completed.
Samuel Morse's electromagnetic telegraph had been perfected in 1844. At
first the federal government ignored its potential usefulness and several
small telegraph companies were formed. By 1851 there were more than fifty
separate companies operating in the United States. By the late 1850s, as the
government began to pay more attention to the telegraph, entrepreneurs

saw a brighter future for the new form of communication and began to gain control of the smaller companies. In Missouri, Charles M. Stebbins had constructed a line in 1858 from St. Louis west along the south bank of the Missouri River to Kansas City, Missouri. The following year, the Western Union Telegraph Company gained control of Stebbins's line. By then Western Union controlled most telegraph lines in the states north of the Ohio River and in parts of Iowa, Minnesota, Kansas, and Missouri.

About two months after the Pony Express service began, Congress passed and President James Buchanan signed the Pacific Telegraph Act authorizing $40,000 a year for ten years to any company constructing a telegraph from the western boundary of Missouri to San Francisco. Hiram Sibley, representing Western Union, won the contract by default in June 1860 after two other bidders dropped out. Sibley sent a representative to California to consolidate two local telegraph companies into the Overland Telegraph Company for the purpose of building the line east from Sacramento. At the other end Sibley hired Edward Creighton to oversee the construction westward, and he divided his eastern crew into specialized groups. One would survey the route, another would install poles, and a third group would string the wires, while a fourth group was responsible for setting up work camps and

This William Henry Jackson painting shows a buckskin-clad Pony Express rider atop his horse, galloping over the Oregon Trail and apparently trying to outrun Indians in the distance. (Courtesy Scotts Bluff National Monument)

This William Henry Jackson painting shows the Three Crossing Pony Express Station west of Independence Rock, and a departing rider. (Courtesy Scotts Bluff National Monument)

feeding the construction workers. Although the westbound line reached Fort Kearny in November 1860 and the equipment was installed in a sod building, the rest of the construction did not begin in earnest until early July 1861, about three months after Confederate cannons bombarded Fort Sumter in Charleston, South Carolina, and the Civil War began.

Migration over the Oregon Trail dropped to perhaps no more than 5,000 in 1861, the year Kansas became a state and Colorado became a territory made up from portions of Kansas, Utah, Nebraska, and New Mexico territories. Some travelers were headed for the goldfields near Denver, C.T., but the majority probably were bound for California and not Oregon because of Indian troubles along the road beyond Fort Hall. One California-bound emigrant, Mallet Case Jackson, left Jackson County, Iowa, in mid-March with an ox-drawn wagon. He joined a company captained by a man named Kennedy. It became known as the Red Horn Company because each ox and cow had one horn painted red for identification. Jackson did not learn of the start of the Civil War until the company reached Fort Laramie.[13] Another traveler over the road in 1860 was Elijah Larken, an Englishman, who left on August 6 by stagecoach from Florence in eastern Nebraska Territory on the

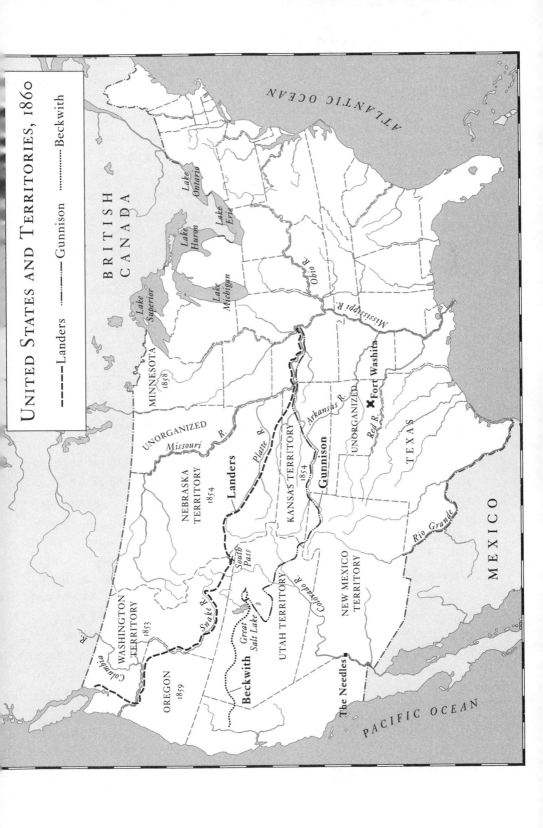

Missouri River, bound for Salt Lake City. He reached Fort Laramie on September 5. When his stagecoach reached the Green River crossing, soldiers ordered the stage to follow the road to Fort Bridger. There the passengers were required to take the citizens' oath of allegiance to the Union.[14]

In the meantime, the transcontinental telegraph construction crews made better time than expected, but on the treeless plains telegraph poles had to be brought in by wagons from where trees were available to be cut. Building the line over the Sierra Nevada and Rocky Mountains was more difficult because of the terrain. The westbound crew following the Oregon Trail reached Fort Laramie on August 5 and then crossed the mountains to Salt Lake City, where the line from Sacramento had already arrived. The construction crews worked rapidly, wanting to finish their job before winter arrived. On October 24, 1861, the two lines were connected at Salt Lake City. The first transcontinental message was sent east to President Abraham Lincoln from Stephen J. Field, chief justice of California, in the absence of the governor. The message read, in part: "The people of California desire to congratulate you upon the completion of the great work. They believe that it will be the means of strengthening the attachment which binds both the East and West of the Union, and they desire . . . to express their loyalty to the Union and their determination to stand by its Government on this its day of trial." The Pony Express was out of business.[15]

By then the Civil War was six months old. In the days after it began, 313 army officers in the West, about a third of the officers in the entire Union army, resigned, most to join the Confederacy. At Fort Kearny, a majority of the soldiers were southern sympathizers. When the war began, tensions were high between them and a minority of staunch Union men. Men on both sides anxiously awaited reports of the war at the post telegraph office. When news came in, copies of the dispatches were made and distributed. Officers at Fort Kearny were also divided in their sentiments. Many were Union men, but those with southern sympathies openly urged secession, including Beverly Robertson of Virginia, who became a general in the Confederate army. When Colonel Dixon S. Miles and the Second United States Infantry were ordered east, a Captain Tyler commanding Company A, Second Dragoons, was given temporary command of Fort Kearny. He spiked fifteen large brass cannon and nearly caused mutiny among Union soldiers. Tyler then left the fort, went south, and joined the Confederate army. He remained there for some time and then decided to travel north to Cincinnati to see his wife. Although he wore a disguise, he reportedly was recognized, arrested, and became a prisoner at Fort Lafayette in New York Harbor.

The Butterfield Overland Stage Company had to cease operations on June 30, 1861, because its route went through the Confederate states of Arkansas and Texas. Another stage line, the Central Overland California & Pike's Peak Express had been started up, although by 1860 it was almost defunct. Ben Holladay, who had amassed wealth during the 1850s in freighting and other business ventures, purchased the line for $100,000 and began what he called the Overland Stage Line. Holladay purchased celebrated Concord stagecoaches and the finest horses and mules he could find. Because the central route across Kansas used by the Central Overland California & Pike's Peak Express had been plagued by hostile Indians, Holladay established a route that ran from the Missouri River town of Atchison, Kansas, northwest to the Oregon Trail and west across Wyoming to Salt Lake City and then west to California. A branch line provided service to Denver. In July 1862 the Post Office Department in Washington ordered Holladay to move his central route across modern Wyoming farther south because of Indian raids along the central route, or the old Oregon Trail. The new route left the Oregon Trail at Julesburg, a trading post named for Jules Beni, a French trader, located close to the Upper California Crossing on the south bank of the South Platte River. The new route went to modern Greeley, Colorado, then a settlement called Latham, and continued through Virginia Dale (Colorado) and Tie Siding (Wyoming), northwest to the Laramie Plains and across Bridger's Pass, and then westward along the modern route of I-80 and the Union Pacific Railroad before rejoining the Oregon Trail at Fort Bridger. Near modern Rawlins, Wyoming, the army sent troops and established Fort Halleck to increase protection in the area. Between 1862 and 1868 about 20,000 emigrants followed this southern route to avoid Indian troubles to the north, and many travelers began referring to the Oregon Trail as the Overland Trail, which it was, because of the growing popularity of Holladay's Overland Stage Line.

Frank Root, then an express messenger with the Overland Stage Line, wrote in 1901:

> There were quite a number of strong secessionists on the "Overland" as there were firm Union men. Neither side hesitated to express itself when occasion demanded. A number of employees didn't "care a continental," they said, how the war terminated, but as for putting themselves up as targets in the service of "Uncle Sam" at thirteen dollars a month—to do that they never would consent. They were being paid too well on the road. Drivers in the employ of the stage company received from $40 to $75 a

month and board; stock tenders, $40 to $50; carpenters, $75; harness-makers and blacksmiths, $100 to $125; and division agents, $100 to $125.[16]

WHEN REGULAR ARMY TROOPS were ordered east soon after the Civil War began, regiments of volunteer troops were also raised. These volunteers enlisted in state or territorial units that were organized under local authority and then sworn into the federal service to be used where needed. In many instances the volunteers were of a higher caliber than the prewar regulars. Many of the officers were former regulars with experience fighting Indians. Fortunately the Indians along the Platte River did not take advantage of the confusion of soldiers leaving forts along the Oregon Trail and the lull before all of the volunteers could take their place. But soon in far western Nebraska Territory—now Wyoming—the Shoshone Indians raided and burned stage stations, attacked stagecoaches, killed drivers and passengers, and drove livestock away. In April 1862, an agent at the Pacific Springs Station near South Pass told his company that he would not send any mail coaches over the line until troops arrived to protect them. Later that month the Post Office Department in Washington ordered all mail to be delivered to California by sea until the interruptions ceased. Through the War Department, President Lincoln asked Brigham Young, president of the Mormon church, to provide temporary protection for the mails and the new telegraph line being constructed in the area near Independence Rock. Young sent more than a hundred troops to patrol the area between Independence Rock and South Pass until voluntary troops arrived. When a detachment of the Sixth Ohio Volunteer Cavalry arrived, the Mormons soon returned to Salt Lake City.

In August 1862 there was a bloody Dakota Sioux uprising in Minnesota after annuity payments were late. Learning the government would not make the customary payments in gold because of the Civil War, traders refused to sell the Indians provisions on credit even though there was widespread hunger and starvation among the Dakota Sioux. Councils were held among the Dakota and most chose war. Four whites were killed near Litchfield on August 17. The next day 44 whites died at the Redwood Agency and among federal troops trying to suppress the uprising. The next day another 16 whites died in and around New Ulm. The Indians took many white captives. After thirty-seven days of fighting, U.S. troops took 1,200 Dakota men, women, and children into custody. During the days that followed, another 800 Dakota surrendered. More than 500 whites had died along with about 60 Dakota during the uprising. Trials followed. Three hundred and twenty-three Dakota Sioux were convicted and 303 sentenced to be hanged, but only 38 Indians were hanged, on orders from President Lincoln. In his book *The Civil War in the American West,* Alvin M. Josephy, Jr., observed that "in the militaristic atmosphere of the Civil War" the Indians were "treated with intolerance and brutality."[17]

Although Minnesota was hundreds of miles to the north of the Oregon Trail, what happened there soon had an impact on the trail. Word spread south quickly to other tribes, and Indians raided and burned stage stations along the trail in the Platte River valley. To the west, other Indian hostilities occurred over the western leg of the Oregon Trail, where in 1862 many of the 20,000 travelers were bound for the new goldfields in eastern Oregon and what is now southwest Montana. Henry Griffin discovered gold in the Malheur River region in October 1861, and gold was found at Bannock in present-day Montana in July 1862. A volunteer troop of Oregon cavalry was sent to eastern Oregon to protect emigrants and gold-seekers. That same year, 1862, two companies of soldiers from Oregon and Washington established Fort Lapwai near modern Lewiston, Idaho, on a new reservation for the Nez Percé. The following year, 1863, Fort Boise was built on the site of present-day Boise, Idaho. To the north, troops from Fort Walla Walla, near the Columbia River, also tried to protect travelers coming up the Oregon Trail from Fort Boise, but there were not enough soldiers to maintain peace. Farther south the Northern Shoshone and Bannock Indians became more intent on resisting the intrusion of whites. Some travelers along the Oregon Trail looked for a safer route and asked Tim Goodale, a guide, to lead them over a cutoff pioneered a decade earlier by John Jeffrey, who had operated a ferry at the mouth of the Blackfoot River. The emigrants hoped the cutoff would also be a more direct route to the goldfields on the Salmon River.

Goodale led the way, beginning on July 22, 1862, and because large numbers would discourage any Indian attacks, he organized a train of 338 wagons with 795 men and 300 women and children, plus about 2,900 head of stock. The wagon train probably was the largest to travel any section of the Oregon Trail up until that time. It took members more than three hours to get into or out of camp. But Goodale got the whole lot through safely. Meanwhile, Bannock Indians had ambushed a wagon train at what became known as Massacre Rock in modern Idaho and killed ten people. Soon travelers were following Goodale's Cutoff instead of the main Oregon Trail to the south along the Snake River. But travel was slow, since Goodale's Cutoff crossed through an area of old lava flows. The lava reduced travel to one lane. Because most of the emigrants followed the cutoff in July when the weather was the hottest, the hot, dry desert air shrank the wood in the wagons and caused wheels and boxes to come apart. Later emigrants who followed Goodale's Cutoff wrote of finding pieces of broken wagons along the route.

One 1862 traveler heading from Omaha to Virginia City, Nevada, was Dr. Charles Lewis Anderson. In letters written to his wife, Dr. Anderson told of more than a thousand teams on the plains moving toward the Pacific. He also saw many trains of disillusioned Mormons "fleeing Zion," plus Confederate sympathizers flying the Confederate flag. At Fort Laramie, Dr. Anderson decided to go to Salt Lake and take a stage to Nevada. He also wrote that many Indian raids along the road had disrupted stagecoach services and the telegraph.[18]

Another traveler that year was Rev. Sherlock Bristol from Wisconsin, who captained a large wagon train bound for Oregon. Near Fort Hall, cattle stampeded, killing a woman and child. After leaving Fort Hall, he learned that Indians had killed six of eight miners going from Boise to Salt Lake. Bristol told of another raid on a wagon train from Iowa City, Iowa, captained by a man named Adams. The Indians were attacking when another wagon train came to the rescue and drove them away, but soon after, the wagon train that came to the rescue was ambushed and two emigrants were killed

Beyond Massacre Rocks, west of American Falls, Idaho, along Interstate 86, one can still see the ruts on a rough stretch of the Oregon Trail. From this point westward the road improved, and a less demanding route lay ahead. (Author's collection)

and its captain wounded. At Rock Creek, Bristol's train was attacked by Indians, but U.S. troops arrived before anyone was injured.[19]

Perhaps the worst Indian attack of 1862 occurred on August 9 along the Snake River west of American Falls in modern southeastern Idaho. Three of four wagon trains were moving west over the Oregon Trail when Indians attacked and killed five emigrants. As wagon trains behind the one that was attacked approached, the Indians fled. The dead were buried and the rest camped for the night and discussed what to do. The next morning a group of thirty armed men went in pursuit of the Indians and located them about seven miles away. When the Indians began firing on the emigrants, most of them turned and ran, but not before four of them were killed. The train then followed the Goodale Cutoff in an effort to avoid the Indians. The site of the attack is just east of what is known today as Massacre Rocks, ten miles west of American Falls, Idaho.

The events along the road in 1862 had a big impact on travelers, but two events that occurred in Washington, D.C., that year would have a far greater effect on overland travel, western settlement, and the future of the Oregon Trail. First, for more than seventy years Congress could not agree on what to do with public lands, but after the southern states seceded from the Union, the Republican-controlled Congress passed and President Lincoln signed the Homestead Act, which became law on January 1, 1863. Any person could file for 160 acres of federal land if he or she was an American citizen, or had filed his or her intention papers. To file, a person had to be twenty-one years old or the head of a family, or to have served fourteen days in the U.S. Army or Navy. Once a qualified person filed on a homestead, he or she could secure a fee-simple title to the land by residing on or farming the claim for five successive years. If a homesteader did not wish to wait five years, 160 acres could be purchased for $1.25 an acre after six months' residence and rudimentary improvements. Second, on July 1, 1862, Congress enacted legislation providing for the construction of the transcontinental railroad from Omaha to Sacramento. Before the Civil War, Congress had appropriated funds to survey various proposed routes for such a line, but lawmakers could not agree on its route until the southern states seceded. The law provided that the railroad be built by two companies, one working from the east, the other from the west. Each company would receive ten alternate sections of federal land per mile on both sides of the route (this amount was doubled in 1864) and a thirty-year government loan paying thousands of dollars for each mile of track constructed. In 1863, when the Union Pacific Railroad began construction from Omaha and the Central Pacific broke ground at Sacramento, it was the beginning of the end for the Oregon Trail.

CHAPTER SIXTEEN

DECLINE OF
THE TRAIL

*The art of progress is to preserve order amid change
and to preserve change amid order.*

Alfred North Whitehead

ROM THE EARLY 1840s into the middle 1850s, most of the Indians living in the regions through which the Oregon Trail crossed came to tol-
erate the seasonal passage of emigrants with their wagons and livestock. The
Indians also accepted the establishment of the military Forts Kearny and
Laramie as they had accepted private trading posts established earlier by the
Hudson's Bay Company. The forts and trading posts provided the Indians
with a place to trade, often with emigrants. Numerous emigrant diaries,
journals, and recollections also tell of Indians trying to beg tobacco or other
things from them on the road. Occasionally, Indians might run off horses or
cattle or steal something from the emigrant camps, but overall those early
years saw mostly peaceful relations between whites and Indians.

Things began to change in the late 1850s when gold was discovered in
what is now Colorado and then in present-day Montana, Idaho, and eastern
Oregon. Gold-seekers seeking shortcuts began to veer off the established
route of the Oregon Trail and cross territory claimed by different tribes to
reach the goldfields. The Indians' view of the white man changed. They
became more resentful of whites and occasionally attacked them. Soldiers
then sought to punish the Indians responsible. By 1862, Mormon settlements
in the Great Salt Lake basin had spread north into Indian territory. Shoshone
Indians under Chief Bear Hunter made scattered attacks on the northernmost Mormon settlements and on emigrants traveling the Oregon Trail to
the north in the vicinity of Bear Lake, which straddles the modern states of
Utah and Idaho. Colonel Patrick E. Connor of the First California Infantry,
stationed at Camp Douglas near Salt Lake City, devised a plan to attack the

Indians with his volunteers, who had been sworn into federal service to patrol the mail road west of Salt Lake City. Learning the Indians were camped on the Bear River about 140 miles north of Bear Lake in Idaho, Connor started north through snow and bitter cold with his 300 volunteer soldiers.

Chief Bear Hunter learned that Connor and his soldiers were coming and resolved to stay and fight. His 300 well-armed warriors made defensive preparations in a steep-sided ravine where their camp was located. On January 27, 1863, Connor and his soldiers reached the area of the Indians' camp and deployed for an attack. When the fighting began, some of the soldiers succeeded in flanking the Indians. The battle lasted about four hours. At times there was hand-to-hand combat between the soldiers and the Indians. When it was over, Chief Bear Hunter and about 250 Shoshones, including 90 women and children, were dead. Connor's command counted at least 14 soldiers killed and more than 50 wounded. Seventy-nine of the soldiers suffered from severe frostbite in what has become known as the Bear River Massacre.[1]

Colonel Connor was promoted to general. His actions did bring temporary peace to the Mormon settlements and in the area along a portion of the Oregon Trail. That year, 1863, more than 3,600 Mormons traveled the road to Salt Lake City, and about 16,000 emigrants and gold-seekers went west to Oregon, California, and the territories of Nevada and Idaho, or what would become Montana Territory the following spring. A large number of gold-seekers only traveled the road west across Nebraska Territory to the South Platte River and then turned south to Colorado Territory.

Many of the emigrants were trying to escape the Civil War, including Arazena Angeline Cooper, who was bound for Oregon. She came from Lawrence County, Missouri, where she had been threatened by guerrilla raids from both Union and Confederate forces. She decided to make a new home in Oregon with her parents and a young daughter, and set out west in 1863. Her husband may have been a soldier. Whether he was dead is not known, but he was not with the party heading west. When they reached Idaho, Arazena gave birth to a son. The family eventually reached the Willamette Valley safely.[2]

Another emigrant fleeing the Civil War was Miles C. Moore, a young man from Wisconsin who wanted to avoid service in the Union army. He joined three other men to seek gold in Idaho. At Council Bluffs they purchased a wagon and mules plus "bacon enough to last a lifetime." In his recollections, Moore remembered that when his party reached Fort Laramie, on an urge, he swam across the dangerous North Platte and back "in a spirit of bravado." When they reached the Sweetwater River, a half-breed tried to talk his party into taking a new route to Montana by way of the Bighorn River. They refused but later followed the Lander Cutoff to Fort Hall. Next they crossed the Snake River on a ferry operated by Mormons and continued to Bannock, where Moore and his companions began prospecting on Grasshopper Creek. Bannock was then in Idaho Territory, but within a year it became part of the new territory of Montana.[3]

This 1863 photo made by C. R. Savage shows a large party of Mormons camped in the Coalville area about thirty miles northeast of Salt Lake City. Coal had been discovered there late in 1858, and by 1863, emigrants who had traveled the Oregon Trail were settling in the area, which is about 5,600 feet above sea level. Coalville, surrounded by mountains and with two rivers flowing nearby, is very picturesque. (Courtesy Kansas State Historical Society)

While other gold-seekers followed the Lander Cutoff to save time, most of those bound for Montana appear to have followed the Oregon Trail to Fort Bridger and then turned north through modern Idaho to Fort Hall and on to the diggings. The only other way to reach the Montana goldfields from the east was to travel up the Missouri River by steamboat to Fort Benton and then to go overland by horseback. It was much longer and more expensive because of the cost of steamboat travel. One 1862 gold-seeker, John M. Bozeman from Georgia, followed the Oregon Trail route, but after getting to the gold diggings was soon convinced there was a shorter route. In March 1863, Bozeman along with John M. Jacobs and his daughter Emma, whose mother was a Flathead Indian, set out from Bannock to scout a new route. They crossed the Gallatin Valley and went over a pass that would later be known as Bozeman Pass into the Yellowstone Valley. Near the mouth of the Bighorn River, they avoided an Indian war party but then came upon James Stuart and his Yellowstone Expedition scouting a wagon road down the Yellowstone River to the mouth of the Bighorn River. Bozeman's party, not realizing they had met Stuart's party, turned and raced away only to run into a large group of Indians who robbed them of their clothes, weapons, and food. Jacobs's daughter was beaten for being in the company of white men. When the Indians left, Bozeman's party continued on and about two weeks later managed to reach the Oregon Trail at the mouth of Deer Creek on the North Platte River, about twenty-five miles southeast of modern Casper, Wyoming.

At Deer Creek Station, they obtained new clothing, food, and supplies, and a few days later Bozeman and Jacobs convinced emigrants in a passing wagon train to take the shorter route. Bozeman hired Rafael Gallegos, a Mexican who knew the region, to lead them. Two days after setting out, a large party of Cheyenne and Lakota Indians stopped them and warned that if they did not turn back, the wagon train would be destroyed. They returned to the Oregon Trail, but after the Indians left, Bozeman, Jacobs, and eight other men on horseback continued over the route via the Bighorn Basin to Montana. The following year, 1864, John Bozeman and others led four large wagon trains with about 1,500 emigrants over what became known as the Bozeman Trail, named for John Bozeman. The wagons were the first to use the trail, the exact route of which shifted a little each year thereafter.

At least 40,000 emigrants traveled the Oregon Trail in 1864. Soldiers, spread thin, did the best they could in escorting emigrants and gold-seekers west, but hostilities still occurred. In July 1864, Thomas and Nancy Morton of Sidney, Iowa, joined a party of emigrants with twelve horse-drawn wagons bound for Denver. They left from Omaha and traveled west over the Oregon Trail to new Fort Kearny, where the post commander assured them there was no danger from Indians. The emigrants had only gone about thirty-five miles west of Fort Kearny when a band of about three hundred Indians swept down on them. As the emigrants tried to escape, Nancy Morton was shot by arrows in her left thigh and side, and her ribs were fractured as the whites tried to escape. The Indians finally got the wagons stopped, killed Nancy's husband, Thomas, and eleven other people, then plundered and overturned the wagons before setting them afire and stampeding the stock. The wounded Nancy and a nine-year-old boy, Daniel Marble, were tied on horses and taken away by the Indians. When army officers at Fort Laramie learned she was still alive, they sent a half-breed to the Indians offering to exchange goods for the woman and boy. The first offer was rejected, but they accepted a second offer and Nancy Morton was released in December 1864. What happened to the boy is not known, but Nancy was treated at the Fort Laramie hospital and then escorted back east.[4]

In another incident during the summer of 1864, a newly married couple, Fanny Kelly, nineteen, and her older husband, Josiah, with a wagon loaded with $6,500 worth of merchandise, followed the road from northeast Kansas toward Montana Territory to establish a store. About eight weeks after starting on their journey, they reached Fort Laramie, where they were told the Indians were peaceable. They continued their journey west, but three days later Sioux Indians attacked their train, killed or seriously wounded a number of the men, plundered the wagons and then took Fanny Kelly and her daughter Mary captive. With her mother's help, Mary escaped but later was found by the Indians and killed. Fanny Kelly learned of her daughter's death when she was finally freed after five months of captivity.[5]

Aside from 1,500 emigrants who followed the Bozeman Trail to Montana Territory in 1864, the others took the long way, following the Oregon Trail over South Pass to Fort Bridger and then north past Fort Hall into Montana Territory. Still others went to California and Oregon, and a large number of gold-seekers went to Colorado Territory. Some Denver-bound travelers were following a new route west across Kansas through territory claimed by Cheyenne and Arapaho Indians. This Kansas route had been used for a number of years, and about three years earlier the government sought to relocate the Cheyennes and Arapahos to reservations, but the Indians refused. Tensions between the Indians and whites increased, and before 1864 ended, two new military posts were built to provide travelers with protection. Fort Sedgwick was established near Julesburg, and Fort Mitchell was constructed on the west side of Scotts Bluff in western Nebraska Territory.

In 1864, Cheyenne and Arapaho chiefs, including Black Kettle, traveled to Denver to talk peace with John Evans, territorial governor of Colorado, and Colonel John Chivington, its military commander. The Indians were unaware that Chivington received a telegram during the talks from his superior, General Samuel Curtis, advising that he wanted no peace until the Indians suffered more. Curtis's views concerning the Indians were in line

*This is Cheyenne Chief Black Kettle, who escaped the
Sand Creek Massacre.* (Courtesy Western History
Collections, University of Oklahoma)

with those of Chivington. When the Indian chiefs left the talks, they thought
they had made peace with Evans and Chivington. The Indians set up camp
on Sand Creek east of what is now Eads, Colorado, close to the western border of Kansas and a little more than two hundred miles south of the Oregon
Trail. After the talks ended, however, Chivington made plans to kill the
Indians.

Early on the morning of November 27, 1864, Chivington, with about
seven hundred Colorado volunteers, swept down on Black Kettle's camp on
Sand Creek with orders to take no prisoners. Black Kettle ran up an American flag given to him a few years earlier by President Lincoln while the chief
was visiting Washington, D.C., along with a white flag of truce on a large
lodge pole in front of his tent, but the mounted troops ignored the flags and
charged. When the attack was over, at least 150 Indians had been killed,
including 8 leading chiefs and many women and children. The soldiers even
scalped many of the Indians. Eight soldiers were killed and 38 wounded.

This drawing depicts the Third Colorado Volunteer Cavalry
charging into Black Kettle's village on November 29, 1864.
(Courtesy Western History Collections, University of Oklahoma)

Although a congressional investigation would later condemn the massacre, no one was ever brought to justice for his actions, but it did result in a reorganization of the western military districts and new leadership.[6]

While Chivington thought Black Kettle had been killed at Sand Creek, the Cheyenne chief and others survived, fled, and spread the news of the massacre. Like a wildfire it spread in all directions across the plains and north beyond the Oregon Trail. First had been Bear River. Now it was Sand Creek. The Indians decided to unite and fight. Although they usually did not make war in the winter, by January 1865 a general Indian uprising was under way. About a thousand Cheyennes and Sioux attacked Julesburg on the South Platte at the junction of the Oregon and Overland Mail trails in northeastern Colorado. The Indians almost succeeded in destroying a garrison of soldiers at Fort Sedgwick. The Indians then attacked stage stations and ranches in raids that were more numerous than those of 1864. When they returned to their camps and showed their plunder, other Indians joined in the attacks. Fortunately it was too early in 1865 for emigrants to have started west over the Oregon Trail.

At one point the army tried to burn out the Indians by setting a three-hundred-mile prairie fire, but the Indians swarmed back, tearing down miles of telegraph lines, raiding more ranches and stage stations, and stopping supply trains, stages, and mail wagons along the Platte River. For many days there was no overland communication between the East and San Francisco, Salt Lake City, and Denver. Early in February, Cheyenne Indians again

Artist Theodore R. Davis depicts Indian prisoners captured by General George Custer and his men, being taken across the plains. The illustration appeared in Harper's Weekly, *December 26, 1868.* (Courtesy Western History Collections, University of Oklahoma)

attacked Julesburg on the South Platte and burned the settlement. Scattered detachments of Ohio and Iowa volunteers guarding telegraph and stage stations could do little but defend themselves. On February 5 and 6, reinforcements from Camp Mitchell and Fort Laramie broke a siege at one telegraph station, but two days later Indians surrounded the troops, who dug in and managed to hold off the Indians. After a couple of days the Indians tired of fighting and left.

Meanwhile, Major General John Pope was appointed head of military operations for a vast area of the West. Pope began making plans to defeat the hostile Indians. He gave General James H. Ford, former head of the Second Colorado Cavalry, the job of going after hostile Indians to the south along the Arkansas River. General Alfred Sully was ordered to break the power of the Western Sioux by taking soldiers across Dakota Territory far to the north of the Oregon Trail and invading the Indians' Powder River hunting grounds, where he built a new fort. General Patrick Connor was charged with protecting the Oregon and Overland Mail trails from Fort Kearny to Salt Lake City and to aid Sully to the north. To replace some of the troops pulled away from the Oregon and Overland Mail trails, Pope used many former Confederate soldiers who had been paroled and recruited at northern

prisoner-of-war camps into volunteer infantry regiments to fight the Indians. They were called "Galvanized Yankees." Six regiments were formed,
and one was given the job of protecting posts and stations along the Oregon
Trail. There were delays in supplying the new troops until the Civil War
ended in April 1865. Then, too, volunteers whose enlistments ended were
mustered out. Soon regular troops freed from service against Confederates
came west to fight the Indians.

News of the general outbreak of Indian hostilities spread to the East.
With the Civil War over, Congress looked westward, and a committee began
to concentrate on Indian uprisings and wars. Their report, however, would
not be released until 1867. In the meantime, when about 25,000 emigrants and
gold-seekers started west in the spring of 1865, there were twice as many soldiers on the frontier than there had been in 1860. Only about 1,300 of the
emigrants were Mormons bound for Salt Lake City. The rest were bound for
other points in the West. Reports of Indian hostilities undoubtedly contributed to a decline in the number of travelers on the Oregon Trail, as did
the end of the Civil War, when Lee surrendered to Grant at Appomattox on
April 9. Abraham Lincoln was assassinated five days later and Andrew Johnson became president.

IN THE SUMMER OF 1865, General Patrick E. Connor left Fort Laramie
with what became known as the Powder River Expedition of 2,600 men to
move north and punish Indians who had been attacking anyone and anything along the Oregon Trail. Meantime, on July 26, about 130 miles up the
Platte River from Fort Laramie, Sergeant Amos Custard was leading a train
of supply wagons from Sweetwater Station at Independence Rock to Platte
Bridge Station near modern Casper, Wyoming. Troops had been stationed at
Platte Bridge Station since 1859 to protect emigrants and the telegraph line.
Around noon, as their wagons neared the station, near Red Buttes, the soldiers were attacked by a large number of Indians. After a four-hour battle,
the troops were overrun, and Sergeant Custard, along with twenty-six of his
men, were killed. That same morning, a troop of men under the command
of Lieutenant Caspar Collins had gone out to assist another supply train
returning to Platte Bridge Station. A mile west of the post, the group was
ambushed by a large contingent of Sioux, Cheyenne, and Arapaho Indians.
As the troops retreated, the Indians killed four men, including Lieutenant
Collins. As a tribute to his memory, the army renamed Platte Bridge Station
Fort Caspar. It was not named Fort Collins because a post in Colorado had

already been given that name to honor the dead lieutenant's father, Colonel W. O. Collins.[7]

Meanwhile, the long columns of General Connor's expedition moved north into the Powder River Basin and established a new route of the Bozeman Trail from the North Platte River near modern Douglas, Wyoming, to just south of present Buffalo, Wyoming. At the crossing on Powder River, Connor's troops constructed a new post called Fort Connor. The expedition then continued north to the Tongue River and attacked nonhostile Arapaho Indians in their village. The soldiers won the battle, but the expedition was a failure. Some of Connor's troops met with bad weather, and in September many horses and mules died and the soldiers struggled to survive. Because the Civil War had ended a few months earlier, many of the volunteers wanted to go home. They simply deserted.

General Connor and other military officers and men were learning that tactics used successfully east of the Mississippi in the Civil War would not work against Plains Indians on horseback, who were highly mobile. Also, the West was sparsely populated, and great distances had to be traversed. Then, too, extreme variations in climate and geography in the West made it difficult to keep soldiers supplied, difficult to maintain communications, and difficult to deploy troops rapidly. While the army had fought Indians in the West after the Mexican War, most of the officers experienced in such warfare had retired. Now new officers on the plains were learning by experience.

General Connor's expedition straggled back to Fort Laramie, and military leaders across the West began to rethink their tactics. By the beginning of 1866, the government in Washington was in financial difficulty because of the cost of fighting the Civil War. Officials realized that gold resources in the West offered potential relief for the nation. Then, too, Americans were enjoying peace in the East and there were calls for peace in the West. In response to the public call, Congress requested a new Indian policy, and officials decided another peace council should be held. Word was sent west and Indian agents sent runners to the Sioux inviting them to a general peace council in June 1866 at Fort Laramie.

As earlier treaties with the Indians had shown, they were only as binding as the power and authority of the chiefs who signed them. An Indian's allegiance to a chief fluctuated. A chief might have the full support of his people when signing a treaty, but weeks or months later, that support might evaporate. There also were problems with treaties on the government's side. While officials who negotiated and signed treaties for the government did so with full authority, the enforcement of those treaties was left to highly independent white men who often failed to live up to their terms. When Indians, whose territory and means of survival were increasingly threatened, became hostile, the military would protect the whites, breaching the treaties and punishing the Indians.

About three months before the Fort Laramie peace council was scheduled to start in the spring of 1866, Spotted Tail, paramount chief of the Brulé Sioux, brought his daughter's body to Fort Laramie, saying he wanted her buried among the whites in the post cemetery. Her name was Ah-ho-ap-pa, which in Sioux means "wheat flour." Several years before, the young girl had been a familiar sight at Fort Laramie. She spent long hours on a bench by the sutler's store watching the white man's way of life, especially the guard mount and the dress parade. It was not uncommon for the officer of the guard to wear a red silk sash, ostrich plumes, shoulder straps, and about two hundred dollars' worth of astonishing raiment. She refused to join other Indian women and children in a circle where soldiers distributed provisions, including crackers. Officers had been told that her father had been offered as many as two hundred ponies for her, but that she refused to marry an Indian. She wanted to marry an army officer. She attempted to learn English and told her people they were fools for not living in houses and making peace. When the Sioux went on the warpath late in 1864, she left Fort Laramie with her father and spent the months that followed in the Powder River region, where she became ill and died during the vicious winter of 1865. Before dying, she told her father she wished to be buried at Fort Laramie. Her father led the funeral procession for more than 250 miles to the post, where the commander complied with the request. Her funeral ceremony was a combination of military pageantry and Brulé traditions. Her body was placed in a coffin on a raised platform a half mile north of the parade grounds.[8]

The commander at Fort Laramie hoped the kindness shown Spotted Tail would strengthen the Indian's friendship during the peace council, which began in June 1866 when about 2,000 Brulé and Oglala Sioux arrived and the peace commissioners began negotiations. Central to the talks was the Bozeman Trail, the road that ran through the best buffalo-hunting land of Chief Red Cloud and the Oglala Sioux. The talks had hardly started when Colonel Henry B. Carrington and a battalion of the Eighteenth Infantry arrived at Fort Laramie. The War Department in Washington had sent Carrington and his expedition to open the Bozeman Trail through the Powder River country to the gold mines in Montana Territory and to build new military forts along the route. The unfortunate arrival of Carrington's expedition, which demonstrated the conflicting policies of the War Department and the Office of Indian Affairs in Washington, caused unrest among the Indians.

Chief Red Cloud supposedly told the peace commissioners that the Great White Father in Washington "sends us presents and wants a new road through our country while at the same time the white chief goes with soldiers to steal the road before the Indian says yes or no." Red Cloud took his party of Sioux and left Fort Laramie. Spotted Tail and his Brulé Sioux remained and agreed to a new treaty, since they did not hunt in the region crossed by the Bozeman Trail. Meanwhile, Colonel Carrington's expedition marched north, opened the Bozeman Trail, and established three new posts, ostensibly to protect travelers. They were Fort Reno, formerly Fort Connor, located east of modern Kaycee, Wyoming; Fort Phil Kearny situated northwest of Buffalo, Wyoming; and Fort C. F. Smith, near Hardin in southeast Montana.

Red Cloud, a Sioux chief, posed for this photo in 1875.
(Courtesy Western History Collections, University of Oklahoma)

Colonel Henry B. Carrington.
(Courtesy Wyoming State Museum)

By now it was clear to the Indians that whites were going to keep coming, pushing them off the plains and killing the buffalo. Red Cloud acted accordingly. His warriors soon began a campaign of harassing soldiers at these posts, culminating with the killing of eighty soldiers under Captain W. J. Fetterman near Fort Phil Kearny on December 21, only a few months after the post was built. A trader and scout named John "Portugee" Phillips then rode 235 miles in four days through bitter cold to Fort Laramie with the news, and troops were sent to the beleaguered garrison.[9]

Two other Indian attacks of note also occurred at about the same time in 1866 and may have been coordinated. At Fort C. F. Smith a detail of soldiers under the command of Lieutenant Sigismund Sternberg was gathering hay outside the post when they were attacked. He and nineteen soldiers and six civilians equipped with converted breech-loading Springfield rifles and a few repeating rifles managed to hold off several hundred Indians in what became known as the Hayfield Fight. Many Indians were killed or wounded, but only three whites were killed and three wounded.[10] At about the same time near Fort Phil Kearny, Captain James Powell and thirty-one men, armed with new breech-loading rifles and barricaded behind wagon boxes that had been removed from their running gears, held off more than a thousand Sioux and Cheyennes for four hours. Again many Indians were killed or wounded, but only three soldiers were killed and two wounded in what became known as the Wagon Box Fight.[11]

John "Portugee" Phillips as he appeared several years after his heroic ride in the winter of 1866. (Courtesy Wyoming State Museum)

In the spring of 1867 there were more Indian attacks from Montana south into Kansas and Colorado Territory. A great many occurred along the Oregon Trail and along the north bank of the Platte River, where Union Pacific construction gangs were pushing westward from Omaha, laying track for the transcontinental railroad. Indians frequently attacked the crews, killing and scalping workers, stealing horses, damaging track, and their raids ran up the railroad's cost of constructing the line. The government often sent troops along with the workers for protection, but if the soldiers were not on hand, half of the graders, tie setters, track layers, and bolters stood guard while the rest worked.

In the summer of 1867, a congressional committee in Washington released its *Report on the Condition of the Indian Tribes.* That report led to an act to establish an Indian Peace Commission to end the wars and bring peace. Headed by General William Tecumseh Sherman, the commission signed treaties in October 1867 with southern tribes at Fort Larned in central Kansas. The commission then traveled to Fort Laramie to do the same with

This illustration depicts John "Portugee" Phillips arriving at Horse Shoe Station, where word of the Fetterman massacre and General Carrington's plea for help were transmitted by telegraph. Phillips, however, did not trust the telegraph and rode on to Fort Laramie, arriving there on Christmas Eve, 1866. (Courtesy Wyoming State Museum)

northern tribes. In the meantime, Crazy Horse, Red Cloud, Sitting Bull, and other Indian chiefs had met on Bear Butte, a sacred mountain in the Black Hills near modern Sturgis, South Dakota, and pledged to stop further encroachments on their land by whites. When it came time for the peace council to begin at Fort Laramie, very few Indians appeared. Chief Red Cloud sent word that no treaty was possible until the forts on the Bozeman Trail and in the valley of the Powder River were abandoned. Another peace council was scheduled for Fort Laramie in the spring of 1868. The peace commission met the Indians' demands and agreed to abandon the military posts along the Bozeman Trail and gave them all of what is now South Dakota west of the Missouri River, plus control and hunting rights in the territory north of the Oregon Trail along the North Platte River and east of the Bighorn Mountains. Both the Brulé and Oglala Sioux signed the treaty, but Red Cloud refused to sign until the soldiers actually left the Powder River country and his warriors had burned abandoned Fort Phil Kearny to the ground. When these things had been done, and with Father De Smet as a witness, Red Cloud signed what became known as "the Great Fort Laramie Treaty of 1868." The Sioux regarded it as a great victory for Red Cloud. It was as though he had beaten the white man in battle. In return, the Sioux agreed to keep the peace with the whites and to permit the Union

"On the Plains—Indians Attacking Butterfield's Overland Dispatch Coach" *is the title of this illustration by Theodore R. Davis that appeared in* Harper's Weekly, *April 21, 1866.* (Courtesy Western History Collections, University of Oklahoma)

This illustration by Theodore R. Davis depicts Cheyenne Indians attacking a construction crew building the Union Pacific Railroad across Nebraska in 1867. The drawing appeared in Harper's Weekly, *August 4, 1867.* (Courtesy Western History Collections, University of Oklahoma)

Pacific to continue building west without interference. The treaty brought peace along the Oregon Trail, but the hostilities of previous years had already reduced travel over the road. Aside from about 3,600 Mormons bound for Salt Lake City, who rode the Union Pacific as far as the tracks had been laid and then traveled overland to Salt Lake City, travel over the Oregon Trail was limited to an unknown but small number of emigrant wagons, some stagecoach and wagon freighting traffic, and military troops.

UNTIL THE 1868 treaty was signed, Indian attacks had slowed the construction of the Union Pacific tracks across Nebraska Territory. The tracks reached Grand Island on the Platte River by July 8, 1866. From Omaha to that point, stagecoaches ceased to run since passengers could travel by train. Frank Root, an employee of the Overland Stage, wrote in 1901 that "the bulk of merchandise transported by the white-covered prairie schooners continued to 'grow small by degrees and beautifully less.' Neither horses, mules, nor oxen could compete with the iron horse in moving freight overland. The frequent stage stations were forever abandoned. The men who kept the trading posts where the railroad ran were forced to abandon them and set up their businesses elsewhere. The continuous passing of freight wagons and stage and emigrant outfits ceased, and not one team could be seen where there were hundreds in the balmy days of overland transportation."[12]

Even before the town of Grand Island was laid out, the railroad's work camp occupied the site. The camp appeared at the end of the tracks as the railroad built west, and it gained much notoriety as the first "Hell on Wheels." It consisted of tents and crude shacks where the construction crews slept, although its residents were not limited to railroad workers. There were many camp followers, who erected an oversized tent a hundred feet long and forty feet wide in the middle of the camp. It contained a bar, a dance floor, and fancy gambling equipment. Bartenders, prostitutes, and gamblers populated the large tent and other smaller tents scattered around the area. They provided relaxation for the construction workers while at the same time relieving them of their pay. Each time the tracks reached a point about sixty miles west of wherever "Hell on Wheels" was currently located, the construction camp was moved to that point. Word of the move quickly passed and everyone pitched in. Tents were folded, shacks dismantled, equipment packed and loaded on flatcars, and "Hell on Wheels" was transported to the western end of the track. There, in a matter of hours, the town reappeared. Sometimes the town had as many as 3,000 people, including wagon freighters meeting the trains to pick up freight.

When Henry Stanley, a reporter for the *Missouri Democrat,* arrived at North Platte, he reported: "Every gambler in the Union seems to have steered his course for North Platte, and every known game under the sun is played here. The days of Pike's Peak and California are revived. Every house is a saloon, and every saloon is a gambling den. Revolvers are in great

EMIGRATION ESTIMATES

YEAR	ESTIMATES		
	MERRILL J. MATTES*	JOHN D. UNRUH, JR.[†]	ONLY MORMONS ANDREW JENSON[‡]
1840		13	
1841	100	58	
1842	200	125	
1843	1,000	913	
1844	2,000	1,528	
1845	5,000	2,760	
1846	1,000	2,700	
1847	2,000	4,450	2,000
1848	4,000	1,700	4,000
1849	30,000	25,450	3,000
1850	55,000	50,000	5,000
1851	10,000	4,700	5,000
1852	50,000	60,000	10,000
1853	20,000	27,500	2,603
1854	10,000	18,000	3,167
1855	5,000	2,000	4,684
1856	5,000	9,000	3,756
1857	5,000	5,500	1,994
1858	10,000	7,500	179
1859	30,000	19,000	809
1860	15,000	10,500	1,409
1861	5,000		1,959
1862	5,000		3,599
1863	10,000		3,646
1864	20,000		2,697
1865	25,000		1,301
1866	25,000		3,333
1867			660
1868			3,232
Totals	350,300	253,397	68,028

*Merrill J. Mattes, *The Great Platte River Road* (Lincoln: Nebraska State Historical Society, 1969). Vol. 25 in the society's publications.

†John D. Unruh, Jr., *The Plains Across* (Urbana: University of Illinois Press, 1979).

‡Andrew Jenson, ed., *The Historical Record* (Salt Lake City: LDS Church, 1889).

requisition. Beardless youths imitate to the life the peculiar swagger of the devil-may-care bullwhacker and blackleg. On account of the immense freighting done to Idaho, Montana, Utah, Dakota, and Colorado, hundreds of bullwhackers walk about and turn the one street into a perfect Babel. Old gamblers who reveled in the glorious day of 'flush times' in the gold districts declare that this town outstrips them all yet."

By then the Union Pacific had a fleet of sixteen locomotives, two hundred platform (flat) cars, twelve passengers cars, and the Lincoln Car, converted for business use. The contractors building the line had their own fleet of six locomotives. On January 2, 1867, the railroad opened its mainline operations to North Platte from Omaha carrying paying passengers. Meanwhile, the construction crews pushed westward, reaching Julesburg about five months later in June 1867, and as far west as the site of modern Cheyenne, Wyoming, which was achieved on November 13. While the construction crews waited for spring 1868, "Hell on Wheels" arrived and the town of Cheyenne was born. It was built so rapidly that the town earned the name "the Magic City." After construction resumed in the spring of 1868 and the Union Pacific reached a point about sixty miles west of Cheyenne, near the site of modern Laramie, Wyoming, "Hell on Wheels moved there, but Cheyenne survived because its location, a hundred miles north of Denver, made it a convenient shipping point for the Colorado goldfields. Freight arrived by rail in Cheyenne and was then shipped by wagon south to Denver and other points. Laramie also survived after "Hell on Wheels" moved farther west, reaching what is now southwest Wyoming in early December 1869.

The building of the Central Pacific Railroad east from Sacramento was also slow at the beginning because rails, wheels, locomotives, and cars had to be made in the East and transported by ship either around the tip of South America or across the Isthmus of Panama and up the Pacific Coast to San Francisco and then taken by steamer or barge up the Sacramento River to Sacramento. Building the line over the Sierra Nevada was difficult, and it was not until June 1868 that the Central Pacific reached the site of modern Reno, Nevada. From there the line was laid east, but there was indecision as to where the Central Pacific would meet the westbound Union Pacific. The problem was resolved when the U.S. Pacific Railroad Commission decided the two railroads should meet at Promontory Summit, north of Salt Lake City, to form one continuous line. On May 10, 1869, the two lines linked and the transcontinental railroad was complete. Regular train service over the line began five days later. Depending upon the comfort desired by a passenger, the one-way fare from Omaha to Sacramento was $111, $80, or $40.

Chinese laborers were employed to help construct the Central Pacific Railroad east from Sacramento, California, over the Sierra Nevada. This illustration appeared in Harper's Weekly, *December 7, 1867.* (Courtesy Kansas State Historical Society)

The completion of the transcontinental railroad marked the death of the Oregon Trail as the principal overland route west for emigrants. Now, instead of taking months, a journey across the West could be made in a few days. Only those who could not afford the railroad fare continued the trek by wagon. Exactly how many emigrants traveled in this manner after 1869 is not known, but according to scattered accounts, occasional emigrant wagons could still be seen on the Oregon Trail into the 1880s. By then no hostile Indians bothered travelers. Fort Kearny and Fort Sedgwick were abandoned in 1871 by the army, which said they were no longer necessary. The Nez Percés under Chief Joseph tried during the 1870s to leave their reservation in the Pacific Northwest but failed. Conflicts with Sioux and Cheyenne Indians on the northern plains ended in 1881 when Sioux Chief Sitting Bull sur-

On May 9, 1869, the Central Pacific and the Union Pacific met at Promontory Point Summit, north of Salt Lake City, and the transcontinental railroad became a reality. It marked the death of the Oregon Trail as the principal overland route west for emigrants. (Courtesy the Bancroft Library, University of California, Berkeley)

rendered. That was about five years after General George A. Custer and two hundred troops died on June 25, 1876, in the Battle of the Little Bighorn. The arrival of the Northern Pacific Railroad in 1883 provided emigrants bound for Oregon with direct and rapid travel. As had been the case along the transcontinental railroad, land grants given to the railroads and offered to settlers saw the population of Oregon increase from 175,000 in 1880 to 300,000 by 1890.

Along the Oregon Trail in Wyoming, Fort Laramie was abandoned in 1891. A few families soon moved into the former post, where the old guardhouse was used as a horse stable. Many buildings became roofless and walls began to crumble. Still, deep ruts over the nearby hills marked the route of the Oregon Trail. A small white schoolhouse was constructed near the corner of the old parade ground, which was grown over with grass. The remains of the dead in the post cemetery were removed and laid to rest at Fort McPherson, to the east in Nebraska.

This is Salt Lake City in 1868, about a year before the transcontinental railroad was completed. Some of the ox-drawn freight wagons in this photo may have traveled west over the Oregon Trail to reach the city. (Courtesy Kansas State Historical Society)

The old ruts and worn road remained, but gradually with the lack of wagon travel, portions of the road from the Missouri River westward across much of Nebraska disappeared as grass and other vegetation covered all but the deepest depressions made by the wagons. In other areas portions of the trail remained and became local roads linking one community with another. But in the drier country from central Nebraska westward, evidence of the old trail remained. There, as to the east, portions of the old road were used for local wagon travel between an increasing number of towns, although inevitably the locations of new communities demanded new roads and eliminated travel over portions of the old Oregon Trail. For new generations along the old road who had not witnessed the countless wagons that traversed the trail, it became nothing more than local history living only in the stories of old-timers. By the late 1890s the Oregon Trail was rapidly becoming forgotten history as the nation prepared to move into a new century.

REBIRTH OF THE TRAIL

History is not a remote Olympian bar of judgment, but a controversial arena in which each generation must make its own estimates of the past.

Allan Nevins

A S THE TWENTIETH CENTURY BEGAN, Francis Parkman's book on the Oregon Trail was reprinted by a New York publisher, but few people paid attention. It was a new century, and transportation by the transcontinental railroad and the automobile were overshadowing the past, including the struggles and hardships endured by those who had traveled overland by wagon over the Oregon Trail. Such things had become old-timer history. The romance and adventure of the Old West were still alive in novels like Owen Wister's *The Virginian* (1902) and in wild west shows, but the real West was changing. Much of the area had been settled, and new towns and cities dotted the western landscape. The railroads had already brought eastern big business west, and with it came corruption, including boss rule in many areas. After timber reserves in the Great Lakes region were nearly depleted, loggers targeted the deep forests of Oregon, and as the twentieth century began, it became the nation's third-ranking lumber-producing state. But then progressives in Oregon overthrew the timber barons' rule and gained the adoption of a series of reform measures, including the initiative, the referendum, recall, and the direct primary. The *initiative* enabled citizens to propose legislation; the *referendum* allowed them to vote for or against laws already passed by state lawmakers; *recall* permitted them to oust corrupt officials; and the *direct primary* (a reform measure first enacted by the Wisconsin legislature in 1903) bypassed party machinery and enabled the voters to choose their party candidates at the polls. Collectively these reforms became known as the Oregon System and were widely adopted in many other areas of the nation to increase popular control of local and state governments.

Although most Americans living between Oregon and the Atlantic coast were too involved in the problems of the present to pay much attention to the past, especially the old Oregon Trail over which so many emigrants had passed to settle the West, not everyone had forgotten. Ezra Meeker, born in Butler County, Ohio, in 1830, had traveled the road to Oregon in 1852 with other emigrants. After an unsuccessful mercantile business in the town of Steilacoom, Meeker settled in the Puyallup Valley, where he founded the town of Puyallup in 1877, located a few miles southeast of modern Tacoma. There he realized the fertile soil could grow abundant crops. He planted hops, used to give the bitter flavor to malt liquors, and by 1885 was wealthy and known as the "Hop King of the World." His business took him to Europe, where in London he met Queen Victoria. Everything was fine until 1891 when an infestation of hop aphids decimated his crops. He lost a fortune but managed to keep his home in Puyallup. Soon he dabbled in other enterprises and made four trips to the Klondike in search of gold. He found little. Back in Puyallup, he began writing a romance novel about coming west, in which he expressed his sympathy for the plight of Indians. He also expressed sympathy for Chinese emigrants who were treated as outcasts in the Pacific Northwest. By 1900 he realized that too many Americans had forgotten the Oregon Trail. Meeker, then seventy-seven, decided to memorialize the road by retracing the route he had taken in 1852 and marking it. As he later wrote:

> The difference between a civilized and an untutored people lies in the application of experiences. The civilized man builds upon the foundation of the past, with hope and ambition for the future. The savage has neither past nor aspiration for the future. To keep the flame of patriotism alive, we must keep the memory of the past vividly before us. It was with these thoughts in mind that the expedition to mark the old Oregon Trail was undertaken.[1]

On January 29, 1906, Meeker left his home in Puyallup, Washington, which he called Camp 1, with what he called his "prairie schooner," whose newly built wagon bed was fashioned as a boat. But Meeker also used hub bands, boxes, and other irons from two old wagons that had actually traveled over the Oregon Trail in 1852. To pull the wagon he used two oxen. One was a seven-year-old named Twist, and the other was an unbroken five-year-old range steer named Dave, who was sixteen hands high and eight feet in girth. "When we were ready to start, Twist weighed 1,470 pounds and Dave 1,560. This order of weight was soon changed. In three months' time Twist gained 130 pounds and Dave lost 80. All this time I fed them with a lavish hand all the rolled barley I dared give and all the hay they would eat," Meeker wrote.[2]

Meeker, with one helper, traveled to Seattle and spent two weeks making preparations for the journey before shipping his oxen and wagon to Tacoma by steamboat. From there he drove them to nearby Tumwater, on the southern edge of Puget Sound, where the first American emigrants had arrived and settled in 1845. Meeker set a post and arranged for a stone marker to be placed on the spot. On February 20, 1906, he sent his wagon, drawn by a team of horses with the oxen following under yoke, to Tenino, Washington, while he took the train. The next day he dedicated another monument at Tenino. As he traveled, Meeker spoke to civic organizations to build interest in the old Oregon Trail and to gain local support for marking the road. Markers were placed at Toledo, Washington, and in Portland, Oregon, where Meeker pitched his tent on a grassy vacant lot in the middle of the city.

On March 10, Meeker, his wagon, and his oxen were taken by boat up the Columbia River to The Dalles, where he set up camp in a park. The women of the town's Landmark Committee provided a monument, and Meeker prepared to deliver the dedicatory address. As Meeker later wrote, the next day

> treated us to some hardships that I missed on the first overland journey. Ice formed in the camp half an inch thick, and the high wind joined forces with the damper of our stove, which had got out of order, to fill the tent with smoke and make life miserable. The fierce, cold wind also made it necessary to postpone the dedication for a day and finally to carry it out with less ceremony than had been planned. Nevertheless, I felt that the expedition was now fairly started. We had reached the point where the real journey would begin, and the interest shown in the plan by the towns along the way had been most encouraging.[3]

On March 14, 1906, Meeker drove his ox-drawn wagon out of The Dalles toward the farming region of eastern Oregon, where farmhouses, red barns, and great wheat fields now covered what in 1852 was barren land. Each night he camped, and soon he saw the Blue Mountains in the distance. When he reached Pendleton, Oregon, fourteen days after leaving The Dalles, he learned that the Commercial Club had raised money for a stone monument, which Meeker dedicated on the last day of March. That evening he visited the Indian school to talk with teachers and students. Meeker was pleased to spend the night in a room, provided at the school, instead of in his wagon. The next morning he learned eighteen inches of snow had fallen in the Blue Mountains. Wondering if he could get his wagon over the mountains,

Ezra Meeker (left) watches as a blacksmith shoes one of his two oxen in Seattle, Washington, before he sets out on his cross-country journey in 1906 to retrace the Oregon Trail. Oxen require two partial shoes on each foot, nailed into the hoof. Although one ox died on the journey, the other had to be shod about seventeen times during the trip. (Author's collection)

Meeker went ahead by train to Meacham, Oregon, where he found an old mountaineer who assured him his wagon could make it. The man promised to bring his team to help Meeker get through the snow. Meeker returned to Pendleton by train and started out with his wagon to climb the Blue Mountains. When he reached the snow line, the mountaineer from Meacham was waiting with his team. Although the snow was axle-deep, by evening they reached Meacham. The next day Meeker dedicated a monument and then crossed the summit of the Blue Mountains and traveled down to La Grande, Oregon, where another monument would be dedicated.

Eight miles out of La Grande, near the mouth of Ladd's Canyon, Meeker placed an inscribed stone marker he had carried in his wagon as children from a nearby school watched and sang "Columbia, the Gem of the Ocean" and "America." From there Meeker drove his wagon to Baker City, Oregon, where a marker was dedicated on the grounds of the high school before a crowd of 2,000 people. Because the actual route of the Oregon Trail was about five miles from Baker City, another marker was set along the trail. Meeker later wrote:

> News of these events was now beginning to pass along the line ahead. As a result the citizens in other places began to take hold of the work with a

Ezra Meeker poses in front of his wagon and oxen in Portland, Oregon, before setting out on his 1906 journey. (Author's collection)

will. Old Mount Pleasant, Durkee, Huntington, and Vale were other Oregon towns that followed the good lead and erected monuments to mark the old trail. A most gratifying feature of the work was the hearty participation in it of the school children.[4]

Meeker and his wagon continued south into Idaho, where he crossed the Snake River just below the mouth of the Boise River. It was there, fifty-four years earlier, that he had made his second crossing of the river coming west, and Meeker made arrangements to place a stone marker that memorialized not only the trail but Fort Boise. Another marker would later be placed at Parma, Idaho. Continuing to Boise, Idaho, Meeker learned that nearly 1,200 contributions had already been made by schoolchildren to erect a monument on the statehouse grounds. Meeker spoke at its dedication as 3,000 people watched.

Meeker crossed southern Idaho, where markers were placed at Twin Falls, American Falls, Pocatello, Montpelier, and Soda Springs. Entering Wyoming, Meeker traveled to Cokeville, northwest of Kemmerer, and then to Pacific Springs, just west of the Continental Divide at South Pass. In his journal, Meeker wrote: "Pacific Springs, Wyoming, Camp No. 79, June 20, 1906. Odometer, 958 [miles registered from The Dalles, Oregon]. Arrived at 6 p.m. and camped near Halter's store and the post office. Ice found in camp during the night." Outside the town, Meeker found a large granite stone and

16. Nooning.

This view shows Ezra Meeker and his helper nooning near Wells Springs, Oregon, in 1906. Meeker is writing in the journal he kept while retracing the Oregon Trail. (Author's collection)

arranged to have it brought into Pacific Springs as a marker. "There being no stonecutter at Pacific Springs to inscribe the monument, the clerk at the store formed the letters on stiff pasteboard. He then cut them out to make a paper stencil, through which the shape of the letters was transferred to the stone by crayon marks. The letters were then cut out with a cold chisel, deep enough to make a permanent inscription. The stone was so hard that it required steady work all day to cut the twenty letters and figure: THE ORE-GON TRAIL, 1843–57," Meeker wrote.[5]

From Pacific Springs, Meeker drove his team to the summit of South Pass and dedicated another monument. The next day, about twenty miles east, he reached the Sweetwater River and found the country was exactly like it had been when he crossed it in 1852. But he noted: "The sight and smell of the carrion so common in camping places in our first trip was gone; no bleached bones even showed where the exhausted dumb brute [ox] had died; the graves of the dead emigrants had all been made level by the hoofs of stock and the lapse of time."[6]

A hundred miles and several days later Meeker came to Split Rock, the first community east of Pacific Springs, and from there he passed Devil's Gate, where in 1852 Meeker's brother Clark had drowned in the Sweetwater River. Meeker drove to Independence Rock, a few miles east, where he took

This postcard, published by Meeker, contains his portrait and scenes that were photographed in 1906 as he retraced the Oregon Trail. (Author's collection)

time to walk around the massive boulder, which covers about thirty acres, reading the inscriptions people had left in the stone. Some were nearly obliterated, others legible only in part. On July 4, 1906, Meeker left Independence Rock, driving his wagon east, and by evening he reached the North Platte River and made camp. The next day he led his oxen and wagon into Casper, Wyoming. That evening the Commercial Club of Casper held a special meeting and agreed to build a monument to mark the trail. Later Meeker learned that a monument twenty-five feet high and costing $1,500 had been erected at Casper.

At Glenrock, east of Casper, the ladies of the town assured Meeker they would erect a marker. To the southeast at Douglas, Wyoming, Meeker learned plans were already under way to erect a monument there. Continuing southeast down the North Platte River, Meeker found ranches and thriving little towns where, of course, there had been none in 1852. He also found the remains of old Fort Laramie. "One of the old barracks, three hundred feet long, was in good preservation in 1906, being utilized by the owner, Joseph Wilde, for a store, post office, hotel, and residence. The guard house with its grim iron door and twenty-inch concrete walls is also fairly well preserved. One frame building of two stories, we were told, was transported by ox team from Kansas City at a cost of one hundred dollars a ton. The old

It is not known if Ezra Meeker used this rope ferry on the Snake River in southern Idaho.
Although the exact location is not known, it was the last operating ferry on the river when
this photograph was made in 1920, showing a Model A Ford being taken across the river.
(Courtesy Kansas State Historical Society)

place is crumbling away, slowly disappearing with the memories of the post," Meeker wrote.[7]

From Fort Laramie, Meeker traveled southeast into Nebraska and found town after town and saw that the Platte River was now being used for irrigation that enabled farmers to produce grain, hay, and beets. He noticed sugar factories, railroads, business blocks, and fine homes in the towns he visited seeking to erect monuments. At Scotts Bluff, Meeker observed that it had not changed. "It still looms up as of old on the south side of the river about eight hundred feet above the trail," he wrote, adding, "About twenty miles from Scott's Bluff stands old Chimney Rock.... A local story runs that an army officer trained a cannon on this spire, shot off about thirty feet from the top, and for this was court-martialed and dishonorably discharged from the army. I could get no definite confirmation of the story, though it was repeated again and again."[8]

When Meeker and his wagon and ox team reached Brady Island, Nebraska, August 9, 1906, and established his Camp 120, tragedy struck. His ox named Twist died. "Yesterday morning Twist ate his breakfast as usual and showed no signs of sickness until we were on the road two or three miles, when he began to put his tongue out and his breathing became heavy. But he leaned on the yoke more heavily than usual and determined to pull the whole load. I finally stopped, put him on the off side, gave him the long

When Ezra Meeker reached Chimney Rock, he posed with his wagon and oxen for the photographer. (Author's collection)

end of the yoke, and tied his head back with the halter strap to the chain, but to no purpose, for he pulled by the head very heavily. I finally unyoked, gave him a quart of lard, a gill of vinegar, and a handful of sugar, but all to no purpose, for he soon fell down and in two hours was dead," wrote Meeker.[9]

Meeker believed that Twist probably died from eating some poisonous plant. He gave the animal a decent burial and erected a headboard. He then hired a man with a team of horses who lived nearby to pull the wagon into Gothenburg, Nebraska, about thirteen miles away. Dave, the surviving ox, was led behind the wagon. At Gothenburg, Meeker hired another horse team to haul the wagon to Lexington, Nebraska. Unable to find another ox or even a steer as large as Dave, he purchased a pair of heavy cows and tried to break them to the yoke. But one of the cows would not pull and Meeker sold her for a loss. Then he hired a horse team to pull the wagon east from Lexington while his ox Dave and the reamining cow were led behind. When Meeker reached Kearney, Nebraska, across the Platte River from the site of new Fort Kearny, he was given a place to camp in the center of town under shade trees. There he was visited by many townspeople who appreciated what Meeker was trying to do. His visit inspired the townspeople to later erect an Oregon Trail monument in Kearney to mark the trail.

Ezra Meeker poses for the camera at Kearney, Nebraska, next to his wagon, his dog Jim, his ox Dave, and the cow he purchased at Lexington, Nebraska. The tepee served as Meeker's kitchen, dining room, and bedroom. (Author's collection)

Horses still pulled the wagon with Dave the ox and the cow following behind as Meeker continued east to Grand Island and then to Fremont, Nebraska. At Fremont, however, he was able to work his ox and cow together to pull the wagon in a parade celebrating the town's first fifty years. From Fremont, Meeker and his wagon traveled to Lincoln, the state capital, and then on to Omaha. There in the stockyards, Meeker was able to find a five-year-old steer, which he bought and named Dandy, who worked well with his ox Dave as Meeker crossed the Missouri River and continued east toward Indianapolis, where he arrived on January 5, 1907.

Meeker had decided to go east to Washington, D.C., with his wagon and team, and from Indianapolis he traveled to Dayton, Columbus, Cleveland, Buffalo, Albany, and New York City. There he was stopped by a policeman and told there was an ordinance against allowing cattle to be driven on the streets. Since Meeker wanted to drive his team down Broadway from one end to the other to attract attention to his cause, he decided to see the city's aldermen. He did, and with encouragement from the *New York Weekly Tribune* and the *New York Herald*, the aldermen passed an ordinance, which the acting mayor signed, making it legal for Meeker to drive his team in New York for thirty days. Large crowds gathered wherever Meeker and his team and wagon went. They were mobbed on Wall Street. He even drove his wagon across the Brooklyn Bridge. On the east side of New York his dog Jim, a collie, was stolen. Meeker had to pay $20 to get him back. Six years later Meeker lost the dog again while traveling by train. He let the animal get off the train for a few minutes. Before Jim returned, the train left. Meeker offered a reward for the dog's return, but no one ever claimed it, and he never saw Jim again.

From New York, Meeker went to Trenton, New Jersey, and then to Philadelphia, Baltimore, and Washington, D.C. He arrived in the capital twenty-two months after leaving his home in Puyallup, Washington. Two members of his state's congressional delegation, Senator Samuel H. Piles and Congressman Francis W. Cushman, took Meeker to the White House to meet President Theodore Roosevelt, who took an interest in marking the old Oregon Trail. Meeker quoted Roosevelt as telling the senator and congressman, "I am in favor of this work to mark this trail. If you will bring before Congress a measure to accomplish it, I am with you and will give my support to do it thoroughly." When Meeker suggested that it might be nice to establish a memorial highway along the old trail, Roosevelt said it would be better if such a highway was proposed by the states crossed by the old trail. Roosevelt then said to Meeker, "Where is your team? I want to see it." The oxen were near the White House. Roosevelt, without his hat, Meeker, and everyone else in the room left the White House to see the oxen and wagon.[10]

President Theodore Roosevelt visits with Ezra Meeker after inspecting Meeker's ox team and wagon just outside the White House in 1907. (Author's collection)

Meeker left Washington on January 8, 1908, shipping his wagon and oxen to McKeesport, Pennsylvania, and then driving the wagon to Pittsburgh, where he put the team into winter quarters and found adequate storage for his wagon. On March 5, Meeker shipped them by boat down the Ohio River to Cincinnati, where he stopped for one day before continuing by rail to St. Louis. Meeker was now determined to retrace the route he had followed in 1852 from east to west. At St. Louis, however, he could not convince city officials to support his plan to mark the trail. Before leaving, though, he did get the endorsement of the city's automobile club and the Daughters of the American Revolution.

After visiting Topeka, Kansas, on May 11, 1908, Meeker headed for St. Joseph, Missouri, where he found vocal support to mark the old trail but no money for a monument. Meantime, he learned that a committee in Congress had approved a bill to appropriate $50,000 to mark the Oregon Trail. So Meeker, now seventy-eight years old, decided to end his wagon journey. He shipped his oxen and wagon to Portland, Oregon. He had been on the road for twenty-eight months, and had succeeded in marking many points along the Oregon Trail. When Meeker, with his oxen and wagon, arrived in Portland, he set out driving them north to Seattle, where he arrived on July 18, 1908. His long journey was over, and as he wrote, "My dream of retracing the way over the Old Trail had come true."[11]

Almost single-handedly Ezra Meeker had focused new attention on the old Oregon Trail. His journey generated much publicity and renewed in the minds of many Americans the saga of the westward movement. Many photographs were taken on his trip, and quite a few were included in his book *The Ox Team; or, The Old Oregon Trail, 1852–1906,* which Meeker first published in Omaha, Nebraska, in October 1906. The first edition only covers his trip as far east as Grand Island, Nebraska, but in each of several revised editions published in the East, his later experiences were added, along with new photographs. His journey caused many Americans to think about the heritage of the Oregon Trail. Most persons his age would sit back and relax after such a journey, but not Meeker. Soon Meeker was making preparations to repeat the trip, which he did between 1910 and 1912, building on the publicity he had already received. He sold postcards with photos from his first journey along with copies of his book to help finance the trip.

About four years after he completed his second journey by wagon, Meeker set out from Washington, D.C., on May 5, 1916, in an 80-horsepower, 12-cylinder Pathfinder automobile with a prairie-schooner top bound for Olympia, Washington. He followed the Cumberland route across Maryland and the old National Road, maintained by the states through which it

In 1910, Ezra Meeker traveled to Los Angeles with his wagon and oxen and appeared at an aviation meet, where this photo was taken. (Author's collection)

passed, west to Vandalia, Illinois, and on to St. Louis and to the Missouri River. He then traveled the modern roads along or close to the Oregon Trail, to Olympia, Washington. He wrote a booklet about this journey by auto, too, which was published in Seattle, Washington, in 1916.

The renewed interest in the Oregon Trail, for which Meeker was greatly responsible, spurred publishers to again reprint Francis Parkman's book, which soon was used in high school literature and history classes. While the events surrounding World War I distracted from Meeker's efforts to keep the old trail in the public eye, he used the time to think and to plan. In 1922, while visiting with friends in Baker City, Oregon, Meeker founded what was first called the Old Oregon Trail Association and was elected its first president. Another strong supporter of memorializing the trail was Walter E. Meacham, who in 1912 became secretary of the Baker County Chamber of Commerce. Meacham, Meeker, and other people in the area organized the first public celebration of the trail in 1923, called "Top O' Blue Mountains Old Oregon Trail Pageant," of which Meacham served as master of ceremonies. With local people playing the parts of historic figures, the program was a blend of patriotism and Oregon's contribution to America. President Warren G. Harding was invited, and he stopped there on a tour of the West. Near the summit of the Blue Mountains, Harding dedicated Emigrant

Springs State Park and placed a marker to the memory of pioneers. A week later Harding died in San Francisco.

The increased attention in the Oregon Trail may have been responsible for the first epic silent Western film, titled *The Covered Wagon*, directed by James Cruze and produced by Paramount Pictures. The movie was based on a novel by Emerson Hough, and it follows a wagon train from Missouri to Oregon, complete with Indian attacks and petty disagreements between the emigrants. The film had beautiful scenery and countless wagons, animals, and actors, although not much of a plot. Still this first Western epic was a great success when it was released in 1923.

Whether or not Meeker saw the film is unknown, but the following year he joined Lieutenant Oakley Kelly in an open-cockpit army de Havilland plane and flew from Fort Vancouver, Washington, over the Oregon Trail and beyond. When the plane landed at Dayton, Ohio, Meeker, then ninety-four, rode in a parade seated next to Orville Wright. A crowd of about 40,000 people cheered and gave Meeker and Wright a great reception. From Dayton, Meeker flew on to Washington, D.C., where he met the new president, Calvin Coolidge, at the White House. Meeker presented him with a plan to create a national highway to honor the Oregon Trail.

President Coolidge apparently liked Meeker's plan, as did some members of Congress. Measures were introduced in the Senate and House of Representatives to "designate the route of the old Oregon Trail." The measures asked for no money but only the designation of the route. On January 23, 1925, the House Committee on Roads began a hearing. Idaho Congressman Addison T. Smith, who was not a member of the committee, testified and cited Ezra Meeker's efforts, adding:

I remember his last visit to this city when he drew up in front of the House Office Building, at the northeast corner, and conversed with those interested in his plans, calling attention to this great historic highway.

From 1910 until 1922 there were a great many articles written in newspapers and magazines in regard to the importance of designating officially this old thoroughfare, and the sentiment was crystallized in 1922 by the formation of what is known as the [Old] Oregon Trail Association, headquarters of which are at Baker, Oreg. The president of this association is W. E. Meacham, who has been devoting his time during the past few years appearing before Commercial, Rotary, Kiwanis Clubs, and similar organizations in the towns along this great thoroughfare, impressing upon the members the importance of having this great thoroughfare designated officially.

We have in the country a great many highways which have been given designations without any more formality than simply having a few men get together and say, "Now this road is to be designated as a certain highway." In certain localities controversies have arisen between towns as to whether or not this road should go through that city or another city, that town or the other town. Automobile and good roads associations have attempted to settle those controversies, oftentimes by arbitrarily saying, "This is the road we are going to designate," and put up signs to that effect.[12]

Other congressmen also spoke during the hearing, which was held on February 13, 19, and 21 in 1925. They cited historical documents and read numerous letters from officials and residents located in communities along the old trail's route. The hearing not only served to attract more attention to the Oregon Trail, but it educated members of Congress and the public about the trail's history, especially after the Committee on Roads ordered a transcript of the hearing published in a 205-page document printed and released later in 1925.

As a direct result of the national attention that Congress gave the Oregon Trail, the Old Oregon Trail Association was renamed the Oregon Trail Memorial Association (OTMA) and was incorporated in 1926 in New York. The National Highways Association provided office space for OTMA in New York City, and a membership drive was started using a list of honorary and life members including President Calvin Coolidge, Secretary of the Interior Ray Lyman Wilbur, Thomas A. Edison, and members of the wealthy and aristocratic clans of Morgan, Astor, and Harriman. To raise some heavy money for office staff, travel expenses, publications, Oregon trail markers, etc., Congress was persuaded to pass a memorial coin bill.

The Memorial Association asked Congress to authorize a half-dollar to "commemorate the heroism of our fathers and mothers who traversed the Oregon Trail to the far West with great hardship, daring, and loss of life, which not only resulted in adding new states to the Union, but earned a well-deserved and imperishable fame for the pioneers." Congress thought the project had national significance and passed legislation on May 17, 1926, authorizing the coining of "no more than six million" commemorative half-dollars. The coin was designed by James Earle Fraser and his wife, Laura, who were responsible for several other commemorative coins. James Fraser was well known as the designer of the buffalo nickel. For the new half-dollar, he created a wagon drawn by oxen, heading into the setting sun with the words IN GOD WE TRUST in an arc above at the rim and the words OREGON

TRAIL MEMORIAL below the wagon. On the opposite side is an Indian, standing erect with outstretched arm, superimposed on a map of the United States showing a line of wagons heading west. The inscription UNITED STATES OF AMERICA is placed around the Indian, and the words HALF DOLLAR are below in an arc.

Here are the front and back of the 1926 Oregon Trail Commemorative Half-Dollar. Between 1926 and 1937 there were fourteen issues of the coin by the U.S. Treasury. (Author's collection)

When the design was approved by the federal Commission of Fine Arts, the models were sent to the Medallic Art Company in New York to make mechanical reductions. The hubs were then shipped to the Philadelphia mint, and in September 1926, 48,000 coins were struck, along with 30 pieces reserved for assay. The coin became known as the "Ezra Meeker issue" since it was produced seventy-five years after Meeker first traveled the Oregon Trail in 1852. The coins sold for $1 each and became very popular. Another issue of 100,000 coins was produced by the San Francisco mint in October 1926 to go to the Oregon Trail Memorial Association for resale to the public, but enthusiasm quickly waned. Only a few coins were sold at the issued price. The Treasury became aware of the unsold coins and ordered the mints to cease production until all of the 1926-S issues were sold.

Meantime, to promote his national highway plan, Meeker gained the support of Henry Ford to make another drive across the country. Ford had a Model A converted to carry a covered-wagon top. On December 3, 1928, before Meeker could complete the trip, he died, just short of his ninety-eighth birthday. By then OTMA had exerted enough pressure for the U.S. Treasury to produce 50,000 more commemorative coins in what was called the "Jedediah Smith issue," a tribute to the mountain man and explorer, but the coins were not released and were placed in the Treasury vaults for five years. When new pressure was exerted in 1933 to strike more coins, the 17,000 unsold 1926-S issues were melted down and the remaining number of "Jedediah Smith" 1928 half-dollars were released before another issue was struck at the Denver mint. More than 5,000 coins were produced. The plan called for them to be sold to visitors at the Century of Progress Exposition in Chicago at a cost of $2 each. When they did not sell, most were sold to speculators by the Scott Stamp & Coin Co. of New York, which also was charged with liquidating the 1928 issues. Eventually, 44,000 of the 1928 coins in storage went into the melting pot.

After Meeker's death and the publicity associated with the commemorative coins, Hollywood released in 1930 a second film, this time with sound, about emigrants on the old trail. *The Big Trail* starred John Wayne and had great scenery, many action scenes with numerous wagons, but still a weak plot. It had moderate success at the box office, and six years later Republic Pictures released *The Oregon Trail,* again starring John Wayne. This film had a fair reception.

By then Howard R. Driggs had succeeded Ezra Meeker as president of OTMA. Under his leadership and with much political help, OTMA had the U.S. Treasury produce other commemorative half-dollars. The Denver mint produced 7,000 coins in 1934 known as the "Fort Hall, Ft. Laramie and Jason Lee issue." Then in 1936 the Philadelphia mint produced 10,000 coins while the San Francisco mint struck 5,000 of the Oregon Trail commemorative half-dollars. In 1937, the Denver mint again produced 12,000, and the final release was a three-piece set containing one coin from each of the three mints in 1938 (a total of 6,000 sets) and in 1939 (3,000 sets). In all, there were fourteen Oregon Trail issues between 1926 and 1939. More recently a leading numismatics authority observed: "Back-room politics have figured in many a decision at the Mint over the years, but the Oregon Trail commemorative program became the biggest abuser in the system."[13]

IN 1930, the Oregon Trail Memorial Association began to organize a series of commemorations called the Covered Wagon Centennial. Between April and December 1930, celebrations were held from Governor's Island, New York, to Portland, Oregon, including a covered-wagon-train reenactment at St. Louis. The main celebration occurred on July 3, 4, and 5 at Independence Rock in Wyoming. Howard R. Driggs later wrote: "Through the patriotic and cooperative efforts of the Wyoming Historical Landmark Commission, the officials and citizenry of Natrona county, in which the old landmark is

*A theater poster for Republic Pictures' The Oregon Trail,
starring John Wayne and directed by Scott Pembroke,
released in 1936.* (Author's collection)

situated, the pioneer campground was made ready for the great rendezvous.
A host gathered there. Nearly a thousand of the Boy Scouts of America with
their leaders came, including a fine troop of young Indians from Lander.
Officers and members of national and state organizations devoted to preserving the story of America's making were there, and with them, to give
reality and precious spirit to the occasion, nearly a score of the covered
wagon pioneers were present as honored guests."[14]

On July 4, 1930, at the north end of Independence Rock, following ceremonies that included talks and songs, a bronze plaque bearing the likeness of
Ezra Meeker was unveiled. At the end of the ceremonies Independence
Rock was dedicated as a national monument to the memory of the coura-
geous pioneers. It was, as Howard Driggs observed, an all-American shrine.

With its 1930 ceremonies, the Oregon Trail Memorial Association had elevated the importance of the old road in the minds of many Americans.

In 1936, the Scotts Bluff National Monument in western Nebraska completed the construction of a new Oregon Trail Museum as part of a federal works project that included installation of new exhibits. When members of the Oregon Trail Memorial Association learned of the new museum and the scheduled dedication, many attended. Merrill Mattes, who had become custodian at the national monument a year earlier, recalled, "We had Indian dances, brass bands and speeches by Howard Driggs and William H. Jackson, president and research director of that organization.... It was the custom of OTMA to go out west every year, dedicating Oregon Trail and Pony Express markers, and to drum up enthusiasm among the different Oregon Trail communities. In 1938 Scotts Bluff was their jumping-off point again, and I remember vividly three things that happened then. Dr. Driggs raising the rafters with his ringing oratory at the banquet held in Scottsbluff; William H. Jackson showing me the exact site of his 1866 encampment when he came through torturous Mitchell Pass, and our big bonfire celebration at Fort Laramie, some 50 miles further west, which had just been proclaimed a National Monument to preserve the priceless remains there."[15]

In 1939, Universal Pictures released a serial titled *The Oregon Trail*, starring Johnny Mack Brown following the format of Hollywood's B-movie Westerns. That same year, a New York publisher released the Federal Writers' Project book *The Oregon Trail: The Missouri River to the Pacific Ocean*, which further helped to attract attention to the old trail. The following year, Driggs, Jackson, and other dignitaries were at Fort Laramie to help dedicate the first phase of the restoration of Old Bedlam, the two-story officers' quarters built in 1849. Later that summer in a meeting at Jackson Hole, Wyoming, OTMA members decided to change the name of their organization to the American Pioneer Trails Association to expand the group's work to help preserve and mark all of the great western trails, including the Santa Fe Trail and the trail followed by Lewis and Clark. But in 1942, William Henry Jackson, the pioneer photographer and artist who had traveled the trail during the 1860s and had served as OTMA's research director, died at the age of ninety-nine, a year or so before the Oregon Trail centennial was to occur. OTMA members began to talk about another celebration, but then the United States entered World War II.

In Oregon, supporters established the Trail Centennial Commission and events were planned. When 1943 arrived, celebrations were held in Baker City, Champoeg, and Portland, Oregon, and a Liberty ship, the *Robert Newell*, was launched with ceremony from the Kaiser shipyard at Portland. But the

Centennial Commission in Oregon was not able to make the year a national celebration. In a time of war other states crossed by the old road had little interest.

In 1945, as World War II was coming to an end, Republic Pictures in Hollywood released another film titled *The Oregon Trail*, starring Sunset "Kit" Carson. A typical B-movie Western with very little about the real Oregon Trail, at least it kept the old road in the minds of Americans. There was far more substance to the outstanding collection of sketches and watercolors owned by the late William Henry Jackson. The collection was offered to the National Park Service by APTA, the American Pioneer Trails Association. Prominent New Yorkers contributed $10,000, and the citizens of Scottsbluff, Nebraska, contributed additional funds to enable the Scotts Bluff National Monument to construct a brick exhibit space, which, along with Jackson's treasures, was dedicated in 1946. Unfortunately, by then the activities of APTA had dwindled, and in 1948 its national headquarters was moved to Kansas City, Missouri. Although APTA supporter Walter Meacham died in

A theater poster for another Hollywood film titled The Oregon Trail, *released in 1959, in CinemaScope, by Twentieth Century Fox Film Corporation. The film starred Fred Mac-Murray, William Bishop, and Nina Shipman, and was directed by Gene Fowler, Jr.* (Author's collection)

Oregon in 1951, Howard Driggs continued as president, and in 1954 he dedicated a Lewis and Clark monument in Omaha, Nebraska, to commemorate the 150th anniversary of the famous expedition. Driggs was then eighty-one years old, and soon the activities of APTA began to fade from the public eye. He died at the age of ninety in 1963.

In the meantime, Twentieth Century Fox released yet another motion picture titled *The Oregon Trail,* this time starring Fred MacMurray. By then entrepreneurs along the trail's route were capitalizing on the attention the old road was receiving and using the name for motels, cafés, and other businesses. Civic organizations, including the Boy Scouts, also adopted the label. Scholars and history buffs began serious research and wrote books and pamphlets detailing various aspects of the trail, keeping the route and its history alive in the West. Then in 1968, Congress passed the National Trails System Act to provide for recreation, public access, enjoyment, and appreciation of the "open-air, outdoor areas and historic resources of the Nation." Initially the legislation recognized the Appalachian Trail from Katahdin, Maine, to Springer Mountain in Georgia, a distance of about 2,160 miles, and the Pacific Crest National Scenic Trail, which stretches 2,650 miles from Mexico to Canada through the states of California, Oregon, and Washington. But ten years later, in 1978, Public Law 95-625 amended the act to create a new category of National Historic Trails, to follow closely original routes of national historic significance. Three years later the Oregon Trail was added along with the Mormon Pioneer Trail, the Lewis and Clark Trail, and the Iditarod Trail in Alaska. Still, it left out the California and Pony Express trails.

In spite of the federal legislation designed to preserve the Oregon Trail, several miles of the old road's ruts were plowed up near Echo, Oregon, and vandalism occurred at Alcove Spring near Marysville, Kansas. There also was the threat of gas and oil exploration and newly planned highways that could or would destroy portions of the old road. These things attracted the attention of Gregory Franzwa, a history buff in St. Louis, who in the spring of 1982 wrote others concerned about preserving the old trail. They met in Denver, Colorado, on August 11, 1982, and formed the Oregon-California Trails Association (OCTA). Attendees included Franzwa, Merrill J. Mattes, Dr. John A. Latschar, Robert D. Tucker, James F. Bowers, Robert Rennels, Troy Gray, Billie Gray, Roger Blair, Dr. Merle W. Wells, and James P. Johnson. After electing officers and board members, a committee was appointed to write bylaws, and plans were made for their first convention. They also agreed to publish the quarterly *Overland Journal,* containing articles on all aspects of the old trails—from the routes followed to the people who traveled them. *Overland Journal* is sent to all dues-paying members as part of the association's efforts to preserve, map, educate, and promote the importance of the trail and its many branches. The organization's membership increased and became a strong and active public voice. Gradually members in different areas along the old roads began meeting to discuss the trails' history and what they could do to better the cause. In 1988, OCTA's bylaws were changed to authorize the formation of chapters. By the year 2000, OCTA had active chapters throughout the West working with state and federal agencies on behalf of the old trails and their history.

By then major interpretative centers had been established along the route to help tell the story of the pioneers who traveled the Oregon Trail. In 1990, the National Frontier Trails Center was opened at Independence, Missouri, in a building owned by the state of Missouri, which renovated a historic mill warehouse and created exhibits about the Santa Fe, Oregon, and California trails, all of which began in Independence. Current and planned exhibits span the period from Lewis and Clark to the arrival of the transcontinental railroad. The headquarters of the Oregon-California Trails Association and the Merrill J. Mattes Research Library are also located in the center's four-building complex. The library is believed to be the largest public research library in the nation focused on western trails.

In 1992 the National Historic Oregon Trail Interpretive Center opened on Flagstaff Hill, five miles east of Baker City, Oregon; it is operated by the

The U.S. Postal Service issued a 29-cent stamp commemorating the 150th anniversary of the Oregon Trail in 1993. The stamp above is on a special first-day-of-issue envelope mailed from Salem, Oregon, on February 12, 1993. (Author's collection)

Bureau of Land Management. The following year the U.S. Postal Service issued a 29-cent stamp commemorating the 150th anniversary of the Oregon Trail. The stamp was released on February 12, 1993, at Salem, Oregon, following a first-day-of-issue ceremony at the state capital that featured Jack Rosenthal, the stamp's designer, Mark Hatfield, U.S. senator from Oregon, and postal officials. The stamp shows a map of the West and the route of the old trail across seven states. Because of space the stamp does not show the thirty-six present-day cities through which the trail passed. Stamp collectors and Oregon Trail buffs across the country made arrangements to receive envelopes with the first-day-of-issue postmark.

Two years later, in 1995, the End of the Oregon Trail Interpretive Center was opened at Oregon City, Oregon, by the Oregon Trail Foundation. In 1999 the National Oregon/Calfornia Trail Center was established at Montpelier, Idaho, by a community volunteer organization, using private funds. In August 2002 the National Historic Trails Interpretive Center opened in Casper, Wyoming; it is operated by the Bureau of Land Management, although it is funded by a private foundation and the city of Casper. Because of the numerous private, state, and federal sites along the Oregon Trail between Missouri and western Oregon, visitors today can gain a better understanding of the old road's place in American history.

Thanks to the efforts of the National Park Service in partnership with the Bureau of Land Management, the Forest Service, state and local governments, OCTA, and private individuals over whose property the old trail crosses, Ezra Meeker's wish that the Oregon Trail not be forgotten has been fulfilled. About three hundred miles of the old road's ruts can be seen today, along with more than two hundred historic sites, not to mention the prairie, plains, mountains, and deserts crossed by the emigrants. Certainly the countless stories told by the emigrants help us to understand their hardships and struggles, but to really appreciate the land they crossed and the vast distances they conquered, one must actually travel the old trail's route. Modern highways make the journey easy. Some have been built over the remains of the old trail or closely parallel the route that is now clearly marked by cities and towns. There are places where one can stop and walk in the tracks where oxen once pulled wagons bound for the emigrants' future homes. Only by retracing the route can one truly experience and appreciate firsthand the accomplishments of those pioneers who traveled the Oregon Trail. It is indeed a national treasure.

Acknowledgments

Thanks go to many people who assisted the author in one way or another in researching this book. A special note of thanks goes to Bill Gulick, in Walla Walla, Washington, the dean of western writers in the Pacific Northwest, who provided much assistance and who escorted the author on a tour of the Whitman mission. The same special thanks go to Robert Clark of the Arthur Clark Co., Spokane, Washington, editor of *Overland Journal*, the quarterly publication of the Oregon-California Trail Association, for his assistance. Thanks also to John Lovett, Western History Collections, University of Oklahoma Libraries; Dean Knudsen, historian, Scotts Bluff National Monument, Gering, Nebraska; Steven R. Fullmer, park ranger, Fort Laramie National Historic Site; Laurie Black, Oregon Trail History and Education Center, Three Island Crossing State Park, Glenns Ferry, Idaho; Judy Austin, recently retired from the Idaho Historical Society; Steve Hallberg and the staff of the Oregon Historical Society, Portland; Nancy Sherbert, Kansas State Historical Society, Topeka; John Carter of the Nebraska State Historical Society, Lincoln; Thomas Robinson of Portland, Oregon; and Megaera Ausman, historian, United States Postal Service, Washington, D.C.

The author owes a debt of gratitude to countless pioneers who wrote diaries and journals or left recollections of their travel over the Oregon Trail, and those scholars whose efforts have contributed to a strong body of research on the road's history, including Merrill Mattes; John Unruh, Jr.; Andrew Jensen; Irene Paden; Louise Barry; Dale Morgan; W. J. Ghent; and many others whose contributions are cited in the bibliography.

Finally, I want to thank my editor Ann Close for her encouragement, guidance, and assistance. I would like to give a special thanks to my wife, Sue, who traveled with me over the trail from the Missouri River to Oregon and back and provided much help and advice on what appears between this book's covers. Our Oregon Trail journey was a lovely adventure we shall never forget.

Appendix A

HISTORIC LANDMARKS

There are many historic landmarks of varying importance along the Oregon Trail. The more significant ones are described in the list below.

Alcove Spring (Kansas). Located on the east bank of the Big Blue River about six and a half miles north of Blue Rapids, Kansas, it was a popular camping site for emigrants. A memorial to Sarah Keyes, an emigrant who died here in 1846, is located at the start of a 250-yard trail that leads to the springs. A portion of the wagon trail once followed by emigrants is still visible near the spring. Nearby is the Independence Crossing of the Big Blue River.

American Falls (Idaho). Located just west of American Falls, Idaho, on I-86, here the Snake River dropped about fifty feet in several ten-foot steps. It was a prominent landmark for early emigrants. Unfortunately, American Falls is no longer visible because it is under the waters of the American Falls Reservoir.

Ancient Bluff Ruins (Nebraska). Located four miles east of Broadwater, Nebraska, on the north bank of the North Platte River, this large formation of eroded sandstone was the first place where emigrants traveling the river's north bank could see Chimney Rock.

Ash Hollow (Nebraska). Located in Garden County, Nebraska, just off U.S. Highway 26 northwest of Ogallala, Nebraska, the hollow is at the bottom of Windlass Hill. A partly spring-fed creek runs through the hollow, which provided emigrants with the best water in the area. In about 1846 someone constructed a small log cabin at the spring, which served as an emigrant post office and remained in operation until about 1850. About one mile up the hollow from the spring, a trading post was established in about 1851 and operated until at least 1853.

Ayers Natural Bridge (Wyoming). Located twelve miles west of Douglas, Wyoming, the natural bridge arches over LaPrele Creek. It is mentioned in the diaries and journals of emigrants.

Battle Mountain (Nevada). Located in north-central Nevada near the Humboldt River and the modern community of Humboldt, the mountain appears to have been named following a series of attacks on emigrants traveling the California Trail in 1857. The attacks were blamed on Indians who actually may have been bandits in disguise.

Beckwourth Pass (California). Located about one mile east of Chilcoot, California, the pass was discovered in 1851 by James P. Beckwourth. At an elevation of 5,221 feet, it was the lowest pass in the Sierra Nevada used by emigrants.

Big Springs (Kansas). *See* Coon Hollow.

Bissonette's Ferry Site (Wyoming). Located about one-third of a mile above the mouth of Deer Creek on the North Platte River, the ferry operated in 1849 and 1850 during the gold rush.

Blue Jacket Crossing (Kansas). Located about five miles southeast of Lawrence, Kansas, this was a crossing of the Wakarusa River.

Blue Mound (Kansas). Located about five miles southeast of Lawrence, Kansas, this is a tree-covered hill nearly one mile long, rising more than 1,000 feet above the surrounding country.

Blue Mountain Crossing (Oregon). Located about nine miles northwest of La Grande, Oregon, off I-84 at exit 248, some of the best preserved wagon-wheel depressions can be seen on a grassy ridge and through stately ponderosa pines in the Wallowa-Whitman National Forest. The site is near the summit of the Blue Mountains at an elevation of 4,193 feet.

Bordeaux Station Site (Wyoming). Located about two miles west of Lingle, Wyoming, this trading post was built in 1849 by James Bordeaux and remained in operation until 1868. Lakota Sioux Indians and emigrants traded here.

Bridger's Ferry Site (Wyoming). Located thirteen miles southeast of Douglas, Wyoming, James Bridger operated the ferry over the North Platte River between 1864 and 1866.

Camp Marshall (Wyoming). Located about ten miles south of Douglas, Wyoming, situated on the west side of LaBonte Creek, this was a temporary military post late in the Civil War, until 1866. The post was named for Capt. Levi Marshall, Co. E, Eleventh Ohio Cavalry.

Camp Mitchell (Nebraska). Located nearly four miles west of Scottsbluff, Nebraska, and three miles west of Mitchell Pass, the post was established on a bend in the North Platte River in 1864 by Capt. Jacob S. Shuman, Co. H, Eleventh Ohio Volunteer Cavalry and named for Gen. Robert B. Mitchell, who ordered the establishment of several substations along the Oregon Trail between Julesburg and South Pass. The post was abandoned in 1867.

Carson Pass (California). Located at California State Highway 88 on the crest of the mountains between Stockton, California, and the Nevada state line, the pass is at an elevation of 8,579 feet in the El Dorado National Forest. It was discovered by John C. Frémont in 1844 and opened by some members of the Mormon Battalion in 1848 returning east to Salt Lake. The heavily traveled Carson Route, which crossed the pass, ran from the Humboldt Sink to Hangtown (now Placerville) and Sutter's Fort via the Carson River.

Chimney Rock (Nebraska). Located almost four miles south of Bayard, Nebraska, this landmark composed of sandstone and clay was given its name because it resembled a tall factory chimney. It is the most frequently mentioned landmark cited in the diaries and journals of emigrants.

City of Rocks (Idaho). Located in a valley of the Albion Mountain range near Almo, Idaho, granite rocks here rise abruptly out of the ground. Emigrants heading for California began to camp in the valley in 1843, and in 1849, James Wilkins, an emigrant, gave the site its name. Later emigrants bound for Oregon camped here after the Applegate Trail, or Southern Route, to Oregon was opened.

Cold Springs (Wyoming). Many emigrants camped near the springs, located nearly two miles southeast of Torrington, Wyoming.

Coon Hollow Site (Kansas). Located near Big Springs, Kansas, this was a popular campground.

Coon Point Campground (Kansas). Located at the mouth of Coon Creek, west of Lecompton, Kansas, many emigrants camped here.

Cottonwood Springs (Nebraska). Located about four miles south of Maxwell, Nebraska, these springs provided the only good water for miles in all directions. The springs may have been named for nearby Cottonwood Canyon, since it is doubtful there were cottonwood tress at the springs during the nineteenth century. The springs were a favorite campground for emigrants. Members of Co. G, Seventh Iowa Voluntary Cavalry, constructed Camp McKean, later known as Fort Cottonwood, in the area. The post was renamed Fort McPherson in 1866.

Courthouse Rock (Nebraska). Located five miles south of Bridgeport, Nebraska, this massive sandstone landmark thrusts upward from the surrounding area and was given its name by emigrants who likened its shape to a courthouse. A smaller sandstone formation to its east acquired the name Jail Rock. They are located south of the Oregon Trail.

Deadman Pass (Oregon). Located eighteen miles southeast of Pendleton, Oregon, on I-84, this is a narrow pass between Telephone Ridge and Emigrant Hill. The Oregon Trail crossed the pass, but it was not named Deadman Pass until 1878 when four teamsters were killed in the area.

Deep Rut Hill (Wyoming). Located near Register Rock, south of Guernsey, ruts worn at least five feet deep may still be seen today. The hill was named in the 1930s by Irene Paden in her book *Wake of the Prairie Schooner.* While the ruts are located on the route followed by many emigrants, there is speculation the ruts were deepened not so much by westbound pioneers but by heavy freight wagons carrying tons of stone from Wyoming quarries late in the nineteenth century.

Devil's Gate (Wyoming). Located on private property about one-half mile north of the Oregon Trail, it can be viewed from Wyoming State Highway 220 to the west of Independence Rock. It is a narrow opening 370 feet deep and 1,500 feet long through which the Sweetwater River flows. Travelers around 1840 began to call the landmark by various names, including Devil's Entrance and Hell Gate. In time, it became known as Devil's Gate.

Dobytown Site (Nebraska). Located about two miles west of new Fort Kearny, a settlement called Kearney City was established in 1859 after a daily stage and mail service began. Kearney City was better known as Dobytown because most of its dozen or more buildings were made of adobe. The place provided soldiers from the fort with saloons, gambling halls, and prostitution. Emigrants who stopped here found blacksmiths and merchants selling provisions. Kearney City became the county seat when the territorial legislature of Nebraska organized Kearney County. After the Union Pacific Railroad was completed north of the Platte River in 1867 and Fort Kearney was abandoned in 1871, the town died. According to tradition, the spelling of Kearney City and later Kearney, Nebraska, was made in error by a post office employee who failed to follow the spelling of Fort Kearny for the town.

Elm Grove (Kansas). *See* Lone Elm Campground.

Emigrant Gap (California). Located on I-80 above Bear Valley, emigrants bound for California first crossed this pass over the Sierra Nevada in 1845. Because of a steep slope to the west, they had to lower their wagons by ropes to the floor of Bear Valley.

Emigrant Gap (Wyoming). Located twelve miles west of Casper, Wyoming, this is a shallow pass through what is today called Emigrant Gap Ridge. Many emigrants chose not to follow this route but to travel instead along the North Platte River.

Emigrant Springs (Oregon). Located three miles northwest of Meacham, Oregon, the springs are at the head of Squaw Creek, just off I-84. Missionary Jason Lee may have discovered them. Emigrants found water here at what is today called Emigrant Springs State Park. A monument dedicated to the early pioneers by President Warren G. Harding on July 3, 1923, may be seen in the park.

Farewell Bend (Oregon). Located in the southeast corner of Baker County, Oregon, this is where the Oregon Trail left the Snake River, which emigrants had followed for more than three hundred miles from Fort Hall.

Fort Bernard Site (Wyoming). Located about five miles southeast of Fort Laramie, Joseph Bissonette built this trading post in 1845 to compete against Fort John (later Fort Laramie), operated by the American Fur Company. Fort Bernard remained in operation until about 1850.

Fort Boise Site (Idaho). Located nearly five miles northwest of Parma, Idaho, the Hudson's Bay Company established a trading post in 1834 on the east bank of the Snake River below the mouth of the Boise River. It remained in operation until 1853, when floodwaters damaged the trading post. Another Fort Boise was established in 1863 by volunteers from Oregon and Washington to protect travelers on the Oregon Trail and gold miners heading for Idaho. This military post, located on the site of modern Boise, Idaho, remained active until 1913. A replica of Fort Boise can be seen in the city park at Parma.

Fort Bridger Sites (Wyoming). Located about one mile north of the modern town of Fort Bridger in southwest Wyoming, James Bridger and Louis Vasquez established their first trading post in 1842 on Black's Fork. About 1844, Bridger and Vasquez established a second trading post of log houses and stock pens on Black's Fork at what is now Fort Bridger State Park, located just off I-80 on U.S. Highway 30 about twenty-five miles east of Evanston. In 1853, Mormons reportedly bought the fort from Bridger for $6,000 in gold, but he later denied it. During the Utah War of 1857, Mormons burned the post as U.S. troops approached the area. It became a U.S. military outpost in 1858 but was abandoned by 1861. It was occupied again by the army in 1862 and remained an active military post until the late 1880s. Today, Fort Bridger is a Wyoming historic site and includes a replica of Bridger's trading post.

Fort Caspar (Wyoming). Located on the outskirts of modern Casper, Wyoming, this military post was established in 1858 and named for Lt. Caspar Collins, Co. G, Eleventh Ohio Voluntary Cavalry, who was killed in action nearby. Two companies of soldiers were stationed there until the fort was abandoned in 1867, after which Indians burned the post. A replica of the fort may be seen today in a city park on the western outskirts of Casper.

Fort Childs (Nebraska). *See* Fort Kearny (new).

Fort Cottonwood (Nebraska). *See* Fort McPherson.

Fort Dalles (Oregon). Located on the southeast side of The Dalles, Oregon, this military post was established in 1850 and was first known as Camp Drum. It was renamed Fort Dalles in 1853. It was established to provide protection for emigrants on the Oregon Trail, and was abandoned in 1867. One remaining building, the quarters of the U.S. Army surgeon, is now a museum.

Fort Grattan Site (Nebraska). Located at the mouth of Ash Hollow just off U.S. Highway 26 about thirty miles northwest of Ogallala, this temporary outpost and supply depot was established by Gen. William S. Harney in 1855 and was garrisoned with a company of soldiers from the Sixth Infantry. The post was nothing more than an adobe building about twenty by forty feet. The post was abandoned a few months later.

Fort Hall Site (Idaho). Fifteen miles northwest of Pocatello, Idaho, on the east bank of the Snake River, Nathaniel J. Wyeth constructed a trading post in 1834. It was sold to the Hudson's Bay Company in 1837 and abandoned in 1856 because of hostile Indians in the area. Fort Hall was an important stop for emigrants. In 1870, the U.S. Army constructed another Fort Hall eight miles east of Blackfoot, Idaho, on Lincoln Creek. Often called New Fort Hall, it was located about twenty-five miles northeast of the first Fort Hall. A replica of the Hudson's Bay Company's Fort Hall has since been constructed in Ross Park in Pocatello, using plans provided by the Hudson's Bay Company.

Fort John (Nebraska). Located seven miles south of Gering, Nebraska, in Helvas Canyon, this trading post was built about 1850 by Pierre Chouteau, Jr. & Co. and managed by Andrew Drips to replace the old Fort John located near the mouth of the Laramie River, which was sold to the U.S. Army in 1849 and renamed Fort Laramie. This new Fort John operated for a few years.

Fort John (Wyoming). Located on high ground about one and a half miles above the mouth of the Laramie River and at the southwest end of the parade ground of the later Fort Laramie, Fort John was sold to the government in 1849. *See* Fort Laramie.

Fort Kearny (new) (Nebraska). Located about forty miles southwest of Grand Island, Nebraska, just off I-80, this military post was constructed in 1848 and named Fort Childs in honor of Col. Thomas Childs of Mexican War fame. It was renamed Fort Kearny in 1848 to honor Col. Stephen Watts Kearny and was the second Fort Kearny in what is now Nebraska. The earlier Fort Kearny was located in what is now Nebraska City, Nebraska, along the Missouri River.

Fort Kearny (old) (Nebraska). Located in Nebraska City, Nebraska, and first called Camp Kearny, the fort began with a blockhouse constructed in 1846 near the mouth of Table Creek. It was the first military post constructed to protect emigrants traveling the Oregon Trail. The Mexican War interrupted further construction, and by 1848 the location was deemed too far east from the main Oregon Trail. A new post was constructed farther west along the Platte River in 1848 and renamed Fort Kearny (new).

Fort Laramie (Wyoming). Located in southeast Wyoming about twenty miles north-west of Torrington on U.S. Highway 26, the trading post was called Fort William when it was constructed in 1834. A few years later it was sold to Milton Sublette and James Bridger and renamed Fort John. In 1849 the government purchased the post, made improvements, and renamed it Fort Laramie because of its location on the Laramie River. Fort Laramie was a major stopping point for emigrants on the Oregon Trail. The abandoned remains of Fort John were demolished in 1862, but other buildings dating back to 1849 can still be seen today.

Fort McPherson Site (Nebraska). Located about fourteen miles east of North Platte, Nebraska, on I-80, and then two miles south, this military post was established in 1863 and first called Camp McKean and then Fort Cottonwood. In 1866 its name was changed to Fort McPherson to honor a Union general. It continued in operation until 1880. Today nothing remains of Fort McPherson, but near its site is a National Cemetery containing the remains of persons first buried in twenty-three cemeteries of long-closed frontier military posts in Nebraska, Colorado, Wyoming, and South Dakota.

Fort Vancouver (Washington). Located in Vancouver, Washington, this Hudson's Bay Company post was established in 1824 and served as the company's headquarters for its trade throughout the Pacific Northwest. Until the California gold rush, Fort Vancouver was the largest trading center in the West. From here Dr. John McLoughlin provided aid to emigrants. The restored post is open to the public today.

Fort Walla Walla Site (Washington). Located at the mouth of the Walla Walla River on the east bank of the Columbia River, this trading post was established by the Hudson's Bay Company in about 1817. The site is today under the waters of Lake Wallula. A replica of the post has since been constructed in a Walla Walla park.

Fort William (Wyoming). The location of the fort appears to have been on the north bank of the Laramie River, six-tenths of a mile above its mouth, and less than a mile east of Fort Laramie. Robert Campbell built the trading post in 1834.

Frémont Springs (Nebraska). Located about four miles south of Diller, Nebraska, the springs are named for John C. Frémont, who camped there in 1842. Frémont and Kit Carson carved their names in sandstone above the springs.

Gate of Death (Idaho). Located about twelve miles west of American Falls, Idaho, this is a narrow break in the rocks through which the Oregon Trail passed. Emigrants apparently feared that Indians might be waiting in ambush at this spot. Ten emigrants died here in August 1862 in a fight with Shoshone Indians. The site was sometimes referred to by emigrants as Devil's Gate. The area is now a state park.

Grattan Massacre Site (Wyoming). It was here, about seven miles southeast of Fort Laramie, that in August 1854, 2nd Lt. John L. Grattan and twenty-eight soldiers with an interpreter and a fieldpiece tried to arrest several Sioux Indians who had killed and eaten a lame cow that had strayed from a party of Mormon emigrants. A fight followed, and all but one of the soldiers and an Indian chief were killed. A wounded soldier carried the news to Fort Laramie before dying.

Ham's Fork Crossing (Wyoming). Located about one mile southwest of Granger, Wyoming, about a mile above the junction where Ham's Fork flows into Black's Fork. In 1857 a bridge was built in the area by the army.

Horse Creek Crossing (Nebraska). Located four miles southwest of Morrill, Nebraska, emigrants here crossed Horse Creek, which was then reported to be about two hundred feet wide, just before its waters flowed into the North Platte River. In 1851, when the Sioux Nation and United States representatives gathered at Fort Laramie, about thirty miles away from Horse Creek Crossing, the ponies ridden by about 10,000 Indians required so much forage that most of those assembled had to move to the meadows at the mouth of Horse Creek in order to feed their animals and sign a treaty.

Independence Crossing (Kansas). Located about seven miles south of Marysville, Kansas, this was a well-known ford of the Big Blue River for emigrants jumping off from Independence and the nearby area. Alcove Springs is located nearby.

Independence Rock (Wyoming). Located forty-eight miles southwest of Casper, Wyoming, this oval-shaped outcrop of granite running southeast to northwest is 1,900 feet long, 700 feet wide, and with a maximum relief of 128 feet above the valley floor. From some distance the rock resembles a very large turtle. It was the most prominent landmark on the Oregon Trail west of Fort Laramie. Located near the road, it was visited by thousands of emigrants, who carved their names and messages in the granite.

Kearney City (Nebraska). *See* Dobytown.

Knob Hill (Wyoming). Located about seven miles south of Douglas, Wyoming, the mound of sandstone or limestone stands out against the surrounding landscape of red earth. It was about one hundred feet west of the Oregon Trail.

Laramie River Crossings (Wyoming). The first crossing was located about one mile above where the Laramie and North Platte rivers join. It could be forded at low water but had to be ferried when the water was high. This was the main crossing of the Laramie River used to reach Fort William between 1834 and 1841, but after Fort Platte was constructed about one mile upstream and Fort William was abandoned, emigrants crossed closer to the new post, thereby establishing a second crossing. A third crossing was less than a mile above the second and was used as the alternate crossing during the gold-rush years. The fourth crossing, about one-half mile above the first crossing, was also used as an alternate during the gold rush. The fifth crossing was located directly east of the Fort Laramie parade ground. In 1873 a wagon bridge was constructed at this crossing and was used until 1884. Nearby was a footbridge constructed in 1869 and used until 1890. A sixth crossing was opposite Fort John, and a ferry service was available there. A seventh crossing of the Laramie River was located southwest of the Fort Laramie parade ground. Another crossing, the eighth, was also located southwest of Fort Laramie, and a ninth crossing was located west of Fort Laramie's parade ground. The numerous crossings of the Laramie River may have been the result of river channels being changed during periods of high water.

Lone Elm Campground (Kansas). Located south of Olathe, Kansas, at the head of Cedar Creek, this was a prominent campground for emigrants. Earlier it was known as Sapling Grove, Round Grove, and Elm Grove, but after emigrants had cut all of the trees in the area for firewood, leaving only a single tree, it earned this name. The lone elm, however, apparently was destroyed by a later party of emigrants.

Lytle Pass (Oregon). Located six miles southeast of Yale, Oregon, emigrants crossed this pass, and wagon ruts can still be seen today.

Mitchell Pass (Nebraska). Located nearly three miles west of Gering, Nebraska, emigrants began using this pass as a route of travel after it was cleared of rock about 1850. It received its name following the establishment of Camp Mitchell in 1864. Before the route was opened, emigrants used Robidoux Pass, farther to the south.

Mormon Ferries (Wyoming). Mormons established a ferry on the Upper Platte River just northwest of modern Casper, Wyoming, in 1847 and operated it through 1851 for emigrants wishing to cross the river during high water. The ferry was built of two dugout canoes about thirty feet long with a three-foot beam covered with wood planks to carry wagons. It cost emigrants four or five dollars to ferry one wagon. Another Mormon ferry was located at the middle crossing of the Green River northeast of modern Kemmerer, Wyoming, in June 1847 and during the summer of 1848. The ferry is described as one boat attached to a rope with pulleys.

Mountain Men's Ferry (Wyoming). Located where the Sublette Cutoff crosses the Green River northeast of modern Kemmerer, Wyoming, this ferry was operated by mountain men from Fort Bridger during periods of high water in 1849 and 1850. The ferry consisted of four canoes lashed together.

North Platte River Crossings (Wyoming). Located north of the fairgrounds at Casper, Wyoming. Emigrants forded the North Platte at this point only when the water was low. A Mormon ferry was established at this crossing in 1847 and continued in use until 1851. In 1858 a log bridge was built by Louis Guinard, eliminating the need for a ferry.

Oregon Crossing (Missouri). A Missouri River crossing located on the border of modern Kansas, Nebraska, and northwest Missouri.

Pacific Springs (Wyoming). Located nearly three miles west of South Pass, the springs are located three hundred feet lower than the pass. In the summer they create a green oasis in an otherwise dry and rather bleak landscape. Emigrants mention the springs in their diaries and journals because it was here that water began to flow westward toward the Pacific Ocean.

Papan Ferry (Kansas). A ferry over the Kansas River at Topeka, Kansas, operated by Joseph and Lewis Papan (sometimes spelled Papin) from about 1844 into the 1850s.

Platte River Crossings (Nebraska and Colorado). Emigrants following the north bank of the Platte River past Fort Laramie did not have to cross the river until they reached the vicinity of modern Casper, Wyoming. Those emigrants traveling along the south bank of the Platte River could cross the stream at one of several points. The eastern-most ford was located about fourteen miles west of new Fort Kearny. Another ford was located about three miles east of North Platte, Nebraska, at the forks of the river. John Frémont crossed the Platte River at this point, sometimes called Fremont's Ford, in 1842. Located nearly four miles west of Brule, Nebraska, is the Lower Crossing over the South Platte River near where it joins the Platte River. It was the first of five other fords or crossings of the South Platte before the Upper Crossing, which became known as the California Crossing. After this crossing the emigrants slowly climbed California Hill to reach a high plateau between both forks of the river. About twenty-two miles up the South Platte, another crossing was established in about 1859 at what is now Julesburg, Colorado.

Register Cliff (Wyoming). Located about four miles south of Guernsey, Wyoming, the soft sandstone cliff stretches about one mile. Beginning in 1847 emigrants carved their initials or names and sometimes their addresses in the stone. Unfortunately the cliff has suffered from vandalism and erosion. What remains is preserved behind protective fencing.

Register Rock (Idaho). Emigrants left their names and dates on this large half-buried boulder located twelve miles southwest of American Falls, Idaho, which is under protective cover today.

Reshaw's Bridge Sites (Wyoming). Crossing the North Platte River near Deer Creek in Converse County, Wyoming, a log bridge was constructed by John Richard in about 1851 but was washed out by high water a year later. Richard then constructed a wooden bridge in 1852 over the North Platte River at modern Evansville, located about three miles northeast of Casper, Wyoming. Richard sold his interests in the bridge in 1865.

Robidoux Pass (Nebraska). Located ten miles west of Gering, Nebraska, emigrants passing Scotts Bluff used this pass extensively until Mitchell Pass was opened in 1850. After that Robidoux Pass was used as an alternate when conditions were bad on Mitchell Pass.

Robidoux Trading Post Site (Nebraska). Located nine miles west of Gering, Nebraska, this post was build late in 1848 about one mile southeast of Robidoux Pass. Established by Joseph E. Robidoux, it offered some supplies, blacksmithing, and whiskey to emigrants. Nearby was a spring with good water. Early in the summer of 1852 the trading post was relocated to the south in Carter Canyon after the opening of Mitchell Pass and a decline in travelers over Robidoux Pass.

Round Grove (Kansas). *See* Lone Elm Campground.

Sapling Grove (Kansas). *See* Lone Elm Campground.

Scotts Bluff (Nebraska). On the south bank of the North Platte River, two miles northwest of Gering, Nebraska, are massive bluffs named for Hiram Scott, an early trapper, who presumably died nearby after being left by a party of trappers. Emigrants often referred to the landmark as Scott's Bluffs, but the singular form is generally used today to describe the large bluff that runs north and south between the Platte River and Mitchell Pass. It is the site today of Scotts Bluff National Monument.

Shoshone Falls (Idaho). About four miles northeast of Twin Falls, Idaho, the Snake River cascades down a 212-foot waterfall. Although located south of the Oregon Trail, emigrants could hear the sound of rushing water for three or more miles away. Some emigrants left the trail to see the falls.

Shunganunga Crossing (Kansas). The crossing of Shunganunga Creek, located on the site of modern Topeka, Kansas.

Smith's Trading Post Site (Idaho). About five miles south of Montpelier, Idaho, mountain man Peg-Leg Smith constructed a trading post in 1848 on the east bank of the Bear River, just below the outlet of Bear Lake. The post was abandoned less than two years later.

Snake River Crossing (Idaho). *See* Three Island Crossing.

Soda Springs (Idaho). Located where the town of Soda Springs stands today on U.S. Highway 30 in southeast Idaho. Emigrants reported springs with water that tasted like soda and beer just west of present Soda Springs in the Bear River valley.

South Pass (Wyoming). Located in Fremont County, Wyoming, this is a shallow pass on the Continental Divide. Emigrants coming from the east climbed a broad, gradual plain to the summit at 7,412 feet. The descent westward is much steeper. Emigrants viewed South Pass as marking their arrival in Oregon Country and also as the halfway point in their journey westward.

Split Rock (Wyoming). Located to the east of U.S. Highway 287 about nine miles west of Muddy Gap Junction, the gun-sight notch in the summit of Split Rock served as something of a compass for emigrants heading to South Pass, which is seventy-five miles to the west.

St. Mary's Mission (Kansas). A Catholic mission established by Belgian Jesuits in 1848 to serve the Pottawatomie Indians. It was located just east of St. Marys, Kansas.

Sutter's Fort (California). Located in the city of Sacramento, it was established about 1839 by John Sutter, who received a 48,000-acre land grant in the Sacramento Valley from the Mexican government. Gold was discovered nearby in 1848. The fort was the destination for countless emigrants bound for California after the gold discovery.

Sweetwater River Crossings (Wyoming). Rising from southwest Fremont County in central Wyoming, the river had to be crossed by emigrants first just southwest of Independence Rock. Emigrants could have cut down on the number of times they crossed the meandering river by traveling along its bank, but this added days to their travel time. Most emigrants chose to move in a straight line, crossing the Sweetwater each time it crossed their route. In all, there were nine crossings between Independence Rock and South Pass.

Thousand Springs (Idaho). About six miles south of Hagerman, Idaho, a series of springs flow from the side of a canyon wall. Emigrants gave the springs their name. For thousands of years volcanic activity spread lava over the Snake River plain, slowly forcing the river south in a great curve. Successive channels of the river and its tributaries were filled with spongy lava, becoming both reservoirs and underground conduits. Here the water from one or more of these buried channels flows from the canyon wall.

Three Island Crossing (Idaho). Two miles southwest of Glenns Ferry in Elmore County, Idaho, many emigrants crossed to the north side of the Snake River to reach a better road to Fort Boise. An Idaho state park is located on the north bank just below the crossing. There were two crossings in this area. At Three Island Crossing emigrants could ford the river without swimming or floating. About one mile upstream was the more difficult Two Island Crossing, where wagons had to be floated across the Snake River. Because most emigrants thought both crossings were the same, the area became known as Three Island Crossing.

Uniontown (Kansas). A Pottawatomie Indian trading post established in 1848 and located about one mile south of the Kansas River about fifteen miles west of Topeka, Kansas. Before a ferry was established on the river in 1850, countless travelers forded the Kansas River at this point.

Vieux Toll Bridge Site (Kansas). Located about five miles northeast of Wamego, Kansas, the bridge was constructed in 1847 or 1848 by Louis Vieux at the crossing of the Red, or Little Vermillion, Creek.

Ward & Guerrier's Trading Post Site (Wyoming). Nearly three miles southeast of Guernsey, Wyoming, two traders named Ward and Guerrier established this trading post in 1841. Whether or not emigrants made much use of the post is not known.

Warm Springs (Wyoming). Located slightly more than two miles west of Guernsey, Wyoming, two free-flowing springs with water warmer than that of the river made this location a popular campground for emigrants.

Whitman Mission (Washington). Located eight miles west of Walla Walla, Washington, this was the site of Marcus Whitman's mission (Waiilatpu). Many emigrants stopped here. It is the site of the Whitman massacre carried out by Cayuse Indians.

Windlass Hill (Nebraska). Located in Garden County, Nebraska, this is a steep hill over which emigrants descended into Ash Hollow. How it received its name is not known, but emigrants had to descend on a slope of 25 degrees for about three hundred feet and let their wagons down by ropes.

Appendix B

CUTOFFS AND OTHER ROADS

As traffic over the main Oregon Trail increased, travelers sought to improve road conditions by seeking alternate routes around rough segments or to reduce the distance traveled. California-bound travelers who followed the Oregon Trail from the Missouri River west looked for the best and shortest route to the goldfields. Cutoffs and other roads were blazed, and some became major routes for emigrants to follow. Below is a summary of the more important named cutoffs and roads that developed during the nineteenth century.

Applegate Cutoff (1846). This route was laid out by Lindsay and Jesse Applegate from near the site of modern Dallas, Oregon, south to what is now Humboldt, Nevada, where it joined the trail to California coming from Fort Hall in Idaho. This became known as the Southern Route among Oregon-bound emigrants traveling from Fort Hall.

Barlow Road (1846). This road was started in 1845 and completed in 1846 by emigrant Samuel Barlow to improve the last leg of travel from The Dalles on the Columbia River around the south side of Mount Hood to the Willamette Valley. Barlow obtained a charter from the Provisional Government of Oregon to construct it and operate it as a toll road. It was almost ninety miles long, with sixty-five of the miles cut through forests and canyons. Before 1846 ended, 145 emigrant wagons, 1,059 horses, mules, and cattle, and one herd of sheep reportedly traveled the Barlow Road.

Beckwourth Cutoff (1851). Blazed about 1850 by James Pierson Beckwourth, a former mountain man turned trader, guide, and scout. It branched off the main California Trail in the area of the Truckee Meadows and the Truckee River near modern Reno, Nevada, and went north and west and then crossed over a pass in the Sierra Nevada, since named Beckwourth Pass. West of the mountain pass the route went north and west along Grizzly Creek and on west to Bidwell's Bar at the confluence of the three forks of the Feather River (now under Lake Oroville) and then south to Marysville.

California Cutoff (1841). The main route started at the Raft River near the City of Rocks in Idaho and angled southwest to the Humboldt River near modern Elko, Nevada. The route followed the river past the site of modern Winnemucca to Humboldt Lake. There the route crossed the Humboldt River and Carson Sink and picked up the Truckee River near what is now Reno, Nevada, and then went over the Sierra Nevada at what is now Donner Pass. Once over the mountains, the route went through the Bear River basin to the Feather and Sacramento rivers. The route along the Humboldt River was first attempted by emigrants in the Bidwell-Bartleson party in 1841, who followed the Bear River south from Soda Springs in present-day Idaho. Two years later Joseph Walker guided Joseph Childs's party to the Humboldt via the Raft River, City of Rocks, Goose Creek, Thousand Springs Valley, and Bishop Creek. This replaced the older route via Bear River and was sometimes called the Fort Hall Road. In 1844 other California-bound emigrants found a more direct route over the Sierra Nevada and soon other improvements were made on what became the main California Trail. (*See* Truckee Route.)

Carson Route (1848). The route, sometimes called the Carson Pass Trail, ran from Carson Sink up the Carson River, passing the site of modern Carson City, Nevada, then crossing the Sierra Nevada south of Lake Tahoe and continuing westward to Placerville and on to the American River and Sutter's Fort in California.

Cherokee Trail (1849). This trail, a link between the Arkansas and Platte rivers, ran along the Front Range of the Rocky Mountains. It apparently was an extension of an old Ute Indian trail that was also used by other tribes. Although few emigrants traveled this trail, it was used by traders from the 1830s. After gold was discovered in California in 1849, it was often called the California Road or the Arkansas Emigrant Train. After two parties of Cherokee Indians used the trail in 1849 and 1850, it became known as the Cherokee Trail.

Childs Cutoff (1850). Emigrants following the north bank of the North Platte River remained on the north side of the stream for this cutoff from Fort Laramie to the Red Buttes area. The cutoff eliminated the need to cross the Platte River at the fort.

Dempsey-Hockaday Road (1856). This road was a variation of the Sublette Cutoff. It stayed to the north of the Sublette Cutoff and went due west from the Green River to the Bear River in Wyoming.

Free Emigrant Road (1853–54). A middle emigrant route across Oregon from the Malheur River near the site of modern Vale to the southern Willamette Valley in Oregon. Stephen Meek first tried to open this route in 1845 but failed to cross the desert portion. Elijah Elliott tried in 1853 and successfully crossed the desert area but became stranded in the Cascade Mountains. William Macy succeeded in crossing the desert and the mountains in 1854. The route is sometimes called the Meek-Elliott-Macy Trail.

Goodale Cutoff (1862). The route left the main trail at Fort Hall in what is now southeast Idaho and went north and northwest toward Big Southern Butte, a landmark on the Snake River Plains, and passed near the site of present-day Arco, Idaho, before winding through the northern part of what is today the Craters of the Moon National Monument. From there it went southwest to Camas Prairie and rejoined the main Oregon Trail at Ditto Creek in the vicinity of Fort Boise. The cutoff was 230 miles in length and required from two to three weeks to traverse. Although the cutoff followed an old Shoshone Indian migration route, John Jeffrey may have been the first white man to travel it in 1852. It was named for Tim Goodale, a native of Illinois and an old mountain man, who in 1862 led a party of emigrants over the route.

Greenwood Cutoff. See Sublette's Cutoff.

Hams Fork Cutoff (1849). This route in Wyoming began at the junction of the Hams Fork and Black's Fork rivers and followed Hams Fork northwest to join the Sublette Cutoff at Emigrant Springs, a popular camping spot for emigrants. It was not used extensively.

Hastings Cutoff (1846). Lansford Hastings, for whom the cutoff is named, led the first wagons over this route through Weber Canyon to the Salt Lake Valley, around the south side of the Great Salt Lake and across what is today called the Bonneville Salt Flats. Once across the desert, the route joined the California Trail near modern Elko, Nevada. Travelers later improved the route by going around the north side of the Great Salt Lake.

Hudspeth Cutoff (1849). Benoni Hudspeth, for whom this cutoff is named, left the California Trail and went west, where the Bear River bends south at Soda Springs in modern southeast Idaho. Hudspeth was guided by John J. Myers. After about 130 miles they rejoined the California Trail where it leaves the Raft River near the site of modern Malta, Idaho. The cutoff did not save much time, nor was the route much better than the California Cutoff.

Kinney Cutoff (1852). This was a variation of the Sublette Cutoff and tracked south following the Big Sandy River to the Green River, thereby avoiding the fifty miles of desert on Sublette's Cutoff. It apparently was blazed by mountain man Charles Kinney and was first used by emigrants in about 1852. After it reached the valley of Slate Creek, it was often called the Slate Creek Cutoff.

Lander Trail (1858). This shortcut between South Pass and the Snake River region was the only portion of the Oregon Trail constructed with government help. The route passed about four miles north of modern Big Piney, Wyoming, went up South Piney Creek through Snyder Basin and Star Valley, and into present-day Idaho, and then past Gray's Lake to Fort Hall. It became known as Lander Road in honor of Frederick W. Lander, an engineer with the U.S. Department of the Interior, who surveyed and constructed it in 1857. More than 1,000 emigrants used this cutoff in 1859.

Lassen Trail (1848). This route was blazed by Peter Lassen leading a small wagon train of emigrants. He followed the Applegate Trail to Goose Lake and turned south along the Pit River. Lassen wanted to blaze a trail to his ranch in the northern Sacramento Valley. Slowed by thick forest, Lassen's party ran out of provisions. Two groups of men from Oregon bound for the California goldfields found Lassen's party, gave them provisions, and helped them reach his ranch. Between then and the late 1850s, the trail was used by thousands of gold-seekers and emigrants. Wagons spent much time going over the rocky-bottomed Pit River.

Meek-Elliott-Macy Trail. See Free Emigrant Road.

Nobles Road (1852). This route in northern California was discovered by William Nobles in 1851 and first used in 1852 by emigrants wanting to avoid the hardships of the Lassen Trail. Nobles's route was an easy wagon road that ran off the Applegate-Lassen Trail from Boiling Spring at Black Rock to Shasta City through the Smoke Creek Desert and Lassen Peak. In 1856 a shortcut was blazed that went around Boiling Spring to Rabbithole Spring and then southwestward.

Salt Lake Cutoff (1848). This cutoff was blazed by Samuel Hensley, a trapper, whose packtrain was mired in mud following the Hastings Cutoff across the desert west of the Great Salt Lake. He returned to the Salt Lake valley and then headed north and west around the Great Salt Lake to reach the California Trail along the Humboldt River. There he met a party of Mormons, who had just opened the Carson Route, and told them about the cutoff. They used it to reach Salt Lake City with their wagons. This cutoff received much use during the California gold rush.

Seminoe Cutoff (1850). The alternate route left the main route just east of the Sixth Crossing of the Sweetwater River and remained south of that stream to avoid four more crossings and Rocky Ridge, a rough segment on the main route. The route probably was named for Basil LaJeunesse, who was known among the Shoshone Indians as Seminoe. Emigrant wagons first used this cutoff in about 1852. It rejoined the main Oregon Trail just west of the ninth and final crossing of the Sweetwater River, just east of South Pass.

Slate Creek Cutoff (1850). This cutoff was another variation of the Sublette Cutoff. Its route was south of the Sublette Cutoff, from the Big Sandy River to the Green River in Wyoming, avoiding the fifty miles of desert found on Sublette's route. *See also* Kinney Cutoff.

Sonora Road (1852). This road was blazed by the Clark Skidmore party of emigrants from Ohio and Indiana in 1852 over the Sierra Nevada via Walker River and Sonora Pass. They spent thirty-five days traveling sixty miles, filling ravines with rock and digging a trench to drain Fremont Lake in order to travel around a cliff. Although some emigrants deserted, those who remained reached the town of Columbia and were met by a cheering crowd and a brass band. The route runs from Leavitt Meadow, Fremont Lake, Emigrant Meadow Lake, Brown Bear Pass, down Summit Creek, Relief Valley, Whitsides Meadow, Burst Rock, Bell Meadow, MiWuk Ridge, N. Twain Harte, Phoenix Lake, Sonora, to Columbia.

Sublette's Cutoff (1826; 1844). This route probably was first blazed by William Sublette in 1826 as a shortcut between South Pass and the Bear River. It saved perhaps seventy miles of travel but included fifty miles of desert located between the Big Sandy River and the Green River. The terrain was difficult. The cutoff was first used by emigrants for wagons in 1844 on the recommendation of Caleb Greenwood, a former mountain man. Between 1844 and 1849, it was called the Greenwood Cutoff, but many emigrants avoided it. Travel over the cutoff increased after 1849 when California-bound gold-seekers traveling light found it saved them time.

Truckee Route (1844). This California route left the main Oregon Trail at the Raft River and went south to the Humboldt Sink, as had earlier emigrants, but in 1844 another party met a Paiute Indian chief at the Humboldt whom they named "Truckee." The Indian gave them directions on how to follow the Truckee River over what is known today as Stephens Pass in the Sierra Nevada. Although it was a difficult route, the emigrants got most of their wagons through, opening the first overland wagon route to California. The following year Caleb Greenwood found a better route through Dog Valley that avoided the Truckee River gorge. Later he found a route for westbound travelers that avoided rugged Bishop Canyon. The new route went to the source of the Humboldt River at Humboldt Wells near modern Wells, Nevada, and turned west. (*See* California Trail.)

Glossary

above my bend. Beyond my capacity

ague. Fever

airtights. Canned goods. The tin-plated can was introduced in America by Peter Durand in 1818, and the following year canned oysters, fruits, meats, and vegetables were introduced in New York. By the 1830s, cookies and matches were sold in tins.

alkali. A powdery, white mineral that salts the ground in western desert areas. A flat stretch of country ruined by alkali was called an alkali flat.

all-a-settin'. In good condition

appola. The stick on which a small piece of meat was roasted over an open fire

apoplexy. Stroke

Arbuckle. Coffee first produced in the late 1860s by the Arbuckle Brothers of Pittsburgh, Pennsylvania, who patented a method of sealing in the roasted flavor by coating the beans with a mixture of egg white and sugar and selling it in paper bags. Sometimes a generic term meaning coffee.

assay. To evaluate precious metals for their value

back home. Wherever they came from

backtrack. To go back over the trail you have been following

bacon. A term meaning "meat from a hog"; sides, hams, or shoulders were often salted and preserved by emigrants at butchering time before leaving on their journey.

ball. The object a flint or percussion muzzle-loading rifle or pistol shoots

Barlow knife. Usually a single-bladed pocketknife

batea. Rough wooded bowl used to wash gold

bear-claw necklace. An Indian neck decoration made of the claws of a grizzly bear

bear grass. A coarse plant found in the high country of Oregon that was not really grass

bear's ass. Common oath

bedding down. Meaning the emigrants' animals were resting for the night

bedrock. Solid rock that alluvial gold rests on

bend an elbow. To drink whiskey

Bible-beater. Usually a preacher or minister

bilious colic. Severe stomach pain

bit. Metal bar placed in a horse's mouth to which the reins are attached

black robe. A Catholic priest, especially a Jesuit

bloomers. Puffy half-length pants worn by some women on the trail beginning in 1852

bluff. Common name for the card game poker from the middle 1840s

bois d'arc. *See* Osage orange

bonnet. The covering on a wagon

boom. A rush of business activity

bread wallet. The human stomach

buck fever. A nervousness when taking aim at a deer or other wild animal

buckskin. Soft leather made from the hide of a buck, or male deer. The name was often used to describe any leather from a deer or elk.

buffalo chips. Buffalo manure, sometimes referred to as bois de vache, booshwa, or bushwah

buffalo gnat. The black fly. Its bite can cause painful swelling in humans.

buffalo grass. A coarse grass on which buffalo feed

buffalo robe. The hide of a buffalo with the hair left on

cabin fever. Human irritability, sometimes depression, when staying in a cabin during a long winter

calf fries. Deep-fried calf testicles, often called mountain oysters

cap-and-ball. A weapon fired by percussion cap

captain. Usually the elected leader of an emigrant company

cartwheel. Usually a silver dollar

chokecherry. A shrub found in the West that bears wild cherries

cinch. A girth for a saddle, made of leather, canvas, or braided horsehair

clap. Gonorrhea

colonel. Usually a title of courtesy and respect without military implications

company. The group of persons in which an emigrant traveled

Conestoga. A large covered wagon first made in Lancaster or Pittsburgh, Pennsylvania, used primarily to carry freight in the West. It was often called a prairie schooner. Because it was very large, heavy, and expensive, emigrants preferred to use smaller farm wagons.

consumption. Tuberculosis of the lungs

corn soup. Made from parched corn

cutoff. Shortcut

desiccated vegetables. Fresh vegetables cut into thin slices and pressed to remove all juice. The remaining solid cake is dried in an oven until it becomes hard. Pieces are cut from the block when needed and boiled in water. The vegetables then swell up and can be eaten.

dinner. Usually the noon meal

doubletree. The crosspiece of a wagon to which two singletrees are attached. One animal was hitched to each singletree.

draw. A gully or ravine; also a form of the card game poker

Dutch oven. A heavy cast-iron pot with a heavy tight lid in which food was cooked over a fire. Hot coals were often placed on the lid so that the food would brown all around.

emigrant. Any person who leaves their country to live elsewhere. The persons who went west over the Oregon Trail were called emigrants and not immigrants because they left settled areas of the nation to travel to areas not yet acquired by the United States.

engagé. A French-Canadian trapper hired for wages

ephedra. A western bush from which Brigham Young supposedly brewed a tea; sometimes called Brigham tea or Mormon tea

Ephraim. A mountain man's nickname for the grizzly bear

Ermatinger money. Currency issued in Oregon Territory in the 1840s and 1850s by the Hudson's Bay Company. Named for Frank Ermatinger, a company trader.

felly rim. A wagon-wheel rim inside the iron tire

fight the bit. To act impatient or unruly (used for a person)

flapjack. A small pancake often cooked in a frying pan

follow the tongue. To place the tongue of a company's lead wagon toward the North Star to enable the emigrants to travel in the right direction the next day

fork. A tributary of a river; also the front of a saddle tree below the horn

forty-niner. Anyone going to California in 1849

four-flusher. A trickster, someone you cannot trust

get aboard. Get on your horse or wagon

goddam. An Indian term for a white man's wagon

green sickness. A green tinge in skin; chlorosis

hard money. Coin and not paper

hardtack. A hard biscuit made from flour and water and baked for a long time in a slow oven. It would keep for a long time.

Hawken. A percussion rifle manufactured in St. Louis from 1822 to 1861

Henry. A repeating rifle manufactured from 1860 to 1866

hoe cake. Cornbread made of cornmeal, hot water, salt, and bacon grease. The term came from the South.

horse canoe. What Indians sometimes called horse-drawn wagons

hunker. To squat on one's heels or the hams of the legs

Idaho brainstorm. A dust devil or dust twister

India Rubber. First patented by Charles Goodyear in 1844, the vulcanized process was used to manufacture books, shoes, bags, blankets, and other products so they would not melt in the summer or get hard in the winter

iron skein. Wagon axle

jamboree. Used after the early 1870s to describe a celebration of dancing and drinking

jerk-line. A single line used to control a team of wagon mules or horses

jerky. Dried meat cut into strips

johnnycake. A baked flat corn cake. The term originated in New England.

jumping-off town. The Missouri River town or settlement from which the emigrants embarked on their journey

Lincoln shingles. A term used by soldiers to describe hardtack after Abraham Lincoln became president

loaf sugar. Small loaves of imported sugar, sometimes called cone sugar

love apple. A tomato

lung fever. Pneumonia

Mackinaw. A flat-bottomed boat

Mackinaw blanket. A warm blanket found in the West beginning in the 1830s. The term derived from the island of Mackinac, where Indians received their grants from the government. In their treaties the Indians asked to receive these blankets.

meat biscuit. Patented by Gail Borden, Jr., and sold in a tin canister or cask beginning in the early 1850s. One pound contained the nutriment of five pounds of fresh beef. One ounce would make a nutritious soup. The meat biscuit could be preserved indefinitely.

middlings. A cheap unrefined flour containing much of the gluten

milk leg. Phlebitis or inflammation in the leg, after giving birth

milk sickness. An illness that often resulted in death caused by drinking milk from cows that ate white snakeroot, a plant containing the toxin tremetol, which causes physical inertia. Some emigrants believed they could get the sickness from eating meat from cattle that grazed on the plant.

Mormon brake. A large log or whole tree dragged behind a wagon to break its speed going down a steep slope

mush. Porridge made from cornmeal. Mush with milk was sometimes a meal for emigrants.

nooning. Taking a midday rest

notions. Trading items related to sewing, including needles, thread, buttons, and ribbons

Osage orange. A bushy hedge tree used by some Indian tribes to make bows. Emigrants sometimes used the wood to make wagon hoops. Used by farmers as a hedge or windbreak.

oso berry. A white-flowering shrub found in Oregon and California bearing blue-black fruit. In Spanish *oso* means "bear."

pemmican. Powdered dry meat, sometimes mixed with berries or melted grease, eaten either raw or mixed with a little flour and boiled

placer. The mining of gold-bearing sand or gravel

physic. Medicine

piker. A nickname for a particular type of Missourian but later applied to anyone from Missouri. According to tradition, among the early emigrants going west were many from Pike County, Missouri, some with the words "From Pike Co., Mo" painted on their wagon covers. When others without such signs were asked where they came from, they promptly answered, "From Pike County, Missouri, by gosh, sir," often with an arrogance that implied they were thereby superior. Soon such a person was referred to as a "piker." In time, the word was also used to describe a person who does business in a small way.

pilgrim. Usually a newcomer to a region, someone inexperienced in western life. The term was also used to describe cows of eastern stock brought west.

pilot bread. Another name for hardtack

pomander. Fruit covered with cloves and other spices, used to scent clothes and bedding and believed to guard against infection

post. A word meaning a "military fort" or "trading post"

prairie buggy. The name soldiers gave to the Indian travois, two trailing poles serving as shafts that bore a platform or net to carry a lodge, camp equipment, or children, which was dragged behind a horse or dog

prairie schooner. A covered wagon with a wooden box or bed about four feet wide and ten to twelve feet long. It stood about ten feet tall with its cover or bonnet, had a wheelbase more than five feet wide, and weighed about 1,300 pounds empty.

prairie wolf. A coyote

ranch. A way station and trading post along the road, usually small, where provisions, including whiskey, were sold. The word comes from the Spanish *rancho*, a place where horses and cattle were raised. Along the Oregon Trail such an establishment was often called a road ranch.

running gear. The parts underneath a wagon

saleratus. Potassium or sodium bicarbonate used like baking soda in cooking

sea biscuit. Hardtack

see the elephant. Although this phrase was used in the 1830s and perhaps earlier, it became closely associated with the gold rush of 1849. When a man has seen enough of whatever he undertakes, when he gets sick and tired of any task, he has seen the elephant.

Shaker's pumpkin. Ground, dried pumpkin prepared by the United Society of Shakers in Massachusetts, used to make pumpkin pies

Sharps. A rifle manufactured by a company of the same name. Nearly forty different models were made between the 1840s and 1881.

shorts. A dense type of cooking flour, something of a cross between wheat bran and whole wheat flour that had to be sifted to remove impurities

skullvarnish. Whiskey to which molasses was added

span. A pair of two draft animals that worked together

spirits. Usually whiskey

spring wagon. A light wagon with a shallow wagon bed. The front wheels are smaller than those at the rear, and each wheel has its own individual steel spring to improve the ride on rough trails.

squaw. An Indian woman who is married or living with a man

States cattle. Cattle brought west from the United States; also called pilgrims

store cheese. Cheddar-style cheese

superfine. Flour ground between two stones with the bran sifted out, similar to today's white flour

sutler. The person responsible for operating the government store at military posts such as Fort Kearny and Fort Laramie

tallow. Animal fat that has been purified by melting

to fork. To mount a horse

to skin. To drive mules

train. What emigrants called their company's line of wagons crossing the plains, prairie, or mountains

wagon bed. The body of a wagon, often called the wagon box

water brash. Similar to heartburn; belching of a thin, watery fluid

wind colic. Distressing pain in the bowels

yellow leg. Nickname for U.S. cavalrymen, who wore yellow stripes down the seams of their pants

yoke. The large wooden bar or frame attached to the necks of oxen working together to pull a wagon. When emigrants said their wagon was pulled by two yoke they meant four oxen; three yoke meant six oxen.

Notes

1. The best source for the history of the Chinook Indians is Robert H. Ruby and John A. Brown's *The Chinook Indians: Traders of the Lower Columbia River* (Norman: University of Oklahoma Press, 1976). Other important tribes in what is now Oregon were the Tillamook, Yamel, Molala, Clackamas, and Multnomah in the northwest; the Santiam and Coos in the southwest; the Cayuse, Northern Paiute, Umatilla, Nez Percé, and Bannock in the dry lands east of the Cascade Range and in the Blue and Wallowa mountains; and the Klamath and Modoc in the south-central region.

2. Instead of writing a journal of his travels, Marco Polo's manuscript contains his observations and detailed descriptions of the people he met, their cultures, and the geography. He describes cities, languages, races, governments, trading practices, the products manufactured, plants, minerals, terrain, and animals, including crocodiles, which had never been seen by Europeans. Before his death in 1324, he was never hailed as an adventurer or explorer. The phrase "It's a Marco Polo" came to denote an exaggerated tale. Late in his life friends feared for his reputation and urged him to recant his stories, but Polo supposedly replied, "I have not written down the half of those things which I saw." It was not until the nineteenth century that what he saw and where he went were corroborated in detail, establishing his credibility. Sources consulted include Manuel Komroff, ed., *The Travels of Marco Polo, the Venetian.* (New York: Boni & Liveright, 1926). The work is revised from Marsden's translation of Marco Polo's manuscript. See also Henry H. Hart, *Venetian Adventurer: Being An Account of the Life and Times and of the Book of Messer Marco Polo* (Stanford: Stanford University Press, 1924). The work includes a facsimile of Marco Polo's will. A more recent work is Frances Wood's *Did Marco Polo Go to China?* (New York: View/HarperCollins, 1996). Wood, head of the British Library's Chinese department, seeks to make a case that Marco Polo did not go beyond Per-

sia and fabricated his story with the help of Arabs and Persians who had visited China.

3. It was not until the mid-1800s that a continental passage was found far to the north, through the ice-filled waters around the northernmost islands of North America, above the Arctic Circle. But it was so treacherous and difficult that it was not until 1903–6 that the route was successfully navigated, by Norwegian explorer Roald Amundsen.

4. George R. Stewart, *Names on the Land: A Historical Account of Place-Naming in the United States* (New York: Random House, 1945), pp. 27–28.

5. Frederic W. Howay, ed., *Voyages of the Columbia to the Northwest Coast, 1787–1790 & 1790–1793* (Portland: Oregon Historical Society Press, 1990), p. 394. This work was originally published in 1941 as vol. 79 of the Massachusetts Historical Society Collections in Boston.

6. Robert Stuart, *The Discovery of The Oregon Trail* (New York and London: Charles Scribner's Sons, 1935), pp. 15–16.

7. Howay, ed., *Voyages of the Columbia*, pp. 398–9.

8. Ibid., pp. 436–38, contains the remnant of the official log of the *Columbia* with an account of her entrance into the Columbia River in May 1792. Biographical material on Robert Gray may be found on pages xiii–xv. This work was first published by the Massachusetts Historical Society in 1941. Biographical material on Robert Gray is also contained in John Scofield's *Hail Columbia, Robert Gray, John Kendrick, and the Pacific Fur Trade* (Portland: Oregon Historical Society Press, 1993), pp. 51–53, 105.

9. Don Alonso Decalves [pseud.], *New Travels to the Westward; or, Unknown Parts of America, Being a Tour of Almost Fourteen Months....* (Boston: Printed and sold by John W. Folsom, 1788), pp. 1–43.

10. Ora Brooks Peaker, *A History of the United States Indian Factory System, 1795–1822* (Denver: Sage Books, 1954), pp. 1–9.

11. James P. Ronda, *Astoria and Empire* (Lincoln: University of Nebraska Press, 1990), p. 44. See also Washington Irving, *Astoria, or Anecdotes of an Enterprise Beyond the Rocky Mountains* (Norman: University of Oklahoma Press, 1964). Irving's work was first published in 1836. This 1964 reprint edited by Edgeley W. Todd demolished charges that Irving's work contained much fiction. Todd's notes leave no question that Astor asked Irving to write the work and that the author was then given full access to records kept by Astor and his associates. For a modern biography of John Jacob Astor, see Axel Madsen, *John Jacob Astor: America's First Multimillionaire* (New York: John Wiley & Sons, 2001).

CHAPTER TWO: ASTORIA

1. Washington Irving, *Astoria, or Anecdotes of an Enterprise Beyond the Rocky Mountains* (Norman: University of Oklahoma Press, 1964), p. 32. Edited by Edgeley W. Todd, this annotated edition of Irving's nineteenth-century work is the best. Todd leaves no doubt that Irving's work is sound, accurate history based upon published and

unpublished accounts by participants, as well as surviving business records of John Jacob Astor's enterprise and other primary sources. The work was first published in Philadelphia in two volumes in 1836. A more recent work on the subject is James P. Ronda's *Astoria and Empire* (Lincoln: University of Nebraska Press, 1990). Ronda relies heavily on Irving's account but places the events within the context of the history of the American West.

2. Ibid., pp. 39–42.
3. Ibid., p. 125.
4. Ibid., p. 136.
5. William Brandon, "Wilson Price Hunt," in *The Mountain Men and the Fur Trade of the Far West*, vol. 6 (Glendale, Calif.: Arthur H. Clark Co., 1968), pp. 182–83. See also *The Overland Diary of Wilson Price Hunt* (Ashland, Oreg.: Oregon Book Society, 1973). This work's seventy-one pages contain Hunt's day-by-day diary of his journey.
6. Brandon, "Wilson Price Hunt," in *The Mountain Men and the Fur Trade of the Far West*, vol. 6, p. 193.
7. Ibid., pp. 194–96.
8. Irving, *Astoria*, p. 40.
9. Ibid., p. 76.
10. Ibid., pp. 107–16.
11. Ibid., pp. 452–57. See also Ronda, *Astoria & Empire*, pp. 277–301.

CHAPTER THREE: DISCOVERING THE OREGON TRAIL

1. Aside from the journals of Lewis and Clark, Robert Stuart's journal is one of the more important documents concerning early exploration in the United States. Stuart titled it "Journal of a Voyage Cross the Continent of North America from Astoria, the Pacific Fur Company's Principal Establishment on the Columbia to the City of New York." He not only details the route he followed and its landmarks, but information on the Indians, wildlife, and even the western and eastern limits of the buffalo (bison). After returning east, and at some point before 1821, Stuart prepared "Travelling Memoranda," perhaps at the request of John Jacob Astor. It was essentially a copy of his journal. A large portion of the "Travelling Memoranda" was poorly translated into French and published in 1821 in Paris. Later the "Travelling Memoranda" was given to Washington Irving either by Stuart or, more likely, by Astor. Much of it was incorporated in Irving's classic book, *Astoria, or Anecdotes of an Enterprise Beyond the Rocky Mountains*, first published in 1836. After Irving's death the copy of "Travelling Memoranda" supposedly was found in a cupboard at his home near New York City. It remained the property of Irving's relatives until the early twentieth century. As for the journal, it remained with Stuart until his death, after which it was owned by his descendents. Today, the original "Travelling Memoranda" and the "Journal" are in the Collection of William R. Coe at Yale University. The first English edition with extensive notes, a lengthy foreword, and editing by Philip Ashton Rollins was published in 1935 by Charles Scribner's Sons, New York, under the title *The Discovery of the Oregon Trail*. A later

publication was titled *On the Oregon Trail: Robert Stuart's Journey of Discovery,* edited by Kenneth A. Spaulding and published by the University Press of Oklahoma in 1953.

2. Rollins, ed., *The Discovery of the Oregon Trail,* pp. 75–76.

3. Ibid., pp. 77–78.

4. Ibid., pp. 108–10.

5. Ibid., pp. 114, 127–28.

6. Ibid., pp. 130–32.

7. Ibid., pp. 134–37.

8. Ibid., pp. 151–53.

9. Ibid., pp. 155–57.

10. Ibid., pp. 158–59.

11. Ibid., pp. 164–65.

12. Ibid., pp. 192–93.

13. Ibid., p. 207.

14. Ibid., pp. 236–37.

CHAPTER FOUR: JOHN McLOUGHLIN AND THE MISSIONARIES

1. Frederick Merk, *The Oregon Question: Essays in Anglo-American Diplomacy and Politics* (Cambridge: Harvard University Press, 1967), p. 26.

2. Alberta Brooks Fogdall, *Royal Family of the Columbia: Dr. John McLoughlin and His Family* (Portland: Binford & Mort, 1982), pp. 59–95. This is a fine scholarly biography of McLoughlin, relying on earlier authoritative sources.

3. For more details on Dr. John Floyd, see Charles H. Ambler's *The Oregon Country, 1810–1830* (Cedar Rapids, Iowa: Torch Press, 1943). For a biography of Hall Jackson Kelley, see Fred W. Powell's *Hall Jackson Kelley, Prophet of Oregon* (Portland, Ore.: Ivy Press, 1917).

4. Washington Irving, *The Adventures of Captain Bonneville U.S.A. in the Rocky Mountains and the Far West* (Norman: University of Oklahoma Press, 1961), pp. 13–16, 48–50. See also Hiram Martin Chittenden, *The American Fur Trade of the Far West* (Stanford, Calif.: Academic Reprints, 1954), 1:396–433.

5. *The Christian Advocate and Journal* (New York), March 1, 1833. Bernard De Voto, in his classic *Across the Wide Missouri* (Boston: Houghton Mifflin Co., 1947), suggests that someone invented the oration, perhaps an editor with the Methodist publication (pp. 6–10).

6. William R. Sampson, "Nathaniel Jarvis Wyeth," in *The Mountain Men and the Fur Trade of the Far West* (Glendale, Calif.: Arthur H. Clark Co., 1968), 5:381–401.

7. John K. Townsend, *Narrative of a Journey Across the Rocky Mountains, to the Columbia River...* (Philadelphia: Henry Perkins, 1839), p. 25.

8. Daniel Lee and Joseph H. Frost, *Ten Years in Oregon* (New York: Published by the authors, 1844), pp. 114–16. Daniel Lee traveled overland, while Frost went to Oregon by ship.

9. Rev. Samuel Parker, *Journal of an Exploring Tour Beyond the Rocky Mountains, Under*

the Direction of the A.B.C.F.M. *Performed in the Years 1835, '36, and '37.* (Ithaca, N.Y.: Published by the author, 1838), pp. 159–60.

10. Mrs. Narcissa Prentiss Whitman, "Letter Written on the Platte River, South Side, Six Days Above the Fort Laramie Fork, Near the Foot of the Rocky Mountains, June 27, 1836." Typed copy in author's library. Original with National Park Service.

11. Eva Emery Dye, *McLoughlin and Old Oregon* (Chicago: A. S. McClure Co., 1900), p. 25.

12. Fogdall, *Royal Family of the Columbia,* p. 74.

13. LeRoy R. Hafen, "Robert Newell," in *The Mountain Men and the Fur Trade of the Far West* (Glendale, Calif.: Arthur H. Clark Co., 1971), 8:272–73. Hafen quotes a statement given by Newell in 1846 when he was Speaker of the House of Representatives in Oregon.

CHAPTER FIVE: THE AMERICAN OCCUPATION OF OREGON

1. Harvey L. Carter, "Ewing Young," in *The Mountain Men and the Fur Trade of the Far West* (Glendale, Calif.: Arthur H. Clark Co., 1965), 2:379–401.

2. Philip Leget Edwards, *The Diary of Philip Leget Edwards: The Great Cattle Drive from California to Oregon in 1837* (Fairfield, Wash.: Ye Galleon Press, 1989), pp. 35–36. Edwards's diary was first printed in 1860 by a California magazine. The diary abruptly ends with the September 18 entry, about a month before the cattle drive reached the Willamette Valley.

3. Ibid., pp. 50–51.

4. Thomas J. Farnham's book, *Travels in the Great Western Prairies, the Anahuac and Rocky Mountains, and in the Oregon Territory,* was first published in Poughkeepsie, N.Y., in 1841. It was reprinted in three separate editions in 1843, again in 1846, and several times since. For a biography of Farnham, see Dan L. Thrapp, *Encyclopedia of Frontier Biography* (Glendale, Calif.: Arthur H. Clark Co., 1988), 1:484.

5. Joseph Williams, "A Tour to the Oregon Territory," typescript copy in the files of the Ripley County (Indiana) Historical Society, Versailles, Indiana, p. 5. Williams died on January 9, 1859, at the age of eighty-one and is buried in Ripley County. See also Louise Barry, *The Beginning of the West* (Topeka: Kansas State Historical Society, 1972), pp. 428–30.

6. *The Fallbrook* (California) *Enterprise,* January 12, 1917. The obituary of Martha Williams Reed, who died at age eighty-seven on January 7, 1917, includes her recollections, dictated to a reporter for the newspaper in September 1913.

7. Williams, "A Tour to the Oregon Territory," p. 6.

8. *Fallbrook* (California) *Enterprise,* January 12, 1917.

9. Ibid.

10. Williams, "A Tour to the Oregon Territory," p. 15.

11. Ibid., p. 18.

12. Ibid., p. 28.

13. Dr. Elijah White, *Ten Years in Oregon: Travels and Adventures of Dr. Elijah White and Lady* (Ithaca, N.Y.: Privately printed, 1848), pp. 138–65.

14. A microfilm copy of Dr. White's 1842 census, in his own handwriting, may be found at the Oregon Historical Society in Portland.

15. Samuel June Barrows, "The Mule and His Driver," in *Exploring the Northern Plains, 1804–1876* (Caldwell, Idaho: Caxton Printers, 1955), p. 331.

16. Peter H. Burnett, *Recollections and Opinions* (n.p., 1880). These recollections were reprinted in Burnett's *An Old California Pioneer* (Oakland: Biobooks, 1946), pp. 59–85.

17. John Charles Frémont, *The Exploring Expedition to the Rocky Mountains* . . . (Buffalo: Geo. H. Derby & Co., 1850), pp. 6–7. This is a later printing of Frémont's 1842 journal that includes reports of his later expeditions.

18. Ibid., p. 54. About a mile to the northeast of Fort Laramie was a lesser-known trading post called Fort Platte, or sometimes Richard's Fort. It consisted of twelve buildings, including a blacksmith shop, surrounded by a large adobe wall. Lancaster P. Lupton started to build the post in 1839 for the fur trade but never finished it. Lupton sold it to Sybille, Adams & Company, who in turn sold it to Bernard Pratte and John Cabanne in 1843. Pratte and Cabanne operated it until about 1845, providing emigrants with a place to rest and blacksmithing service, although they never carried much in the way of groceries or other supplies. Their principal trade was in whiskey, which sold for $4 a pint.

19. Ibid., p. 55.

20. Ibid., p. 75.

21. Ibid., p. 65.

CHAPTER SIX: THE EMIGRANTS OF 1843

1. Harvey L. Carter, "John Gantt," in *The Mountain Men and the Fur Trade of the Far West* (Glendale, Calif.: Arthur H. Clark Co., 1968), 5:101–15. Carter points out that Gantt was born on the eastern shore of Maryland and that his father, Edward S. Gantt, served five terms as chaplain of the United States Senate. In 1808, the family moved to Louisville, Kentucky, where in 1817 John Gantt was appointed a second lieutenant in the U.S. Army. He served in the West and was promoted to captain in 1823. Gantt took part in an army expedition up the Missouri River to the Yellowstone River before being found guilty by court-martial of falsifying pay accounts and kicked out of the army.

2. Edward Henry Lenox, *Overland to Oregon* (Fairfield, Wash.: Ye Galleon Press, 1993), p. 39. This is a reprint of the 1904 first edition published in Portland, Oregon, titled *Overland to Oregon in the Tracks of Lewis and Clarke*. The reprint edition has a new introduction by Glen Adams.

3. Matthew C. Field, *Prairie and Mountain Sketches* (Norman: University of Oklahoma Press, 1957), p. 26. Field's diary and letters were edited by Kate L. Gregg and John F. McDermont.

4. Lenox, *Overland to Oregon*, p. 36.

5. Ibid., p. 44.

6. Jesse Applegate, *A Day with the Cow Column* (Fairfield, Wash.: Ye Galleon Press, 1990), pp. 26–27. Applegate's narrative first appeared in *Transactions of the Oregon Pioneer Association* (Portland: Oregon Pioneer Association, 1876).

7. Ibid., 27–43.

8. Nancy M. (Hembree) Bogart, "Reminiscences of a Journey Across the Plains in 1843 with Dr. Marcus Whitman's Caravan." Original nine-page manuscript in the Bancroft Library, University of California, Berkeley.

9. Sarah Damron Adair, "Recollections," in *Transactions of the Oregon Pioneer Association* (Portland: Oregon Pioneer Association, 1900), pp. 65–82.

10. John A. Stoughton, "Recollections," *Washington Historical Quarterly* 15 (1924): 208–10.

11. Lenox, *Overland to Oregon*, pp. 48–51.

12. Much of Hiram Scott's life and death are clouded in mystery. The closest thing to a biography is Merrill J. Mattes's "Hiram Scott," in *The Mountain Men and the Fur Trade of the Far West*, 1:355–66.

13. John D. Unruh, Jr., *The Plains Across* (Urbana: University of Illinois Press, 1979), p. 251.

14. Jesse A. Applegate, "Recollections of My Boyhood," in *Westward Journeys* (Chicago: R. R. Donnelley & Sons Co., 1989), pp. 34–37.

15. John C. Frémont, *Oregon and California: The Exploring Expedition to the Rocky Mountains, Oregon, and California* (Buffalo: Geo. H. Derby & Co., 1850), p. 173.

16. Ibid., 174–75.

17. Applegate, "Recollections of My Boyhood," pp. 46–49.

18. Ibid., pp. 55–56.

19. Ardis M. Walker, "Joseph R. Walker," in *The Mountain Men and the Fur Trade of the Far West*, 5:373–74. See also *California History Quarterly* 22 for a brief biography of Reading. Much detail on the California-bound travelers may be found in "Journal of John Boardman," *Utah Historical Quarterly* 2 (1929): 99–121.

20. John Burch McClane, "Recollections," thirteen-page manuscript in the Bancroft Library, University of California, Berkeley.

CHAPTER SEVEN: SELF-RULE AND MORE EMIGRANTS

1. F. T. Young, "Ewing Young and His Estate," in *Oregon Historical Society Quarterly*, 21 (September 1920): 197–215. In 1854, fourteen years after Ewing Young died, a young man named Joaquin Young arrived in Oregon from Taos, New Mexico. He carried papers showing that he was the son of Ewing Young and Maria Josepha Tafoya. The Territory of Oregon awarded Joaquin Young $4,994.64 to settle the estate.

2. Hubert Howe Bancroft, *The History of Oregon* (San Francisco: History Co., 1886), 1: 448–49.

3. Thomas A. Rumer, *The Wagon Trains of '44: A Comparative View of the Individual Caravans in the Emigration of 1844 to Oregon* (Spokane, Wash.: Arthur H. Clark Co., 1990), p. 158. The full recollections of B. F. Nichols may be found in "Across the Plains in 1844," published in the *Laidlaw Chronicle*, Crook County, Oregon, November 16, 1906.

4. Catherine Sager Pringle, *Across the Plains in 1844* (Fairfield, Wash.: Ye Galleon Press, 1993), pp. 5–8. Her recollections were first published in *Whitman College Quarterly* (1897): 30–31.

5. John Minto, "Reminiscences," *Oregon Historical Quarterly* 2 (1901): 119–67. See also Taylor Quintard, *In Search of the Racial Frontier: African Americans in the American West, 1828–1990* (New York: W. W. Norton, 1998). Bush's friend Michael T. Simmons, a legislator, attempted to change the antiblack laws in 1854 to help Bush get title to his land, but failed. Bush was finally granted official title to his property by a special waiver from the U.S. Congress in 1855. Later, one of Bush's sons, William Owen Bush, became a member of the first state legislature in Washington State. He introduced the bill to the legislature that created what is now known as Washington State University, founded in 1890.

6. Charles L. Camp, "James Clyman," in *The Mountain Men and the Fur Trade of the Far West* (Glendale, Calif.: Arthur H. Clark Co., 1965), 1:248. See also Aubrey L. Haines, *Historic Sites Along the Oregon Trail* (Gerald, Mo.: Patrice Press, 1981), p. 230.

7. Doyce B. Nunis, Jr., "Andrew Whitley Sublette," in *The Mountain Men and the Fur Trade of the Far West*, 8:360. See also Edward Evans Parrish's journal "Crossing the Plains in 1844," in *Transactions of the Oregon Pioneer Association* (1888): 82–122.

8. Thomas A. Rumer, ed., *The Emigrating Company: The 1844 Oregon Trail Journal of Jacob Hammer* (Spokane, Wash.: Arthur H. Clark Co., 1990), pp. 76–77.

9. Ibid., p. 77.

10. Ibid., pp. 86–88.

11. Ibid., p. 117.

12. Ibid., pp. 120–21.

13. Ibid., p. 122.

14. Ibid., p. 125.

15. Merrill J. Mattes, *Platte River Road Narratives: A Descriptive Bibliography of Travel over the Great Central Overland Route to Oregon, California, Utah, Colorado, Montana, and Other Western States and Territories, 1812–1866* (Urbana and Chicago: University of Illinois Press, 1988), pp. 60–61.

CHAPTER EIGHT: FIFTY-FOUR FORTY OR FIGHT

1. President Martin Van Buren was the likely candidate of the Democratic Party in 1844, but he detested the annexation of Texas and was not popular in the South and West. When Van Buren failed to be nominated on the seventh ballot at the Democratic National Convention, Polk, a likely vice presidential candidate, was nominated on the ninth ballot, becoming the first so-called dark horse candidate to win an American presidential nomination. In the election Polk's bold talk of expansion enabled him to win all western states except Tennessee and Ohio. He won, however, because a third candidate, James G. Birney of the antislavery Liberty Party, captured enough votes in New York to give Polk, and not his other opponent, Henry Clay, the state. Polk captured 170 electoral votes compared to Clay's 105. See Charles G. Sellers, Jr., *James K. Polk, Jacksonian, 1795–1843* (Princeton: Princeton University Press, 1957); and Bill Severn, *Frontier President: The Life of James K. Polk* (New York: Ives Washburn, 1965).

2. *St. Joseph Gazette,* June 6, 1845, as cited by Louise Barry, *The Beginning of the West* (Topeka: Kansas State Historical Society, 1972), p. 539.

3. Fred Lockley, *Captain Sol. Thetherow, Wagon Train Master* (Portland, Ore.: Privately printed by the author, n.d.), p. 27.

4. Barry, *The Beginning of the West*, pp. 539–41.

5. Ibid., p. 543.

6. Ibid., pp. 543–44.

7. Joel Palmer, *Journal of Travels over the Rocky Mountains, to the Mouth of the Columbia River*... (Cincinnati: J. A. & U. P. James, 1850), pp. 15–16.

8. Ibid., pp. 17–18.

9. Ibid., p. 18.

10. Ibid., pp. 18–19.

11. Ibid., pp. 19–20.

12. Ibid., pp. 20–21.

13. Ibid., p. 20.

14. Ibid., p. 21.

15. Ibid., p. 23.

16. Ibid., pp. 25–26.

17. Ibid., p. 33.

18. Ibid., pp. 141–43.

19. Diary of James Field's overland journey, 1845. Original copy held by the Oregon Historical Society, Portland. Typed copy consulted, p. 51.

20. Sarah Fisher Hamilton and Nellie E. Latourette, eds., "Correspondence of Rev. Ezra Fisher, Pioneer Missionary of the American Baptist Church Home Mission Society," *Oregon Historical Quarterly* 16 (1915): 379–412.

21. Palmer, *Journal of Travels over the Rocky Mountains*, pp. 62–63.

22. Harvey E. Tobie, "Stephen Hall Meek," in *The Mountain Men and the Fur Trade of the Far West* (Glendale, Calif.: The Arthur H. Clark Co., 1965), 2:225–40.

23. Palmer, *Journal of Travels over the Rocky Mountains*, p. 84.

24. *Missouri Republican*, June 14 and July 3, 1845.

25. Matthew Field, *Prairie and Mountain Sketches* (Norman: University of Oklahoma Press, 1955), p. 150.

26. Eugene E. Campbell, "Miles Morris Goodyear," in *The Mountain Men and the Fur Trade of the Far West*, 2:179–88.

CHAPTER NINE: THE YEAR OF DECISION

1. *Oregon Spectator*, February 18, 1847. The Oregon Lyceum, an association of settlers, was founded in Oregon City in 1844 for the purpose of establishing a newspaper for the growing community. Shares were sold to finance and purchase a Hoe printing press, several fonts of type, a supply of paper, ink, and other printing supplies, which were shipped to Oregon City. On February 5, 1846, the *Oregon Spectator* appeared. It was the first in Oregon Country. Col. William G. T'Vault, who came overland in 1845, was the first editor. Two months later he was succeeded as editor by Henry A. G. Lee. John Fleming was the printer of the newspaper, and when Lee retired in 1846, Fleming served as editor for two months until George L. Currey took the position in October 1846. Eighteen months later Currey resigned to start

the *Oregon City Free Press.* Currey purchased secondhand type from some Catholic missionaries, but the type lacked lower case *w*'s. Currey made his own *w*'s by whittling them out of hard wood. He constructed his press out of wood and scrap iron. The *Free Press* operated for less than eight months.

2. Louise Barry, *The Beginning of the West* (Topeka: Kansas State Historical Society, 1972), p. 572.

3. Ibid., p. 576. See also John D. Unruh, Jr., *The Plains Across* (Urbana: University of Illinois Press, 1979), p. 119.

4. Louis Barry, *The Beginning of the West,* pp. 588–89. See also *Autobiography of John Brown* (Salt Lake City: Privately printed, 1941), pp. 66–87.

5. Dale Morgan, ed., *Overland in 1846: Diaries and Letters of the California-Oregon Trail* (Lincoln: University of Nebraska Press, 1993), 1:150–58. This two-volume work was first published in 1963.

6. Edwin Bryant, *What I Saw in California* (New York: D. Appleton & Co., 1848), p. 15. Bryant's work is one of the most detailed and reliable books on overland travel. It was very popular and went through numerous reprintings, especially after the discovery of gold in California.

7. Ibid., pp. 87–89.

8. Ibid., pp. 90–91.

9. Francis Parkman, *The Journals of Francis Parkman* (New York and London: Harper & Brothers, 1947), 2:447, 625.

10. Ibid., p. 440.

11. Edwin Bryant, *What I Saw in California,* p. 144.

12. Ibid., pp. 173–74.

13. Ibid., p. 248.

14. Virginia Reed Murphy, *Across the Plains in the Donner Party* (Fairfield, Wash.: Ye Galleon Press, 1998), pp. 24–25.

15. Ibid., pp. 36–37.

16. Dale Morgan, ed., *Overland in 1946,* 1:361–63.

17. Henry R. Wagner and Charles Camp, *The Plains and the Rockies: A Critical Bibliography of Exploration, Adventure, and Travel in the American West* (San Francisco: John Howell, 1982), 4th edition, revised, enlarged, and edited by Robert H. Becker, pp. 258–59.

18. Bernard De Voto, *The Year of Decision, 1846* (Boston: Little, Brown & Co., 1943), p. 4.

CHAPTER TEN:
NEW ZION, MORE EMIGRANTS, AND A MASSACRE

1. Louise Barry, *The Beginning of the West* (Topeka: Kansas State Historical Society, 1972), pp. 676–77.

2. *William Clayton's Journal* (Salt Lake City: Privately printed, 1921), pp. 71–90.

3. Will Bagley, ed., *The Pioneer Camp of the Saints: The 1846 and 1847 Mormon Trail Journals of Thomas Bullock* (Spokane: Arthur H. Clark Co., 1997), pp. 124–25.

4. Ibid., pp. 22–23.

5. Ibid., pp. 177–78.

6. Ibid., p. 263.

7. Ibid., pp. 21, 140.

8. Barry, *The Beginning of the West*, pp. 677, 681.

9. Thomas C. McClintock, "Henderson Luelling, Seth Lewelling, and the Birth of the Pacific Coast Fruit Industry," *Oregon Historical Quarterly* 60, no. 2 (June 1967): 153–74.

10. Albert Briggs, recollections, manuscript, pp. 1–8, in the Bancroft Library, University of California, Berkeley.

11. Hugh Cosgrove, "Reminiscences of Hugh Cosgrove," *Oregon Historical Quarterly* 1 (1900): 353–69.

12. Dr. Benjamin Cory, journal, manuscript, pp. 4–75, Society of California Pioneers, San Francisco.

13. Elizabeth Dixon Smith Geer, "Diary of Elizabeth Dixon Smith Geer," ed. George H. Himes, *Transactions of the Oregon Pioneer Association* (1907): 153–79.

14. Barry, *The Beginning of the West*, pp. 680–81.

15. James Jory, "Reminiscences of James Jory," ed. H. S. Lyman, *Oregon Historical Quarterly* 3 (1902): 271–86.

16. Erwin N. Thompson, *Shallow Grave at Waiilatpu: The Sagers' West* (Portland: Oregon Historical Society, 1973), p. 85.

17. Undated letter written by Mary Mash Carson, in the files of the National Park Service, Washington, D.C.

18. Harvey E. Tobie, "Joseph L. Meek," in *The Mountain Men and the Fur Trade of the Far West* (Glendale, Calif.: Arthur H. Clark Co., 1965), 1:313–35. See also Stanley Vestal, *Joe Meek, the Merry Mountain Man: A Biography* (Caldwell, Idaho: Caxton Printers, 1952), pp. 282–309.

CHAPTER ELEVEN: A LULL BEFORE THE RUSH

1. John A. Sutter, "The Discovery of Gold in California," in *Hutchings' California Magazine*, November 1857. While John Marshall's 1848 discovery of gold received widespread publicity, resulting in the California gold rush, gold had been found by José Francisco de García López, a cattle rancher in Live Oak Canyon in Santa Clarita Valley, six years earlier. The gold was taken to Los Angeles and word of the discovery sent to Mexico City. An assay showed the gold to be .926 fine. Prospectors from Los Angeles and Sonora flocked to Live Oak Canyon, which was renamed Placerita Canyon. Between 1842 and 1847, about 1,300 pounds of gold were found, but when California became part of the United States in 1850, the miners, including those from Sonora, went home.

2. Louise Barry, *The Beginning of the* West (Topeka: Kansas State Historical Society, 1972), pp. 779–80, 787–88.

3. Ibid., pp. 744–46.

4. Kenneth L. Holmes, ed., *Covered Wagon Women: Diaries and Letters from the Western Trails, 1840–1890* (Glendale, Calif.: Arthur H. Clark Co., 1983), 1:216–18.

5. Ibid., pp. 222–23.

6. Ibid., pp. 225–27.

7. Merrill J. Mattes, *Platte River Road Narratives* (Urbana and Chicago: University of Illinois Press, 1988), p. 112.

8. James D. Miller, "Early Oregon Scenes: A Pioneer Narrative," *Oregon Historical Quarterly* 31 (1930): 55–68. See also Honoré-Timothée Lempfrit, *His Oregon Trail Journal and Letters from the Pacific Northwest, 1848–1853* (Fairfield, Wash.: Ye Galleon Press, 1985), pp. 41–193.

9. Thomas Stock Bayley recollections, "First Overland Mail Bag to California," eight-page manuscript, California State Library, Sacramento.

10. Bruce Cornwall, *Life Sketch of Pierre Barlow Cornwall* (San Francisco: A. M. Robertson, 1906), pp. 14–28. See also Nicholas P. Hardeman, "Charles A. Warfield," in *The Mountain Men and the Fur Trade of the Far West* (Glendale, Calif.: Arthur H. Clark Co., 1969), 7:358.

11. Mattes, *Platte River Road Narratives,* pp. 114, 116.

12. Ibid., p. 114.

13. Ibid.

14. Charles Emerson Griffin recollections, nine-page manuscript, Utah Historical Society.

15. Mattes, *Platte River Road Narratives,* p. 120.

16. Barry, *The Beginning of the West,* pp. 772–73. See also Will Bagley, ed., *Scoundrel's Tale: The Samuel Brannan Papers* (Spokane: Arthur H. Clark Co., 1999).

17. 30th Cong., 2nd sess., H. Ex. Doc. No. 1 (Serial 537).

CHAPTER TWELVE: THE GOLD RUSH OF 1849

1. Rudolph Friedrich Kurz, *Journal of Rudolph Friedrich Kurz: An Account of His Experiences Among Fur Traders and American Indians on the Mississippi and the Upper Missouri Rivers During the Years 1846 to 1852.* Bulletin, Smithsonian Institution, Bureau of American Ethnology, no. 115 (Washington, D.C.: U.S. Government Printing Office, 1937), p. 46.

2. W. J. Ghent, *The Road to Oregon: A Chronicle of the Great Emigrant Trail* (London and New York: Longmans, Green & Co., 1929), pp. vii–viii.

3. *St. Louis Republican,* April 7–May 2, 1849.

4. Louise Barry, *The Beginning of the West* (Topeka: Kansas State Historical Society, 1972), p. 849.

5. Albert Watkins, ed., *Publications of the Nebraska State Historical Society* (Lincoln: Nebraska State Historical Society, 1922), 20:190.

6. Barry, *The Beginning of the West,* pp. 807–8.

7. Louise Barry, "Charles Robinson—Yankee '49er: His Journey to California," *Kansas Historical Quarterly* 34 (1968): 179–88.

8. *St. Louis Republican,* August 5, 1849.

9. Barry, *The Beginning of the West,* pp. 848, 870–71. See also Merrill J. Mattes, *Platte River Road Narratives* (Urbana and Chicago: University of Illinois Press, 1988), p. 2.

10. William J. Watson, *Journal of an Overland Journey to Oregon Made in the Year 1849* (Fairfield, Wash.: Ye Galleon Press, 1895), pp. 3–48.

11. Virginia Watson Applegate recollections, eighteen-page manuscript, Oregon Historical Society, Portland.

12. John McWilliams, *Recollections of John McWilliams: His Youth Experiences in California and the Civil War* (Princeton, N.J.: Privately printed, 1919), pp. 46–69.

13. Mattes, *Platte River Road Narratives,* p. 126.

14. John D. Unruh, Jr., *The Plains Across* (Urbana: University of Illinois Press, 1979), p. 170.

15. Watkins, *Publications of the Nebraska State Historical Society,* 20:193–206.

16. Mattes, *Platte River Road Narratives,* p. 136.

17. J. Goldsborough Bruff, *Gold Rush: The Journals, Drawings, and Other Papers of J. Goldsborough Bruff* (New York: Columbia University Press, 1944), 1:1–353.

18. Henry Austin diary, in the Bancroft Library, University of California, Berkeley.

19. *Columbus* (Ohio) *Dispatch,* April 2–August 26, 1949. The newspaper published excerpts from Dr. Charles E. Boyle's diary during this five-month period.

20. Mattes, *Platte River Road Narratives,* pp. 141–42.

21. Barry, *The Beginning of the West,* pp. 835–37.

22. Mattes, *Platte River Road Narrative,* pp. 197–98.

23. Ibid., p. 125.

24. Merrill J. Mattes, ed., "From Ohio to California: The Gold Rush Journal of Elijah Bryan Farnham," *Indiana Magazine of History* 46 (1950): 297–318, 403–20.

25. Watkins, *Publications of the Nebraska State Historical Society,* 20:208.

26. Ibid., pp. 212–13.

27. Ibid. See also Barry, *The Beginning of the West,* pp. 875–76.

CHAPTER THIRTEEN: THE HECTIC YEAR OF 1850

1. Louise Barry, *The Beginning of the West* (Topeka: Kansas State Historical Society, 1972), p. 913.

2. *New York Weekly Tribune,* February 23, 1850.

3. Barry, *The Beginning of the West,* p. 903.

4. Ibid., p. 905.

5. Ibid., p. 907.

6. Ibid., p. 903.

7. Eleazer S. Ingalls, *Journal of a Trip to California in 1850–51* (Waukegan, Ill.: Tobey & Co. Printers, 1852), pp. 6–51.

8. Albert Watkins, ed., *Publications of the Nebraska State Historical Society* (Lincoln: Nebraska State Historical Society, 1922), 20:224.

9. Ibid., pp. 228–29.

10. Ibid.

11. Dr. Samuel Matthias Ayres's letters are in the joint collection of the University of Missouri Western History Manuscript Collection and Missouri State Historical Society manuscript section, Columbia, Missouri.

12. Kenneth L. Holmes, ed., *Covered Wagon Women: Diaries and Letters from the Western Trails, 1840–1890* (Glendale, Calif.: Arthur H. Clark Co., 1983), 2:214–16.

13. Merrill J. Mattes, *Platte River Road Narratives* (Urbana and Chicago: University of Illinois Press, 1988), p. 3.

14. Andrew Child, *Overland Route to California* (Los Angeles: N. A. Kovach, 1946), pp. 20–21.

15. Watkins, *Publications of the Nebraska State Historical Society,* 20:222–27.

16. John D. Unruh, Jr., *The Plains Across: The Overland Emigrants and the Trans-Mississippi West, 1840–1860* (Urbana: University of Illinois Press, 1979), pp. 106–7. See also Morris W. Werner's unpublished manuscript "Wheelbarrow Emigrant of 1850" (Lawrence: University of Kansas—Kansas Heritage server, n.d.).

17. Barry, *The Beginning of the West,* pp. 902, 941–42, 957.

18. Ibid., pp. 925–27.

19. Ibid.

20. Ibid., p. 942.

21. Ibid., p. 937.

22. Ibid., p. 957.

CHAPTER FOURTEEN: THE CHANGING ROAD

1. "Letter of Quincy Adams Brooks," *Oregon Historical Quarterly* 15 (1914): 210–15.

2. Kenneth L. Homes, ed., *Covered Wagon Women: Diaries and Letters from the Western Trails, 1840–1890* (Glendale, Calif.: Arthur H. Clark Co., 1984), 3:131–32.

3. Louise Barry, *The Beginning of the West: Annals of the Kansas Gateway to the American West, 1840–1854* (Topeka: Kansas State Historical Society, 1972), pp. 982–83.

4. Percival G. Lowe, *Five Years a Dragoon ('49 to '54) and Other Adventures on the Great Plains* (Kansas City, Mo.: Franklin Hudson Publishing Co., 1906), pp. 79–81.

5. Albert Watkins, ed., *Publications of the Nebraska State Historical Society* (Lincoln: Nebraska State Historical Society, 1922), 20:236–37.

6. Francis Paul Prucha, S. J., *American Indian Treaties: The History of a Political Anomaly* (Berkeley: University of California Press, 1994).

7. J. P. Dunn, Jr., *Massacres of the Mountains: A History of the Indian Wars of the Far West* (New York: Harper & Brothers, 1886), pp. 189–218.

8. Gilbert L. Cole, *Overland Trail in Nebraska in 1852* (Kansas City, Mo.: Franklin Hudson Publishing Co., 1905), pp. 14–15.

9. Barry, *The Beginning of the West,* pp. 1078–79.

10. Watkins, *Publications of the Nebraska State Historical Society,* 20:239–40.

11. Barry, *The Beginning of the West,* pp. 1083–84. See also John D. Unruh, Jr., *The Plains Across* (Urbana: University of Illinois Press, 1979), p. 120. The Mormon estimate was made by Andrew Jenson, "Emigration to Utah, 1847–1868, Statistics," in the archives, Church of Latter-Day Saints, Salt Lake City.

12. "Journal of Henry Allyn," *Transactions of the Oregon Pioneer Association* (1921): 372–435.

13. Count Leonetto Cipriani, *California and Overland Diaries of Count Leonetto Cipriani,* trans. and ed. Enest Falbo (San Francisco: Champoeg Press, 1962), pp. 71–129.

14. Harriett Sherrill Ward, *Prairie Schooner Lady,* ed. Ward G. DeWitt (Los Angeles: Westernlore Press, 1959), pp. 57, 70.

15. Judge T. H. Cann, "From Mississippi to the Valley of the Sacramento: Memories of Fifty Years," *Overland Monthly* 45 (1905): 526–28.

16. Unruh, *The Plains Across,* p. 120. See also Andrew Jenson's "Emigration to Utah, 1847–1868, Statistics," in the archives, Church of Latter-Day Saints, Salt Lake City.

17. Albert Watkins, ed., *Publications of the Nebraska State Historical Society,* 20:259–60.

18. Merrill J. Mattes, *Platte River Road Narratives* (Urbana: University of Illinois Press, 1988), p. 449.

19. Loring Samuel Comstock, *A Journal of Travels Across the Plains in the Year 1855* (Oskaloosa, Iowa: Privately printed, n.d.), pp. 6–33.

20. Watkins, ed., *Publications of the Nebraska State Historical Society,* 20:278–90.

CHAPTER FIFTEEN: MORE CHANGE AND CIVIL WAR

1. Original letter in the archives of the Church of Latter-Day Saints, Salt Lake City.

2. William Audley Maxwell, *Crossing the Plains, Days of '57: A Narrative of Early Emigrant Travel to California by the Ox-Team Method* (San Francisco: Sunset Publishing House, 1915), p. 24.

3. Ibid., pp. 57–58.

4. J. Robert Brown, *Journal of a Trip Across the Plains of the United States from Missouri to California in 1856* (Columbus, Ohio: Privately printed, 1860). Yale University has the only known copy.

5. *Missouri Republican,* August 12, 1857.

6. Lt. Col. Philip St. George Cooke, "March of the 2nd Dragoons," ed. Hamilton Gardner, *Annals of Wyoming* 27 (April 1955): 43–60.

7. The Mormon migration estimate is that of a church historian, Andrew Jenson, and contained in "Emigration to Utah, 1847–1868, Statistics" in the archives, Church of Latter-Day Saints, Salt Lake City. The other estimates are from John D. Unruh, Jr., *The Plains Across* (Urbana: University of Illinois Press, 1979), p. 120; and Merrill J. Mattes, *The Great Platte River Road* (Lincoln: Nebraska State Historical Society, 1969), p. 23. Mattes's work is vol. 25 of the society's publications.

8. Richard Thomas Ackley, "Across the Plains in 1858," *Utah Historical Quarterly* 9 (1941): 190–228.

9. Anselm Holcomb Barker, *Anselm Holcomb Barker, Pioneer Builder and Early Settler of Auraria: His Diary of 1858* (Denver: Golden Bell Press, 1959), pp. 45–67.

10. William N. Byers and John H. Kellon, *Hand Book to the Gold Fields of Nebraska and Kansas . . .* (Chicago: D. B. Cooke & Co., 1859), pp. 12, 22–25.

11. David Dary, *True Tales of Old-Time Kansas* (Lawrence: University Press of Kansas, 1984), pp. 38–47.

12. C. M. Clark, M.D., *A Trip to Pike's Peak and Notes by the Way, etc.* (San Jose, Calif.: Talisman Press, 1958), p. 44.

13. Merrill J. Mattes, *Platte River Road Narratives* (Urbana: University of Illinois Press, 1988), p. 538.

14. Journal of Elijah Larkin, manuscript, Harold B. Lee Library, Brigham Young University, Provo.

15. Robert L. Thompson, *Wiring a Continent: The History of the Telegraph Industry in the United States, 1832–1866* (Princeton: Princeton University Press, 1947), pp. 367–68.

16. Frank Root and William Elsey Connelley, *The Overland Stage to California* (Topeka: Privately printed, 1903), p. 73.

17. Alvin M. Josephy, Jr., *The Civil War in the American West* (New York: Alfred A. Knopf, 1991), p. 268.

18. Mattes, *Platte River Road Narratives*, p. 542.

19. Ibid., p. 543.

CHAPTER SIXTEEN: DECLINE OF THE TRAIL

1. Brigham D. Madsen, *The Shoshone Frontier and the Bear River Massacre* (Salt Lake City: University of Utah Press, 1985). This 285-page work contains a good account of the massacre, which at the time did not gain much notice in the East because of the Civil War. More Indians died in the Bear River Massacre in 1863 than in any of the five other Indian massacres that occurred from 1863 to Wounded Knee in 1890.

2. Arazena Angeline Cooper recollections, typescript, Oregon Historical Society, Portland.

3. Miles C. Moore recollections, manuscript, Denver Public Library.

4. Merrill J. Mattes, *Platte River Road Narratives* (Urbana: University of Illinois Press, 1988), pp. 586–87.

5. Fanny Kelly, *Narrative of My Captivity Among the Sioux Indians* (Cincinnati: Wilstach, Baldwin & Co., 1871).

6. *The Sand Creek Massacre: A Documentary History* (New York: Sol Lewis, 1971). This 418-page work is a compilation of government documents, including the report of the Joint Committee on the Conduct of the War, *Massacre of the Cheyenne Indians*, 38th Cong., 2nd sess., 1865, and a report of the Secretary of War, 39th Cong., 2nd sess., Senate Executive Document No. 26 (Washington, D.C., 1867). A more recent study of the Sand Creek Massacre is Bob Scott's *Blood at Sand Creek: The Massacre Revisited* (Caldwell, Idaho: Caxton Printers, 1994).

7. Agnes Wright Spring, *Caspar Collins: The Life and Exploits of an Indian Fighter of the Sixties* (New York: Columbia University Press, 1927). See also Alfred James Mokler, *Fort Caspar (Platte Bridge Station): Comprising a Description of the Killing of Lieutenant Caspar W. Collins and the Massacre of Sergeant Amons J. Custard and Twenty-four of Their Comrades, July 26, 1865* (Casper, Wyo.: Prairie Publishing Co., 1938).

8. Eugene Ware, *The Indian Wars of 1864* (Topeka, Kans.: Crane & Co., 1911). Ware's Appendix A contains a detailed account of the young Indian woman.

9. *Massacre of Troops near Fort Phil. Kearney* (Fairfield, Wash.: Ye Galleon Press, 1987). This booklet is a reprint of the 1867 government report to Congress examining the Fetterman massacre.

10. Jerome A. Greene, "Hayfield Fight: A Reappraisal of a Neglected Action," *Montana Magazine* (Autumn 1972): 30–43.

11. Roy E. Appleman, "The Wagon Box Fight," in *Great Western Indian Fights* (New York: Doubleday & Co., 1960). This work was published by the Potomac Corral of the Westerners. Appleman was a professional historian with the National Park Service.

12. Frank A. Root and William E. Connelley, *The Overland Stage to California* (Topeka: Published by the authors, 1901), p. 502.

CHAPTER SEVENTEEN: REBIRTH OF THE TRAIL

1. Ezra Meeker, *Ox-Team Days on the Oregon Trail* (Yonkers-on-Hudson, N.Y.: World Book Co., 1925), pp. 165–66. This work was written by Meeker in collaboration with Howard R. Driggs.
2. Ezra Meeker, *The Ox Team; or, The Old Oregon Trail, 1852–1906* (Omaha: Published by the author, 1906), p. 85. This work was written by Meeker.
3. Ibid., p. 107.
4. Meeker, *Ox-Team Days,* pp. 192–93.
5. Meeker, *The Ox Team on the Old Oregon Trail,* pp. 135–36.
6. Ibid., p. 140.
7. Meeker, *Ox-Team Days,* p. 261.
8. Meeker, *The Ox-Team,* pp. 173–74.
9. Ibid., pp. 176–77.
10. Meeker, *Ox-Team Days,* p. 220.
11. Ibid., pp. 224–25.
12. *The Old Oregon Trail, Hearings Before the Committee on Roads, House of Representatives, Sixty-Eighth Congress, Second Session on H.J. Res. 232, H.J. Res. 328, and S. 2053, January 23, February 13, 19, and 21, 1925* (Washington, D.C.: Government Printing Office, 1925), p. 4.
13. David W. Lange, research director, Numismatic Guaranty Corporation (NGC), Sarasota, Florida. NGC has produced histories of all U.S. coins to accompany photographs of coins submitted to NGC for documentation.
14. Howard R. Driggs, *Westward America* (New York: G. P. Putnam's Sons, 1942), p. 99.
15. Merrill J. Mattes, "A Tribute to the Oregon Trail Memorial Association," *Overland Journal* (Winter 1984): 29–36.

Bibliography

BOOKS

Akin, James, Jr. *The Journal of James Akin, Jr.* Fairfield, Wash.: Ye Galleon Press, 1999. A reprint of the 1919 first edition.

Allen, Martha Mitten. *Traveling West: 19th Century Women on the Overland Routes.* El Paso: Texas Western Press, 1987.

Ambler, Charles H. *The Oregon Country, 1810–1830.* Cedar Rapids, Iowa: Torch Press, 1943.

Applegate, Jesse A. *A Day with the Cow Column.* Fairfield, Wash.: Ye Galleon Press, 1990.

————. "Recollections of My Boyhood," in *Westward Journeys.* Chicago: R. R. Donnelley & Sons Co., 1989.

Bagley, Will, ed. *The Pioneer Camp of the Saints: The 1846 and 1847 Mormon Trail Journals of Thomas Bullock.* Spokane: Arthur H. Clark Co., 1997.

————, ed. *Scoundrel's Tale: The Samuel Brannan Papers.* Spokane: Arthur H. Clark Co., 1999.

Bancroft, Hubert Howe. *The History of Oregon.* Vol. 1. San Francisco: History Co., 1886.

Barker, Anselm Holcomb. *Anselm Holcomb Barker, Pioneer Builder and Early Settler of Auraria: His Diary of 1858....* Denver: Golden Bell Press, 1959.

Barry, Louise. *The Beginning of the West.* Topeka: Kansas State Historical Society, 1972.

Beeson, Welborn. *The Oregon and Applegate Trail Diary of Welborn Beeson in 1853.* Edited by Bert Webber. Medford, Oreg.: Webb Research Group, 1987.

Brett, Maurice. *Flying the Oregon Trail.* Dorset, Eng.: Cirrus Associates, 2000.

Brown, J. Robert. *Journal of a Trip Across the Plains of the United States from Missouri to California in 1856.* Columbus, Ohio: Privately printed, 1860.

Brown, John. *Autobiography of John Brown.* Salt Lake City: Privately printed, 1941.

Bruff, J. Goldsborough. *Gold Rush: The Journals, Drawings, and Other Papers of J. Goldsborough Bruff.* New York: Columbia University Press, 1944.

Bryant, Edwin. *What I Saw in California.* New York: D. Appleton & Co., 1848.

Burnett, Peter H. *An Old California Pioneer.* Oakland: Biobooks, 1946. Burnett's recollections were first published in 1880.

Child, Andrew. *Overland Route to California.* Los Angeles: N. A. Kovach, 1946. The guide was first published in 1852 under the title *New Guide for the Overland Route to California.*

Chittenden, Hiram Martin. *The American Fur Trade of the Far West.* 2 vols. Stanford, Calif.: Academic Reprints, 1954.

Cipriani, Count Leonetto. *California and Overland Diaries from 1853 through 1871.* Translated and edited by Ernest Falbo. San Francisco: Champoeg Press, 1962.

Clark, C. M., M.D. *A Trip to Pike's Peak and Notes by the Way, Etc.* Edited by Robert Greenwood. San Jose, Calif.: Talisman Press, 1958. First published in Chicago in 1861.

Clark, Malcolm, Jr. *Eden Seekers: The Settlement of Oregon, 1818–1862.* Boston: Houghton Mifflin Co., 1981.

Clayton, William. *The Latter-Day Saints' Emigrants' Guide.* Fairfield, Wash.: Ye Galleon Press, 1974. A reprint of the 1848 first edition published in St. Louis.

————. *William Clayton's Journal.* Salt Lake City: Privately printed, 1921.

Cole, Gilbert L. *Overland Trail in Nebraska in 1852.* Kansas City, Mo.: Franklin Hudson Publishing Co., 1905.

Comstock, Loring Samuel. *A Journal of Travels Across the Plains in the Year 1855.* Oskaloosa, Iowa: Privately printed, n.d.

Cooke, Lucy Rutledge. *Crossing the Plains in 1852.* Modesto, Calif.: Privately printed, 1923.

Cornwall, Bruce. *Life Sketch of Pierre Barlow Cornwall.* San Francisco: A. M. Robertson, 1906.

Cross, Osborne. *The March of the Mounted Riflemen: First United States Military Expedition to Travel the Full Length of the Oregon Trail from Fort Leavenworth to Fort Vancouver, May to October, 1849. . . .* Glendale, Calif.: Arthur H. Clark Co., 1940.

Dary, David. *True Tales of Old-Time Kansas.* Lawrence: University Press of Kansas, 1984.

Decalves, Don Alonso (pseud.). *New Travels to the Westward; or, Unknown Parts of America: Being a Tour of Almost Fourteen Months. . . .* Boston: Printed and sold by John W. Folsom, [1788].

De Voto, Bernard. *Across the Wide Missouri.* Boston: Houghton Mifflin Co., 1947.

————. *The Year of Decision, 1846.* Boston: Little, Brown & Co., 1943.

Dickenson, Luella. *Reminiscences of a Trip Across the Plains in 1846 and Early Days in California.* Fairfield, Wash.: Ye Galleon Press, 1977.

Dodd, Lawrence. *Narcissa Whitman on the Oregon Trail.* Fairfield, Wash.: Ye Galleon Press, 1985.

Driggs, Howard R. *Westward America.* New York: G. P. Putnam's Sons, 1942.

Dunn, J. P., Jr. *Massacres of the Mountains: A History of the Indian Wars of the Far West.* New York: Harper & Brothers, 1886.

Dye, Eva Emery. *McLoughlin and Old Oregon.* Chicago: A. S. McClure Co., 1900.

Edwards, Philip Leget. *The Diary of Philip Leget Edwards: The Great Cattle Drive from California to Oregon in 1837.* Fairfield, Wash.: Ye Galleon Press, 1989.

————. *Sketch of the Oregon Territory, or, Emigrant's Guide.* Fairfield, Wash.: Ye Galleon Press, 1992. A reprint of the first edition published in 1842 in Liberty, Missouri.

Elliott, T. C. *The Earliest Travelers on the Oregon Trail.* Fairfield, Wash.: Ye Galleon Press, 1975. A reprint of a 1912 work published by the Oregon Historical Society.

Ellison, Robert S. *Fort Bridger, Wyoming: A Brief History.* Illustrated by William H. Jackson. Foreword by J. Cecil Alter. Casper: Historical Landmark Commission of Wyoming, 1931.

———. *Independence Rock, the Great Record of the Desert.* Casper, Wyo.: Natrona County Historical Society, 1930.

Evans, James R., with Bert Webber. *Flagstaff Hill on the National Historic Oregon Trail, Baker City, Oregon: An Interpretive Guide.* Medford, Oreg.: Webb Research Group, 1992.

Farnham, Thomas J. *Travels in the Great Western Prairies, the Anahuac and Rocky Mountains, and in the Oregon Territory.* Poughkeepsie, N.Y.: Killey & Lossing, 1841.

Federal Writers' Project. *Oregon: End of the Trail.* Portland, Oreg.: Binfords & Mort, 1940.

———. *The Oregon Trail: The Missouri River to the Pacific Ocean.* New York: Hastings House, 1939.

Field, Matthew C. *Prairie and Mountain Sketches.* Collected by Clyde and Mae Reed Porter. Edited by Kate L. Gregg and John Francis McDermott. Norman: University of Oklahoma Press, 1957.

Fogall, Alberta Brooks. *Royal Family of the Columbia: Dr. John McLoughlin and His Family.* Portland, Ore.: Binford & Mort, 1982.

Franzwa, Gregory M. *Maps of the California Trail.* Tucson: Patrice Press, 1999.

———. *Maps of the Oregon Trail.* Gerald, Mo.: Patrice Press, 1982.

———. *The Oregon Trail Revisited.* Gerald, Mo.: Patrice Press, 1967. Reprinted in 1973 and 1976.

Frémont, John Charles. *The Exploring Expedition to the Rocky Mountains....* Buffalo, N.Y.: Geo. H. Derby & Co., 1850.

———. *Memoirs of My Life.* New York: Cooper Square Press, 2001. A reprint of the 1886 first edition, with a new introduction by Charles M. Robinson III.

Fuller, Emeline L., and Carl Schlicke. *Left by the Indians,* and *Massacre on the Oregon Trail in the Year 1860.* Fairfield, Wash.: Ye Galleon Press, 1992.

Furniss, Norman F. *The Mormon Conflict, 1850–1859.* New Haven: Yale University Press, 1960.

Ghent, W. J. *The Road to Oregon: A Chronicle of the Great Emigrant Trail.* London, New York, and Toronto: Longmans, Green & Co., 1929.

Gillette, Martha Hill. *Overland to Oregon and in the Indian Wars of 1853....* Ashland, Ore.: Lewis Osborne, 1971.

Hafen, LeRoy R., ed. *The Mountain Men and the Fur Trade of the Far West: Biographical Sketches of the Participants by Scholars of the Subject.* 10 vols. Glendale, Calif.: Arthur H. Clark Co., 1965–72.

Hafen, Mary Ann. *Recollections of a Handcart Pioneer of 1860: A Woman's Life on the Mormon Frontier.* Lincoln: University of Nebraska Press, 1983.

Haines, Aubrey L. *Historic Sites Along the Oregon Trail.* Gerald, Mo.: Patrice Press, 1981.

Hart, Henry H. *Venetian Adventurer, Being an Account of the Life and Times and of the Book of Messer Marco Polo.* Stanford: Stanford University Press, 1942.

Hastings, Lansford W. *The Emigrants' Guide to Oregon and California.* Bedford, Mass.: Applewood Books, n.d. A reprint of the 1845 first edition.

Hayden, Mary. *Pioneer Days.* Fairfield, Wash.: Ye Galleon Press, 1979. A reprint of the 1915 first edition.

Hixon, Adrietta Applegate. *On to Oregon! A True Story of a Young Girl's Journey into the West.* Weiser, Idaho: Signal-American Printers, 1947.

Holmes, Kenneth L., ed. *Covered Wagon Women: Diaries and Letters from the Western Trails, 1840–1890.* 11 vols. Glendale: Arthur H. Clark Co., 1983.

Howay, Frederic W., ed. *Voyages of the Columbia to the Northwest Coast, 1787–1790 and 1790–1793.* Portland: Oregon Historical Society Press, 1990.

Hulbert, Archer Butler. *1830–1930, the Oregon Trail Centennial: The Documentary Background of the Days of the First Wagon Train on the Road to Oregon.* Missoula: State University of Montana, [1930].

Hunt, Wilson Price. *The Overland Diary of Wilson Price Hunt.* Ashland, Ore.: Oregon Book Society, 1973.

Hutchison, Daniel J., and Larry R. Jones, eds. *Emigrant Trails of Southern Idaho.* Boise: Bureau of Land Management and Idaho State Historical Society, 1993.

Ingalls, Eleazer S. *Journal of a Trip to California in 1850–51.* Waukegan, Ill.: Tobey & Co. 1852.

Irving, Washington. *The Adventures of Captain Bonneville U.S.A. in the Rocky Mountains and the Far West.* Norman: University of Oklahoma Press, 1961.

———. *Astoria; or, Anecdotes of an Enterprise Beyond the Rocky Mountains.* Edited by Edgeley W. Todd. Norman: University of Oklahoma Press, 1964. Irving's work was first published in Philadelphia in 1836.

Isham, G. S. *Guide to California, and the Mines, and Return by the Isthmus.* New York: A. T. Houel, Printer, 1850.

Jackson, William Emsley. *William Emsley Jackson's Diary of a Cattle Drive from La Grande, Oregon, to Cheyenne, Wyoming, in 1876.* Edited by J. Orin Oliphant. Fairfield, Wash.: Ye Galleon Press, 1983.

Kellom, John N. *A Handbook to the Gold Fields.* Chicago: D. B. Cooke & Co., 1859.

Kelly, Fanny. *Narrative of My Captivity Among the Sioux Indians.* Cincinnati: Wilstach, Baldwin & Co., 1871.

Knudsen, Dean. *An Eye for History: The Paintings of William Henry Jackson, from the collection at the Oregon Trail Museum.* Gering, Neb.: Scotts Bluff National Monument, the Oregon Trail Museum Association, 1997.

Komroff, Manuel, ed. *The Travels of Marco Polo, the Venetian.* New York: Boni & Liveright, 1926.

Lee, Daniel, and Joseph H. Frost. *Ten Years in Oregon.* New York: Published by the author, 1844.

Lempfrit, Honoré-Timothée. *His Oregon Trail Journal and Letters from the Pacific Northwest, 1848–1853.* Fairfield, Wash.: Ye Galleon Press, 1985.

Lenox, Edward Henry. *Overland to Oregon.* Fairfield, Wash.: Ye Galleon Press, 1993.

Leonard, H. L. W., Esq. *History of the Oregon Territory from Its First Discovery up to the Present Time.* Fairfield, Wash.: Ye Galleon Press, 1980. A reprint of the 1846 first edition published in Cleveland, Ohio.

Lockley, Fred. *Captain Sol. Thetherow, Wagon Train Master.* Portland, Ore.: Privately printed by the author, n.d.

Lowe, Percival G. *Five Years a Dragoon ('49 to '54) and Other Adventures on the Great Plains.* Kansas City, Mo.: Franklin Hudson Publishing Co., 1906.

Madsen, Axel. *John Jacob Astor: America's First Multimillionaire.* New York: John Wiley & Sons, 2001.

Madsen, Brigham D. *The Shoshone Frontier and the Bear River Massacre.* Salt Lake City: University of Utah Press, 1985.

Martin, Clinton S., ed. *Boy Scouts and the Oregon Trail, 1830–1930: The Story of the Scout Pilgrimage to Independence Rock, Wyoming, to Hold Rendezvous in Honor of the Pioneers Who "Won and Held the West."* New York: G. P. Putnam's Sons, 1930.

Massacre of Troops Near Fort Phil. Kearney. Fairfield, Wash.: Ye Galleon Press, 1987. A reprint of the 1867 government report to Congress examining the Fetterman massacre.

Mattes, Merrill J. *Platte River Road Narratives: A Descriptive Bibliography of Travel over the Great Central Overland Route to Oregon, California, Utah, Colorado, Montana, and Other Western States and Territories, 1812–1866.* Urbana and Chicago: University of Illinois Press, 1988.

Maxwell, William Audley. *Crossing the Plains, Days of '57: A Narrative of Early Emigrant Travel to California by the Ox-Team Method.* San Francisco: Sunset Publishing House, 1915.

May, Christina Rae. *Pioneer Clothing on the Oregon Trail.* Pendleton, Oreg.: Drigh Sighed Publications, 1998.

McWilliams, John. *Recollections of John McWilliams: His Youth Experiences in California and the Civil War.* Princeton, N.J.: Privately printed, 1919.

Meeker, Ezra. *Ox-Team Days on the Oregon Trail,* Yonkers-on-Hudson, N.Y.: World Book Co., 1925.

———. *The Ox Team; or, The Old Oregon Trail, 1852–1906.* Omaha: Published by the author, 1906.

———. *Story of the Lost Trail to Oregon.* Fairfield, Wash.: Ye Galleon Press, 1998. A reprint of the 1915 first edition published in Seattle.

Merk, Frederick. *The Oregon Question: Essays in Anglo-American Diplomacy and Politics.* Cambridge: Harvard University Press, 1967.

Merrill, Julius. *Bound for Idaho: The 1864 Trail Journal of Julius Merrill.* Moscow: University of Idaho Press, 1988.

Mokler, Alfred James. *Fort Caspar (Platte Bridge Station): Comprising a Description of the Killing of Lieutenant Caspar W. Collins and the Massacre of Sergeant Amons J. Custard and Twenty-four of Their Comrades, July 26, 1865.* Casper, Wyo.: Prairie Publishing Co., 1938.

Morgan, Dale, ed. *Overland in 1846: Diaries and Letters of the California-Oregon Trail.* 2 vols. Lincoln: University of Nebraska Press, 1993.

Morgan, Murray. *Puget's Sound: A Narrative of Early Tacoma and the Southern Sound.* Seattle: University of Washington Press, 1979.

Munger, Asahel, and Eliza Munger. *Diary of Asahel Munger and Wife.* Fairfield, Wash.: Ye Galleon Press, 1992.

Murphy, Virginia Reed. *Across the Plains in the Donner Party.* Fairfield, Wash.: Ye Galleon Press, 1998.

Myres, Sandra L., ed. *Ho for California! Women's Overland Diaries from the Huntington Library.* San Marino, Calif.: Huntington Library, 1980.

Old Oregon Trail Centennial Commission. *Wagons West, 1943; Old Oregon Trail Centennial, 1943.* Salem: Oregon Trail Commission, 1943.

Oregon State Highway Department. *Route of the Oregon Trail: Fort Boise, Idaho, to The Dalles, Oregon.* Portland: Oregon State Highway Dept., n.d. This booklet contains ten maps.

Oregon Trail Memorial Association. *Covered-Wagon Centennial and Ox-Team Days.* Yonkers-on-Hudson, N.Y.: Oregon Trail Memorial Association, 1932.

————. *Oregon Trail, a Plan to Honor the Pioneers.* New York: Oregon Trail Memorial Association, [1929].

Oregon Trail Overlands: Journal of Medorem Crawford; the Diary of Jared Fox; Oakley's Oregon Expedition; Journal of John Spencer. Fairfield, Wash.: Ye Galleon Press, 2001.

Palmer, Joel. *Journal of Travels over the Rocky Mountains, to the Mouth of the Columbia River....* Cincinnati: J. A. & U. P. James, 1850.

Palmer, Rosemary Gudmundson. *Children's Voices from the Trail: Narratives of the Platte River Road.* Spokane: Arthur H. Clark Co., 2002.

Parker, Rev. Samuel. *Journal of an Exploring Tour Beyond the Rocky Mountains, Under the Direction of the A.B.C.F.M. Performed in the Years 1835, '36, and '37.* Ithaca, N.Y.: Published by the author, 1838.

Parkman, Francis. *The California and Oregon Trail: Being Sketches of Prairie and Rocky Mountain Life.* New York: George P. Putnam, 1849.

————. *The Journals of Francis Parkman.* 2 vols. New York and London: Harper & Brothers, 1947.

Parrish, Rev. Edward Evans. *Diary of Rev. Edward Evans Parrish.* Fairfield, Wash.: Ye Galleon Press, 1988.

Payette, B. C., ed. *The Northwest.* Montreal: Payette Radio Limited, 1964.

————. *The Oregon Country Under the Union Jack: Postscript Edition.* Montreal: Payette Radio Limited, 1962.

Peaker, Ora Brooks. *A History of the United States Indian Factory System, 1795–1822.* Denver: Sage Books, 1954.

Peltier, Jerome. *Madame Dorion.* Fairfield, Wash.: Ye Galleon Press, 1980.

Powell, Fred W. *Hall Jackson Kelley, Prophet of Oregon.* Portland, Ore.: Ivy Press, 1917.

Pringle, Catherine Sager. *Across the Plains in 1844.* Fairfield, Wash.: Ye Galleon Press, 1993.

Prucha, Francis Paul, S.J. *American Indian Treaties: The History of a Political Anomaly.* Berkeley: University of California Press, 1994.

Quintard, Taylor. *In Search of the Racial Frontier: African Americans in the American West, 1828–1990.* New York: W. W. Norton, 1998.

Roberts, Sidney. *To Emigrants to the Gold Region: A Treatise, Showing the Best Way to California, with Many Serious Objections to Going by Sea....* New Haven, Conn.: Privately printed, 1849.

Root, Frank A., and William E. Connelley. *The Overland Stage to California.* Topeka, Kans.: Published by the author, 1903.

Root, Riley. *Journal of Travels from St. Josephs to Oregon, with Observations of That Country, Together with a Description of California....* Galesburg, Ill.: Gazetteer & Intelligencer Prints, 1850.

Ronda, James P. *Astoria and Empire.* Lincoln: University of Nebraska Press, 1990.

Ruby, Robert H., and John A. Brown. *The Chinook Indians: Traders of the Lower Columbia River.* Norman: University of Oklahoma Press, 1976.

Rumer, Thomas A. *The Wagon Trains of '44: A Comparative View of the Individual Caravans in the Emigration of 1844 to Oregon.* Spokane, Wash.: Arthur H. Clark Co., 1990.

————, ed. *The Emigrating Company: The 1844 Oregon Trail Journal of Jacob Hammer.* Spokane, Wash.: Arthur H. Clark Co., 1990.

The Sand Creek Massacre: A Documentary History. New York: Sol Lewis, 1971.

Schlissel, Lillian. *Women's Diaries of the Westward Journey.* New York: Schocken Books, 1982.

Scofield, John. *Hail Columbia: Robert Gray, John Kendrick, and the Pacific Fur Trade.* Portland: Oregon Historical Society Press, 1993.

Scott, Bob. *Blood at Sand Creek: The Massacre Revisited.* Caldwell, Idaho: Caxton Printers, Ltd., 1994.

Sellers, Charles Grier. *James K. Polk, Jacksonian, 1795–1843.* Princeton: Princeton University Press, 1957.

Severn, Bill. *Frontier President: The Life of James K. Polk.* New York: Ives Washburn, 1965.

Shepherd, James S. *Journal of Travel Across the Plains to California and Guide to the Future Emigrant.* Fairfield, Wash.: Ye Galleon Press, 1978. This work was first published in 1851.

Shupe, Verna I. *The Argonauts and Pioneers.* Pocatello, Idaho: Graves & Potter, Tribune Press, 1931.

Spring, Agnes Wright. *Caspar Collins: The Life and Exploits of an Indian Fighter of the Sixties.* New York: Columbia University Press, 1927.

Stewart, George R. *The California Trail: An Epic with Many Heroes.* New York: McGraw-Hill Book Co., 1962.

———. *Names on the Land: A Historical Account of Place-Naming in the United States.* New York: Random House, 1945.

Stuart, Robert. *The Discovery of the Oregon Trail.* New York and London: Charles Scribner's Sons, 1935.

———. *On the Oregon Trail: Robert Stuart's Journey of Discovery.* Edited by Kenneth A. Spaulding. Norman: University of Oklahoma Press, 1953.

Thompson, Erwin N. *Shallow Grave at Waiilatpu: The Sagers' West.* Portland: Oregon Historical Society, 1973.

Thompson, Robert L. *Wiring a Continent: The History of the Telegraph Industry in the United States, 1832–1866.* Princeton: Princeton University Press, 1947.

Thrapp, Dan L. *Encyclopedia of Frontier Biography.* 4 vols. Glendale, Calif.: Arthur H. Clark Co., 1988.

Townsend, John K. *Narrative of a Journey Across the Rocky Mountains, to the Columbia River....* Philadelphia: Henry Perkins, 1839.

Tyler, Ron, ed. *Alfred Jacob Miller: Artist of the Oregon Trail.* Fort Worth: Amon Carter Museum, 1982.

Unruh, John D., Jr. *The Plains Across.* Urbana: University of Illinois Press, 1979.

Vestal, Stanley [Walter S. Campbell]. *Joe Meek, the Merry Mountain Man: A Biography.* Caldwell, Idaho: Caxton Printers, 1952.

Wagner, Henry R., and Charles Camp. *The Plains and the Rockies: A Critical Bibliography of Exploration, Adventure, and Travel in the American West.* San Francisco: John Howell, 1982. Fourth edition, revised, enlarged and edited by Robert H. Becker.

Ward, Harriett Sherrill. *Prairie Schooner Lady.* Edited by Ward G. DeWitt. Los Angeles: Westernlore Press, 1959.

Ware, Eugene. *The Indian Wars of 1864.* Topeka, Kans.: Crane & Co., 1911.

Ware, Joseph. *The Emigrants' Guide to California.* Fairfield, Wash.: Ye Galleon Press, 1999. A reprint of the 1849 first edition published in St. Louis.

Watkins, Albert, ed. *Publications of the Nebraska State Historical Society.* Vol. 20. Lincoln: Nebraska State Historical Society, 1922.

Watson, William J. *Journal of an Overland Journey to Oregon Made in the Year 1849.* Fairfield, Wash.: Ye Galleon Press, 1895.

Whitney, Asa. *Project for a Railroad to the Pacific....* New York: G. W. Wood, 1849.

White, Dr. Elijah. *Ten Years in Oregon: Travels and Adventures of Dr. Elijah White and Lady West of the Rocky Mountains....* Ithaca, N.Y.: Privately printed, 1848.

Williams, Jacqueline. *Wagon Wheel Kitchens: Food on the Oregon Trail.* Foreword by Samuel P. Arnold. Lawrence: University Press of Kansas, 1993.

Wilson, D. Ray. *Fort Kearny on the Platte.* Dundee, Ill.: Crossroads Communication, 1980.

Winther, Oscar O. *The Transportation Frontier.* New York: Holt, Rinehart & Winston, 1964.

Wood, Frances. *Did Marco Polo Go to China?* New York: View/Harper Collins, 1996.

Wyeth, Capt. Nathaniel J. *The Journals of Captain Nathaniel J. Wyeth's Expeditions to the Oregon Country, 1831–1836.* Fairfield, Wash.: Ye Galleon Press, 1997.

ARTICLES

Ackiley, Richard Thomas. "Across the Plains in 1858." *Utah Historical Quarterly* 9 (1941).

Adair, Sarah Damron. "Recollections." In *Transactions of the Oregon Pioneer Association.* Portland, 1900.

Allyn, Henry. "Journal of Henry Allyn." In *Transactions of the Oregon Pioneer Association.* Portland, 1921.

Appleman, Roy E. "The Wagon Box Fight." In *Great Western Indian Fights.* New York: Doubleday & Co., 1960.

Barrows, Samuel June. "The Mule and His Driver." In *Exploring the Northern Plains, 1804–1876.* Caldwell, Idaho: Caxton Printers, Ltd., 1955.

Barry, Louise. "Charles Robinson—Yankee '49er: His Journey to California." *Kansas Historical Quarterly* 34 (1968).

Boardman, John. "Journal of John Boardman." *Utah Historical Quarterly* 2 (1929).

Brandon, William. "Wilson Price Hunt." In Hafen, ed., *The Mountain Men and the Fur Trade of the Far West.* Vol. 6.

Brooks, Quincy Adams. "Letter of Quincy Adams Brooks." *Oregon Historical Quarterly* 15 (1914).

Camp, Charles L. "James Clyman." In Hafen, ed., *The Mountain Men and the Fur Trade of the Far West.* Vol. 1.

Campbell, Eugene E. "Miles Morris Goodyear." In Hafen, ed., *The Mountain Men and the Fur Trade of the Far West.* Vol. 2.

Cann, Judge T. H. "From Mississippi to the Valley of the Sacramento: Memories of Fifty Years." *Overland Monthly* 45 (1905).

Carter, Harvey L. "Ewing Young." In Hafen, ed., *The Mountain Men and the Fur Trade of the Far West.* Vol. 2.

———. "John Gantt." In Hafen, ed., *The Mountain Men and the Fur Trade of the Far West.* Vol. 5.

Cooke, Lt. Col. Philip St. George. "March of the 2nd Dragoons." Edited by Hamilton Gardner. *Annals of Wyoming* 27 (April 1955).

Cosgrove, Hugh. "Reminiscences of Hugh Cosgrove." *Oregon Historical Quarterly* 1 (1900).

Fisher, Rev. Ezra. "Correspondence of Rev. Ezra Fisher, Pioneer Missionary of the American Baptist Church Home Mission Society." Edited by Sarah Fisher Hamilton and Nellie E. Latourette. *Oregon Historical Quarterly* 16 (1915).

Geer, Elizabeth Dixon Smith. "Diary of Elizabeth Dixon Smith Geer." Edited by George H. Himes. *Transactions of the Oregon Pioneer Association* (1907).

Greene, Jerome A. "Hayfield Fight: A Reappraisal of a Neglected Action." *Montana Magazine*, Autumn 1972.

Hardeman, Nicholas P. "Charles A. Warfield." In Hafen, ed., *The Mountain Men and the Fur Trade of the Far West*. Vol. 7.

Hafen, LeRoy R. "Robert Newell." In Hafen, ed., *The Mountain Men and the Fur Trade of the Far West*. Vol. 8.

Jory, James. "Reminiscences of Jory James." Edited by H. S. Lyman. *Oregon Historical Quarterly* 3 (1902).

Mattes, Merrill J. "Hiram Scott." In Hafen, ed., *The Mountain Men and the Fur Trade of the Far West*. Vol. 1.

———. "A Tribute to the Oregon Trail Memorial Association." *Overland Journal*, Winter 1984.

———, ed. "From Ohio to California: The Gold Rush Journal of Elijah Bryan Farnham." *Indiana Magazine of History* 46 (1950).

McClintock, Thomas C. "Henderson Luelling, Seth Lewelling, and the Birth of the Pacific Coast Fruit Industry." *Oregon Historical Quarterly* 60, no. 2 (June 1967).

Miller, James D. "Early Oregon Scenes: A Pioneer Narrative." *Oregon Historical Quarterly* 31 (1930).

Minto, John. "Reminiscences." *Oregon Historical Quarterly* 2 (1901).

Nichols, B. F. "Across the Plains in 1844." *Laidlaw Chronicle* (Crook County, Oregon), November 16, 1906.

Nunis, Doyce B., Jr. "Andrew Whitley Sublette." In Hafen, ed., *The Mountain Men and the Fur Trade of the Far West*. Vol. 8.

Parrish, Edward Evans. "Crossing the Plains in 1844." *Transactions of the Oregon Pioneer Association* (1888).

Sampson, William R. "Nathaniel Jarvis Wyeth." In Hafen, ed., *The Mountain Men and the Fur Trade of the Far West*. Vol. 5.

Stoughton, John A. "Recollections." *Washington Historical Quarterly* 15 (1924).

Sunder, John E. "Telegraph Beginnings in Kansas." *Kansas Historical Quarterly* 25 (1959).

Sutter, John A. "The Discovery of Gold in California." *Hutchings' California Magazine*, November 1857.

Tobie, Harvey E. "Joseph L. Meek." In Hafen, ed., *The Mountain Men and the Fur Trade of the Far West*. Vol. 1.

———. "Stephen Hall Meek." In Hafen, ed., *The Mountain Men and the Fur Trade of the Far West*. Vol. 2.

Walker, Ardis M. "Joseph R. Walker." In Hafen, ed., *The Mountain Men and the Fur Trade of the Far West.* Vol. 5.

Young, F. T. "Ewing Young and His Estate." *Oregon Historical Quarterly* (September 1920).

GOVERNMENT DOCUMENTS

Fox, Florence C. *Notes on the Oregon Trail, Arranged as New Materials of Instruction in Geography, Civics, and History for Elementary Schools.* Washington, D.C.: U.S. Government Printing Office, 1930. This forty-eight-page work provided background material and guidance for the teaching of Oregon Trail history in elementary schools.

Harding, Warren G. *Address of the President of the United States on the Oregon Trail at Meacham, Oreg., July 3, 1923.* Washington, D.C.: U.S. Government Printing Office, 1923.

Kurz, Rudolph Friedrich. *Journal of Rudolph Friedrich Kurz: An Account of His Experiences Among Fur Traders and American Indians on the Mississippi and the Upper Missouri Rivers During the Years 1846 to 1852.* Bulletin, Smithsonian Institution, Bureau of American Ethnology, no. 115. Washington, D.C.: U.S. Government Printing Office, 1937.

Lander, Frederick W. *Additional Estimate for Fort Kearny, South Pass, and Honey Lake Wagon Road: Letter from the Acting Secretary of the Interior, Transmitting a Communication from Colonel Lander in Regard to the Fort Kearney, South Pass, and Honey Lake Wagon Road.* Washington, D.C.: House of Representatives, 1861.

United States Congress, House Committee on Roads. *The Old Oregon Trail. Hearings Before the Committee on Roads.* House of Representatives, 68th Cong., 2nd sess., on H. J. Res. 232, H. J. Res. 328, and S. 2053. January 23, February 13, 19, and 21, 1925. Washington, D.C.: U.S. Government Printing Office, 1925.

United States Congress, House. *Presidential Message. James Polk.* 30th Cong., 2nd sess., H. Ex. Doc. No. 1 (Serial 537).

United States Congress, Senate Committee on Banking and Currency. *Commemorative Coin—Oregon Trail. Hearings.* Washington, D.C.: U.S. Government Printing Office, 1926.

MANUSCRIPTS AND LETTERS

Applegate, Virginia Watson. Recollections. Manuscript. Oregon Historical Society, Portland.

Austin, Henry. Diary. Bancroft Library, University of California, Berkeley.

Ayres, Dr. Samuel Matthias. Letters. Joint collection, University of Missouri Western History Manuscript Collection and Missouri State Historical Society, Columbia, Missouri.

Bayley, Thomas Stock. "First Overland Mail Bag to California." Manuscript. California State Library, Sacramento.

Bogart, Nancy M. (Hembree). "Reminiscences of a Journey Across the Plains in 1843 with Dr. Marcus Whitman's Caravan." Original nine-page manuscript. Bancroft Library, University of California, Berkeley.

Briggs, Albert. "Recollections of Albert Briggs." Manuscript. Bancroft Library, University of California, Berkeley.

Carson, Mary Marsh. Undated letter in the files of the National Park Service, Washington, D.C.

Cooper, Arazena Angeline. Recollections. Typescript. Oregon Historical Society, Portland.

Cory, Dr. Benjamin. Manuscript journal. Society of California Pioneers, San Francisco.

Field, James. Typescript copy of diary. Oregon Historical Society, Portland.

Griffin, Charles Emerson. Recollections. Manuscript. Utah Historical Society, Salt Lake City.

Jenson, Andrew. "Emigration to Utah, 1847–1868, Statistics." Archives, Church of Latter-Day Saints, Salt Lake City.

Larkin, Elijah. Original journal of Elijah Larkin. Harold B. Lee Library, Brigham Young University, Provo.

McClane, John Burch. "Recollections of John Burch McClane." Manuscript. Bancroft Library, University of California, Berkeley.

Moore, Miles C. Recollections. Manuscript. Denver Public Library, Western History Collections.

Whitman, Mrs. Narcissa. Letter, June 27, 1836, typescript in author's library.

Williams, Joseph. "A Tour to the Oregon Territory." Typescript copy in the files of the Ripley County (Indiana) Historical Society, Versailles, Indiana.

Young, Brigham. Letter dated 1855, describing the construction of handcarts. Archives, Church of Latter-Day Saints, Salt Lake City.

JOURNALS

Annals of Wyoming
California Historical Quarterly
Kansas Historical Quarterly
Oregon Historical Quarterly
Overland Journal (Oregon-California Trail Association)
Transactions of the Oregon Pioneer Association
Utah Historical Quarterly
Washington Historical Quarterly

NEWSPAPERS

Adventure (St. Joseph, Missouri)
Christian Advocate and Journal (New York)
Democrat (Boonville, Missouri)
Dispatch (Columbus, Ohio)
Fallbrook Enterprise (California)
Gazette (St. Joseph, Missouri)
Intelligencer (St. Louis)
Leslie's Illustrated Weekly (New York)

Missouri Republican (St. Louis)
Oregon Spectator (Oregon City)
Republican (St. Louis)
Weekly Tribune (New York)

EMIGRANT GUIDES

Abbey, James. *California: a Trip Across the Plains, in the Spring of 1850....* New Albany, Ind.: Kent & Norman, and J. R. Nunemacher, 1850.

Aldrich, Lorenzo D. *A Journal of the Overland Route to California....* Lansingburgh, N.Y., 1851.

Bryant, Edwin. *What I Saw in California....* New York: D. Appleton & Co., 1848.

Child, Andrew. *Overland Route to California....* Milwaukee: Daily Sentinel Steam Power Press, 1852.

Clapp, John T. *A Journal of Travels to and from California....* Kalamazoo, Mich., 1851.

Clayton, William. *The Latter-Day Saints' Emigrants' Guide....* St. Louis: Missouri Republican Steam Power Press, 1848.

Drake, F. M. *The Emigrant's Overland Guide to California.* Fort Madison, Iowa, 1853.

Farnham, Thomas Jefferson. *Travels in the Great Western Prairies, the Anahuac and Rocky Mountains, and in the Oregon Territory.* Poughkeepsie, N.Y., 1841.

Hastings, Lansford Warren. *The Emigrants' Guide to Oregon and California....* Cincinnati: George Conclin, 1845.

Horn, Hosea B. *Horn's Overland Guide....* New York: J. H. Colton, 1852.

Ingalls, Eleazar Stillman. *Journal of a Trip to California, by the Overland Route Across the Plains in 1850–51....* Waukegan, Ill., 1852.

Isham, G. S. *Guide to California, and the Mines, and Return by the Isthmus....* New York: A. T. Houel, 1850.

Johnson, Overton, and William H. Winter. *Route Across the Rocky Mountains, with a Description of Oregon and California....* Lafayette, Ind.: John B. Semans, 1846.

Johnson, Theodore T. *Sights in the Gold Region, and Scenes by the Way.* New York: Baker & Scribner, 1849.

Keller, George. *A Trip Across the Plains, and Life in California....* Massillion, Ohio: White's Press, 1851.

Kelly, William. *An Excursion to California over the Prairie, Rocky Mountains, and Great Sierra Nevada....* London: Chapman & Hall, 1851.

Marcy, Randolph B. *The Prairie Traveler. A Hand-book for Overland Expeditions....* New York: Harper & Brothers, 1859.

McNeil, Samuel. *McNeil's Travels in 1849, to, Through and from the Gold Regions in California....* Columbus, Ohio: Scott & Bascom, 1850.

Palmer, Joel. *Journal of Travels over the Rocky Mountains, to the Mouth of the Columbia River....* Cincinnati: J. A. & U. P. James, 1847.

Parker, Rev. Samuel. *Journal of an Exploring Tour Beyond the Rocky Mountains....* Utica, N.Y.: M. M. Peabody, 1838.

Parkman, Francis, Jr. *The California and Oregon Trail....* New York: George P. Putnam, 1949.

Platt, P. L., and Nelson Slater. *The Travelers' Guide Across the Plains....* Chicago: Daily Journal, 1852.

Roberts, Sidney. *To Emigrants to the Gold Region: A Treatise, Showing the Best Way to California....* New Haven, Conn., 1949.

Root, Riley. *Journal of Travels from St. Josephs to Oregon....* Galesburg, Ill.: Gazetteer & Intelligencer Printers, 1850.

Shepherd, Josiah S. *Journal of Travel Across the Plains to California....* Racine, Wis., 1851.

Sherwood, J. Ely. *California: Her Wealth and Resources....* New York: George F. Nesbit, 1848.

Steele, Oliver G. *Steele's Western Guide Book, and Emigrant's Directory....* Buffalo: Oliver G. Steele, 1949.

Street, Franklin. *California in 1850, Compared with What It Was in 1849....* Cincinnati: R. E. Edwards & Co., 1851.

Tarbell, J. *The Emigrant's Overland Guide to California.* Fort Madison, Iowa, 1853.

Thompson, Jessy Quinn. *Oregon and California in 1848....* New York: Harper & Brothers, 1849.

Ware, Joseph E. *The Emigrants' Guide to California, Containing Every Point of Information for the Emigrant....* St. Louis: J. Halsall, 1949.

Watson, William J. *Journal of an Overland Journey to Oregon, Made in the Year 1849....* Jacksonville, Ill., 1851.

Wilkes, Charles. *Western America, Including California and Oregon....* Philadelphia: Lea & Blanchard, 1849.

Wood, John. *Journal of John Wood as Kept By Him While Traveling from Cincinnati to the Gold Diggings in California in the Spring and Summer of 1850....* Chillicothe, Ohio: Addison Bookwalter, 1852.

Index

Page numbers in italics refer to illustrations

A NOTE ON THE TYPE

This book was set in Janson, a typeface long thought to have been made by the Dutchman Anton Janson, who was a practicing typefounder in Leipzig during the years 1668–1687. However, it has been conclusively demonstrated that these types are actually the work of Nicholas Kis (1650–1702), a Hungarian, who most probably learned his trade from the master Dutch typefounder Dirk Voskens. The type is an excellent example of the influential and sturdy Dutch types that prevailed in England up to the time William Caslon (1692–1766) developed his own incomparable designs from them.

ORIGINALLY COMPOSED BY NORTH MARKET STREET GRAPHICS, LANCASTER, PENNSYLVANIA

ORIGINALLY PRINTED AND BOUND BY BERRYVILLE GRAPHICS, BERRYVILLE, VIRGINIA

MAPS BY DAVID LINDROTH, INC.

DESIGNED BY ROBERT C. OLSSON